Megeu

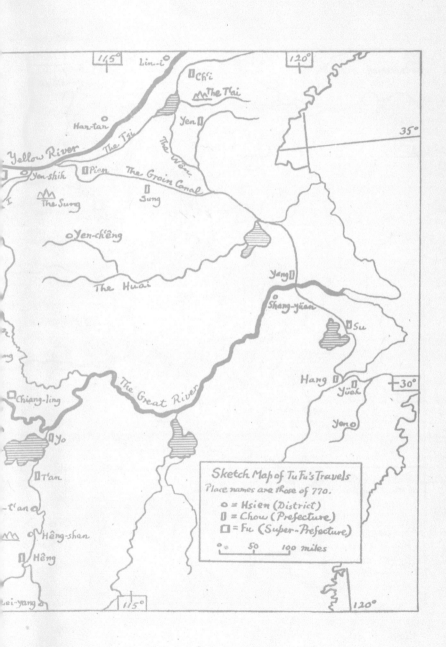

Sketch Map of Tu Fu's Travels
Place names are those of 770.

o = Hsien (District)
▯ = Chow (Prefecture)
▢ = Fu (Super-Prefecture)

0   50   100 miles

"True literature lasts a thousand ages"

TU FU, A.D. 767

TU
FU

China's
Greatest
Poet

by William Hung

HARVARD UNIVERSITY PRESS

CAMBRIDGE 1952

To Rhoda Kong Hung

How did I come to write this book? When I was a boy of thirteen, my father gave me a set of Tu Fu's works in Yang's edition. My father told me that Tu Fu was a man of ambition, character, and humor. "He was that type of man," said my father, "who, if he had luck, would succeed, and if he had no luck, would not fail." When I grew up, I learned to like the Bible as the best of books. Next only to the Psalms, the poems of Tu Fu have given me the greatest fascination, joy, and consolation. My understanding and appreciation of the man and the poet grew during the forty years of frequent reading and consultation.

During the months of my imprisonment by the Japanese army in 1942, I requested a copy of the Bible. It was denied me. Then I requested a set of Tu Fu. When Wên T'ien-hsiang (1236–1282) refused to serve the Mongols and was in prison awaiting execution, he occupied himself by using the original lines of Tu Fu to fashion two hundred new poems of his own. I thought I might enjoy the same game. My request was again refused; no reading of any kind was permitted. In my prayers and meditations, I resolved on a number of things I should do if I survived my imprisonment. To study Tu Fu with greater concentration was one of these.

During 1947–48, when I was invited once more to teach at Harvard University, I offered a course on the Historical Background of Tu Fu. I believe my students liked the course. Some of them urged me to write a book in English on the subject. In February 1948 I delivered the Woodward Lectures at Yale University; I lectured on Tu Fu. A number of my listeners also advised me to prepare a book in English. This book is now offered with the humble hope that it may help to enhance the appreciation of China's greatest poet and to enlarge the sympathetic understanding of China's people.

My thanks are due to the authorities of Yenching University, Harvard University, and the Harvard-Yenching Institute, and especially to Professor Serge Elisséeff, Director of the Institute, for the opportunity given me to study and teach the subject. To the Trustees of the Harvard-Yenching Institute I wish to express my gratitude also for their generous grant toward the cost of publication. I wish to thank my friends and colleagues, Professors James Roland Ware and Francis Woodman Cleaves, for lending me rare items from their own collections; Dr. Alfred Kaiming Ch'iu, Librarian of the Chinese-Japanese Library of the Harvard-Yenching Institute at Harvard University, for giving me excellent facilities for using the collections under his charge; Miss Alice Reynolds, in charge of Interlibrary Loans at Harvard College Library, for helping me to borrow books from libraries at some distances from Cambridge; and Mr. Hung-shun Ch'ên, Librarian of the Yenching University Library, for sending me extracts and copies of items not available in America.

My manuscript was completed two years ago. The delay of its acceptance for publication was due mainly to my failure to separate the parts of interest primarily to the Sinological specialist from those that may interest the general reader. Professor Elisséeff very kindly suggested the idea of two volumes—one for the text and the other of notes.* Dr. Thomas James Wilson, Director, and Miss Eleanor R. Dobson, Editor, of the Harvard University Press, very graciously appointed Mrs. Chase J. Duffy to assist me in making the needed revision. I am grateful to Mrs. Duffy for numerous suggestions on organization and style and especially for reducing the instances of my inadequate handling of English idioms.

More than to any other human being, I owe to my wife the encouragement and help without which this book might never have been written or completed. In order to give me more time and freedom for my work, she has taken upon herself much of the burden of duties and cares that is properly my share in our home. I dedicate this book to her very much in the spirit of Tu Fu when he said of his wife:

"In a poor home, everything depends on a good mother."

WILLIAM HUNG

September, 1951
Cambridge, Massachusetts

* The text, consisting of the biography of Tu Fu and translations from his poems, is contained in the present volume. A supplementary volume, of notes addressed to the specialist, is also scheduled for publication under the auspices of the Harvard-Yenching Institute in 1952. HARVARD UNIVERSITY PRESS.

CONTENTS

x

杜甫

"The sea monster and the purple phoenix
Are inverted on the short skirts."

China's eighth-century poet Tu Fu has been introduced to the West as the Chinese Virgil, Horace, Ovid, Shakespeare, Milton, Burns, Wordsworth, Béranger, Hugo, or Baudelaire. How can one poet be like so many unlike ones? The truth of the matter is that Tu Fu is not like any or all of them. Tu Fu is unique.

Even among the thousands of Chinese poets, Tu Fu is unique. He is the only one whose influence grows with time. He was not one of the popular poets of his own day, but forty years after his time, poets began to realize that he was one of the greatest masters of their craft, and some of them would not hesitate to say that he was the greatest. Three centuries after his death, scholars began in earnest to collect his works, to edit them, and to provide them with commentaries. They began to study the incidents of his life in the light of his poetry and to understand his poetry in terms of his life and time. Thus the admiration of the man came from the fascination of his poetry, and the admiration of the poetry was further strengthened by the more detailed knowledge of the poet's life.

Throughout the centuries, there have been indeed critics who would praise this or that poet in preference to Tu Fu. The overwhelming majority of Chinese historians, philosophers, and poets would, however, confirm Tu Fu in the first place of honor; and this because, to them, Tu Fu the man represents the widest sympathy and the highest ethical principles, while Tu Fu the poet commands the largest variety of artistry and the deepest reality of art. If an exhaustive bibliography of the partial and the complete editions of Tu Fu's works should be compiled, the titles would run into hundreds. If a complete list were attempted of the works that contain more or less appreciative studies or commentaries on our poet, the titles would run into thousands.

Even today in China, when all standards of morality and literature have been thrown into doubt and confusion, the position of Tu Fu in man's fascination and respect remains alone unchallenged. Even those who adhere to the extreme right in defense of the status quo claim him because he stands for unswerving loyalty to the government and unhesitating opposition to rebellion. Even those who move toward the extreme left in support of a bloody revolution quote him because he describes the most moving scenes of suffering and cries out the most indignant condemnation of injustice. Conservative students of literature admire Tu Fu's breadth of learning, mirrored in his rich and elegant display of terms and allusions culled from all types of historical and literary works and applied aptly to the subjects and situations he portrays. They are fascinated by his clever manipulation as well as his strict observance of the rules of prosody in various standard forms of poetry. The iconoclasts, on the other hand, delight in his daring innovations in subject matter, in form, and in diction. The advocates of vernacular literature point to his frequent use of dialectic vulgarisms and proudly proclaim him as one of the earliest masters to challenge the right of the dead classical usage to shackle living moods and creative thoughts. If one should try to collect from the publications of past and present poets and versifiers those pieces that suggest Tu Fu's influence either in form or in spirit, the number might run into hundreds of thousands.

A Western student who wants to know something about Tu Fu will very likely consult first the *Chinese Biographical Dictionary,* a very convenient, easily accessible, and on the whole, good volume by the celebrated Sinologue, the late Professor Herbert Allen Giles of Cambridge University. In almost all of the short notices about Tu Fu by writers in several European languages the influence of Giles's account of our poet is easily discernible, whether or not openly acknowledged. As recently as 1934, a selection of Tu Fu's Szechuan poems were translated into English and published with a biographical account of the poet in the preface. Many of the statements are almost verbatim from the biographical dictionary.

Unfortunately, Giles's account of our poet is very unsatisfactory. It is amazing how so many errors can get into so little space. Those inaccuracies which the learned compiler might have inherited from generations of our Chinese scholars are easily recognizable; I was, however, very much puzzled by a few ridiculously incorrect items that could hardly be of Chinese origin. After some search, I was finally led through the like-

2

wise inaccurate accounts by d'Hervey and Rémusat to what is probably the earliest biographical study of Tu Fu in a Western language. This was written by Father Amiot of the Jesuit Mission in Peking, and was published in 1780 in the fifth volume of the *Mémoires concernant les chinois*. During the century and a half since the work of Amiot, there have been quite a few long or short accounts of Tu Fu's life by Western scholars. Fortunately, they are on the whole less incorrect. Unfortunately, they are also less interesting.

In China, the knowledge of Tu Fu's life and the understanding of his poetry has been a matter of gradual growth during the centuries. The process of discovery is by no means complete. The first biographical account of our poet was not written until 813. It left out many important facts of his life, such as the dates of his birth and death, which were, only after several hundred years of research, correctly determined to be 712 and 770. The first attempt at getting together a complete collection of Tu Fu's writings was as late as 1039. The collection in twenty *chüan* (fascicles) then contained 1,405 poems and 29 pieces of prose. And the canon, so to speak, was not closed until 1667, when the numbers stood at 1,457 and 32 respectively.

The task of reconstructing the poet's life would have been easy if all of his writings had been clearly dated by Tu Fu himself, as a few were; if they had been arranged by him in a chronological order (as he might have very likely done in the original manuscript collection reported to be sixty *chüan* in bulk, which was probably lost or scattered shortly after his death); if many of the poems that concerned important events of his time were not phrased in masquerading metaphors and elusive allusions; if all of the poems in the transmitted collection were really authentic; and if the texts were free from the errors and changes introduced by generations of editors, copyists, and printers.

As it is, the situation is like an intriguing, but in spots hopeless, jigsaw puzzle. Suppose you have a bag full of small irregular pieces which when put together will show the city map of classical Rome; but the drawings are faint, and the readings uncertain. You know that the set is not complete. The edges of many pieces had been chewed by rats. Some of the pieces have been discovered to belong to other maps, and you do not know how many more foreign pieces have gotten into the bag. As you examine and compare the pieces, moving them back and forth on the table, you experience the annoyance of their refusing to fit well and also the thrills of finding many perfect fittings. There is fascination in the game.

The first scholar to try the jigsaw puzzle and build up a *nien-p'u* or chronological table of Tu Fu's life was Lü Ta-fang (1027–1097). Evidently, he put back into the bag most of the pieces that tried his patience too much; the resulting chronology was very sketchy, and many pieces were wrongly placed. After Lü, many others tried the game. By 1153, the chronology prepared by Lu Yin assumed a dignified size, and a number of the incidents of Tu Fu's life were so well placed that subsequent scholars were satisfied to leave them alone.

Huang Ho was the most ambitious of the players. He labeled every piece with a date and frequently with his argument for the assignment. It is significant, however, that his edition of 1226 did not arrange the poems according to his chronological sequence, but left them as they were in the older editions. The reason is obvious. The incongruities, uncertainties, and impossibilities might become too apparent. It remained to men like Ch'ou Chao-ao and Yang Lun to rearrange the poems according to Huang's dating and to move some of the pieces backward or forward as might be justified. If in their editions, published in 1713 and 1791, there are still many difficulties, the blame would be Huang's, not theirs. Ch'ou's edition represents an incessant labor of twenty-four years. It contains the most minute explanations of Tu Fu's allusions and the fullest discussions of his poetics, both of which Ch'ou selected from previous masters accessible to him, with amazing diligence, if not always with astute discrimination. By eliminating what he regarded as irrelevant or unnecessary, Yang cut the unwieldy bulkiness of Ch'ou's edition to a convenient size. This, together with other features, such as further rearrangement of the pieces, the addition of some new explanations and selected comments, and especially the complete suppression of Ch'ien Ch'ien-i—whom I shall mention later—accounted for the wide circulation and popularity of Yang's edition for a century and a half.

The most recent attempt to reconstruct the chronology of Tu Fu's life was that of the late Professor Wên I-to of Tsinghua University, in a long paper published in 1930–31. Wên very wisely avoided the handling of the many poems with no clues for dating and confined his attention to those that yielded information about Tu Fu's life and experience. I regret, however, that Wên did not give attention to the development of thought in the poet's life. He did not discriminate often enough against the spurious pieces which only confuse our understanding of the man and the poet. His work also relies too much on Ch'ou—without the benefit of some of the chronologically preferable rearrangements in Yang's edition.

I have been asked: Why burden poetry with chronology? My answer has to deal with both the general and the particular situations. When we listen to the spring song of a bird, we have an inkling of what he is saying because we know and appreciate the background: the air, the sunshine, the green leaves, the colorful flowers, the flying insects—everything, including ourselves, in a springtime mood. Suppose we make a record of the bird's song and play it somewhere near the North Pole, in icy darkness. We can still imagine the background of the bird's singing

4

and appreciate at least in part its meaning. Would a polar bear who happens to be listening appreciate it as much? The polar bear has no knowledge of the atmosphere of spring.

To us, a poet generally sings more intelligibly than a bird. A poem often supplies its own background, but not always. Even in ordinary conversation, we depend on the context in order to understand the words. A written communication, like a cablegram, can hardly be understood without a knowledge of the sender, the time, and the place. A Chinese poem is very much like a telegram wherein verbal economy is very desirable. Pronouns and conjunctions are almost always omitted. A word or two frequently indicates an allusion to a very complex thought or situation which may require paragraphs of elucidation.

Compared with that of Western poetry, the subject matter of Chinese poetry may be said to cover a similar range of themes, though the relative prominence given to these themes may not be the same in both cases. As Mr. Arthur Waley has admirably observed in the Preface to his *Translations from the Chinese* (New York, 1919, 1941) that while Western poets are often preoccupied with love, love as a theme is on the whole less prominent than the theme of friendship in Chinese poetry. Regarding the mechanical aspects of poetics, Mr. Waley also observes the strong resemblance between the old Chinese poetic form and traditional English verse in the importance attached to rhyme and meter— meter with the Chinese, however, is not concerned with the various combinations of syllabic stresses, but with those of syllabic tones. The most noticeable difference between Chinese poetry and the poetry of the West, I may add, is the brevity of the average Chinese poem. The Chinese poet uses his pen to mark only the heights of his ecstasy and inspiration. The scene may be rich and the story complicated with details. These details the poet will attempt to leave as much as possible to the ingenuity and imagination of his readers.

In Tu Fu we meet a poet who delights in telling the most with the least number of words. Frequently we have to imagine a background and supply the missing items between words and lines before we can appreciate the logical completeness of his message. The less accurately we know the time, the place, and the circumstances in the background, the more liable we are to imagine it incorrectly, and the result will be that we either misunderstand the poem or fail to understand it altogether.

Moreover, most of Tu Fu's poems are of a social nature. They contain vital messages of societal importance. The controlling ambition of Tu Fu's life was to serve his country through statesmanship. Even during the last three years of his life, when his increasing illness convinced him that all hopes of service at the court must be abandoned, his poems to his friends were mainly concerned with urging them to be good officials and loyal subjects. He had indeed great confidence in his poetic ability, and he was proud of his own poetry. But poetry was, to him, only an advocation, not a vocation. The idea of being a professional poet was far from his thoughts—there was no such profession in China. Except in the recent years of commercial journalism, poetry hardly has been a salable merchandise.

Tu Fu wrote poems as letters to his friends. He wrote poems to express his feelings of joy or sadness. A person may sing when he is happy; Tu Fu sings his own song of the occasion, and sometimes we can almost imagine his dances and pantomimes accompanying his singing. A person may weep when he is very unhappy; Tu Fu writes his poems with his tears, and we often feel some of his lines still wet. Since he wanted to be a statesman and held the country and the people close to heart, his anxieties and aspirations were mainly concerned with the good or bad aspects of government, with the welfare or misfortunes of the people, with peace or war. Because his observations are very keen, and his portrayals very vivid, his poems have been generally regarded as indispensable for the study of the history of his time. And what a time it was! The world's most glorious empire, which had enjoyed decades of peace, prosperity, and brilliant culture, suddenly was thrown into the deepest chaos and misery by political intrigue, misgovernment, and war.

One of the writers of the tenth century reported that because Tu Fu's poems reflected so completely and accurately the history of his time, his contemporaries called him the poet-historian. I doubt that the importance of Tu Fu's poetry to history was appreciated as early as that. We have a few of the poems written to Tu Fu by his friends; there is no hint about the poet-historian. His contemporaries did not need his poems to inform them of the institutions and events of their own time. The historical aspect of his poetry could, however, be widely appreciated half a century after his time, after his poetic fame had risen to the heights, and after new generations had become inquisitive about the amazing times of their grandfathers.

It was said that Emperor Wên-tsung (827–841) liked to read Tu Fu's poems. From "Lamentation by the River" [Poem LXXV] he realized that before the capital had suffered the havoc of wars there were beautiful palaces on both banks of the Meandering River, and he decided to rebuild some of them. It is probably from about this time onward that scholarly minds came to appreciate the intimate relation between Tu Fu's poetry and the history of his time. We shall see in some of the chapters to follow how some of the poems would be meaningless to us without the knowledge of their immediate historical background. We shall see also how some of the poems help us to fill in some important omissions and to correct some mystifying errors in the historical records of T'ang. It is important, therefore, that Tu Fu should be read, as far as possible, in the right chronological order.

A selection of Tu Fu's poems, not arranged chronologically, can be justified only if the intention is to illustrate Tu Fu's poetic technique by classifying the selected pieces according to subjects or styles. A volume of translations of his poems like the one brought out in 1929 by Edna Worthley Underwood and Chi-Hwang Chu can hardly be justified. This volume completely lacks any principle of arrangement. Sometimes the same poem is rendered in varying translations, given different titles, and placed at random among the 290 selections. The liberty the translators take with Tu Fu's poetry is at times startling. I do not mean mistranslations, additions, or subtractions among the lines. Even the best Chinese scholars frequently misunderstand this or that poem. When they translate Tu Fu's poems from Chinese poetry into Chinese prose, they invariably have to add many words and subtract a few. A poet is entitled to poetic license. Tu Fu took plenty of it. He could hardly object to his interpreters' and translators' taking some also, if the motive is conscientiously to convey his thought and intention. On the other hand, he might find it difficult to applaud the license that involves cutting up his poems and grafting part of one to part of another. He might even be astounded by the instances wherein a poem originally composed in French in nineteenth-century Europe reappears in an English version as a translation of his Chinese text.

The works on Tu Fu by Florence Ayscough and Erwin von Zach are entirely free from such gratuitous practices. Mrs. Ayscough's two volumes, published in 1929 and 1934, contain over 470 titles, completely or partially translated into English, arranged more or less chronologically, and clearly referred to the pagings of the Chinese originals in the Yang edition. The late indefatigable Sinological translator, Dr. von Zach, published a complete German translation of Tu Fu's poetry in two periodicals and one additional volume during the years 1932–1938. The translation was based on the text and commentary in the edition in twenty *chüan* of Chang Chin, which was completed in 1673 and published probably in 1698; the translated poems naturally follow the same order.

Von Zach's choice of the text was not so well advised as Mrs. Ayscough's. Though he also had studied Tu Fu for twenty-four years, Chang Chin was not a critical scholar, and his approach was amateurish. His edition was based on that of Hsü Tzŭ-ch'ang, under the pretentious title of "One Thousand Commentators' Combined Edition," printed during the first half of the seventeenth century, which in its turn traced its origin to an edition by Kao Ch'ung-lan in 1303. As regards the arrangement of the poems, Chang's edition inherits, therefore, indirectly that of Kao, who merely followed the chronological order of Lu Yin with slight modifications in the light of Huang Ho. This arrangement cannot, of course, compare with that of Yang, which had the benefit of several centuries more of discussion.

7

In the matter of interpretive guidance, Chang's edition is again inferior to Yang's. Yang had the benefit of Ch'ou's industrious labors. Chang inherited Kao's hardly thorough prunings of the multitudes of commentators of the eleventh to the thirteenth centuries. Chang's own contribution to the interpretive aspect of the work was somewhat aided by his readings of the works of two of his contemporaries, Ch'ien Ch'ien-i and Chu Ho-ling, and consisted chiefly of his prose paraphrasings of the parts of a given poem. Von Zach's prosaic translation shows a too heavy dependence on these frequently mediocre interpretations. Though von Zach never mentioned it, he must have been at times bored by or annoyed with the Chang edition, and turned from it to the bulky Ch'ou edition. Quite a few pieces of von Zach's translation were really made according to Ch'ou's interpretation, including such matters as Ch'ou's rearrangement of groups of lines in a given poem. There are, however, a few cases where one might wish that von Zach had also compared Chang with Ch'ou, for had von Zach done so, he would certainly have suppressed in his translation the unfortunate blunders that Chang had transmitted and Ch'ou corrected.

Compared with Dr. von Zach's work, Mrs. Ayscough's represents two other advantages. She was wise to realize that Tu Fu the man was inseparable from Tu Fu the poet. While von Zach was content to translate the poems alone, she made a special effort to introduce the man and his time. Though much of the effort was wasted on trivial matters of doubtful historicity, though her comments are frequently inaccurate, and though the chronology she followed needs considerable revision, these are excusable shortcomings in her case. Her reading ability in literary Chinese was limited, and she depended largely on her Chinese teacher and helper, of whom she spoke with charming generosity in her book. This gentleman, who is made known to us only through his *nom de guerre,* Mr. Cultivator-of-Bamboos, might be an erudite man in many ways, but his acquaintance with T'ang history is rather superficial and his knowledge of Tu Fu's life especially inadequate. At least, some of Mrs. Ayscough's astonishing observations must have resulted from his erroneous information. Yang's text and commentary are in no wise responsible.

Mrs. Ayscough had another advantage in the idea of translating only a selection and not the entire collection of Tu Fu's poems. Dr. von Zach's determination to translate all of the more than fourteen hundred poems —genuine and otherwise; good, bad, and indifferent—was really more ambitious than wise. A few poems of Tu Fu are so fancifully illogical, whimsically ambiguous, and purposely vague that though we suspect he must have some hidden message under the bizarre surface, we cannot get at it because of our inability to build a background with defensible historicity. A good commentator would not hesitate to acknowledge his

8

inability to deal with them. A poor commentator would continue to hand out old absurdities or proceed to make new ones. A wise translator will do well to stay away from them. Mrs. Ayscough did stay away from them. Her principle of selection was to give preference to those poems she regarded important for illustrating Tu Fu's life and those poems she liked.

When we come to the question of translation, we have to acknowledge that Dr. von Zach had the advantage of a master Sinologue and an experienced translator. Except for places where Tu Fu's text was difficult and Chang Chin's interpretation misleading, and except for occasional slips, he gave an accurate, though prosaic, translation. Mrs. Ayscough's translation suffers badly by comparison. She was very proud of her new method in translation. But alas! It is indefensible. The origin of this method went back to the time when Mrs. Ayscough and Amy Lowell were collaborating on an anthology of Chinese poetry in English translation, published in 1921 as *Fir-Flower Tablets*. The method is described at the beginning of the book, again in the prefaces of Mrs. Ayscough's two volumes on Tu Fu, and finally in a charming volume of the correspondence between the two ladies, published in 1942 by Mrs. Ayscough's second husband, the late Professor Harley Farnsworth MacNair of the University of Chicago.

The basic assumption of the method was that the etymological derivations of the Chinese ideographs (or characters, or words) composing the lines in a poem were of great importance. Suppose there are two characters having the same meaning in current usage. Why should the poet choose the one instead of the other? The ladies believed that the choice was determined according to how well the "descriptive allusions" or the "undercurrent of meaning" would enrich the "perfume" of the poem. In order to get at the descriptive allusions and meaningful undercurrents, the translator must study the structure and the component parts of the character and know its "ancestry." A philological approach to the learning of words in any language is, of course, a sound one, but I consider it unsound to assume that among synonyms the poet's choice is primarily concerned with archaic meanings and associations. A poet's discrimination between synonyms is very frequently concerned with the difference in sound values. It often has to do with usage, the relation of the word to the other word or words in the line. If the poem is intended to appeal to the general public, the poet would prefer the current and conventional usage. If the poem is to appeal to learned readers, he would want the combination to be acceptable in the sense that an example or an analogy could be cited from some acknowledged masterpiece to justify it, and he would want it to be fresh in the sense that it has not been overworked in current and conventional usage. The obscure and archaic origins and associations of a word are seldom capitalized upon by a poet

9

unless he wants to convey some cryptic message—in which rare case he would have to employ the word in a startling and puzzling combination so as to force his reader to fish in the undercurrents of the etymological depth.

Let us see in an example how Mrs. Ayscough's method is not justifiable. In Tu Fu's poem, "A Poetry Contest after Dinner at the Tso Villa" [Poem I], the words in the first line and their immediate meanings are as follows:

fêng	lin	hsien	yüeh	lo
wind	forest	slender	moon	drops

There are various ways to translate the line into an acceptable English sentence. For reasons of symmetrical balance with the next line and contextual harmony with the whole poem, it might be rendered somewhat as follows:

Behind the windy forest, the slender moon has dropped.

Mrs. Ayscough's translation is entirely different:

Wind weaves,   of forest shadows   and fallen   moon-light,
    a pattern, white in warp and black in weft;

In the Preface to her first volume, she cited this translation to illustrate her method. In her efforts to scrutinize the ancestry of characters, she discovered in a dictionary that the character *hsien* had, besides the usual meaning of "slender," the rather unusual meaning of "silk woven with a white warp and a black weft." So this was the stray ancestor that should be dragged into the translation to enrich the poetic perfume of the line. And she felt that Tu Fu purposely used this "silk woven with a white warp and a black weft" as a figure to describe the moonlight he saw. As a faithful translator, she must not abbreviate this beautiful figure.

I have grave doubts. In the first place, I wonder whether a piece of fabric with any design of weaving could be an apt figure for moonlight through a forest. Granting that it could be, wouldn't it be more likely a piece that is woven with a black warp and a white weft? In the second place, it is generally better poetry to lead the reader to see the sight for himself than to tell what it is like, especially when it is difficult to describe. Tu Fu is a good poet precisely because with only five simple words he has led our imagination to see the faint moonlight filtered through the madly dancing foliage of a forest. He would be a very tiresome and bad poet, if after taking us to the sight, he goes on to tell us which particular kind of fabricated merchandise should be compared with what we see before us.

In the third place, though it is bad poetry, the translation can still be justified, if it is merely Mrs. Ayscough's reading into Tu Fu's line what she imagined she would see after the poet had led her to the scene. But it cannot be justified on the strength of the tiny character *hsien*. With or without ancestry, the character cannot bear that burden while it is standing in that particular spot in the line. Controlled both ways by word order in the line and by antithetical balance with the third word in the next line, it has to be a modifier, modifying the next word, "moon." It has to be the adjective "slender" and cannot be the noun "silk woven . . ."

In the last place, Mrs. Ayscough liked to mention *Shuo wên* (A.D. 121) as the source of information on Chinese etymological derivations. This ancient philological treatise gave only the meaning of "slender" for *hsien*. A writer toward the close of the second century, commenting on a defective text in one of the later classics, where *hsien* appeared in what was thought to be a substantive position, made the wild guess that it meant a woven fabric white in warp and black in weft. This peculiar meaning is applicable only to this one doubtful passage, though lexicographers have kept on transmitting it in dictionaries. This meaning, therefore, instead of being an ancestor, was only an imaginary distant cousin!

When Miss Lowell and Mrs. Ayscough were collaborating on their anthology, the plan was for Mrs. Ayscough to prepare first a word-for-word translation of the original, as literal as possible and with as much as possible of the "splitting" of the characters into component ancestral pictures. Then Miss Lowell would work over the draft and reduce it to a poem. As a, if not the, leading imagist, Miss Lowell was naturally enthusiastic about the abundance of images that resulted from the "splittings." Just imagine the one word "slender" split up into so many interesting things! With her fine poetic training and experience, Miss Lowell did produce in *Fir-Flower Tablets* many readable, intelligible, and good, if not always accurately translated, poems.

The translation of Tu Fu was also intended to be a collaborative work of the two ladies. After Miss Lowell's death in 1925, Mrs. Ayscough revised her own draft for publication. From the standpoint of readability, it could hardly be compared with the few selections of Tu Fu included in *Fir-Flower Tablets*. The line we quoted as an example is one of the best that has resulted from the peculiar method of translation. In many other places, Tu Fu appears to be babbling strings of idiotic nonsense. One cannot help being well impressed by Mrs. Ayscough's warm enthusiasm for our poet, her excellent planning for a historical presentation of him and his poetry, and the meticulous care she takes in her work. But then one might wonder how the selected poems were worthy of her good intention and conscientious efforts. One should know it is the novel method of translation that is at fault.

In the following chapters, my general plan is somewhat similar to Mrs. Ayscough's. The general theme is: Tu Fu's life and time, interpreted according to my understanding and appreciation and illustrated with my translation of 374 of his poems. In the portrayal of Tu Fu's time, I shall emphasize certain political, economic, and social details that should give more intimate glimpses into the poet's life and thought. I shall deliberately neglect many institutions and personalities that might be important for a complete picture of the period, but which are not sufficiently relevant to the life of Tu Fu. Likewise, I shall accentuate Tu Fu's more important friendships; but shall not mention the many friends and acquaintances who had no great influence on him, unless the contacts happen to be usable clues in solving some of the difficult problems of chronology. I shall advocate the revision at a number of points of the chronology of Yang, which was followed by Mrs. Ayscough. I am reminded of how Tu Fu described the patched embroidery on his two daughters' robes by saying that some of the pictures were upside down on the skirts [LXXXIX]. In the repatching of fragmentary information to make a new picture of Tu Fu's life, I hope I have succeeded in setting right some of the hitherto inverted details. My fear is that there might still be too many inversions in the picture I present.

Since I do not wish to have the book larger than a convenient-sized volume, I have been very sparing in the selection of poems to be translated. The first preference is given to those that contain important information about the life of Tu Fu. A few of these are rather mediocre from the literary standpoint. If they are not spurious, I shall include them merely for the sake of history. I shall include also most of the poems that are justly famous. The Roman numerals accompanying the poem titles represent the order of the appearance of the poems in my book as well as what I regard to be the time sequence in which Tu Fu composed them. Tu Fu knew that his poetry would live forever. Hence, I chose the first line of one of his poems [CCCXXIV] to appear on the title page of this book.

In the matter of translation, my principle is to tell what I think the poet is trying to communicate in the light of the text and the context which generally extends far beyond one individual poem. It will not be literal. Literal translation of vernacular Chinese is easy and practicable. Literal translation of documentary Chinese is possible and desirable. Literal translation of literary Chinese is not only difficult but also misleading. To enjoy a social dinner, it is not necessary to swallow the table decorations. But the spirit of hospitality and friendship should not be missed. In literary Chinese, table decorations are generally thrown in to satisfy the mechanical requirements. The spirit is often evident only between courses.

I have found it difficult to cast my translation in English meter and rhyme. It is almost impossible to avoid "paring down the foot to fit the shoe," as an ancient Chinese adage says. I try, therefore, to convey only Tu Fu's thought and spirit, and cease to worry over form. My general procedure was to draft my own translation first, and then to compare it with such other translations as are accessible to me. These are listed in the Notes, which are to be published in a supplementary volume. I am grateful to most of them, for frequently they inspired or provoked me to revise my draft translations. Except in cases of extraordinary errors, I refrain from commenting on the other translations. Von Zach's work frequently gives indications of other translations. His references have led me to a number of stray pieces the existence of which I would not otherwise have known. Mrs. Martha Davidson, who has been preparing a bibliography of translations of Chinese texts, has been so kind as to give me a number of titles containing translations of Tu Fu. These are specifically acknowledged in my notes.

Something has to be said about the text back of my translation. As matters stand now, Tu Fu cannot be translated from any one single text. The variant readings have to be sorted and choice made according to some principle of selection. In my prolegomena to the *Concordance to Tu Fu* (Harvard-Yenching Institute, 1940) I have given an extensive discussion of the genealogical relationships of the important editions. I called attention to the need of exercising caution in the use of Ch'ien Ch'ien-i's edition (1667) and almost all of the editions after it, for they were more or less influenced by Ch'ien.

Ch'ien Ch'ien-i (1582–1664) was a man of masterly erudition, persuasive literary ability, and rather doubtful character. He made some important contributions to the interpretation of Tu Fu and to the correction of many of the erroneous notions that had been transmitted through the centuries. His influence on scholars of Tu Fu during and after his time was due to his great fame, his real contribution to the study, and especially his edition of the text. His edition was based on what he claimed to be an edition of 1133 by Wu Jo, which contained an impressive display of textural variants. Ch'ien also employed a younger scholar, Chu Ho-ling (1606–1683), to pick up more variants from a few other works, such as early anthologies which included selections from Tu Fu, and to add them to the "Wu Jo" variants. Later on, the two men quarreled over the work, the collaboration was ended, and each went ahead to publish an edition. Ch'ien's edition did not appear until three years after his death, the supervision of its printing being entrusted to a partisan pupil and clansman of his. Chu's edition appeared shortly after. Of these two editions, the interpretive aspect differs in that Ch'ien's was the more brilliant and Chu's the more cautious. Subsequent commentators have generally taken their choice from one or other of these works.

13

In the textural aspect, Ch'ien's work was generally recognized as the best. However, Emperor Ch'ien-lung (reigned 1736–1795) felt an intense animosity against the memory of Ch'ien and ordered the complete destruction of all of his literary products. From 1776 to almost the end of the nineteenth century, books in Ch'ien's name and books quoting Ch'ien by name could be obtained only in secret and at some risk. Nevertheless, Ch'ien's influence continued, especially in matters relating to Tu Fu. A number of new editions followed principally Ch'ien's text without mentioning his name.

In my judgment, the so-called Wu Jo text with its fine display of variant readings—a hand-copy of which was in the possession of Ch'ien alone, but was nowhere to be found shortly after his time—was a clever forgery made by plagiarizing a plagiarist's edition of 1204 and by putting in a number of additions and alterations. Circumstantial evidence seems to point to Ch'ien himself as the forger. The details of my research and conclusion are in the prolegomena mentioned above. I mention this matter here mainly to indicate that when my translation differs from that of the other translators, aside from other causes, it may also be due to a difference in the textual basis. I refer every poem to a page and a serial number in the second volume of the *Concordance*, which contains a reprinting of the text edited in 1183. I generally give preference to the readings in this text. When the question of variants should be considered, I turn next to Ch'ien or Ch'ou, or both. If an apparently desirable variant appears with some priority claim—especially the claim of a high position on the genealogical table—I may accept it only after confirming it by such other early editions as the bogus Wang edition of the thirteenth century and the plagiarist Ts'ai edition of 1204, both of which are now accessible in reprints. The first volume of the *Concordance* contains a cross-reference table which will give the exact location of any given poem in numerous other editions.

Take, for instance, the line about the dropping of the slender moon behind a windy forest. Ch'ou's text reads *lin fêng*, not *fêng lin*. Why did Ch'ou accept this inversion? Not only because it seemed to him better, but also because Ch'ien's "Wu Jo" indicated this variant as one from a text as early as 945! Since I cannot confirm it by other means, I drop it as one of the items forged by Ch'ien.

I have intended this volume mainly for scholars who are not Sinologues. Sinologues would naturally prefer to enjoy Tu Fu in the original Chinese. Since, however, I have advanced a few new hypotheses concerning Tu Fu's life and times, some Sinologues may be interested; and I shall welcome their criticism. The notes in the supplementary volume and the Chinese characters in the index in that volume are mainly for their convenience.

In my reconstruction of Tu Fu's life, I use strictly the geographical names of the times concerned. During Tu Fu's lifetime the name of a place generally had been changed three times. These changes and the dates and the modern location of the places are indicated in the index. The maps locate only the places relevant to the present study. I do not propose to include in this volume any pictures of Tu Fu. None of them is authentic.

"One remembered, ten forgotten."

CHAPTER ONE

In China, the family and the clan occupy a central position in a man's thinking. The Tu clan is no mean one. Their genealogy claims an origin from the great Emperor Yao of hoary antiquity, with the legendary chronology of 2357–2257 B.C., and boasts of numerous men of virtue and achievement and many members of the feudal nobility throughout the centuries. One of the most illustrious was Tu Yü (A.D. 222–284) of the Tu or Tu-ling District in the Ching-chao (or Capital) Prefecture, who married a princess of the imperial family, was ennobled as a marquis, and rose to the rank of the highest generals of the army and the highest prefect of the state; who left a widely read commentary on one of the most important Confucian classics; and who, above all else, was admired by posterity as a man of good character and sound scholarship, worthy of his place among the immortals in the Confucian temple.

Tu Fu (A.D. 712–770, known also as Tu Tzŭ-mei) was very proud of this ancestor, from whom he considered himself a descendant of the thirteenth generation. Of the more immediate progenitors, custom requires a man, for all legal purposes, to identify his descent from the great-grandfather downward, and here again the list shows that Tu Fu did not come from an obscure and poor family. His great-grandfather, Tu I-i, was the magistrate of Kung District, a position that corresponded to the sixteenth step from the bottom on the ladder of officialdom, which required thirty steps to the top. His grandfather, Tu Shên-yen, passed the imperial literary examinations in 670 and, after a checkered official career, died in 708 in the position of what might be called an associate professor in the Peers' College, and was posthumously promoted to be a

Writer of the Bureau of Literary Composition, a position on the eighteenth step. He was regarded as one of the four foremost men of letters of his time. When Tu Fu said, "Poetry is the distinction of our family," he was without doubt thinking of the grandfather whom he had not the good fortune of seeing.

Of Tu Fu's father we know very little. The name was Tu Hsien according to Yüan Chên (779–831), who wrote the text for Tu Fu's funerary tablet in 813, wherein it was also said that Tu Hsien was magistrate of Fêng-t'ien District. This identification has been followed by all biographical accounts of Tu Fu to our own day, and the tendency has been to make Tu Hsien die as magistrate of Fêng-t'ien. *The Compendium of Genealogies,* compiled in 812, added that Tu Hsien had been police commissioner of Wu-kung district before he became magistrate of Fêng-t'ien. This constituted no difficulty, for the earlier position was lower in rank than the later one, and it could be understood that some promotion had taken place. A difficulty arises, however, in Tu Fu's text, dated 744, for the funerary tablet of his step-grandmother. There, Tu Hsien was said to have died on the nineteenth step up the ranking ladder—as the assistant prefect of Yen-chou Prefecture. Commentators and biographers of Tu Fu, without reading the text of this funerary inscription carefully, mistakenly concluded that the poet's father was assistant prefect before 744 and district magistrate sometime after 744. The late Professor Wên I-to even ventured the guess that Tu Hsien probably died sometime after 751.

These scholars have neglected to give close attention to the relative rankings of local functionaries in the T'ang system and have forgotten that the frequent changes in geographical nomenclature constitute an important criterion in questions of chronology. My own hypothesis is that Tu Hsien probably entered officialdom by way of the T'ang system of *yin* (or heritage of grace) allowed a son of an official from the seventeenth rung upward. A few years after the death of his father Tu Shên-yen, he would be entitled to an appointment with a ranking not higher than the fourth step up, and the police commissioner of Wu-kung was ranked on the third step. There is no way to tell how long he stayed in that position, for though an official might be promoted in rank according to periodical accounting of accumulated merits, a change of employment did not necessarily follow. When he became magistrate of Fêng-t'ien, Tu Hsien had reached the sixteenth step. The ranking of an assistant prefect of Yen-chou Prefecture corresponded to the nineteenth rung. It would seem, therefore, that Tu Hsien's Yen-chou appointment came after his Fêng-t'ien service. Yen-chou was renamed Lu-chün in 742, and this means that his whole official career and his death were all before that date.

Tu Fu did not know his own grandmother, the first Mrs. Tu Shên-yen, née Hsüeh. After giving birth to three sons and three daughters, she died in 691, while most of the children were still young. The second Mrs. Tu Shên-yen, née Lu, brought up these children as well as one son and two daughters of her own. She died in 744 in her sixty-ninth year; and in her funerary inscription Tu Fu spoke of her as a lady who understood well the rules of propriety.

On his mother's side, our poet descended from the imperial Li family of the T'ang dynasty. His maternal grandmother, a Mrs. Ts'ui, was a great-granddaughter of Emperor T'ai-tsung (reigned 627–649), one of the best and ablest rulers in Chinese history. We doubt that Tu Fu ever saw this maternal grandmother, though he held her memory in great respect because of her heroism in daring to visit and to bring food to her parents, who were first thrown into prison and later killed by the usurper Empress Wu in the persecution of 685–688 which wiped out most of the princes and princesses of the imperial Li family.

Several centuries after Tu Fu's death, a legend developed gradually that the name of the poet's mother was Hai-t'ang (or Crab Apple) and that she was a concubine of Tu Hsien. This represented only a vain attempt to explain away two apparent puzzles. Our poet spent almost ten of his later years (759–768) in Shu, now Szechuan Province, and wrote poems on practically every kind of flower. There was no poem of his on the crab-apple blossom, for the beauty and profusion of which the Shu regions were famous. Was he observing the taboo wherein one, out of deep respect, never mentioned certain personal names—principally those of the emperors of the dynasty and those of one's own immediate forebears? Hai-t'ang would sound like a feminine name, and so a writer of the eleventh century made the wild guess that the poet's mother was so named.

Moreover, since Tu Fu's maternal grandmother was a Mrs. Ts'ui, his mother must be, of course, née Ts'ui. But in the funerary inscription of his step-grandmother, her oldest stepdaughter-in-law was given as née Lu. A writer of the seventeenth century jumped to the conclusion that whereas Mrs. Tu Hsien, née Lu, was the legal spouse, Tu Fu's mother, Ts'ui Hai-t'ang before marriage, was only a concubine. The guesser might indeed consider himself clever, for the crab-apple blossom being a common flower of no great value, a maiden so named was likely to become a servant girl or a concubine. He had forgoten that the grand-daughter of a prince and great-granddaughter of an emperor was unlikely, before the collapse of the dynasty, to be given into concubinage.

The solution to the riddle is hinted in the story of Tu Fu's aunt, whom he immortalized in a beautiful funerary inscription dated 742. Mrs. P'ei Jung-chi was the second daughter of Tu Shên-yen by the first marriage, and she probably exercised more than any other woman an inspiring influence on Tu Fu's life. He proposed to have her known to posterity as the Righteous Aunt of T'ang Dynasty. While still an infant, he was in her care. It was perhaps during an epidemic that Tu Fu and her son both became very ill. A sorceress who came to the house predicted that only the child placed in the southeastern corner of the bedroom would be saved. The aunt took her own son out of the crib in the southeastern corner and placed little Tu Fu therein. "On this account," said Tu Fu, "I lived, and my aunt's son died." The example of her character can explain a number of decisions in our poet's life, wherein he deliberately chose self-denial. The story incidentally explains his relation to his own mother, who was not once mentioned either in his prose or in his poetry: she must have died shortly after he was born. Tu Fu had no recollection of her.

Was Tu Fu the only son of this Mrs. Tu Hsien, née Ts'ui? His contemporaries sometimes referred to him as Tu Number Two. This would oblige us to assume that he had either an elder brother or an elder cousin. The *Old T'ang History* mentioned Tu Hsien as the second son of Tu Shên-yen. This might favor the assumption that Tu Hsien had an elder brother who had a son older than Tu Fu. That Tu Hsien was the second son of Tu Shên-yen was, however, not confirmed by the *Compendium of Genealogies* of 812 and could be repudiated by citations from Tu Fu's text for the funerary tablet for his step-grandmother. We may assume, therefore, that Tu Fu had an elder brother. Since this elder brother was never mentioned in Tu Fu's writings, we may assume further that he must have died very young.

According to my interpretation of the historical source material, Mrs. Tu Hsien, née Lu, was simply Tu Fu's stepmother, who was married to his father after the death of the first wife, née Ts'ui. In Tu Fu's poems, three younger brothers and one younger sister are frequently and affectionately mentioned. These were, of course, the children of his father and the stepmother. There is, however, complete silence about this stepmother, who was certainly still alive in 744. This silence, I suspect, speaks volumes to account for so much of our poet's absence from home during boyhood, youth, and early manhood.

We do not know where Tu Fu was born. The term "native place" is an ambiguity in Chinese documents. It might indeed refer to a birth place, but it might allude to a locality chosen for permanent residence, a district where the old homestead of the family is to be found, or a prefecture wherein the clan had originated. In formal documents, our poet refers to himself as Tu Fu of Ching-chao, which in his time was the first prefecture of the empire, containing the capital city known popularly as Ch'ang-an and some twenty districts. The first of these districts was Wan-nien, which contained the suburb Tu-ling, located only a few miles to the south of the capital city. In his poetry, Tu Fu called himself an old rustic of Tu-ling or of Shao-ling—Shao-ling being an area of slight elevation in Tu-ling. The reference to Ching-chao might indicate only the origin of the clan. Many of the Tu families of his time were indeed still inhabiting Tu-ling, but it is doubtful that he had a home there until after he had acquired some farm property in the neighborhood in his early forties.

At the foot of the famous Shou-yang Hills in the Yen-shih District, some three hundred miles to the east of the capital Ch'ang-an, Tu Fu's illustrious ancestor Tu Yü was buried; so were his grandfather and grandmothers, and if my guess is correct, also his father and mother. He had built a house in the district and owned some land. He and his brothers probably lived there for a time. Thus Yen-shih might also be said to be his home place. Since it was a district of the Prefecture of Honan and bordered on the west the principal city, Lo-yang (or Eastern Capital), some scholars were led to think that Lo-yang was his home city. But he himself did not think so, for the opening line of his first poem to Li Po [ix] says, "I was two years a sojourner in the Eastern Capital."

Ever since biographical accounts of Tu Fu appeared in the *Old T'ang History* (945) and the *New T'ang History* (1060), there has been a persistent effort to regard Hsiang-yang (about 275 miles south of Lo-yang, slightly to the west) as the native place of our poet. But neither in Tu Fu's poems nor in the existent poems of his grandfather was Hsiang-yang ever mentioned in such a way as to indicate it as the place of the home or the temple. We have no right to make Hsiang-yang the native place of Tu Fu, in whatever interpretation, since he refers to himself as belonging to other places. Modern scholars have also a tendency to regard Kung, an adjacent district to the east of Yen-shih, as the home district of Tu Fu. The supposition is that since his great-grandfather had been the magistrate of Kung, the family had continued to live there. But there is no such indication in Tu Fu's writings.

Nor do we know the date of Tu Fu's birthday. It took several hundred years for scholars to determine the correct year of his birth, 712. But the year 712 is one of those confusing years of T'ang chronology, wherein one can easily make a mistake as regards the reigning emperor and the reigning period. The days of 712 before March 1 belong to the second or third year of the Ching-yün period of Emperor Jui-tsung. From March 1 to April 20 the time belongs to the first year of the T'ai-chi period of the same emperor. From April 21 to September 11 it was the first year of the Yen-ho period of the same Emperor Jui-tsung. On September 8 the emperor abdicated in favor of his son, the great Emperor Hsüan-tsung, more popularly known as Ming-huang, but did not, however, relinquish some of the most important authorities of government until July 31 of the following year, 713. From September 12 to the end of 712 the days belong to yet another period, the first year of the Hsien-t'ien period. Of which emperor? The historian is free to choose Jui-tsung or Ming-huang. The biographers and commentators of our poet generally say that he was born in the first year of the Hsien-t'ien period of Emperor Jui-tsung or Emperor Ming-huang. This is of course hazardous, since there is no way of knowing the day, or month, or even the season of his birth.

From his later poetic reminiscences, we can draft a rough sketch of Tu Fu's early life. In the winter of 767 in the house of a friend in K'uei-chou, he saw a special dance given by a Madame Li and recalled that he had seen the same sort of dance some fifty-odd years previously, in the year 715, performed in Yen-ch'êng by Madame Li's teacher, Madame Kung-sun [cccxxx]. One of the earliest biographers indeed doubted such prodigy of observation in a boy in his fourth year. A later editor indicated a variant reading which would change 715 to 717. It seems to me neither necessary to assume that a man could not remember an impressive experience at the age of three, nor wise to preclude the possibility that the memory of such an experience in early boyhood might have been freshened and explained by elders as the boy grew up. It should be noted that Yen-ch'êng was about 150 miles south and slightly east of Lo-yang and was nowhere near the places Tu Hsien was reported to have been an official. Could little Tu Fu still be with his aunt, and could P'ei Jung-chi be at that time an official in Yen-ch'êng? We have no literary evidence to answer these questions one way or the other.

In a long poem entitled "Brave Adventures" [ccxi], which I would date in the year 761, we have most of Tu Fu's reminiscences of his youth. He says in the poem that in his seventh year his thoughts already tended to be heroic, and his first song was concerned with the fabulous phoenix which, in the Confucian tradition, was supposed to harbinger an age of sagacious government. In his ninth year, he began to practice calligraphy in large characters, and his writings soon filled a bag. When he was between thirteen and fourteen, if we take his word, he had already ventured into the arena of letters, and two famed writers of the time even saw in him a possible reincarnation of some of the greatest literary masters of antiquity.

Unfortunately, we know nothing about Tu Fu's schooling. Neither where, nor how. The eighth-century T'ang system of education was, of course, very different from the twentieth-century republican system of schools which are somewhat modeled after American and European patterns. In the T'ang empire there was indeed a system of public schools with limited enrollments open to the sons of the privileged. None of these, however, was open to boys under thirteen years. So the early schooling of our poet was probably obtained in one of the private schools, which were usually maintained jointly by the families that could afford to hire teachers to instruct the children in classical literature. In the

T'ang system of imperial examinations, candidates were sent up either by the public schools, mainly to qualify for the *ming-ching* degree of proficiency in canonical classics, or by the prefectures, mainly to qualify for the *chin-shih* degree of skill in writing prose and poetry. Since in his "Brave Adventures" Tu Fu mentioned his being sent up by his home prefecture, we may safely conclude that he did not go to a public school even after he reached the age of thirteen. But he must have gone to some school or schools, for in one of his poems written in 766 [CCLXXXIII] he said that many of his schoolmates were enjoying position and affluence in the neighborhood of Ch'ang-an. And this may prompt us to guess that his schooling was at least in part in the Ching-chao Prefecture. Indeed, since in another of his later poems he contrasted his growing old in K'uei-chou with his boyhood north of the Wei River, we may be justified in believing that some of his schooling was in the neighborhood of Wu-kung or Fêng-t'ien, both north of the Wei, both belonging to the Ching-chao Prefecture, and both about fifty miles from Ch'ang-an.

If Tu Fu's literary ability at the early age of thirteen or fourteen was good enough to impress some of the masters of the time, it must imply not only prodigious intelligence, but also unusual diligence in study. It does not necessarily mean, however, that the boy did not have boyish activities. In yet another poem [CLXXXII] containing early reminiscences, he recalled how at the age of fourteen he was running about like a healthy calf, and how he climbed trees to pluck pears and dates a thousand times a day.

Tu Fu traced his habit of drinking to early youth and justified it by saying that it was needed to soften an uncompromising inner self that had an intense hatred of wickedness. We wonder what sort of wickedness a boy in his teens could know. At home, or in society? At any rate, he said that he detached himself from those who were superficially clever and associated only with the grayheads. Exhilarated by wine, Tu Fu and his older companions cast their glances over the entire universe and all vulgar worldliness dwindled into oblivion. The eighth century, we may understand, was long before the advent of our modern crusades for temperance or prohibition. There has been in China very little condemnation of the moderate use of alcoholic drinks on moral or physiological grounds. Even Confucius was said to have drunk wine without limit, though always short of "disorder." In Tu Fu's time the ordinary wine was very likely taken warm as it is done in China today. Its effect comes and goes quickly. Excessive drinking as portrayed in "Eight Immortals of the Wine Cup" was rare; and even there the inordinate inebriation has generally been regarded with more pleasantry than deprecation. Wine was always served on festive occasions. In Tu Fu's poetry there were the pepper wine and the cypress-flavored wine for the New Year's festival; there were the chrysanthemum wine and the bamboo-leaf wine for the Double Ninth (the ninth day of the ninth month) festival. Such home-brews were considered to be good for health and longevity, and even children were permitted to drink them. We need not, therefore, be surprised that some of the eighth-century grayheads should encourage juvenile Tu Fu in the drinking of wine.

When he was still in his late teens, Tu Fu had already started to roam far and wide. Travel in China in those days lacked the speed and comfort possible on vehicles driven by steam, gas, and electricity. The horse, the donkey, the wooden cart, and the wooden boat were the only means, if one did not want to walk, wade, and swim. But then Tu Fu's early travels for pleasure were again different from his later travels from necessity. It is not only the motives of travel that make a difference. The times too give a sharp contrast: peace, prosperity, and hospitality on the road in the earlier period; war, poverty, and brigandage to be met in Tu Fu's last years.

Unfortunately, we know very few of the particulars of his earliest travels. We can only guess why a boy should be permitted long and far away from home. Perhaps, it was deemed a safe enough and possibly desirable experience for the lad, and for the home folks, especially the stepmother, a relief from some of the strained feelings. At any rate, off he went. He crossed the Yellow River and visited the district of I-shih in P'u-chou Prefecture. We know of this only from some casual mentions in later poems. We know also that he made an extensive trip to the southeastern coast of the empire, visiting the places of scenic beauty or historical interest in the prefectures of Su-chou, Hang-chou, Yüeh-chou, and T'ai-chou and musing over the contrast of his age with the times of heroism and intrigue and of refinement and vulgarity centuries ago. Among the friends he made, he mentioned with affection, about thirty years later, a venerable Buddhist monk in Chiang-ning District [CVI] with whom he wrote poetry, played chess, and went boating. This southern trip possibly took several years. He had wished to sail farther south along the enchanting Yen River. He had engaged a ship with the hope of exploring the islands of the eastern sea. He had to give up. Why? Was it repeated letters from home, urging him to return and get ready for prefectural and imperial examinations? At all events, it seems reasonable to suppose that he did get to Ch'ang-an in the later part of 735 to take the prefectural examinations in order to qualify as one of the candidates from the Ching-chao Prefecture for the imperial examinations to be given in the spring of 736.

At the conclusion of the southern trip, Tu Fu was already in his twenty-fourth year. He must have written, of course, many pieces of prose and of poetry. With the possible exception of one little poem, they are not transmitted in the present collection of his works.

The slender moon has dropped behind the windy forest. A lute, moist with dew, lies untouched in the open. A hidden brook rushes beneath the flower path; Above the thatched roof the firmament is studded with spring stars.

We consult books, aware of the candles' burning short; We reëxamine the sword, still taking time to sip our cups. The poems are finished, then chanted in the Wu dialect. The allusion to Fan Li's little boat is hard to forget.

We do not know who Tso was, or where the villa was situated, or when Tu Fu wrote this poem. In a poetry contest the candles were generally marked to indicate the time allowed the versifiers. The sword could have been a family heirloom, and it might be the subject on which the poems were to be written. In literary allusions, books and swords refer, as a rule, to one's readiness to serve his country with knowledge and prowess. Fan Li of the fifth century B.C., having helped his prince to defeat the Prince of Wu, disdained any reward for his extraordinary service and sailed away in a light boat, never to return. The Wu dialects spoken in the Su-chou, Hang-chou, and nearby prefectures differed greatly from those of the capital and other northern prefectures. Since Tu Fu had traveled for some time, possibly several years, in the south, he could have learned enough of the Wu dialect to understand the poems chanted—certainly enough to catch and be impressed by the allusion to Fan Li's leisurely sailings after a victorious career. Was our poet thinking of the opportunities of public service after the examinations? Was he regretting the necessity of postponing to the indefinite future the more extensive sailing trips he had planned? I am inclined to think that the poem becomes more meaningful if we assign it to the late spring of 735, toward the end of his southern trip.

What have become of the other writings of this early period, 712–735? They might simply have been lost, as were many of Tu Fu's writings of other periods. He may have thrown away those early pieces when he found them too short of the standard he set himself in later years. Unfortunately, because of the loss of these, we are obliged to reconstruct this early period of his life mainly from reminiscences and casual mentions in his later prose and poetry. What we have gleaned is very little. Borrowing one of his lines from an entirely different context, we may even say, "One remembered, ten forgotten."

"More than eight years of lively freedom."

CHAPTER TWO

In Tu Fu's time, promising scholars of the empire aspired to pass the *chin-shih* examinations. An official appointment followed this success as a matter of course, and the climb up the ladder of officialdom could be rapid. Annually, only about thirty among the many hundreds of candidates at the imperial examinations would be passed. The difficulty of attaining success accounted for much of its honor and glamor.

A scholar must first apply to the prefectural government for preliminary examinations to qualify himself as a candidate. The subjects examined were similar to those at the imperial examinations: first, prose and poetry; then five essays on some specified current problems of government; and then a few questions from the classics of the Confucian and Taoist canons. Prefectural officials generally examined the applicants very thoroughly, for they would be given demerits if they failed to send up really qualified candidates or if too many of their candidates showed too poorly at the imperial examinations. By midwinter, the chosen candidates had to present themselves at the Executive Division of the Imperial Government to go through the routines of registration and certification. The imperial examinations were given the following spring, with the chief officer of the Bureau of Examinations in the Ministry of Appointment as the chief examiner.

Before the candidates were locked up in the examination halls, how would they spend their time in Ch'ang-an? We might expect them to keep themselves busy with books. As a matter of fact, probably very few were so engaged. It had gradually become customary for a candidate to do a good deal of self-advertising. This was many centuries before the practice of sealing up the names of the candidates was adopted. Since the examiners could read the candidates' names on their papers, it was but natural that they would be somewhat influenced in evaluating a particular paper if they happened to know the candidate personally, to know of his powerful relatives or patrons at court, or to know of his popular renown as a man of letters. Hence the custom developed of the candidates' trying to bring their own names into prominence. Spring was a gay time in Ch'ang-an, and there were many parties. If a talented scholar wrote a clever song, it would soon be on the lips of the singing girls; and this was one of the quickest ways to achieve popularity. Most of the scholars, however, spent their time in calling on prominent officials who had some genuine or feigned interest in literature. Under the pretext of seeking criticism and guidance, a candidate would present an official a roll containing sample writings in poetry or prose, or both. If the great man happened to be well impressed with a passage or a couplet, he might quote it to his friends, and the fame of the writer would soon be circulated.

What did Candidate Tu Fu do in Ch'ang-an in the late winter of 735 and early spring of 736? I am inclined to believe that he attended very little to self-advertising. He probably felt no need to do so, for he had complete confidence in his own ability to win high honors in the examinations. Two later poems [xxv, ccxi] tell us that, before the examinations, he had worn out ten thousand rolls of books by reading, and whenever he put words on paper, he felt divine inspiration in every thought. He would compare himself with only the greatest of the past, and he had no fear of the competition of his contemporaries. Granted, there are poetic exaggerations in the lines conveying such memories. At least, circumstances seemed to encourage him in his youthful pride. Was he not the grandson of Tu Shên-yen, famous as much for literary skill as for proud contempt of all rivals? Was he not a candidate offered by the Ching-chao Prefecture, whose chief city was the cultural as well as the political center of the empire? Of students who had come from among the "barbarians" beyond the frontiers to get an inkling of the learning and wisdom in store in the great city—of these alone, there were eight thousand. Naturally, the candidacy-qualifying examinations given by the Ching-chao Prefecture would be very "stiff." The fact of being a candidate from Ching-chao was already a rare honor, and the Ching-chao candidates were seldom known to fail in the imperial examinations. Moreover, our poet was not without fame in the city at this time. Among the elder officials, there were Li Yung and Wang Han, both long celebrated for literary success. Tu Fu had not called on them. But Li himself sought the acquaintance of the young man. And Wang even wanted to live close to the proud candidate.

The imperial examinations of 736 became famous because of a bitter quarrel which brought about a change in the administration of sub-sequent examinations. The chief examiner was Li Ang, a cantankerous man who wanted to show that he passed the papers entirely on merit. He took the unnecessary measure of calling the candidates together and of criticizing the literary blemishes of those who had tried to influence him by devious means. One of the latter inquired if it might be allowed an unsuccessful candidate to reciprocate such a generous gift of sharp criticism. "Yes," answered Li angrily. The candidate cited two lines:

> My ears are washed in the clean waters of the Wei,
> And my mind is as free as the white clouds above;

and asked whether these celebrated lines had not been written by the great examiner. "Yes, but what is the matter with them?" The candidate proceeded to show that the story of the ear-washing related to a hermit who wanted to hear nothing of the abdication of the emperor in his favor. He went on to ask if it was not lese majesty for a person to assume that the present emperor was to yield the throne to him. The chief examiner was so angered and frightened that tears came to his eyes. He went to complain to the court, and this resulted in the imprisonment of the unsubmissive candidate. But the emperor thought that the prestige of a bureau chief was not sufficient to awe the candidates. He decreed that henceforth one of the vice-ministers of the Ministry of Propriety should be the chief examiner.

The wording in one of Tu Fu's lines indicates that he took the imperial examinations before this administrative change had taken place. Tu Fu said, moreover, that after the examination he had "more than eight years of lively freedom" before returning to Ch'ang-an again; he returned in 745. This places the examination in 736, and not, as commonly assumed, in 735.

Tu Fu did not pass the imperial examinations. We do not really know why. I am inclined to believe that our poet had himself to blame. He was born in a period when the great literary renaissance of T'ang had just begun to take shape. In prose, the movement to revive rugged vigor did not reach its peak until about half a century after his time. He himself, riding on the new tide, did try conscientiously to write in the style of the masters of the Han period (206 B.C. to A.D. 220). Of the thirty-two prose pieces that remain in his collection, there are indeed several that are vigorous in thought and masterly in form. There are also those in which the attempt at ruggedness shows too much sacrifice of smooth reading, and there are passages almost impossible to punctuate. In poetry, Tu Fu embodied the highest achievements in loftiness of aspirations, in depth of pathos, in variety, in metrical technique, in the meticulous patness of literary allusions, and in the revolutionary daring of appropriating some colloquial terms. But the majority of his poems lack those popular characteristics—simplicity of diction, smoothness of flow, rapidity of pace—which quickly attract attention and stimulate admiration. Readers can appreciate his poetry only after prolonged study. His own wide reading also gave rise to the habit of using obscure allusions. There are many lines that a thousand years of erudition have not succeeded in elucidating.

How did Tu Fu write his prose and poetry in his examinations? Did he write only what he wanted to say and only in the forms he deemed sufficiently good, or did he write only what the examiners could understand and be pleased to read? I fear it was the former and not the latter. In which case, his success or failure would have to depend on whether or not his examiners happened to have both the learning and the patience needed for a proper appreciation of what he wrote.

The failure was, of course, unexpected. A line in "Brave Adventures" says, "I went alone to say good-by to the prefect of Ching-chao." Here the word "alone" contains a painful sadness. All the other candidates from Ching-chao had passed; some had received appointments, others were waiting to be appointed; he alone had failed and had marred the enviable distinction of the prefecture in the choice of candidates.

It was not only good-by to the prefect of Ching-chao, but farewell also to all thought of official career or examinations. Though Tu Fu probably departed from Ch'ang-an with a very heavy heart, the life which he lived after this contained experiences which he in later years looked back upon with longing relish. He called the period between this departure from Ch'ang-an and the next return to it "more than eight years of lively freedom." Since we know that Tu Fu got back to Ch'ang-an late in the autumn or early in the winter of 745, the present departure was probably early in 737. What did he do during the months between failing the examinations and his actual departure? We have no information at all.

Of course, he would have to face his disappointed father and stepmother. This meeting may have occurred in the spring or summer of 737 in Yen-chou (about 632 miles east and slightly north of Ch'ang-an) where his father was the assistant prefect. There is one poem in Tu Fu's collection which may reasonably be assigned to this time.

II   ON YEN-CHOU CITY-WALL TOWER

To an eastern prefecture I have come to pay a son's respect; Now I take my first chance to enjoy the view from the South Tower. Floating clouds connect the T'ai Mountain and the Eastern Sea; A vast plain stretches over ancient regions of Ch'ing and Hsü. On that lonely peak once stood a tyrant's monument, In yonder desolate city were the ruins of a good prince's palace. Always have I valued the importance of antiquity, Other sight-seers have departed; I alone hesitate to leave.

Tu Fu probably did not stay in Yen-chou long. He left his parents once more to roam for pleasure. We may pause here to ask: could his family afford it? His father's earnings were sufficient to provide for his traveling expenses to the south for several years; there is no reason to suppose that the family income had deteriorated now. As a matter of fact, we can make a rough estimate of how the Tu family at this time might compare economically with the average family in the empire.

The average family would be a farming family of seven on a land grant of, say, 300 *mou*, capable of producing annually about 160 *hu* of grain. One-third of this amount would be kept for food and the rest sold for the money needed to buy the other necessities and comforts of life, to meet social obligations, and to pay taxes. Tu Hsien's family, being an official family, was exempt from taxes and corvée labor. As the assistant prefect of Yen-chou, Tu Hsien would have two kinds of land grants and would receive two kinds of salaries. If we calculate the rental he might collect from the tenants on his land, and if we compute all his cash receipts in terms of grain, we might say that the annual income from his official position alone was about 1,796 *hu*—in other words, eleven times the income of the average comfortable family.

This calculation does not include the houses allowed Tu Hsien by the local government—or the horses, office expenses, other privileges and services. Nor have we put down the land and other property which he inherited from his father and grandfather, nor his own savings and investments; but our guess is that the income from these sources was probably quite sufficient for the maintenance of his stepmother who lived in Pien-chou, possibly with her children and possibly also his two widowed sisters-in-law. His immediate family living with him in Yen-chou would be his wife and their children, perhaps at this time already five in number. Let us allow him five servants or slaves living on his earnings. The Yen-chou household might consist of twelve, but his earnings were sufficient to maintain several times that number. Of course he could afford to provide for his eldest son's travels.

The allowance must have been quite generous, for we know our poet traveled about in grand style. He wore fine furs and rode fine horses. He spent most of his time sightseeing and hunting in the areas north and northwest of Yen-chou, on both sides of the Yellow River valley in the territories known as Ch'i and Chao at the time of the ancient Warring Kingdoms (403–222 B.C.). These regions do not yield good hunting today, but in Tu Fu's time the population of China was only about one-tenth of what it is now (48,143,609 was the census figure for 740). The countryside must have been still thickly wooded. In "Brave Adventures," he recalled shooting birds, chasing wild animals, and playing with hunting falcons, in the woods and on the hills. It was probably in this period that he learned to master horsemanship and archery, two nonacademic talents which he wanted to display even in his later years, when he was in poor health. It was during this period that he won the friendship of an older scholar, Su Yü, who took him on hunting trips and regarded him as a pleasing and skilled companion.

Again, unfortunately, we do not have many of the poems that Tu Fu wrote during this period. The three poems that follow can reasonably be assigned here. He might have written "Gazing up the T'ai Mountain" [III] before he left Yen-chou or very shortly after he started northward, for the T'ai Mountain was only ten miles north of Yen-chou. In the poem, Tu Fu alluded to his desire to climb to the top. This, according to a later reminiscence, he actually did, but there is no poem in the existent collection of his works which paints the view from the highest peak.

"Officer Fang's Ferghanian Horse" [IV] and "Painting of a Falcon" [V] could be assigned to some other period of the poet's life, but they seem to fit best with the days of roaming on horseback and playing with hunting falcons.

III   GAZING UP THE T'AI MOUNTAIN

How becomes the T'ai a worshipful mountain? See how the greenness of the surrounding plains is never lost. Creation has lavished there its mysterious wonders; The sunny and shady sides fashion dawn and dusk at the same moment.

The growing layers of clouds might scour one's bosom of worldly thoughts; To follow those returning birds would strain my eyes. One day I shall climb like Confucius to the top To see how the surrounding hills dwarf into moles.

IV   OFFICER FANG'S FERGHANIAN HORSE

This is one of the famed Ferghanian horses. See his wiry build, almost angular and rugged. See his two ears, erect and sharp like bamboo strips. See his four hoofs, fleeting with the wind.

This is a horse for the conquest of space. To him, one may entrust one's life. When one has a flying steed like this, A few thousand miles are nothing!

V   PAINTING OF A FALCON

Extraordinary portrayal of a blue falcon! Frosty winds rise from the pale silk. Is he intently watching for a fleeing rabbit? Why does he look askance like an annoyed barbarian?

The bright chain and ring are of course for one to unfasten; His perch is so near, let us call him. When are you to strike those common warblers And scatter their blood and feathers on the prairie?

Of course Tu Fu did not spend all of this period of more than eight years in sightseeing and hunting. We do not know how soon he had to come to a halt. I speculate that his father died in 740. In that case, he would have to return to Yen-chou to wind up his father's affairs and to look after the funeral arrangements. The burial place might very well be in Yen-shih in the family graveyard where his grandfather, grandmother, and very likely also his mother were buried. As the head of the family now, Tu Fu would have to find a place where his stepmother and the rest of the family could move to and live. Yen-shih would of course be the natural place. The family must have already owned some property there, since it was the site of the family graveyard, and the Confucian code of ancestral worship required frequent visits to the grave, especially during the twenty-seven months of mourning.

This hypothesis will help to explain Tu Fu's presence in Yen-shih and his building a house in the neighborhood of the Shou-yang Hills. The completion of the new house was the occasion of a libation panegyric, dated 741, to his ancestor Tu Yü. This document seems to indicate that he was then the head of the family, and that he and his brothers were then living in Yen-shih. Since Yen-shih was only twenty-three miles northeast of Lo-yang, where his beloved aunt, Mrs. P'ei Jung-chi, was then living, it is natural to suppose that Tu Fu would frequently visit her, and she was perhaps already in poor health. If he went from Yen-shih to Lo-yang, he might very easily pass a famous temple to Lao-tzŭ. We find among his poems one entitled "A Visit in Winter to the Temple of His Mystical Majesty North of the City of Lo-yang" [VI]. The question when he wrote this poem is important. We want to know how early in his life the struggle to maintain an equilibrium between his understanding of practical Confucianism and his appreciation of the occult mysteries became evident. We want to know what personal problems in which period of his life might have put him in the quandary vaguely alluded to in the last lines of the poem. Though the dating of the poem in 749 by the commentator of 1226 has been universally accepted, I find his arguments not really obligatory. On the other hand, the title of the poem furnishes a compelling clue. Writing in 749, Tu Fu would have referred to the temple in question as the Grand Infinitesimal Palace. It was only during the short period between the early spring of 741 and the late autumn of 742 that the official appellation of the edifice was, as our poet gave it, the Temple of His Mystical Majesty. His visit must have been late in the year 741, because winter is evident in the poem.

This is one of those poems wherein some satirical subtlety is couched in terms of extravagantly elegant praise. The Taoist cult had been steadily gaining the support of the T'ang emperors. As early as 620 the first emperor of the dynasty was informed that he should consider himself a descendant of Lao-tzŭ, whose family name according to a legend was thought to be Li (plum). By 666 the title "Mystical Emperor" was conferred on this ancient philosopher, an elder contemporary of Confucius (551–479 B.C.), and author of *The Canon of Virtue*. Emperor Minghuang himself published in 733 a commentary on this book and ordered its study in all schools. It was thought regrettable that the first of the standard histories, the *Historical Memoirs* of Ssŭ-ma Ch'ien (135–87 B.C.), had not given Lao-tzŭ a preëminently honorable place, and the emperor ordered in 735 a rearrangement of this historical work. The gradual elevation of the cult of Lao-tzŭ followed miraculous discoveries or messages transmitted generally by imposters.

How would Tu Fu, the descendant of the great Confucian classicist Tu Yü, regard the cult of Lao-Tzŭ? Would he not be hostile to it? But he was never that sort of an orthodox Confucianist who would frown upon other religious systems. Moreover, he was living in an age wherein Taoistic alchemy and the search for the elixir of life were still current in man's thinking, and, as we shall see soon, he himself was, for a time at least, considerably influenced thereby. But as a diligent and astute scholar, he could not have failed to see that, as taught in *The Canon of Virtue*, the "hollow spirit" emptied of all exertion and pretense could hardly have any use for the entire paraphernalia of imperial dignity and affluence. The last two lines of the poem are intriguingly ambiguous. The term "clumsiness" was more likely intended to apply to the poet himself. Was he then already thinking of leaving the home in Yen-shih?

VI A VISIT IN WINTER TO THE TEMPLE OF HIS MYSTICAL MAJESTY NORTH OF THE CITY OF LO-YANG

Mysterious indeed is the mystic capital beside the polar star. The fences stretch up the hill to keep intruders out. The priestly officer is strict about all ceremonies, And the guards are empowered to take all precautions.

The green tiles on the roof will keep out the cold of the early winter. This golden pillar in the yard will transmit the unity of cosmic essence. Mountains and rivers display their support of the painted doors. The sun and the moon revolve around the carved beams.

Sturdy are the spreading roots of the immortal plum tree; Apt is the metaphor of fragrant orchids of illustrious generations. Though the ancient historian had neglected to honor him with a princely place, Our reigning emperor has succeeded with The Canon of Virtue.

Among painters, many famed masters are to be counted, But the art of Wu Tao-hsüan excelled theirs by far. He transported the landscape and the scene And made them shine with exquisite liveliness on the palace walls.

Five majestic sages in dragon robes follow one another closely; A thousand officials appear like a line of geese. Each tassel of each headgear dazzles with light; Every banner flutters with motion.

On the temple grounds the green cedars cast deep shadows. The pears are reddish, tinged by severe frost. From the eaves comes the music of the jadelike hangings driven by wind. On the exposed well stands the windlass frozen like silver.

When he retired, the Chou Dynasty was humbled. When the canon was transmitted, the Han emperor did well. If the hollow spirit is indeed deathless, Where may clumsiness be maintained?

We find our poet again in Lo-yang in 742. Mrs. P'ei Jung-chi died either in the autumn or winter, and Tu Fu had come for the funeral. During the same year, he probably made a trip about 120 miles eastward to visit his step-grandmother in Pien-chou, which in that year was renamed Ch'ên-liu. There he wrote a little poem of no especial significance on a rockery built by a relative to please the old lady.

During the larger part of the following two years, 743 and 744, Tu Fu was a sojourner in Lo-yang, trying to eke out a living for himself—possibly by teaching pupils, more likely by being a sort of unofficial secretary or ghost writer to some dignitary in the Eastern Capital. Thus he began to taste poverty. But why did he not stay in Yen-shih? My guess is that after the death of his father, not only the family income would necessarily be very much reduced, but also the costs of the funeral, of moving the household, and of building the new house would have consumed much of the family savings. Was his stepmother quite satisfied with the reduced standard of living? Since the period of mourning would be over by 742, why did he not seek some official appointment? Though he had not passed the imperial examinations of 736 and had refused to try subsequent ones, he could at least enter government service by taking advantage of the *yin*, for his father's official ranking had not only reached the seventeenth step but was actually two steps above it. Why did he not do it? Here I shall venture another guess. Tu Fu gave this privilege to his younger brother, or rather half brother, Tu Ying. This should of course please the stepmother immensely, and it would be like our poet to make such an unselfish decision. This conjecture should help to explain the fact that in 746, and possibly also 745, we find one of Tu Fu's younger brothers, very likely Tu Ying, as an assistant magistrate of the District of Lin-i, a petty official on the third rung of the ranking ladder, while the elder brother Tu Fu was still only a private individual and a roaming free-lance writer.

We may give here two of Tu Fu's poems written in the neighborhood of Lo-yang. Exact dating is not possible. I propose to assign them to the years 743–744. "Passing Mr. Sung Chih-wên's Old Villa" [VII] has been very poorly read or translated. The villa was in the Lu-hun Hills in the District of I-ch'üeh, which was twenty-three miles southwest of Lo-yang. Our poet might have gone to the Lu-hun Hills to visit a distant cousin, Tu Tso, whom we shall meet in another chapter. Sung Chih-wên, an auxiliary secretary of the Bureau of Examinations, an intimate friend of Tu Fu's grandfather, enjoyed a very popular fame as a poet during his lifetime. His two younger brothers were also often mentioned in T'ang writings. The last two lines of Tu Fu's poem, according to a note probably by the poet himself, concern the third brother, a good and brave general. But there is a difficulty. According to the order of the names of the three brothers as given in the *New T'ang History*, the third would appear to be Sung Chih-sun, a gifted calligrapher. There was a notorious case in 706, in which an assassination plot failed because the chief plotter's intimate friend had treacherously turned informer. In some documents, this informer was said to be Sung Chih-sun; in others, it was either Sung Chih-wên, or Sung Chih-wên and Sung Chih-sun together. Now our poet was a man who valued loyalty in friendship as one of the dearest things in life; how could he refer to the youngest brother of the Sungs with implied approbation and to the eldest without implied disapproval? I found the solution to the riddle in the *Compendium of Genealogies* of 812, wherein Sung Chih-sun was the second and Sung Chih-ti the third brother. It seems then that only Sung Chih-sun was responsible for the betrayal of friendship; Tu Fu mentioned the poet and the soldier, but held the calligrapher beneath notice.

VII PASSING MR. SUNG CHIH-WÊN'S OLD VILLA

Mr. Sung's old pond and villa Are now too desolate to sustain the muse. Once, one could reach this place only by detour And would be reinvited only if he left a poem.

I linger just to hear the tales from the aged neighbors; Then we sit in sad silence, facing the landscape. Indeed, the big tree there reminds one of a good general; But as the sun goes down, weeping winds issue from the leaves.

Was our poet feeling keenly the vanity and impermanence of power and influence—even of achievement and fame? There is probably more of this feeling in the poem "Visiting the Fêng-hsien Monastery at Lung-mên" [VIII]. Lung-mên, also in the District of I-ch'üeh, was about ten miles south of Lo-yang, where the I River ran between two cliffs—hence the term "Heaven's Gap" in the poem—and was the flourishing center of Buddhistic sculpture, which had been chiseled on the rocks under the patronage of Empress Wu Chê-t'ien about seventy years before this time.

34

Our poet might have stopped at the monastery on his way to, or on his way back from, the Lu-hun Hills.

VIII VISITING THE FÊNG-HSIEN MONASTERY AT LUNG-MÊN

Earlier I visited the grounds with the monks, Now I have spent the night in the monastery. The music of stillness rises in the dark ravine, The radiance of moonlight is filtered through the forest. The Heaven's Gap seems to press upon the constellations. Sleep among the clouds has chilled my clothes. The early prayer bell struck as I was about to wake, Am I awake with my soul as well as with my senses?

Tu Fu's sojourn or temporary employment in Lo-yang was doubtless interrupted by the death of his step-grandmother in midsummer of 744 in Ch'ên-liu; she was buried in the family graveyard in Yen-shih in midautumn. After the burial was over, our poet might have returned to Ch'ên-liu, to see to some property sales. It was very likely here that he first met two brilliant poets, the irresponsible Li Po, who was already famous, and the ambitious Kao Shih, who was to become famous later.

Li Po was older than Tu Fu by eleven years. He had been brought up in Shu, had roamed about the empire, had committed murder, squandered a fortune, taken wives, acquired concubines, and played with prostitutes; had demonstrated a heroic capacity for loyal friendship; had manifested a devout fondness of Taoistic magic and alchemy; had excited people's jealousy and hatred by his drunken haughtiness; and had inspired widespread admiration for his exhilarating prose and even more exhilarating poetry. About two years before this time, the fame of this private individual thought to be the incarnation of some immortal genius reached the ears of Emperor Ming-huang. Li Po was called to Ch'ang-an and given a post in the Han-lin Academy (Academy of Letters), a sort of private secretariat of His Majesty. One account says that Li Po's brilliant pen aroused the envy of Chang Chi, a son-in-law of the emperor. Another story has it that in a moment of drunken exhilaration, Li stretched out his feet and ordered the head eunuch, Kao Li-shih, to pull off his boots. Smarting under this insult, Kao set the emperor's favorite concubine against Li by suggesting that one of Li's poems written in her honor contained a historical allusion that was insulting. Whether advised by his son-in-law or his concubine, the emperor donated to Li Po a good sum of money and dismissed him from service. We do not know exactly when this took place, but Li was still in Ch'ang-an in the early spring of 744. According to one of his poems, Li left Ch'ang-an for the east after his dismissal and was already in the Prefecture of Ch'ên-liu in midsummer.

Kao Shih was about six years older than Tu Fu. In 735, at the age of twenty-nine, he answered a call to Ch'ang-an, but was not successful in obtaining an official appointment. Returning to Lo-yang, he moved his family to the Yü-ch'êng District of Sung-chou, where he said that he took to farming. In reality, he traveled about a great deal and was evidently in touch with officials and scholars. The biographical accounts in various historical works generally say that he did not begin to write poetry until his fiftieth year. Actually, we find in the collection of his poems excellent pieces which must be dated a number of years before then. We know for certain that he was visiting in the prefectures of Ch'ên-liu and Sui-yang (Sung-chou before 742) in 744, and that by the end of autumn he was about to travel south along the eastern coast of the empire.

By comparing the time schedules of the three great poets, it becomes quite evident that they met in Ch'ên-liu in the late autumn of 744. In a poem of reminiscences, written many years later, Tu Fu mentioned that his friendship with Kao and Li began in a wineshop, that these two masters of literary elegance were happy to have his association, and that when they were sufficiently inebriate, the three of them mounted together the historic Blow Tower to view the landscape and to muse over antiquities. From Ch'ên-liu, they probably traveled together about one hundred miles southeastward to Yü-ch'êng. In yet another poem, Tu Fu recalled that they ascended in the evening the Shan-fu Tower, built in commemoration of an excellent magistrate. By early winter, Kao Shih probably took his departure from the two friends. Did Li Po and Tu Fu proceed further and visit other places then? We have no record of such travels, nor indeed do we know of any poem on either of the two famous towers, which these poets might have written together.

Tu Fu's poem, "Presented to Li Po" [ix], was perhaps written in Ch'ên-liu shortly after he made the acquaintance of the elder poet.

IX PRESENTED TO LI PO

I was two years a sojourner in the Eastern Capital, And in my experience, I saw enough of tricks and intrigues. A country person like me hungers for vegetable foods, Not for the meat and fish on the tables of the rich and the powerful. Is there really no rice cooked according to an ancient recipe That will give me health and color? The trouble is I have no money to buy the ingredients; That is why I have not withdrawn to the mountains and woods.

Mr. Li was an honored member of the Goldern Court, But he has left it to seek quiet explorations. He too is visiting in the Liang and Sung regions, Let us hope the precious herbs will really be found.

From Sui-yang it was about 133 miles northeastward to Lu-chün, the erstwhile Yen-chou. By the early spring of 745, our poet was again in the prefecture where his father had been an assistant prefect. We do not know where he made his headquarters this time. Possibly he borrowed or rented a place to live in a suburb east of the prefectural city, a place called Stone Gate. An early eighteenth-century scholar of the neighborhood said that this name came from a little hill with two rocky cliffs facing each other like a gate. Tu Fu might have lived in a village at the foot of the hill, and he did go up-hill to visit a hermit, Mr. Chang. There are two poems on this visit, or visits, and we shall translate only the first one.

X   I WRITE TWO POEMS ON THE WALL OF HERMIT CHANG'S HOUSE

I

Spring has brought me to find you in these hills. The sound of chopping wood emphasizes the quietness of the place. Crossing the rills yet covered with snow and ice, I followed the slanting sun rays from the Stone Gate cliffs to reach this wooded spot. You see by night the aura of hidden gold and silver and care for nothing; You associate daily with deer and learn how they escape harm. We tramp around and soon lose ourselves; We are as carefree as a pair of empty boats adrift.

In the summer of 745, Tu Fu was in Lin-tzŭ Prefecture, 110 miles north of Lu-chün. Here he met a boyhood friend, Li Chih-fang, who had been a bureau official in Ch'ang-an and had recently come to Lin-tzŭ as a prefectural official. He met again Li Yung, whom he had seen in Ch'ang-an and Lo-yang, and who now as the prefect of Pei-hai (about 100 miles to the east) had come to Lin-Tzŭ on a visit. There were of course parties and poems about them. Then Tu Fu went twenty miles north to Lin-i, a subsidiary district of Lin-tzŭ, and the purpose of the visit might have been merely to see his brother Tu Ying, who was possibly already an assistant magistrate there. By autumn, our poet was back in Stone Gate again. From here, he went out with friends to visit various places. Here he invited friends to meals with him. Some of the visitors brought along a feast, and they had a glorious party together.

XI   FEAST AT STONE GATE WITH LIU, PROSECUTOR OF LU-CHÜN PRE-
FECTURE, AND CHÊNG, MAGISTRATE OF HSIA-CH'IU DISTRICT

The autumn water is clear and bottomless, It quietly cleanses the hearts of visitors. Frequently, officials taking time off duty Come on horseback to these wild woods. Now, two of the ablest, like a pair of gems, Have brought a sumptuous dinner, worth a piece of gold. The sound of the flutes at dusk is good, Even the dragon under water joins in the music.

Li Po was probably one of those who came to visit Tu Fu at Stone Gate. The two poets would, of course, go out together to drink and to visit friends. And naturally Tu Fu would write poems about these events. The first of the following two poems has been generally misread and mistranslated. Poetic wording in Chinese is terse, and personal pronouns are generally left out. Here, it will not do to supply the second person pronoun and to make the poem sound as if the elder poet were being chided as a worthless boy.

XII TO LI PO

Autumn again. We are still like thistledown in the wind. Unlike Ko Hung, we have not found the elixir of life. I drink, I sing, and I waste days in vain, Proud and unruly I am, but on whose account?

XIII LI PO AND I CALL ON HERMIT FAN

The beautiful lines of Mr. Li Often resemble those of Yin K'êng. I, too, am a visitor in the Tung-mêng Hills, And I love him like a brother. Inebriate, we sleep in the same bed in autumn; Hand in hand, we walk together daily. When we want to find a quiet rendezvous, We come to call on the scholar of the north suburb. Our admiration bounds as soon as we enter the gate To find the attendant boy so handsome and so polite.

As the sun declines, we hear the mallets, pounding on washings, We see the clouds hovering above the ancient city. Accustomed we are to sing the "Praise of the Evergreen Citron"; What officers really retire because of liking vegetable soup? Let us drop all reference to rank and power; Let our thoughts and feelings roam only above the distant seas.

Some critics have tried to read the reference to Yin K'êng as Tu Fu's veiled criticism of Li Po's poetry. They argue that Yin K'êng of the sixth century had hardly reached the poetic heights of Li Po. They forgot that Tu Fu was a warm admirer of Yin's achievements, and the compliments to his elder friend were, therefore, entirely sincere. It is hardly necessary for us to follow those critics who assumed that there must be jealousy between two great poets. They would also read the thistledown poem as Tu Fu's giving a stern rebuke to Li Po. They would even quote "Teasing Tu Fu" as if it were a genuine poem of Li Po:

> *Here on the Rice Muffin Hill is Tu Fu,*
> *Wearing a bamboo hat under the noon sun.*
> *You have grown too thin since we parted,*
> *Perhaps you labor too hard on your poems.*

The truth of the matter is that this poem was not really in the collection of Li Po's poems and was found in a collection of gossipy anecdotes about poets, compiled more than a century after Li and Tu's time. A bamboo hat would indicate summer; but we know only of two meetings of the poets, both in autumn. The text of this poem is not worthy of Li Po's pen, nor its spirit worthy of the friendship that existed between him and Tu Fu. We must, therefore, accept the judgment of the best of scholars on these poets, that this poem is spurious.

We do have two of Li Po's poems to Tu Fu, both written in the autumn of 745. In one of these, "Seeing Tu Fu off from Stone Gate . . ." Li Po regrets that the thistledown will be blown apart and advises that the cups in hand be drained, for such enjoyable companionship is not likely to be repeated in Stone Gate. We do not know where Tu Fu was going this time. But toward the later part of the same autumn, Tu Fu was probably sailing southward on the Wên River on his way back to Ch'ang-an and Hsien-yang, and Li Po sent him a poem from an unidentified place, doubtless in an area not very far from Lu-chün. In "Written by the Sand Hill City and Sent to Tu Fu," the elder poet says that the wine no longer tastes good, that the songs he hears are no longer inspiring, and that while listening to the autumn sound of the old trees by the Sand Hill City, his affection follows the Wên River southward with his friend. It is a beautiful expression of his esteem of the younger poet.

But what caused Tu Fu to return to the West again? Of course, he had no idea of the ten tortuously up-and-down years that were ahead of him. While in the East, his thoughts were those of an otherworldly hermit, a seeker of the alchemical transformation of life. Why should he return to the capital, the center of political intrigues and competitions? Had he run out of money? Was there some new development that would bring him to the West? We really do not know. There is, however, in the collection of Tu Fu's works a short piece of prose curiously entitled "Miscellanies." It must have been written in one of the cities in the neighborhood of Lu-chün, perhaps during the autumn of 745.

MISCELLANIES

Let us ask: Which is considered better at present? To rely on one's own abilities, or to make use of others' talents? If the latter, the two talented scholars in Lu, Chang Shu-ch'ing and K'ung Ch'ao-fu, with their wisdom and eloquence, their depth of insight and breadth of view, should surely be able to win friendship, extend fame, be given responsibility and succeed with it—all as fast as a whirlwind. Why do they appear so gloomy and famished—not even so well off as the slaves in the rich houses? What hope have they of good clothes and fine carriages? Was it that the governors of the East wanted merely to shut the doors against you? Or was it that they had not heard about you from those higher up? Was it providence? Was it fate? Messrs. Ts'ên Shên and Hsüeh Chü have indeed brought each month to your hotel dozens and hundreds of well-known scholars to hear your poetry. This is only superficial reputation. Beware, beware! When the wise men of antiquity knew that it was not possible to be on the top of the world, they decided to remain low. When they found it impossible to lead the masses, they chose to follow them. O Shu-ch'ing, you have a sharp and powerful pen, you are wildly ambitious and do not seem to be capable of quiet planning. If you will really accept me as an informed and helpful friend, you will keep still and think. O Ch'ao-fu, you are accustomed to moderation and meekness; I cannot advise you to change. The T'ai Mountain seems to be unconscious; but it rises to great heights. The Ssŭ River seems to be shallow; but it overflows and is clear. O my friends, when may we meet again in His Majesty's Capital? When shall you toast me again with cheap wine and address me again as an elder brother?

With the exception of Chang Shu-ch'ing, the other men mentioned here will appear in later chapters. Hsüeh Chü was a successful candidate at the imperial examinations of 731, and Ts'ên Shên passed those of 744. They were at this time already literary celebrities, and they doubtless had been given government posts. Was our poet impressed by the fact that unless one had succeeded with the powerful in the capital, it would be difficult to depend on the favors of local dignitaries to make ends meet? This might have been the very reason that sent him back to Ching-chao.

"More than three years on a donkey's back."

CHAPTER THREE

Li Lung-chi (685–762) is known in history by his posthumous title Hsüan-tsung, or more popularly as Ming-huang or the Brilliant Emperor. In the summer of 710, while only a prince of twenty-four, he was at the head of a *coup d'état* which avenged his uncle, Emperor Chung-tsung, by killing the latter's wife and murderess, Empress Wei, together with her paramours and conspirators. He then placed on the throne his own father, Emperor Jui-tsung. Jui-tsung was a well-intentioned and self-effacing man. So was his eldest son, the Prince of Sung, who insisted that the younger brother, Li Lung-chi, should be made the crown prince. On September 8, 712, Jui-tsung announced his own abdication in favor of the crown prince, though as emperor emeritus he still retained some important powers.

The most powerful person in the state at that time, however, was neither the emperor nor the emperor emeritus, but Princess T'ai-p'ing, the aunt of the former and sister of the latter. Of the seven highest ministers of state, five were completely under her sway. Thus the young emperor, for his own benefit, had to plan another *coup d'état*, which took place at the end of August of 713. After the partisans of the ambitious princess had been slain by palace troops, the princess herself and her children were granted the favor of ending their own lives. The emperor emeritus then relinquished all powers of government to the emperor, and spent the remaining three years of his life in complete retirement, keeping busy perhaps with classical exegesis and calligraphy, at which he was said to be quite expert.

The Brilliant Emperor's reign lasted forty-three years. During the first half of this period, he gave himself unsparingly to the duties of government, to the practice of economy, to strengthening the military defense of the empire both internally and on the frontiers, to the improvement of the lot of the common people, and to the promotion of literature and the arts. As the head of an absolute monarchy with unlimited powers, he certainly could do a great deal; and he did accomplish a great deal. Men of character and ability served him as the highest ministers of state. One of them lived in a temple in order to save the expense of maintaining a house, and another died so poor that an old servant sold himself into slavery in order to get enough money to bury the master. Under the T'ang system of official remuneration, it is difficult to see why a high minister should be so poor, unless he refused to accept what was rightly due him or chose to give away what he got. Such extreme examples of frugality and self-denial were of course unusual, but they did have some influence on the officialdom of the empire: corruption was indeed the exception rather than the rule.

Because the emperor chose good and brave generals for the defense of the frontiers, the encroachments of the barbarians were gradually pushed further and further back. In 742, the empire consisted of 362 prefectures (not counting the 800 barbarian prefectures loosely attached to the empire); 1,528 districts; 16,829 villages; 8,525,763 households; and a population of 48,909,800. On the frontiers there were already a number of important military outposts, each headed by a governor general. In the northeast, the Fan-yang governor general with his capital at Fan-yang and the P'ing-lu governor general at Liu-ch'êng were to watch over the barbarians known as Hsi, Shih-wei, Mo-ho, and Kitai in the territories later known as Manchuria and Inner Mongolia. The Koreans, having submitted to Chinese suzerainty some seventy years previously, required no Chinese military precaution against them. Toward the west the Ho-tung governor general at T'ai-yüan and the Shuo-fang governor general at Ling-wu were mainly concerned with repulsing the raids of the Turks from Mongolia. In the early years of the Brilliant Emperor's reign, the Turks created considerable havoc on the northern frontier; but gradually weakened by internal dissension and defeats inflicted by the Chinese armies, they seldom made trouble after 721. By 743 most of the power of the Turks passed to one of their affiliated tribes, the Uighurs, who remained friendly to the T'ang government.

Toward the southwest was the Ho-hsi governor general at Wu-wei, whose territory stretched northwestward, roughly corresponding to the present province of Kansu, and whose chief duty was to prevent the Turkish tribes on the north and the Tibetans on the south from joining forces to attack China. Still further southwestward, the governor general of Lung-yu at Hsi-p'ing had the duty of resisting the main thrust of the

Tibetans upon China. Further south, the Chien-nan governor general at Shu-chün was likewise to ward off the Tibetans from the west, and in addition, was to pacify the southern barbarians who were in the territories that constitute the present province of Yünnan. Though the sgam-po or ruler of the Tibetans was given in 707 a T'ang princess in marriage and became thus a sort of son-in-law of the T'ang court, the warlike barbarians of Tibet, then known as T'u-fan, did not cease to make raids on the border. They received, however, more defeats than victories, and by 730 they were more eager for peace than for war. On the southern coast of the empire, the Ling-nan governor general at Nan-hai had the duty of pacifying the various aborigines in the mountainous areas in the present Kuangsi and western Kuangtung, and in addition, was responsible for southern coastal defense, for at this time Nan-hai was already a flourishing center of foreign trade, with numerous foreign merchants in the city and many Arab ships in port.

These eight important military outposts, which together with three minor garrisons for southeastern and eastern coastal defense (chiefly against piracy), constituted the military bulwark of what has been known in modern times as China Proper. Two other important governors general were in the vast northwestern territory known today as the province of Hsin-chiang or Chinese Turkestan. The Pei-t'ing governor general at Pei-t'ing, about 1,760 miles northwest of Ch'ang-an, had charge of the northern part of this vast area, watching over the Western Turks, now on the whole submissive to the T'ang authority, and extending his military power westward beyond the regions between the lakes Balkash and Issykul into what is now popularly called Russian Turkestan. A few hundred miles to the southwest of Pei-t'ing, the An-hsi governor general at Ch'iu-tzŭ (Kucha) controlled the famous four garrisons at Ch'iu-tzŭ, Yen-ch'i (Karashahr), Yü-t'ien (Khotan), and Su-lê (Kashgar) of the Tarim basin, flourishing Indo-European communities that had for centuries served as transmitters of Buddhism and Greco-Indian art into China. The An-hsi governor general also extended his power westward beyond the Pamirs to protect the principalities of Ferghana, Transoxiana, and to some distance south of the River Oxus, which generally preferred China's lenient suzerainty to conquest by either the Arabs or the Tibetans.

These establishments for the defense of the frontiers entailed armed forces of 490,000 men and 80,000 horses. The Brilliant Emperor realized that mobility was of supreme importance to the army, and wisely gave attention to the acquisition and breeding of good mounts. By 725, it was said the horses in the imperial studs, mostly in Lung-yu, numbered 430,000.

Prosperity followed peace. The distribution of land was generous, the taxation light. Commodities were plentiful, and prices low. No one needed to find it difficult to make a living, and many were comfortably off. Travelers could find hospitality all along the road. Communications were well maintained, and there were plenty of donkeys for hire in the hotels. There was no banditry, and one might travel hundreds of miles with no need of any weapon for self-protection. Crime was rare; in 730 there were only twenty-four executions in the whole empire. Even with light taxation, the imperial receipts were annually over 2,000,000,000 in copper coins; 19,800,000 *hu* (an undetermined measure) of grain; 7,400-000 *pi* (about 1.89 by 42 feet) of woven silk; 10,800,000 *liang* (one and one-third ounces) of floss silk; and 10,350,000 *tuan* (about 52.5 feet) of flax cloth.

With peace and prosperity came cultural brilliance. The emperor himself was quite a scholar, and he naturally gave much attention to education. He ordered the establishment of new schools and extended some of the government-supported enrollments. He frequently conducted special examinations in addition to those held annually; through these, he thought more men of talent could find their way into public service. Moreover, when he heard of an unusual man, he sometimes employed him without any examination, as he did in the case of Li Po. Some scholars simply sent their writings to him, and if he was pleased with them—as we shall see in the case of Tu Fu—he would order the government to examine these writers and to try them with some employment. Indeed, he liked to show himself always ready to use good men and would resent any insinuation to the contrary. One story has it that the hermit poet Mêng Hao-jan, on a visit to the great poet and painter Wang Wei (701–761)—who was already a high official and very much in His Majesty's favor—hid under the bed when the emperor came to Wang Wei's room. The emperor ordered the hermit to come out and wanted to hear some of his poems. When the recitation came to the line, "His Majesty has no use for an untalented man like me," the emperor was offended. "You yourself sought no employment," said His Majesty; "why blame me for it?"

The scholarly emperor regretted that the imperial library collections begun by his great-grandfather had been neglected for many years, and in 715 he appointed a board to put the collections in order and bring them up to date by the addition of new works to be copied from private collections. After a few years, the board completed the work and reported that the four collections (classical, historical, philosophical, and literary) totaled 3,600 titles in 51,852 rolls, besides 2,500 titles of Buddhistic and Taoistic works in 9,500 rolls. Two hand-copies were made of each book on I-chou paper, for the imperial libraries in Ch'ang-an and Lo-yang.

The emperor was the founder of two important literary institutions. The Chi-hsien Yüan (Academy of Talents) was mainly concerned with

44

the writing and compiling of books, and the chief officers therein would frequently read to and discourse with His Majesty. The Han-lin Yüan (Academy of Letters) was a sort of private secretariat of the emperor, composed of the best writers of prose and poetry that the emperor could find to draft documents for him. Surrounded with the literary celebrities from these academies as well as from other offices of the government, His Majesty frequently gave social parties at which many poems were written in commemoration. This practice originated long before his time, but it was during his regime that the dignity and elegance of this kind of literature rose to a height unsurpassed by any other age.

The Brilliant Emperor was also a great patron of art and was himself a gifted musician. He employed some of the finest painters in his service: Wang Wei in landscape, Wu Tao-hsüan with human figures, and Han Kan with horses were among those thought to have achieved perfection in their lines. He collected promising boys and girls into the palace, and he himself and some of the master players and singers would teach them. The drama and dancing received considerable encouragement. Games and sports of various sorts obtained imperial patronage, especially cock-fighting and dancing horses. The prizes presented from His Majesty were generally lavish.

In short, though in his later years he was guilty of some unpardonable stupidities, his people continued to remember him as the Emperor Brilliant. They remembered him as having given them many years of peace, prosperity, and brilliant culture. They remembered him as a talented, generous, kindly, and jolly prince. Few sovereigns in history have so endeared themselves to their people. And this faithfulness and devotion on the part of his subjects will help to explain the next ten tortuous years of Tu Fu's life, during which he was unable to decide definitely whether to wait in the capital for an opportunity to serve the emperor, or to leave. This helps to explain also many of his later poems in which he looked back upon the earlier portion of the Brilliant Emperor's reign with a peculiar mixture of nostalgia and regret.

By the time our poet was in Ching-chao again, in the later part of 745, the seeds of disaster for the T'ang empire had all been sown, and some had already begun to grow. The sharp decline and near fall of the world's most brilliant empire of the eighth century constitute a favorite subject for moralizing among historians. Those who were for Confucian orthodoxy have deprecated the growing popularity of literary attainment at the expense of sound doctrinal training in the classical studies. The rise of treason and rebellion could indeed be ascribed to the displacement of ethical loyalties by ambition and lust. A case could be made against the emperor's growing interest in Taoistic superstition. The selfish desire for longevity by the practice of alchemy and Taoistic rites would distract him from the duties of government. Uncritical acceptance of super-

45

natural pretenses and tolerant treatment of exposed imposters tended of course to encourage deception and disloyalty in official ranks.

Those historians who have sought economic causes could show that during the Brilliant Emperor's reign economy had given rise to abundance, abundance to extravagance, extravagance to the fear of scarcity, and the fear of scarcity led not back to economy, but headlong to extortion. In the matter of extravagance, the emperor's lavish gifts and the high cost of maintaining and increasing the frontier defenses were already impressive. The size of officialdom was becoming burdensome also. At the beginning of the dynasty, the emperor's great-grandfather had tried to govern the empire with only 730 officials. This was of course soon found to be impractical. Under the Brilliant Emperor, in the year 733, the civil service had grown to number 17,686 officials and 57,416 minor officials.

Extortionary measures began innocently enough in the government, in the form of trying to catch up with tax evaders. But success in increasing receipts brought promotion and power to those economic experts who vied with one another in devising and enforcing policies to maintain the further extravagance of the government and the privileged at the expense of the people. A Confucianist once said that an extortionate minister who enriched the state was more dangerous than an embezzler who enriched himself. The truth of the matter was that a minister whose usefulness to the emperor was to augment the imperial treasuries seldom failed to expand his own.

In 752 one such minister got into trouble and was executed, and his property was confiscated. It took the confiscating officers several days just to compile an inventory of the houses the man owned. Extravagance, extortion, and corruption were as contagious as an epidemic. The people naturally suffered. If toward the middle of the Brilliant Emperor's reign the people were on the whole contented with their tolerably comfortable livelihood, the situation was entirely changed toward the close of the reign. The rich were restlessly getting richer, while the poor were getting restlessly poorer. We can gather from the poems of Tu Fu the social injustice in the sharp contrast between the powerful and the victimized, between the fabulously rich and the miserably poor. The stage was ready for rebellion and the collapse of His Majesty's government.

Those historians who have emphasized the importance of military institutions trace the collapse of the imperial power to the change in 722 from the old system of military conscription to that of hired service. The conscriptive system took the soldiers from, and returned them to, the farm. The machinery of administration became, after the long period of peace, ineffective in coping with evasion, substitution, and desertion. It was thought easier to maintain an able-bodied soldiery by hiring men and granting them some privileges as inducements. When the induce-

46

ments soon appeared to be less attractive and the risks more real, the army became again depleted and weak. Whenever there was need, as for frontier defense, recruiting had to rely on impressment. It did not take long for the governors general to grow strong by fashioning their own armies, having their own armaments, and collecting their own revenues. Only the defense of the capital continued to grow weaker. When the strongest of these governors general, An Lu-shan, chose in 755 to rebel, such defense as the emperor could put up for his own safety was smashed with ease.

Whether it was moral depravity or institutional foolery, or both, that must account for the fall of a dynasty, Chinese historians are agreed that the first misstep is usually the employment of the wrong men in the government. The Brilliant Emperor made the irretrievable mistake of appointing a brilliant crook as a minister of state. Prime Minister Li Lin-fu was not a well-lettered man. Though he was fond of making literary pretenses, he was found to have made laughable errors in diction. What he lacked in proficiency with the written word, he more than made up, however, with his unusual oral eloquence. When his contemporaries counted the vast number of those who fell victim to his charming, persuasive, but deadly advices, they realized that he was a man whose words were steeped in fragrant honey, but whose intentions always contained a murderous dagger.

The emperor was a willing victim to Li's pleasing flatteries and in 734 made him one of the three highest ministers of state. Two years later, he became the highest minister, in which position he continued for seventeen years until his death in 752. By skillful bribery he had the important eunuchs keep him fully informed of every move and every word of the emperor. Knowing His Majesty's intentions well in advance, he plotted to make the once brilliant emperor gradually into a complete fool. No matter how bad a thing was, so long as His Majesty was inclined to do it, he would always have the encouragement and support of Li Lin-fu, who also saw to it that none in the empire would dare to advise against it.

In 737, the emperor killed three of his own sons, including the crown prince. Shortly after 737, he took the wife of another son of his into his own harem, and in 745 publicly made her his favorite concubine. This woman, known in history as Yang Kuei-fei, was said to have been plump and beautiful, gifted in music, and endowed with an unusual perspicacity, which she used expertly to capture the love of the emperor. She was soon regarded by everyone in the palace as the empress, and her three talented and pretty elder sisters, Mrs. Ts'ui, Mrs. P'ei, and Mrs. Liu frequented the palace as sisters-in-law and also as favorites of the emperor and were ennobled as the Lady of Han, the Lady of Kuo, and the Lady of Ch'in respectively. Of Yang Kuei-fei's three cousins, one

47

was given a daughter of the emperor in marriage; another was at once made assistant attendant to His Majesty, a high position on the twenty-second step up the official ladder; and the third, known later as Yang Kuo-chung—a poorly educated, vagabonding, but handsome, eloquent, and clever rascal, a paramour of the widowed Lady of Kuo—started at first as His Majesty's gambling companion, then became the Secretary of the Bureau of Public Finance with a growing number, until over forty, of concurrent positions, and finally became the highest minister of state to succeed his long friend and ally but at last rival and enemy, Li Lin-fu.

Had the Brilliant Emperor ever stopped to think what a distance he had traveled downward? In the earlier years of his reign, he was affectionate and generous to his brothers and nephews, giving them his personal attention and lavishing upon them many and rich gifts. But he never allowed them to have any part in government, and he saw to it that they had no influence whatever with government personnel. He knew the dangers of nepotism. Now the four Yang sisters and the three Yang cousins exercised a tremendous influence, both direct and indirect, on the government. They took bribes freely. They lived and moved about in amazing grandeur and extravagance. They took no precaution to hide their power and affluence. On the contrary, they boldly and proudly displayed them. Had the emperor reflected, he might have realized that he was guilty of what Chinese historians had always condemned as the worst kind of nepotism—the kind caused by a woman. The Brilliant Emperor had, however, no time to think. He was too busy with charming company, with games and gambling, and with superstitious practices in the hope of prolonging indefinitely this pleasure-filled life. He actually said in 744 that since the world was at peace and at its best, he had better enjoy himself and leave the government to Li Lin-fu.

This would suit Li Lin-fu well. The brilliant crook's main anxiety was that his own position might not be permanently secure. He had seen to it that of all the corrupt persons he had supported or tolerated in the government or in the emperor's favor, there should be none as able as he himself was in the mastery of intrigue and strategy. He had yet to weed out all of those who for one reason or another might not admire or fear him and who might rise into a position to challenge his supremacy. Among these, the new crown prince, the later Emperor Su-tsung, was a thorn in his flesh. The new crown prince might have perished as did his three brothers, were he not advisedly cautious in all his doings and contacts, and had he not the helpful intercession of the chief eunuch, Kao Li-shih, and the emperor's son-in-law, Chang Chi.

Wei Chien, the brother of the crown prince's wife, was one of those who aspired to be an economic expert in order to gain imperial favors.

Since his wife was a cousin of Li Lin-fu, he had at first considerable support from the prime minister. As the imperial commissioner of taxation and transportation for the southeastern areas, he succeeded, after considerable hydraulic engineering, in bringing ships of the Yangtze valley, laden with the rich and dazzling produce of distant regions, clear to the waters outside the imperial palace in Ch'ang-an. The arrival of hundreds of such ships was managed with impressive pageantry and music, and Wei Chien at once rose high in the emperor's favor. Li Lin-fu regretted that he had not foreseen such ability in his protégé. The possibility of Wei Chien's becoming also one of the chief ministers of state became a matter of grave concern, not only because he was the brother-in-law of the crown prince, but also because he had such important friends as the powerful Huang-fu Wei-ming, governor general of both Ho-hsi and Lung-yu, and State Minister Li Shih-chih, whose position in the government was second only to that of Li Lin-fu. Li Shih-chih, one of Tu Fu's "Eight Immortals of the Wine Cup," was a famous scholar and poet who had a wide circle of friends among upright and courageous men. Since Li Shih-chih had the confidence of the emperor and was in a position to rally opposition, Li Lin-fu undertook first to alienate him from the emperor.

The brilliant crook casually mentioned to Li Shih-chih one day that His Majesty did not yet know of the possibility of mining the Hua Mountain for minerals. The connoisseur of wine was not a connoisseur of politics and fell into the trap. He went to the emperor to suggest a mining project. When the emperor consulted the prime minister, the latter said, "I have known of this mining possibility for a long time; but as the spirit of the Hua Mountain is generally regarded as the guardian spirit of Your Majesty's longevity, I cannot advise the cutting, digging, or tunneling of this mountain." His Majesty's warmth toward the second minister of state suddenly chilled to such an extent that Li Shih-chih thought it wise to resign. This happened in the summer of 746. Many of the guests that usually came to share his wine and food fell away for fear of Li Lin-fu. Whereupon the slighted ex-minister wrote a poem:

> Avoiding the split, I have left the cabinet.
> Enjoying the unmingled, I sip the cup.
> I shall inquire of my usual guests:
> How many will come today?

These lines became widely admired for the clever use of terms applicable to wine and politics alike. Li Lin-fu's displeasure was, however, not to be regarded in jest. By the spring of 747, Huang-fu Wei-ming, Wei Chien, Wei Chien's brothers, Li Shih-chih, and Li Shih-chih's son were all dead by execution or suicide. Even old Li Yung, Prefect of Pei-hai, was flogged to death. Assistant Chancellor Fang Kuan, a friend of Li Shih-chih and Tu Fu, was banished from the capital.

While the wicked prime minister was plotting the fall of these prominent friends of Tu Fu, where was our poet, and what was he doing? We know neither what Tu Fu did for a living nor where he lived after his return from the East to Ching-chao in the winter of 745. My guess is that he probably depended on gifts in return for some free-lance literary service and that he lived mostly in inns in the neighborhood of Ch'ang-an and Hsien-yang. "Thinking of Li Po on a Winter Day" [xiv], however, could have been written in the house of a friend or relative where he perhaps had been given the use of a couple of rooms. "What a Night!" [xv] concerned the New Year's Eve of the Chinese calendar, the Julian equivalent of which might be January 25, 746. "Remembering Li Po on a Spring Day" [xvi] was probably written in the late spring of 746 when the elder poet was already on the southeastern coast. "Letter from My Brother in Lin-i . . ." [xvii] has puzzled commentators as to proper dating. I have found that the flood referred to in the poem probably occurred in the early autumn of 746. The last two lines of Tu Fu's poem hinted that since he was mingling with the grandees in the capital (Li Shih-chih, Fang Kuan, et cetera), he could help the government to understand that the inundation of the dykes was caused by the unusual flood and that a petty official like his brother, Tu Ying, should not be blamed for it. "Eight Immortals of the Wine Cup" [xviii] was written between the resignation and suicide of Li Shih-chih. If composed after the catastrophe had occurred, it would be bad taste to portray Minister Li with pleasantry. The eight immortals were, of course, contemporary drinking friends in Ch'ang-an. The period of time was limited, because we knew Li Po did not arrive in Ch'ang-an earlier than 742, and Ho Chih-chang had left in the spring of 744. A discrepancy occurs in the inclusion of Su Chin who died in 734. It might be a slip of the pen on the part of Tu Fu, or a corruption in the transmitted text.

XIV THINKING OF LI PO ON A WINTER DAY

In this quiet and lonely study, The whole day I think of you. I turn again to the classical story of friendship, Once more I am reminded of your brotherly song. Here I feel the bitter cold through shabby clothing; There you are still searching for the elixir of life. I cannot follow the impulse to go at once to see you; In vain have we thought of hermitage together.

XV WHAT A NIGHT!

What a night! The year is departing. The watches are long, the candles bright; none is to be wasted. But in the Hsien-yang inn is there any-

thing to do? Let us throw dice for fun. One leans over the table to shout for five whites; Another bares his arms to throw: no winning faces! Great men are sometimes like these, And a chance meeting is not necessarily meaningless. Do not laugh. Remember how the undistinguished Liu I Owned nothing and was willing to lose a million!

XVI REMEMBERING LI PO ON A SPRING DAY

Li Po's poetry is unrivaled. His soaring thoughts are unique. His freshness reminds me of Yü Hsin; His delicacy, of Pao Chao. Now as I look upon the spring trees north of the Wei, He is probably watching the evening clouds east of the Chiang. When can we meet over a pot of wine, Again to study and discuss literature?

XVII A LETTER FROM MY BROTHER IN LIN-I TELLS OF THE LONG RAIN AND THE FLOOD OF THE YELLOW RIVER. AS AN ASSISTANT MAGISTRATE, HE IS WORRIED ABOUT THE RUIN OF THE DYKES UNDER HIS CHARGE, AND I SEND THIS POEM TO REDUCE HIS ANXIETIES.

Since the dual principles of the universe add up to storm and rain, A hundred mountain gullies pour down torrential streams. I am told that the Yellow River has broken its bounds, And that one sheet of high water stretches clear to the sea. Every official is burdened with worries, Every prefecture is complaining of disaster. My brother, in a humble district, As an assistant magistrate is charged with conservancy. A letter that came two days ago Told of frequent repairs of dykes, And of how he wished he might have the turtles and alligators of ancient times, Or the fairy crows and magpies all to help. Farm crops south of Yen are ruined, Even the weeds of the Tsi valley are all under water. Snails and clams have been found near the city walls, Serpents and dragons roam in every pool. I can imagine how the water would be deep by the Hsü Pass, How the inundation of the Chieh-shih Hill would leave a tiny peak, How villages would disappear with only solitary trees left, How under the blue sky even ten thousand ships are useless.

My own humble lot resembles a floating twig: Can I sail on it to reach the eastern sea and the land of the mystical peaches? I shall nevertheless cast a fishing line across the continent To hold the watery monster in check for you.

XVIII EIGHT IMMORTALS OF THE WINE CUP

Ho Chih-chang rides his horse as though he were sculling a boat, And is quite willing to tumble into a well asleep.

The Prince of Ju-yang had his three gallons before going to Court; Yet a passing brewer's cart makes his mouth water And his heart long for a transfer as Prince of Wine Spring.

Ten thousand coins a day our Second Minister spends On the drinks he takes as a whale the waters of the sea; Yet says he, "I like the un-mingled and avoid the split."

Ts'ui Tsung-chih—a young man handsome and carefree—With bland eyes lifts his cup to the blue skies And stands like a sparkling jade tree in the wind.

Honoring an embroidered Buddha, Su Chin is a vowed vegetarian; But how he enjoys his lapses whenever he is drunk with wine!

A hundred poems Li Po will write for a gallon And will sleep in a wine shop in the market of Ch'ang-an. Disobeying the Imperial command to board the barge, He says, "Your Majesty's servant is an immortal of the cup."

Give three cupfuls to Calligrapher Chang Hsü, Even before dignitaries he will throw off his cap And draw clouds on paper with his brush.

Chiao Sui will need at least five gallons to be awake—To startle the company with eloquence in discussion or debate.

Perhaps even in 746 Tu Fu had not realized how much evil was being brewed by Li Lin-fu. When 747 came, however, he was not only to see his friends banished, driven to suicide, or beaten to death, but also to taste for himself some of the bitterness that was the brilliant crook's concoction.

The emperor had wanted to give another chance to the scholars who had failed the imperial examinations in the past. Even if a man was proficient in no more than one subject, he was now urged by His Majesty to come and be specially examined. Li Lin-fu feared that some of the examination papers might contain information that he did not want the emperor to have. He therefore persuaded His Majesty not to conduct the examinations in person and to have officials appointed for the purpose. Finally, Li reported to the throne that all the candidates had failed, and that he must congratulate His Majesty for having already unearthed all the empire's talent. We know that the gifted Yüan Chieh (723–772) was one of those who failed this time. From a reference in one of Tu Fu's poems [xxv] we know that he was another. I am inclined to think that K'ung Ch'ao-fu might be a third.

According to Tu Fu's farewell poem to K'ung [xxi], it seems that K'ung was determined to leave Ch'ang-an and would not listen to his friends' entreaties to stay longer. Perhaps it was not only his disappoint-ment with the special examinations but also his disgust with the moral depravity of the politics of the time that confirmed his determination on a departure which might have taken place in the spring of 748. We find in the winter of 747, while Li Lin-fu had not yet closed the cases against the friends of Wei Chien, Li Yung, and others, that he had started new programs of persecution. He had the ability to make his henchmen turn on their own relatives and friends. This might have been the background of Tu Fu's quatrain on "Friendship" [xx].

These were the times when a man of Tu Fu's patriotic and affectionate nature would be exposed to amazing and rapid alternations between hope and disappointment, joy and sadness, the possibility of service and the fear of persecution, appreciation of friendship and indignation on its betrayal. "The Mei-pei Lake" [xix] reflects somewhat these changing moods. Our poet wrote several poems relating to Mei-pei, and on at least two occasions he was with Ts'ên Shên, who, though younger than he was, was already an official and a better-known poet. I venture to place this poem in the early autumn of 747, partly because of the moods expressed therein, and partly because it sounds as though it was written on our poet's first visit to the famous lake about twenty-three miles southwest of Ch'ang-an.

XIX THE MEI-PEI LAKE

Ts'ên Shên and his brother are fond of the wonders of nature, And they have invited me for a sail on the Mei-pei Lake. Suddenly the darkening universe takes on a strange color, And we find before us a vast stretch of breakers breaking like glass.

We cast the boat loose to float among the crystal madness—An unusual daring that rouses a hundred fears. How can we be sure of the absence of whales and alligators, Should the wicked wind and waves really work their worst?

Presently it clears. Our boatmen busy themselves merrily; Our hosts help to unfurl the brightly embroidered sail. Songs of the oars burst while geese and gulls fly in disorder, And pipes and strings harmonize to welcome the blue of the sky. Poles and cords will not fathom the depth of the water Which washes the aquatic leaves and blossoms fresh and immaculate.

As we approach the center of the oceanlike expanse, We see in the downward darkness the Southern Mountains dropped, Inverted, and immersed in the farther half of the lake, Quivering here and there with rhythmic shadows of quiet ease. Will our boat collide with the Temple of the Cloud Edge Peak? Watch how the moon swims out of the Lan-t'ien Pass!

53

Now is the time the Black Dragon should offer his fabulous pearl. Let the guardian spirit of the waters beat the drums to the movement of the little dragons, Let the Princess of the Hsiang and the Maidens of the Han come out to dance Amidst the flickering lights of the green flags and silvery poles.

Still there is the lurking fear that a thunderstorm might strike at any moment. What after all is the intention of unpredictable Providence? How long can the illusions of youth last in the reality of age! How many rapid turns of joy and sadness in an interval so brief!

XX FRIENDSHIP

One turn of the hand, it might be either rain or storm. Such fickleness in countless instances everywhere! Do you not see that the permanent loyalty so beautiful in classical friendship Is now trampled as dirt under foot?

XXI FAREWELL TO K'UNG CH'AO-FU, WHO, ON THE PRETEXT OF ILLNESS, IS LEAVING FOR THE SOUTHEASTERN COAST. PLEASE SHOW THIS TO LI PO.

K'ung Ch'ao-fu shakes his head and will not stay, He will follow the eastward clouds to the sea. While his poems continue to be admired by men, His fishing line will dangle over the coral trees.

The spring is cold, the sky overcast, the weather gloomy, But the deeper into the mountains, the nearer by the marshes, the farther you are from vipers and serpents. The heavenly maiden of the fairy isles has turned her chariot in the clouds To point you the way to blissful vacuousness.

How are ordinary people to know That you have immortality in your bones? We love and want desperately to keep you: Have we forgotten that wealth and prominence are less stable than dew on the grass?

Only Mr. Ts'ai, the quietist, speaks more with his silence And chooses this fine night to spread a feast on the veranda. As I finish playing the lute, the moon glints sadly upon us all. When will you drop me a letter from space? If you meet Li Po by the sea, please tell him: "Tu Fu wishes to inquire about your health."

"Twenty-two Rhymes to His Excellency Wei Tsi" [xxv] is one of Tu Fu's three poems to his elderly friend who in 748 was promoted from the position of the prefect of Ho-nan to that of an assistant controller of the Executive Division (twenty-fourth step up the ladder), an important position in the capital with some supervisory powers over the Ministry of Appointments, the Ministry of Economics, and the Ministry of Propriety. This particular poem was written either at the end of 748 or in the beginning of 749. I am inclined toward the later date. In one of the lines the text reads, "Thirty years on a donkey's back." A seventeenth-century commentator observed that while still in his thirties, Tu Fu could not have had thirty years on a donkey's back, and suggested amending the text to read "thirteen years." Though this amendment has been generally accepted, I find it difficult to reconcile these thirteen years of beggarly existence with the more than eight years of lively freedom which must constitute a large part of the thirteen. I propose therefore to amend the two characters *shan shih* (three ten) to read *shan ssŭ* (three four), which would be Tu Fu's way of saying "more than three." This poem sums up our poet's life in the neighborhood of Ch'ang-an from the later part of 745 to the early part of 749. It is not certain that the poems, "Summer Outing at Chang-pa Creek . . ." [XXII, XXIII] and "Lo-yu Park" [XXIV] were written during this period. Nor is there any evidence against their assignment here. They help, however, to explain our poet's feelings in the poem to Wei Tsi.

XXII SUMMER OUTING AT CHANG-PA CREEK WITH YOUNG ARISTOCRATS
AND GEISHAS: RAIN CAME TOWARD EVENING (TWO POEMS)

I

It is pleasant to board the barge as the sun sinks low And the light breeze slowly beats up the ripples; Now we pass between thick bamboo groves; Now we reach the fresh coolness of the water lilies.

While the young gentlemen mix the icy drinks, And the pretty girls are slicing the delicious lotus roots, I see a patch of clouds darkening over us; This means rain to hasten my poetry.

XXIII   2

The shower has bathed our seats; The wind beats hard against the boat. Drenched are the red skirts of the southern girls, Wretched the painted faces of the northern beauties. The mooring line is cutting into the willow. The curtains are sprinkled with curling foam. I see our return will be chilly; We shall feel autumn at the height of summer.

XXIV LO-YU PARK

The old Lo-yu Park is open and spacious, With continuous acres of soft, luxuriant grass. Our aristocratic young host has chosen the highest knoll for a sumptuous picnic: We can see the distant rivers as flat as our palm, as shiny as wine. Impulsively we gulp from big wooden ladles, Hilariously we mount saddled horses and gallop.

*The verdant spring is reflected in the ripples of the Princess' Pond,
The drums thunder from within the walled Imperial Passageway. We
pass the palace gates open wide to the broad sunshine; By the Meandering River we meet curtained chariots with silver plates. We watch the
dancers' flying sleeves skimming the water; We follow the singers' rising tunes spiraling to the clouds.*

*Of course, I remember getting drunk each year at this season, But now
I am too sad before I am drunk. This poor head with thin white hair
is worth nothing, I shall not refuse to drink even a hundred forfeits.
The great Court has found no attraction in a humble scholar; Every
mouthful comes only by the grace of God. After the party is over, what
will become of me? I shall stand alone, lost in my songs.*

XXV TWENTY-TWO RHYMES TO HIS EXCELLENCY WEI TSI

*Those who wear silk underwear never starve. An academic cap is apt
to ruin a life. If my venerable elder will quietly listen, I shall humbly
offer my dissertation.*

*When I was still in my youth, I was a candidate for the Imperial exam-
inations. With thousands of volumes worn by reading, Whenever I
took a pen, my thoughts were inspired. My prose was thought to rival
Yang Hsiung's, My poetry was regarded as approaching that of Ts'ao
Chih. Even the great Li Yung wanted to make my acquaintance, And
the brilliant Wang Han wished to lodge near me. I thought, of course,
I was extraordinary, And should immediately climb to an important
position, To help my sovereign to succeed better than even the best,
And to restore the purity of culture and civilization.*

*But all these hopes were sadly shattered. I gleaned to live in an un-
willing hermitage. Now for more than three years on a donkey's back,
I have been fed on the spring air of the flowery capital. Mornings, I
knock on the doors of rich youth, Evenings, I follow in the dust of
the fast horses. Left-over wine and the roast that is cold I swallow together with my pride and my tears. In answer to His Majesty's recent
command, I leaped in the hope of vindication. But I was a bird dropped
from the blue sky with folded wings; I was a carp thrown upon a reef
and not allowed to swim.*

*Though I hardly deserve your generosity, I do appreciate your genuine
kindness; And I know that frequently among your associates, You
have quoted good and fresh lines of mine. One moment, I rejoice in
your recent promotion, The next, I detest my own poverty. I know I
should not have allowed the heart to be restless; But how am I to*

give rest to my weary feet? Now I am about to go eastward toward the sea; And that means I shall quit Ching-chao in the west. I do still love the look of these Southern Mountains, Many a time I shall remind myself of the clear Wei. A grateful heart will find it hard not to remember a simple meal; And still harder to forget a great statesman. But when the white seagull disappears in the vast expanse, Who will be able to tame him from afar?

"No beating of the wings will enable the poor bird to rise."

CHAPTER FOUR

In his "Twenty-two Rhymes to His Excellency Wei Tsi" [xxv], Tu Fu mentioned that he was about to start eastward toward the sea. There are other poems which show that at this time—the first part of 749— he was considering a boat trip to the east coast. To set the record right, we should ask afresh, "Did he actually go east?" Most of Tu Fu's biographers would reply that he did, because they found him visiting the Temple to His Mystical Majesty in Lo-yang in the winter of 749. Since we have demonstrated in the second chapter that this visit took place in the winter of 741, not 749, and since we can find among his poems or in his prose no evidence of Tu Fu's being in the east in 749, we are more likely correct if we conclude that, though he had thought of leaving Ching-chao, he did not actually go. The tone of the last few lines of his poem to Wei sounds as though he were saying, "Unless you do something, I shall surely leave." It is not impermissible to speculate that Wei did do something. He could at least have given Tu Fu money for temporary relief. Even had he thought it unwise to recommend Tu Fu for employment, he might have persuaded his friends to befriend the poor poet with more generous gifts. Tu Fu was a man of extremely affectionate nature who delighted in the company of friends. Unless there were an ethical issue at stake, it would not require very much persuasion to get him to tarry. This happened again and again during his life.

Moreover, some poetic exaggeration should be allowed the description of his beggarly existence. Not all of the generosities which he received were such as to make him conscious of condescension. There was genuine friendship with at least one good and famous prince. Li Chin, the Prince of Ju-yang, one of Tu Fu's eight immortals of the wine cup, was the eldest son of the emperor's eldest brother, the erstwhile Prince of Sung, who refused the right of succession in favor of the emperor and who, upon his death in 741, was honored as the Self-denying Emperor and was buried with imperial rites, despite the humble remonstrance of the son. As the emperor's beloved nephew, the Prince of Ju-yang, though having no part in government, was naturally very well off. "Twenty-two Rhymes Presented to the Prince of Ju-yang" [xxvii] shows that the prince must have been very fond of our poet.

It is difficult to determine precisely when Tu Fu wrote this poem. It must have been presented before the death of the prince in 750. In "Brave Adventures" [ccxi], our poet recalled that when he returned to Ching-chao following more than eight lively years in the East, famous men of letters appreciated his talent and a good prince liked his company. The men of letters might have been Ts'ên Shên, K'ung Ts'ao-fu, and others. The good prince was, of course, the Prince of Ju-yang. But how soon after our poet's return to the West in the winter of 745 did he come in contact with the prince? The present poem shows that the first meeting was late in autumn; it could not then have been earlier than the autumn of 746. Since spring and summer are also mentioned, the poem could not have been written earlier than the summer of 747. The time of the poem should therefore be between 747 and 750 inclusive.

The lines referring to living in a shut-in dwelling high up among the cliffs present a difficulty. They seem to indicate that our poet was living in real or semi-hermitage. This would be too much of a contrast with the life depicted in the poem to Wei Tsi. Perhaps the poem "Go" [xxvi] will help us to solve the riddle. "Go" has generally been dated by commentators and biographers in the latter part of 755, after Tu Fu had accepted an official appointment. This dating I cannot agree with, since the acceptance of an official appointment meant for Tu Fu the abandonment of plans for hermitage. I am very much tempted to place "Go" in 749, and to hypothesize that after receiving donations from Wei Tsi and others, our poet gave up the idea of going to the east coast and went only for a temporary retreat in the jade-producing hills of Lan-t'ien, about ten miles southeast of Ch'ang-an. The short retreat was perhaps terminated when he was again cordially invited to enjoy the hospitality of the Prince of Ju-yang.

XXVI GO

Do you not see that as soon as it is fed, The falcon will leave the arm-let and soar away? You cannot expect it to imitate the swallow, To carry mud and seek shelter under a roof. An unconventional rustic is indeed thick-skinned, But should he remain long among princes and nobles? Still untried is the recipe for preparing the elixir with jade, I shall retreat into the Lan-t'ien Hills tomorrow.

XXVII   TWENTY-TWO RHYMES PRESENTED TO THE PRINCE OF JU-YANG

Your Royal Highness is an example to the entire nobility, Your elevated position is due to personal virtue as well as to heavenly origin. You remind one of the historical comparison of a good prince with a stalwart steed, And of the fabulous story of the gigantic bird with wings touching heaven. In matters of propriety you neglect not the infinitesimal, When duty calls, you forget all your own comforts. His Majesty's favors are continuously upon you, But away from court you behave like a humble subject. The finest of wines that you share with your guests, The rarest of birds like the imperial eagle Are among the gifts brought to your unsoiled doors By the palace messengers that almost daily come. Of late you have accompanied His Majesty on outings less often, But your usual filial piety and righteousness are no less well known. It was His Majesty's own devotion to brotherliness; Not your desire for the imperial rites for your father.

A learning that is as rich as that of a refined scholar, A literary proficiency that qualifies a gifted master, And a calligraphy that is as beautiful as a peacock, All combine to account for the impressive elegance of your writings. With understanding, eloquence, and humor, You have formed friendships with no self-consciousness. Your appreciation is always ready to recognize the slightest merit, Your generosities are never accompanied with condescension.

I already have the rare honor of serving a most talented prince, Your Royal Highness surprises me by regarding me as an equal and a friend. I have been invited many times to share Your Royal Highness' hospitality; The weight of such kindness is almost beyond my strength. I recall the evening of our first meeting, how it was like the clearing of a fog, How the autumn was at its peak of clean freshness, How winepots and wine cups were placed near the edge of the pond, And how we watched the sleeping ducks and geese by the light of the lanterns. I recall how we spent a whole flowery month in visiting and feasting. I recall how I escaped the stifling heat of the summer days Writing with a pen dipped in your cold inkwell, Or listening to the sound of ice from the striking jade pendants of your palace eaves.

I have been a hermit possessing half a gourd for a drinking cup, And living in a shut-in dwelling high up among the cliffs. Now I presume to face your largeness as a little shell might measure an ocean, Not to say your generous wine is as plenty as the water of the Shêng! Are the secrets of everlasting life forever hidden? There must be steps that will lead to them. So long as the immortal prince will keep his friend, He will never need to suffer the lack of friendly advice.

While we cannot and perhaps need not be sure that the poem to the Prince of Ju-yang was presented in 749, we can and should be fairly certain that "The Kokonor Steed of Governor General Kao" [xxviii] was written, as traditionally dated, in that year and not, as more recently redated, three or four years later. On the choice between the earlier and the later dating depend some very serious issues in our study of the character and intelligence of Tu Fu. The ostensible subject of the poem is the horse; the real subject is the governor general. Our poet openly praises Governor General Kao's victories and subtly hints that Kao should not be kept in the capital but should be encouraged to continue his victorious exploits on the western frontiers.

In 749, after some successful campaigns beyond the Hindu Kush, An-hsi Governor General Kao Hsien-chih, a Korean, returned to Ch'ang-an, received an additional appointment and a promotion, stayed for several months, and was sent west again the same year. Early in 751 Kao, again victorious, made a second visit to Ch'ang-an, was again promoted, and once more returned to duty in the west. After suffering a disastrous defeat by the Arabs beyond the Pamirs, Kao returned for the third and last time to the capital, presumably in the early part of 752, and did not reappear in an expedition until the end of 755, only a few weeks before his execution for some alleged failures. The redating of Tu Fu's poem is based mainly on the assumption that Kao's short stay of a few months in Ch'ang-an in 749 does not seem to justify our poet's hint as well as Kao's longer inactivity after his third return in 752. A plausible enough argument. But its acceptance will pose for Tu Fu some very embarrassing questions. When he wrote the poem in 752 or 753, had he known of Kao's miserable defeat in the west? If he had, was he not guilty of flattery at the expense of veracity? If he had not, was he not rather poorly informed? Was he not rather rash to venture his hint? Were not his aspirations to sound statesmanship rather ridiculous?

Fortunately, we need not accept the new dating and may even confirm the old one. The titular reference to Kao in the poem and its title would be inappropriate for Kao's higher ranking and different appointment after 751, but would fit him well in 749. The hint in the poem had to do, of course, with his new concurrent appointment to a *gendarmerie* generalship, which would enable him to stay, if he desired, indefinitely in the capital. Moreover, as we shall see, our poet had come to condemn frontier expansions by 750. After 750, it would have been quite impossible for him to laud Kao's military exploits as he did in the present poem.

XXVIII THE KOKONOR STEED OF GOVERNOR GENERAL KAO

The blue Kokonor steed of the Governor General of An-hsi, Has acquired a sudden reputation in the East. We are told that he has long been unrivaled in battle, And that he has always shared his master's purpose of achieving victories. The victories won, he deservedly receives generous care everywhere, And now he has arrived here from faraway Takla-makan. His powerful build belies long stabling, His warlike spirit recalls the tactics of the battlefield. Such springy ankles with high hoofs hard as wrought iron Must have almost shattered the packed ice of the Turfan rivers. Admire him not for the fine-tasseled mane like a rainbow over his body; Only after thousands of miles will you appreciate the famous blooded breed. None of Ch'ang-an's cavaliers dares to ride him; Everyone recognizes his gallop—a lightning speed. But if he is to grow old with those blue-ribbons on his head, How is he ever to issue forth on the road out of the West Gate?

The new policy of frontier defense, put into effect by Li Lin-fu, has been condemned by historians as one of Li's worst crimes. It had been customary for the T'ang court to appoint promising statesmen in civil service to military posts on the frontiers. Many of those who had distinguished themselves in the victorious defense of the empire against the barbarians would be called back to the capital and made ministers of state, and some of these had been men of the highest literary reputation. Since Li Lin-fu's main concern was to keep away from the central government men who might supplant him in power and influence, he had to put an end to the practice which might give him rivals in the government who had literary ability, administrative experience, and military prestige. After he had brought about the downfall of those governors general whom he feared most either by charging them with seditious crimes or by accusing them of obstructive conservatism in military movements, he chose to support the rapid advancement of soldiers of foreign extraction to commanding positions on the frontiers. If these barbarians were poorly educated in Confucian political philosophy, or if some of them were utterly illiterate, so much more would they be free from the restraints of moderation and pacific proclivities, and so much more likely would they be to become aggressive and daring in an expansionist program on the frontiers—a program in which the prime minister took pains to encourage His Majesty.

The successful military exploits of these men in extending the boundaries of the empire would be rewarded with higher ranking honors and greater powers as governors general. They would not be given high ministerial positions in the government, for their educational qualifications would make them appear ridiculous in civil service. Li Lin-fu could thus rest in peace. But the new policy spelt disaster for the T'ang empire. Adventurous barbarian soldiers, scantily acquainted with the ethical principles of loyalty and patriotism, invested with vast military, political, and economic powers in vast areas on the frontier—might they not be tempted to covet the imperial throne? Li Lin-fu apparently did not bother himself with such questions.

Among the soldiers of foreign extraction thus elevated to power, the three outstanding figures were Kao Hsien-chih, Ko-shu Han, and An Lu-shan. On account of his disgraceful defeat by the Arabs in 751, Kao Hsien-chih, the Korean, was kept in the capital with a high-sounding military title but with no armed forces under his command. He did not prove to be a threat to imperial security. Ko-shu Han, a fierce fighter of mixed barbarian blood, the governor general of Ho-hsi and Lung-yu combined, had a record of victories over the unsubmissive Tibetans; commanded tremendous power, prestige, and wealth; and had in his service some of the ablest scholars of the time. Because of excessive drinking and debauchery, his health broke down in the spring of 755, and he had to stay in Ch'ang-an, exercising only an indirect command over the territories and armies under his charge. Nor did he turn out to be a danger to imperial authority.

With An Lu-shan, however, the case was entirely different. This cowardly scoundrel, also of mixed foreign blood, had won some advantages over the barbarians of the Northeast mainly through treachery. The prime minister espoused especially his rapid advancement because An had the admirable qualification of being a complete illiterate. By 742 this uneducated schemer was already governor general of P'ing-lu. After he came to pay court in Ch'ang-an, he wormed himself into the confidence of the emperor and gained the love of the imperial concubine, Yang Kuei-fei.

By the most lavish use of bribery, An Lu-shan had everybody in the palace loud in his praise; he knew everything that was going on in the government or at court. Though he was sharply suspicious and cunning at heart he had a disarming appearance of innocent simplicity. He was ridiculously short and fat, with a protruding and hanging belly, said to weigh alone at least four hundred pounds. He was delighted to have men laugh and women giggle at him and was never slow to join in general hilarity. The emperor jokingly pointed to his belly and inquired what might be in that enormous bag. "Nothing whatever, Your Majesty," said An, "save loyalty." He induced the Yang sisters and cousins to adopt him as a brother, but once in the inner palace through their introduction, he had Yang Kuei-fei adopt him as a son. Once he celebrated his birthday in the palace. The pretty imperial concubine had a multitude of women carry him around in an enormous diaper made of silk brocade. Attracted by boisterous laughter the emperor went to the scene and was told that the adopted mother had just bathed her adopted infant. Our Brilliant Emperor had grown sufficiently stupid to be very pleased with such an abundance of happiness and never suspected that there might be something improper in the adoption.

By 751, An Lu-shan had become governor general of the three areas Fan-yang, P'ing-lu, and Ho-tung combined. He feared only the resourceful Li Lin-fu. After Li's death in the winter of 752, his rebellious plans developed with rapidity. But we are getting too far ahead of our chronology. We shall come back to An Lu-shan in later chapters.

In 749 Tu Fu was, of course, not yet aware of the disastrous tendencies in the government's military policy. He doubtless shared the popular exhilaration at the news of frontier victories. But he was soon to realize, at least partially, the harmful aspects of the program of military expansion. "The Song of War Chariots" [xxix] must have been written toward the close of 750, because it refers to the troops of Kuan-hsi sent on an expedition against the Tibetans. Moreover, the poem mentions the sending of recruits to the North and to the West but not the infamous recruiting in 751 for an expedition to the Southwest against the rebellious barbarians in the area of what is now Yün-nan. It must, therefore, have been written before 751. "Frontier Duties" [xxx–xxxiv], five of nine poems under the same title, might have been written about the same time as "The Song of War Chariots," for the sentiments expressed are somewhat similar. The captured kings mentioned in the poem might be those who fell to Kao Hsien-chih in Kashmir and Tashkent and who were offered by him to the court early in 751.

XXIX THE SONG OF WAR CHARIOTS

Chariots rumble, horses neigh, Men are marching with bows and arrows. Parents, wives, and children rush to bid them farewell; The rising dust obscures the Hsien-yang Bridge. They clutch at the soldiers' clothes, stumble, and bar the road; Their cries pierce the clouds.

Let the passer-by question the marchers: "Just another recruitment," they reply. "Some of us were sent north at fifteen to guard the Yellow River, Now at forty we are going to garrison the West. Last time, caps of manhood were forced upon us by the village chief. Just home with white hair, we go again to the frontiers, Where enough blood has been shed to form a sea; Still His Majesty will not cease to expand our Empire. Have you not heard that in the two hundred eastern prefectures Thousands upon thousands of villages are overgrown with weeds? Even where there are strong women to try farming tools, No

64

man will be able to recognize his own field at harvest. Moreover, since the soldiers from Ching-chao are noted for endurance, So must they be driven about like dogs and fowls. You are indeed kind to ask about our troubles; How dare we to air our grievances? Let us just take the present winter: You know the Kuan-hsi troops have not yet returned. The government is ruthlessly collecting taxes; Where are the taxes to come from? Now we have learned how unfortunate it is to have sons— Better to have brought up daughters instead. Girls can be married in the neighborhood, Boys are born to perish among unfamiliar weeds. Do you not know that in the region near Kokonor Since ancient times human bones have been left to bleach in the sun? New ghosts murmur while the old ones weep, You can always hear them when night or rain comes."

XXX FRONTIER DUTIES (NINE POEMS)

I

With heavy hearts we leave our home village; We are going far, far to Turfan. The government has set a time limit, Deserters will surely be caught and punished. Is not His Majesty's empire vast enough? Why does he want to extend the boundaries? We are now forever severed from our parents' love: We swallow our sobs, take up our arms, and march.

XXXI   4

There is the village elder responsible for every recruit. Here am I, destined for the faraway frontiers. Life or death, I am going forward; You, officer, have no need to be angry. I may meet an acquaintance on the road, Let him take a letter home. Alas, we shall be forever parted, Without hope even of suffering together.

XXXII   6

Trying bows, we try the taut ones; Choosing arrows, we choose those that are long. Shooting the enemy, we shoot their horses first; Capturing them, we commence with their king. There must be a limit to killings; For a country, there must be some boundary. Since it is enough to repulse an invasion, What good can result from inflicting more casualties?

XXXIII   8

The barbarian ruler dares to attack our forts; For miles the air is thick with rising dust. We wave our swords only a few times: This army stampedes before us. We bring back their famous king a prisoner; With a cord around his neck, we deliver him to headquarters. Since soldiering is our lot, One victory is nothing!

With twelve years of service in the army, There must be some record of merit. The others all claim more than they should, If I speak out, I might appear to resemble them. Back in the interior there are fights and quarrels; What can you expect from barbarians in the North or the West? A man's ambition should be aimed far, Why should he become restless with present hardship?

In the autumn of 750 a new educational institution was established at the capital, mainly to accommodate a very famous scholar. Chêng Ch'ien was perhaps the most talented and learned man of the time. He was well versed in geography, astronomy, pharmacology, and military history, and had written extensively on these subjects. He was a renowned calligrapher, painter, and poet. Once he presented to the emperor a roll of beautiful landscape painting, explained with elegant poetry exquisitely handwritten. The emperor wrote at the end of the roll, "Three perfections of Chêng Ch'ien." Later, Chêng had been accused of attempting an unauthorized history of the dynasty and was banished. Now he was recalled to the capital. Since Chêng—a self-indulgent man who drank a great deal—was not accustomed to the routine duties of a government office, the emperor ordered the creation of the College of Literary Extension and appointed him the first professor. We do not know when the warm friendship between the poor professor and the poorer poet began. I am inclined to think that "Visiting General Ho's Country Villa with Professor Chêng" [xxxv–xxxviii] was written in the late spring of 751. The estate was in the southwestern suburb of Ch'ang-an. The title covers ten little poems in all, but we shall translate only four of them.

XXXV   VISITING GENERAL HO'S COUNTRY VILLA WITH PROFESSOR CHÊNG
CH'IEN (TEN POEMS)

I

I never knew the road to the South Pond, Now I know it is beyond the Fifth Bridge. A famous garden stands by the green waters; Wild bamboos shoot toward the blue skies. I am always fond of secluded places, How happy I am to be invited here. As long as it is for an inspiring retreat, I have never grudged to ride far.

XXXVI 4

I like these tall bamboos flanking the hut And those flowers on the old fence glowing in the sunset. That puddle in the track might be deep enough to drown a horse, Those thick wisteria vines wind very much like snakes. What good can result from mere skill in poetry and prose? Retirement into the hills and woods is not beyond reach. I am thinking of offering my whole library for sale! Maybe I can buy a hut in this neighborhood.

XXXVII 9

Tall trees in the yard seem to brush the clouds. In the rooms, books piled on beds almost reach the ceiling. The general is one who dislikes war; All his children can write well. A light breeze blows as I wake from wine. After we listen to the poems, it is quiet midnight. The climbing vines make shadows on our thin robes; A cold moon scatters broken pieces of whiteness outside.

XXXVIII 10

Quiet thoughts suddenly are tinged with sadness, For we should not tarry and must return. Beyond the gate we shall follow the water that flows on, Leaving behind us these white clouds. I can only laugh at myself when I dance before the light of the powerful, Who really cares for the songs I sing after I have drunk the wine of the rich? The only right thing to do is to follow my friends, To come here often, whether it rains or shines.

It is reasonable to suppose that Tu Fu wrote these poems before he presented to the Brilliant Emperor three long masterly *fu*. A *fu* is a literary piece which is like prose because of its length and the full development of thoughts in logical order with little regard to the economy of words, but like poetry in that the lines are generally antithetical in structure and are rhymed. These three *fu* were to commemorate three stately ceremonies—impressive sacrifices offered by the emperor on specifically chosen dates in the early part of the year 751 to the Temple of Lao-tzŭ, to the Imperial Ancestral Temple, and to the Altars of Heaven and Earth. In a memorial accompanying the *fu*, Tu Fu begs to inform His Majesty that he is in his fortieth year; that since his late teens he has traveled far and lived humbly, circumstances owing to his own failure to pass either the regular or the special examinations given by the imperial government; that while making a humble livelihood in the capital through the generosity of friends, he had the unusual opportunity to witness and record these wonderful ceremonies; and that though these *fu* might not be deemed worthy of His Majesty's attention or of being handed down in history, he nevertheless made bold to place them in the Imperial Hope Chest because he did not want to die unknown and unrecognized.

The Imperial Hope Chest, with a reception officer in charge, was an institution of long standing devised to help aspirants seeking recognition or employment. When our poet made use of the Imperial Hope Chest, he was of course hoping that it might result in some literary appointment. The chest must have been filled with documents each day and undoubtedly only a few pieces ever reached His Majesty after the critical sorting by the reception officer. This worthy was evidently one of Tu Fu's acquaintances, for we shall see that he had a poem for him three years later.

The three *fu* were written in the best style of the Han masters, rich in descriptive imagery, elegant in literary allusions, suggestive in historical analogies, and clever in disguising advice in the form of praise. The third piece ends with these words:

Thereupon His Majesty meditated thoroughly and long. That which he was to achieve, he wanted to last always. There is no glory in receiving tributes from distant regions. There is no need to multiply useless temples. Dazzling edifices for strange worship add nothing to government. Bright corals and shiny gems are also ordinary things, without doubt. "I shall treasure only the precepts of Heaven," decided His Majesty, "and the teachings of my ancestors. I shall strive toward the perfect government in accordance with the teachings of the *Canon of Changes.*"

What happened when the Brilliant Emperor read the three magnificent *fu?* Tu Fu says in his "Brave Adventures" that the emperor interrupted his meal to issue a summons—a historical allusion which means that the good emperor was impressed and acted at once. The summons seemed only to be for the poet to report to the Academy of Talents and to await further orders. It might be because he had to wait that we find him still in Ch'ang-an, at the end of the year 751, spending New Year's Eve in the home of a distant cousin. What I suspect is that he had no real home of his own to which to go. The distant cousin in question was Tu Wei, a son-in-law of Prime Minister Li Lin-fu! Tu Wei's house was in the southeastern section of the city of Ch'ang-an, near the beautiful Meandering River.

XXXIX NEW YEAR'S EVE IN THE HOUSE OF TU WEI
To see the year depart at a brotherly home, To participate in the songs and toasts with the pepper-wine, I can hear from the stable the noisy horses of the guests, I can see the crows leaving the trees because of the torches. By tomorrow, I shall no longer be forty; The evening of life will be fast coming upon me. Of what use is it to be cautious and to exercise restraint? Let me forget it all by being utterly drunk.

The five poems "Another Visit to General Ho" [XL-XLII] may have been written in the spring of 752 while Tu Fu was still impatiently awaiting His Majesty's further orders. He was perhaps beginning to feel the futility of official service, and for the moment, it was the monetary aspects of an appointment that most appealed to him. Only three of the five poems under the title are presented here.

XL ANOTHER VISIT TO GENERAL HO (FIVE POEMS)

I

I wrote to inquire about the bamboos by the east bridge, And the general wrote a reply: "Get on a horse and come at once," said he, "Make my house your own, sleep, and have sweet dreams." The oriole snatches a falling flower as if it were a butterfly. An otter pursuing a fish magnifies the splash of the brook. It is pleasant to come again to this place for rest—An ideal dwelling for rustics.

XLI   3

It is good to drink tea in the spring breeze, At sunset, on this flat terrace. Inking my pen on the slanting stone balustrade, I sit down to write a poem on a wu-t'ung leaf. Here is a kingfisher singing on a bamboo clothes rack; There is a dragonfly clinging to a fishing line. Now that I know what quiet enjoyment is, I shall come here again and again.

XLII   5

Whenever I come I shall stay at least overnight; With such welcome, I can stay a whole year! A stumbling life! It is late enough! Only vain longings after a good place of hermitage! When will I be able to have a salary, Go back to the village and buy a little farm? Even the present venture may result in nothing; Holding my untasted wine cup, I am lost in sadness.

Orders from His Majesty did come at last: Tu Fu was to take another examination. The affair was evidently quite formal. The celebrities congregated at the hall of the Secretarial Division with all their official paraphernalia. Prime Minister Li Lin-fu wrote the questions. The Minister of Propriety helped to grade the papers. The high officers of the Academy of Talents stood like a wall surrounding Tu Fu, who sat down to write bravely and with pride.

The result? Well, it was not an outright failure. Li Lin-fu's heart might have been somewhat softened by the intercession of his son-in-law, Tu Wei. Or the old rascal might have deemed it prudent not to abuse too harshly a scholar who had already attracted the emperor's attention. But he would want to see to it, of course, that the report of the examination would be such that the skilled writer so eager to serve the emperor with loyal advice should be thought not good enough for any literary service to His Majesty—which, as we shall see, was really Tu Fu's earnest hope. Further orders from His Majesty were to the effect that the examinations might be considered satisfactory and that the candidate might proceed to the Bureau of Appointments and wait for his turn to be given a job. This procedure was one allowed any student after passing the annual examinations, or any young man coming up under the *yin* system, or any office clerk, after long service, beginning to climb the first step of the official ladder. From Tu Fu's standpoint it was equivalent to failure. Naturally he felt very much as he had some fifteen years earlier.

XLIII FAREWELL TO THE HONORABLE TS'UI KUO-FU AND THE HONORABLE YÜ HSIU-LIEH, TWO HIGH OFFICERS OF THE ACADEMY OF TALENTS

A white-haired man under this brilliant dynasty Knocked on the heavenly gate only when no other way was open. The audacity indeed reached beyond the stars, But the writing was good enough to move His Most Exalted Majesty; His Excellency the Prime Minister wrote the examination questions; His Excellency the Propriety Minister reviewed the dissertations. But the flying seagull, having lost its way, Has to endure the chattering swallows and sparrows. The swimming carp, failing to reach the Dragon Gate, Is thrown into company with miscellaneous water snakes. Though the blue sky is still there for one to reach, No beating of the wings will enable the poor bird to rise. Sound learning proves to be indeed a handicap, Though the reputation of the family is somewhat vindicated.

Back in the home hills there are many herbs of immortality; The landscape is as beautiful as the Valley of Peach Blossoms. As I am about to take my departure and go back, I cannot forget my experience in the Academy near the palace walls. You two gentlemen have generously praised my three fu; I do not know how I can requite your kindness.

The commentators who thought that by "home hills" Tu Fu meant the District of Kung or the Prefecture of Hsiang-yang were of course mistaken. Could he mean Yen-shih or Tu-ling? Documentary evidence tends to indicate the latter. In "Brave Adventures" he wanted his readers to understand that after the examination in the hall of the Secretarial Division, he left without receiving anything, and contented himself with drinking and poverty. Then he went on to describe the scene in the Tu Village, or Tu-ling, how he was regarded as one of the village elders and was busy with the social duties of the Tu clan. It would seem that he did go to Tu-ling to live for awhile at least.

"The thought of returning to the home hills is ended!"

CHAPTER FIVE

A problem that has long puzzled all biographers of Tu Fu is: when was he married? Wife and children began to be very much in evidence in 754. Was he already married before 752, and had he left his family in Yen-shih? During the 745–752 Ch'ang-an period could he not have made trips of a few days' journey on donkey or horse three hundred miles back to Yen-shih? But I find it difficult to understand why he did not go home even for New Year's as most people would do. His later poetry shows him to be a very affectionate husband and father, and there was always a tone of nostalgia in his poems whenever he was separated from his wife and children. With the possible exception of one short poem—which I shall assign to 755—there is complete silence about his family in the writings that could be dated between 745 and 752. More-over, we have found that our poet's thoughts vacillated between the hope of serving the emperor and the wish to withdraw from society for the cultivation of his individual immortality. This contrasts very sharply with the later Tu Fu, who was very much a family man and who re-garded his duties toward his dependents very seriously. I venture there-fore to introduce the bold hypothesis that Tu Fu married late, and in 752.

The fact that Mrs. Tu Fu, by the autumn of 757, had become the mother of five children will necessitate the supposition of not only a close succession of births but also of twins. This is of course not very common, but has occurred in a few instances to my knowledge. That

Tu Fu observed his New Year's Eve in the home of a distant cousin militates against the supposition of his marriage before 752. In 751, moreover, Tu Fu, in his fortieth year, though the son of a good official family, was a poor man with no prospect of official employment or assured income and was known to have been frequently drunk and liable to run away alone to some distant and inaccessible spot in the empire. It would have been difficult for him to marry a girl from a tolerably good official family. In his forty-first year, the situation was considerably changed. Suddenly he had become famous: his three *fu* had moved His Majesty! A good appointment with steady income was thought to be very likely. With a good appointment, and if also with a good wife, he would hardly want to run away, and he might even drink less. The matchmakers would get busy. There must be beautiful maidens of good families whose marriage, for one reason or another, had been delayed long enough.

Tu Fu's bride, the daughter of Yang I, vice-president of the Court of Agriculture (ranking on the twenty-second step from the bottom), might already have been fatherless, for we know nothing of him except his name and title. She might have been in her twenties, for we know she died in her forty-ninth year, probably a few years after 770. Judging by the affection and respect Tu Fu expressed for her in some of his poems, the matchmaking must have been fairly easy.

Upon his second visit to General Ho [XLII, 5], our poet was strangely thinking not only of salary but also of some farm property. This was quite unlike the man who had left, probably to his half brothers, the house he had built and the property he had inherited in Yen-shih. Was the marriage in contemplation or had it already taken place? The desire to have some official appointment—not to roam on the southeastern coast or to retreat high up among the cliffs of Lan-t'ien, but to take up village life in the neighborhood of the capital—might also indicate an economic prudence made necessary by the acceptance of new responsibilities.

We find Tu Fu visiting the famous Buddhistic Pagoda of Mercy and Grace [XLIV] near the Meandering River—a few hours' walking distance from Tu Village—together with four other poets, Kao Shih, Hsüeh Chü, Ts'ên Shên, and Ch'u Kuang-hsi, in the autumn of 752. The five of them, of course, wrote poems. The date is certain, because it was the only autumn that the five poets could have been together in Ch'ang-an or its neighborhood. Kao had passed a special examination in 749 and had been made a district police commissioner, a job which he found distasteful, particularly the flogging of subordinates and common people. So he left the job to come to the capital in search of better employment. In his poem, he expressed disappointment in not having found it. Ts'ên Shên stated in his poem that he was about to terminate his official life;

he was evidently dissatisfied with his minor and nominal position attached to a garrison commander's office. Censor Ch'u said in his poem that the towering pagoda must crumble, and those who lived there should be warned not to remain long. The poem written by Hsüeh, at this time a junior officer in one of the ministries, is no longer existent.

Comparing the several poems, literary critics are agreed that Tu Fu's is the best. His is certainly the most difficult to translate. Without the historical background of the time as a guide to the hidden meanings under the rich imagery and historical allusions, the poem might appear illogical and meaningless. The dragons and serpents, for instance, represented the intricacies of high politics, which could affect the fortunes of even a humble scholar like Tu Fu. The Heavenly River (Milky Way) flowing west might refer to the exhaustion of the manpower and wealth of the empire for military exploits mostly in the west. The clouds that obscure the mountain were Li Lin-fu and his allies, who deceived the emperor. The clear Wei and the muddy Ching got mixed in the same way, since there was no longer any standard for judging good and bad. The sagacious Emperor Shun of remote antiquity refers, of course, to the Brilliant Emperor, and the Fairy Queen Mother of Han Dynasty mythology was indeed Yang Kuei-fei. The yellow cranes were good men who were leaving the capital. The flying geese were Kao Shih, Hsüeh Chü, Ts'ên Shên, Ch'u Kuang-hsi—each worried about his livelihood.

XLIV CLIMBING THE PAGODA OF MERCY AND GRACE WITH SEVERAL GENTLEMEN

On this height astride the sky, The piercing wind never ceases. Since one cannot be free from care, This climb evokes more fears. The power of religion revealed in externals Commands one to pursue a quiet search. When I peep through the dragon-and-serpent crevices, I am amazed at the mystery of spans and supports within.

I see clearly the seven stars of the Dipper, But I hear the sound of westward currents of the Heavenly River. The sun is being driven downward, The clear autumn moon is trying to rise. Suddenly the clouds shatter our great mountain into pieces; The clear Wei and the muddy Ching are mixed and lost. Looking down, you find only one misty blur—How can you tell it is our august Empire?

I turn toward the nebulous sadness above his grave, And shout for the great Shun to wake. Alas! at the feast by the mythical Lake of Jade, The Fairy Queen Mother is drinking as the sun sets behind K'un-lun. The yellow cranes are fleeing and will not stop; With all their plaintive cries, where can they go? You observe those flying geese in the sunset: Each one seeks only food.

73

"Meandering River" [XLV] was very likely written in the same season of the same year as the pagoda poem. We give here only one of the three stanzas under the title. It may be noted that Tu Fu had now acquired some farm land in Tu-ling. We know not how he managed it. He might have come into a small sum of money for having done some writing for those who could afford to pay well. Or, he might have been helped by a retired military grandee whom he called eulogistically Li Kuang. Li Kuang was a Han Dynasty general, good and brave, but unlucky in his official career. Mistaking a rock for a tiger, he shot an arrow and pierced it. The allusion in the poem probably referred to a friend or patron—perhaps General Ho?—a military man living in retirement who privately minced no words about such political tigers as Li Lin-fu and his confederates.

XLV MEANDERING RIVER (THREE STANZAS)

3

I have decided not to blame Heaven for this life of mine, For I am really fortunate to have some farms near the Tu Village. I might purposely move to live nearer the Southern Mountains. Clothed like a farmer, mounted on a horse, I shall keep you company, Li Kuang, And end my years contentedly, just watching you shoot tigers.

The poem "Given to Cousin Tu Tsi" [XLVI] was evidently written while our poet was concerned with some Tu Village affairs. This distant cousin was to turn up in prominent positions in Tu Fu's later life. Clearly, they were not on intimate terms. According to the Tu genealogy, Tu Tsi was one generation below Tu Fu. But Tu Fu always addressed him as belonging to the generation of his grandnephews—obviously the text of the *Genealogical Compendium* is defective.

XLVI GIVEN TO COUSIN TU TSI

On a donkey's back, early in the morning, I had to decide at which house to call. No agreement can be reached with the high and mighty; I thought it best to see you, my distant cousin. You are poor and unemployed, Your houses are like a deserted village. Bamboos grow in front of the main hall; Day lilies were back of it. The day lilies died in the autumn; Frost now harms the bamboos.

To wash rice, not much water need be drawn: Too many drawings will make the well muddy. To cut the sunflower, be gentle with your hand: You might injure its root, if you swing the axe too hard. I am an old man, lazy, and long in idleness. You, my boy, can walk or run as you please.

*I have come on the business of our clan, Not at all for a bowl of porridge.
Mean fellows love to wiggle their tongues: Idle gossip hardly deserves
attention. Do not allow the outsiders to instigate trouble; The ancients
taught that the clan must stand united.*

While Tu Fu, abandoning the thought of serving the government
dominated by Li Lin-fu, retreated to the Tu Village and busied himself
with the affairs of the Tu clan, Li Lin-fu continued to make himself the
most feared man of the empire. Even powerful and cunning rascals like
Yang Kuo-chung and An Lu-shan cringed at the very thought of incur-
ring his anger. But Li Lin-fu was also the man most afraid of other men
in the empire. Having unjustly brought about the death of countless
human beings, he was apprehensive of revenge. His magnificent mansion in Ch'ang-an was a veritable fortress with reinforced walls, secret
chambers, and underground communications. None of his numerous
concubines, twenty-five sons, and twenty-five daughters knew in which
room he might choose to sleep at night. But illness could attack him anywhere. By early winter in 752 he was a very sick man, and on January 3,
753, he died. Thus ended a powerful career at the top of the government—nineteen continuous years of the most cunning deceit and the
most ruthless cruelty, which poisoned the world's most brilliant empire,
seeping to its very foundations. Few men in history gave by their death
as much momentary relief and rejoicing to their contemporaries as did
this wicked prime minister.

Yang Kuo-chung, who, we may recall, was the emperor's gambling
companion and the imperial concubine's cousin, succeeded Li Lin-fu as
the highest minister of state. He began to fabricate charges against his
dead friend and rival. Moved to anger, the emperor proceeded to deal
out punishments. All of Li Lin-fu's titles and honors were annulled, his
coffin was opened, his corpse stripped of all finery, gems, and pearls, and
all his relatives sent into exile. Some fifty of his henchmen in the government were banished.

That Yang Kuo-chung was not an honest, forthright man by any
standard should not have been unknown to Tu Fu. Tu Fu would be
quite correct, however, if he thought that Yang could not be as poisonous as Li. It would be quite human for one momentarily to feel warmth
toward the murderer of one's worst enemy. Moreover, Yang Kuo-chung
also started some calculated pretenses to endear himself to those who
had been long frustrated in seeking official appointment. He expedited
the business of appointments with amazing speed, and the grateful recipients of jobs even set up a stone monument in his praise. Yang called
to the capital a well-known literary scholar, Shan-yü Chung-t'ung, a
patron of Yang in the earlier days in Shu-chün, and made him the
prefect of Ching-chao. Tu Fu's poem to Shan-yü Chung-t'ung [XLVII]

was undoubtedly written in 753, because Shan-yü's biographer tells us that he soon was disliked by his erstwhile protégé and was banished in the same year, 753. After the death of Li Lin-fu and the new appearance of the appointment program, Tu Fu probably thought that with Shan-yü's help he would not have to wait many months or years at the gate of the Ministry of Appointments in the company of those whom he likened to chattering sparrows and water snakes.

XLVII TWENTY RHYMES PRESENTED TO PREFECT SHAN-YÜ CHUNG-T'UNG

There are many scholars in the Empire, But how many are really good men? A rare talent should rise occasionally; It is not difficult to discern it. Now I have discovered the great Prefect—He is indeed the one to stand near His Majesty. A wonderful charger has opened the road for the other horses; The great eagle has soared high as an example to the birds in the dust. Countless marquises and barons already fill the capital, But you rise because of literary excellence. You have flown far past fellow men of letters, The erstwhile obscurity can be easily forgotten. Leaving behind the fishing line in the old place of hermitage, You are holding the axe and hammer to build a new administration. The Ching-chao Prefecture is already near the clouds, What could be nearer to the stellar position of the State Council?

That all of your sons are excellent boys, That new guests are welcome to your patronage, I have heard with grateful expectations, Though because of past defeats, I have hesitated to approach you at once. I know not which direction to take on the long journey; I hesitate to make another appeal to lofty heaven. I, too, am a scholar with training in poetry And was once an examination candidate sent up by the Prefecture. It was my lot to regret my own failure And be left behind to admire the success of the others.

At times I have doubted whether a literary training was of any use; Then again I remembered men who succeeded only late in life. Through the Imperial Hope Chest my writings caught His Majesty's gracious attention. Though I had not bowed below the audience hall, I did have the chance to meet with the great celebrities And to have them witness the display of my humble talents. It was frightful to live under the last administration, For then a sinister plotter was alone at the control of things. That even a humble creature should be made an object of attack Has turned every thought into bitter tears. Now you are associated with a new and colorful government At a time when grace is to rain upon a scorched earth; That a good scholar dreads starvation, Will you not soon inform His Excellency the Prime Minister?

76

Hoping that the poem would be effective in bringing him employment, Tu Fu now issued forth from his retreat in the Tu Village, to take up in Ch'ang-an where he had left off the previous year. The duties of a clan elder were generally concerned with officiating at weddings and funerals; collecting contributions to repair the clan temple, to bury the insolvent dead, or to give relief to poor widows and orphans; and with patching up petty quarrels among the kinsmen. If there were many instances of Tu Tsi's type of noncoöperation, Tu Fu could hardly be blamed for leaving the job by moving to Ch'ang-an. We find him in the rainy months of 754 living in a house close to the south wall of the city of Ch'ang-an. He might very well have been in that house already in the summer of 753 and received the call of the Honorable Mr. Li [XLIX].

With Yang Kuei-fei in the palace and Yang Kuo-chung in the premiership, the other five Yangs became even more loud in the garish display of their affluence. Each of the five households would dress up the retainers, servants, and guards in one particular color. Occasionally there would be a parade of the five colors through the streets, with a mistress in a carriage or a master on a horse at the head of each column. Prime Minister Yang Kuo-chung would precede the rainbow-colored columns with the brilliant military paraphernalia of the governor general of Chien-nan, a position he held concurrently. "Pretty Women" [XLVIII] gives us a glimpse of the Yangs on a festival day, possibly April 10, 753. The mention of the pink kerchief has been thought to be a faint hint of illicit union.

Since Tu Fu's estimate of the character of Prime Minister Yang Kuo-chung was so low, we need not wonder that at times he must have wanted to berate himself for having to beg help from such a scoundrel. "White Silk" [L] might be taken to be evidence of some such struggle with his conscience. And no wonder he cast a covetous eye toward the West in his farewell poem to Kao Shih [LI], who went to Wu-wei in the summer of 753 to be Governor General Ko-shu Han's secretary. Though Tu Fu still had misgivings about Ko-shu's expansionist tendencies, he realized that under Ko-shu's patronage a man of Kao Shih's caliber could make rapid advances in official career.

XLVIII PRETTY WOMEN

There is a freshness in the air this Third of Third, a spring festival day. I see by the Meandering River of Ch'ang-an many fair women With distant looks but frequent smiles, sweet and real. With delicacy of complexion and symmetry of form, They appear in silken dresses embroidered with golden peacocks Or silvery unicorns, dazzling in the sunshine of late spring. What do they wear on their heads? Kingfisher head-dresses with jade-leaves over the temples. What do you see on their backs? Pearl-trimmed capes cut perfectly to fit. You can spot the Imperial relatives among those rainbow-screens—Among them the Lady of Kuo and the Lady of Ch'in. The purple steak of dromedary hump, broiled in a shining pan, The white meat of raw fish served on crystal plates, Are not inviting enough to the satiated palate. All that is cut with fancy and prepared with care is left untouched. Palace messengers come on light steeds, galloping without dust, Continuously bringing the rarest delicacies from His Majesty's kitchens. Strings and pipes now accompany the feasting with music, weird enough To move ghosts—not to mention the hoard of guests and retainers, each of commanding importance. You see the last comer, who approaches leisurely on his horse, Dismounts near the screens, and steps on the flowery carpet. Willow catkins drop like snow to confuse the white frogbit; A blue bird flies away with a pink kerchief in its beak. The Prime Minister is so powerful, his mere touch will scorch. Approach not, lest you anger him.

XLIX   THE HONORABLE MR. LI CALLS ON A SUMMER DAY

My noble friend has come to call on me Here among the trees where the summer heat is light. My poor dwelling is near the south city wall tower In a remote area very much like a deserted village. I have found the neighborhood wholesome and simple, And what I need is easy to get. I shout from my yard to the household on the west, And ask if they could let me have some wine. Home-brew is passed over the wall; With it, we can go to the bank of the stream and spread a mat. A fresh breeze comes from the right and the left; My guest is surprised at the feeling of autumn. In their several nests, birds are quarreling; Among the thick leaves, the cicadas buzz. We are often annoyed by their cries, Who says that my hut is quiet? The aquatic blossoms look clean in the sunset, They invite us to linger a while longer. I fear there is not much left in the winepot, Let me rise to get more for you.

L   WHITE SILK

Reeling silk off cocoons, you want the threads long, not necessarily white; They may be for Yüeh gauze or Shu brocade to be measured by a gold-inlaid yardstick. Delicate hands may need a profusion of red on the ivory frame To embroider hundreds of flowers among thousands of grasses for shining contrast.

Yes, you may grieve to see pure material dyed to suit fashion; Wait till you see under the creaking loom the broken bits in the dazzling light. The fair one will tenderly press the finished piece smooth and flat, Will cut and trim to hide all traces of needles and threads. She may wear it as a spring gown to dance for you, While the butterflies flutter and the orioles chat, While the willows coquettishly swing their wands in the wind, And drop their catkins to float lightly in the sunshine. Let dust or

78

perspiration but once soil the finery, It will be discarded to make room for a new dress.

Do you not see, wise men know the hazards of seeking aid, It is the fear of abandonment that detains them in strange places?

LI FAREWELL TO SECRETARY KAO SHIH

The wheat near the K'ung-t'ung Mountains will soon be ready for harvest, Let us hope there will be no war. Please ask your Governor General: What is the use of acquiring barbarian territories? When a falcon hungers for food, He will fly low to follow his master. Mr. Kao, astride a saddled horse, Appears like a frontiersman from the Northeast. Now that you are rid of the duties of a police commissioner, You must be happy to drop the whipping rods. Let me ask what appointment it is That takes you to Wu-wei in such hot weather. "Only a secretaryship," you answer; "But I am trusted as though I were the Empire's best man." But can you trust him as much? It will be advisable to be careful with yourself. After ten years of service with a Governor General, You, yourself, may head a large area. Since this trip seems to promise much, I am very happy for you. A man may well be satisfied with the attainment of success and fame, Even though it comes late in life.

I regret that the joy of our meeting has been short; often we have been separated in different corners of the world. Now again we are to be like morning and evening stars, One can only long for the other in the pathos of not meeting. The dreaded wind will soon carry off the great crane, I can watch, but cannot follow. Every time I think of yellow dust darkening the deserts, I shall wonder why you should not come back. On the frontiers, if you have free time, Do send me poems about your military experience.

In 754, Tu Fu was desperate. Shan-yü Chung-t'ung had gone. No encouragement had come from the Ministry of Appointments. A baby, or perhaps twins, must have arrived the previous year. With an enlarged family and very likely additional servants or wet nurses, the economic pressure must have been high. If the new prime minister, whose rank had been advanced late in the spring to that of Ssŭ-k'ung—on the highest step of the ladder—would not help, could the emperor be appealed to again?

Into the Imperial Hope Chest our poet put another *fu*. This time it was to recommend that His Majesty might go ahead with the investiture ceremonies conferring special honors upon the Hua Mountain, astrologically the guardian spirit of His Majesty's life. It was without doubt calculated to appeal to the emperor's superstitious fancy and pride. Not wanting to repeat the sad experience he had had with the late Li Lin-fu,

Tu Fu even tried to placate the new prime minister, Yang Kuo-chung, by stating in the accompanying memorial: "Moreover, the great Hua has brought about the birth of our Ssǔ-k'ung in order to give him to Your Majesty as the first helper." We cannot help feeling that all this is not worthy of our good and upright Tu Fu. We must, however, sympathize with his desperate state of mind, for the real purpose of this new venture was simply to tell His Majesty that he had waited for two years in the routine machinery of appointments without getting anything, and that since he was frequently sick because of some trouble with his lungs (not necessarily tuberculosis, perhaps merely an allergic asthma), he feared death before having a chance to serve his sovereign.

Tu Fu also presented a poem to Tien Ch'êng, the reception officer in charge of the Imperial Hope Chest. The allusion to Yang Hsiung (53 B.C.–A.D. 18) was to hint that the present *fu*, like the last ones, contained important advices for His Majesty.

LII PRESENTED TO RECEPTION OFFICER T'IEN CH'ÊNG

The Reception Office is high up near the source of rains and dews, The charge is so important that it can be trusted only to a superior man. Our officer is so diligent that he collects the documents even after office hours, The palace ladies will approach the throne with opened envelopes. Early in the morning you hasten to the gate of the palace, During the day you sort out the best pieces under a bright window, Yang Hsiung now has another good fu, It needs only your help to be wafted to heaven.

Most of Tu Fu's critics have not thought highly of the literary quality of this poem, and I place it here merely for the sake of history. It was perhaps hastily composed, and I doubt if T'ien Ch'êng was well impressed. I doubt also if the *fu* in question ever reached the emperor. If the *fu* was placed in the chest during the summer, T'ien Ch'êng—despite Tu Fu's poetic description of diligence—might not work so eagerly in the heat over an enormous pile of papers. If he had not reached Tu Fu's *fu* until autumn, just a hasty glance would be sufficient to determine his dropping it into the waste basket. For the autumn of 754 started with a continuous rain which lasted more than sixty days. Houses in the capital were crumbling, and crops in the neighborhood were ruined. Famine had begun. In 750, the investiture of the Hua Mountain had been considered, but postponed because of a drought—too little rain, too little water. The Hua would not be deserving of so great an honor since it failed to prevent such a calamity. Now, in 754, there was too much rain and too much water. It was, of course, unthinkable to present Tu Fu's *fu* to His Majesty. His Majesty might even become angry with both the poet and the reception officer.

Waiting is not pleasant. Tu Fu was waiting for the rain to cease, for the price of food to come down, for word to come from the emperor or from the Ministry of Appointments. His Majesty was kind enough to allow a million *hu* of rice to be taken out of the reserve granaries for rationed sale at a reasonable price to the starving population of Ch'ang-an. But each household was allowed daily only a five-hundredth of a *hu*, sufficient for two and a half persons. We find that Tu Fu's household consisted of about ten persons the following year. At this time he might have had to provide for half a dozen or more. What could he do? Well, he could write some poems about the rain. We give here one of the three poems, entitled "Sighing over the Autumn Rain" [LIII]. Another thing he could do was to go to his friend Professor Chêng Ch'ien and get drunk with him [LIV]. "To Tease Professor Chêng Ch'ien; Also to Show Dean Su Yü" [LV] might or might not have been written in the year 754. Our poet's old friend, Su Yü, could not have come to Ch'ang-an as a Dean of the Imperial University before the autumn of 753, nor after the winter of 755. I give this poem here to indicate the intimate friendship among the three men.

LIII   SIGHING OVER THE AUTUMN RAIN (THREE POEMS)

2

Continuous storm and rain have spoiled the autumn. One stretch of clouds over the whole world Darkens the days. One cannot tell horses from oxen, going or coming. The rivers are flooded, none can tell the clear Wei from the muddy Ching. Fungi cover the trees, grains rot in the fields. Neither cereals nor vegetables have come from the farms. In the city you barter your bedding for two days' supply of rice. You are lucky! Who talks about old prices?

LIV   DRUNK

The dignitaries are promoted one by one, up and up. In his cold office the honorable professor alone is forgotten. In the many mansions they feast on choice meats; The honorable professor has not enough rice to eat. He is a better man than exemplary saints; He writes better than the revered masters. If the present generation cannot recognize you as the best of men, What is the use of trying to leave a great name for later ages?

The Rustic of Tu-ling is even more laughable—An old fellow with scanty gray hair, with ill-fitting, shabby clothes. He goes daily to the Imperial Granary to buy five shêng *of rice, Then he comes frequently to old Chêng for company. When there is money, one will find the other; It matters not who buys the wine; wine they will get. All formali-*

*ties of polite address can be dropped, One admires the other for the
mastery of the drinking cup. We pour the spring brew late into the
quiet night; Rain drips from the eaves while the snuffs of the candles
drop. So long as we feel our lofty songs arouse the spirits, Why worry
about starvation and death in the gutters!*

*The literary genius Ssŭ-ma Hsiang-ju was a dishwasher, The learned
scholar Yang Hsiung tried suicide by jumping from a tower. It is better,
O Professor, to retire early—Even to an unproductive farm and a dilapidated hut covered with moss. After all, what is Confucianism to us?
Confucius and Bandit Chê—are they not both dust? Let us not sadden
ourselves with this sort of talk; So long as we are alive and can meet,
let us drink the cup.*

LV   TO TEASE PROFESSOR CHÊNG CH'IEN; ALSO TO SHOW DEAN SU YÜ

*The Professor arrives at the college; He ties his horse before the steps of
the hall. When drunk, he mounts his horse to leave, Leaving his superior
officers to curse after him. Though he has had literary fame for thirty
years, He is still too poor to provide cushions for visitors. It is good that
there is Dean Su Yü From whom he can beg money for wine.*

It was possibly in the latter part of the autumn, after Tu Fu realized
that his second use of the Imperial Hope Chest had amounted to nothing, that he turned earnestly to explore the possibilities of an employment on the western frontiers. Indeed, the failure of the central government to make adequate use of good and able men had driven more and
more of them to the service of military magnates in the outlying territories. Poet Kao Shih had been working in Wu-wei for Governor General Ko-shu Han for more than a year. Poet Ts'ên Shên, another of Tu
Fu's friends, had also left Ch'ang-an to enter the employment of the
stern disciplinarian, clubfooted Governor General Fêng Ch'ang-ch'ing
of An-hsi. It was but natural for Tu Fu to wonder whether he should not
follow the example of Kao and Ts'ên. It happened that Ko-shu Han's
messenger at court was about to return to Wu-wei. Tu Fu presented him
with a farewell poem and sent by him another poem for presentation
to Governor General Ko-shu. The latter poem was practically an applica-
tion for employment. This was of course a vain step, for the grandiose
warrior had only to ask Kao Shih to find out about the applicant's anti-
war views. It was, however, a step which Tu Fu would hardly have
taken had he not been in terribly distressing circumstances—ceaseless
rain, poverty, hunger, and cold.

Perhaps thinking it easier to find food in the village than in the city,
Tu Fu took his family back to the Tu Village—either in the rain or as
soon as the rain stopped in late autumn. But it was doubtful that he

82

could obtain much grain in time of famine from the tenants on his farms. Not much relief could be expected from the clan, since the famine must have affected everyone. The only practical thing to do was, of course, to move again—to an area which the famine had not reached, or where it was light. We find in Tu Fu's collection a long poem addressed to a group of officers in charge of the Imperial Mausoleum of Jui-tsung in the District of Fêng-hsien, about eighty miles northeast of Ch'ang-an. This poem states that because of famine he and his family, including the undernourished children, had bid Lower Tu Village farewell, had crossed the muddy Ching River, and had arrived in Fêng-hsien late in the evening, in tears, and like the autumn fireflies, had been given temporary shelter in some unused quarters of the mausoleum. He must have had some friend or relative in Fêng-hsien who, he hoped, would help him find more permanent quarters.

I am inclined to think that Tu Fu stayed in Fêng-hsien through the winter of 754 and barely managed to provide for himself and his family with loans and gifts that he might have picked up in the neighborhood. "Sandy Park Stud" [LVI] was very likely written during this winter; the stud was in the neighborhood, a few miles to the southeast. The last few lines of the poem allude to An Lu-shan.

In Tu Fu's collection there is a poem which he wrote in support of another poem, by a Mr. Kuo, on the subject of a deep pool located east of the Hua-ch'ing Palace hot springs below the Li Hills (official name for Lan-t'ien Hills). Here Tu Fu mentioned among other things:

There on the slope, a golden toad Appeared for a definite reason. His Majesty only laughed at it; The Fairy Queen Mother would not keep it. After it returned to the bottomless deep, It was to turn into a dragon-like monster.

While it is not possible to indicate definitely the time and place of a poem written in support of another, it is reasonable to assume that Tu Fu wrote this poem after the spring of 754, and after An Lu-shan had left Ch'ang-an for Fan-yang. The toad of course was An Lu-shan, and the dragon was a symbol of sovereignty. It is recorded that considerable jealousy and ill feeling had sprung up between An and Prime Minister Yang Kuo-chung. Yang warned the emperor, "An Lu-shan will surely rebel. Suppose you send for him; he will not dare come." The emperor did summon An—who came promptly, early in the spring of 754. He was royally entertained in the Hua-ch'ing Palace. The emperor made up his mind not to doubt An's complete loyalty. Taking advantage of this trust, the villain got His Majesty to appoint him General Supervisor of the forty-eight Imperial Studs; he then proceeded to order a selection of many thousands of fine horses, to keep them apart from the weak ones, and finally to have them sent to his own armies. Moreover, he obtained from the emperor signed certificates of appointments for 500 generals and 2,000 colonels with blank spaces left for the names of the appointees to be filled in by An! An filled in the names of foreign soldiers whom he could trust with his rebellious plans. When he left the capital in the latter part of the spring of 754, he was afraid that Yang Kuo-chung might interfere with his journey, and he traveled by boat day and night without stopping, back to Fan-yang. A few persons ventured again to tell the emperor of An's rebellious preparations: His Majesty had them arrested and sent to An for punishment!

LVI SANDY PARK STUD

Have you not seen in the P'ing-i Prefecture white sands as white as water, Surrounded by a wall forty miles in length? In ancient times imperial steeds were reared by the waters of Wo-wa, Now the blooded breeds are offered from here. Three thousand stallions and mares in this park Graze on the fresh, green grass that flourishes even in winter. Such well-fed, strong horses are not found even in the West Regions; The colts foaled here each year excel those of the frontiers. His Majesty has a brave officer in charge of the stud, Within which the Imperial stables are grouped like thick clouds. A snow-white courser alone is chosen for His Majesty; Twice in the year, spring and autumn, he goes to Court.

Of the hundreds of thousands in the stables or pastures Of the Empire, which one can compare with him? As the fleetest of foot he is already peerless, Not to speak of his heroic loyalty and resourcefulness.

I see horses dash among sandy mounds, I see them jumping and leaping across the streams. Entering the woods, they play and wrestle with wild deer; Floating on the ponds, they disturb the turtles and water-lizards. Beware! There appears a giant fish as big as a man. It has golden scales and a vermilion tail. Has a monstrosity anything in common with righteousness? It is frightening, though it is not really a dragon.

Tu Fu returned to Ch'ang-an probably early in the spring of 755, leaving his family in Fêng-hsien. "Moon on the One Hundred and Fifth Night" [LVII] is a love poem in which our poet is thinking of his wife. Counting the days from the winter solstice, the 105th was the Cold Food Festival in memory of a heroic tragedy. Chieh Chih-t'ui of the seventh century B.C., forgotten by his marquis in the distribution of rewards for loyal service, retired to the woods and perished there when the marquis set fire to the woods to force him to come out to receive his well-deserved reward. In remorse, the marquis ordered the cessation of fire or cooking on the memorial day. This love poem of Tu Fu has been

84

generally assigned to the spring of 757. I have found this to be incorrect, for on the night of the Cold Food Festival of that year, there was only a half moon in the sky, but a full moon is demanded in this poem. There are only three possible times in Tu Fu's adult life when a full moon shone on the night of the festival: 747, 755, and 763. In 763 he was with his family. In 747, he was probably not yet married. I date this poem, therefore, April 1, 755.

Critics consider this poem one of the cleverest from Tu Fu's pen in the use of allusions to folklore. We need to explain only that the cowboy and the spinning maiden refer to two stars on two sides of the Heavenly River (Milky Way), and that the girl was thought to meet the boy once every year by crossing the river on the seventh day of the seventh month. The faint shadow in the full moon was thought to represent the cassia plant.

LVII   MOON ON THE ONE HUNDRED AND FIFTH NIGHT

I have no home on the night of the Cold Food Festival. I have only tears like silvery waves. If one can cut away the cassia in the moon, Surely there will be more of the clear light. Separated from me, she will not wear red flowers; I imagine her brows are drawn in sadness. We are now like the cowboy and the spinning maiden, but we mustn't complain, Let us hope to cross the river in the autumn.

When Ko-shu Han arrived in the capital in the spring of 755, so sick that he had to request indefinite leave of absence from his post, Tu Fu's hope of employment by the governor general of Ho-hsi and Lung-yu must have evaporated like thin air. He now presented a long poem to Wei Chien-su, who in the previous autumn had been appointed a state minister, second in command next to Yang Kuo-chung. Wei was a kindly, elderly man, who after passing the imperial examinations had spent many years slowly climbing the official ladder. He was, however, a timid man. Even if he appreciated Tu Fu's needs, he was not likely to do anything unless he was certain of Yang Kuo-chung's approval.

Late in the spring, however, Tu Fu probably had a temporary respite from his impoverished state. He wrote a magnificent text to be inscribed on the tombstone of a long-deceased imperial concubine, the mother of a princess married to Chêng Ch'ien-yao. Chêng Ch'ien-yao, said to be a nephew of Professor Chêng, was more probably his second cousin, and it was very likely Professor Chêng who recommended our poet for this composition. Literary labors of this sort were customarily rewarded with fees. To judge from our poet's several poems on visiting the gardens of the princess and on outings together with her husband, this daughter and son-in-law of the emperor were evidently well-off. The fee could have been a handsome one. In the inscription, Tu Fu compared himself rather immodestly, but quite justly, with the best ancients in this type of composition. At the same time, he humbly acknowledged Her Royal Highness' gracious notice of a white-haired rustic without any official rankings whatever. Was he hoping that the emperor, reading the elegant portrayal of the virtuous and beautiful concubine of his younger years, might be reminded that the same author—whom the emperor had admired four years previously—was still without an appointment? If our Tu Fu had so hoped, he hoped in vain.

When autumn came, there was still no prospect of official appointment for our poet. In desperation he went to the Imperial Hope Chest for the third time. "The *Fu* on the Eagle" and its accompanying memorial contain no clue for precise dating. I am inclined to think that it was this *fu* that finally hastened the authorities to give the poor poet an appointment, either late in the same autumn or early in the winter. In the memorial, Tu Fu hinted to His Majesty that he wanted no appointment through the ordinary mill and preferred to serve His Majesty in some literary capacity, as his grandfather once served in the court of Emperor Chung-tsung. In the *fu* he described beautifully the hunting activities of the eagle in autumn. He was implying, of course, that he would serve the emperor by being that brave and fearless eagle to extirpate the old foxes and the cowardly rabbits in the government.

If the emperor had done anything in response to this *fu*, our poet would certainly have aired his gratitude or disappointment in a number of his poems. I doubt also that this *fu* went beyond the pigeonhole or the wastebasket in the Reception Office. The tone was too bold and the request too extraordinary. When the news got round to the foxes and rabbits, some of them must have deemed it wise to get this fool of a poet out of the capital before he did something really rash. Accordingly, an appointment came down from the Ministry of Appointments. Tu Fu was named police commissioner of the District of Ho-si, not far from Fêng-hsien. What generosity! Imagine appointing a great poet with the deepest kindness and the widest sympathy—a man sensitive to even the suffering of beasts—to a job whose chief duty was to administer whippings to the draft evaders and the tax delinquents!

Fortunately, the T'ang system allowed an appointee to refuse an unsuitable appointment. We know nothing of the details of the change. But a change evidently was soon made. "Teasing Myself after the Appointment Was Settled" [LVIII] was probably written in the early winter of 755. Under the title is a note: "At this time I was relieved of the post of Police Commissioner of Ho-si and became Registrar in the Right Commandant's Office of the Crown Prince's Palace."

It may be said that the work of the various commandants attached to the Crown Prince's Palace had by this time become more nominal

86

than real and that the registrar had hardly any duties to perform. The official ranking was the fifth step up the ladder. An appointment with this rank would entitle the recipient to the assignment of 200 *mou* of land for permanent possession, 250 *mou* during tenure of office, an annual grant of 134 *hu* of rice, a monthly salary totaling 35,640 coins for the year, and a few other advantages, such as the free service of two servants, the use of a horse, and so forth. Such an income should have enabled our poet to maintain moderately a household of about ten persons.

In Tu Fu's self-teasing poem the term "back-breaking" came from the story of the famous T'ao Ch'ien (372–427), who resigned from office because he did not want to break his back by frequent bows to superiors merely on account of the small salary of half a *hu* of rice. Our poet might have used the allusion playfully to indicate the back-breaking of others before the police commissioner. Judging by his poem to Kao Shih [LI], we need not doubt that to him the most distasteful aspect of that job was the punishing of subordinates and common people.

LVIII TEASING MYSELF AFTER THE APPOINTMENT WAS SETTLED

Because of the unhappiness of back-breaking, You do not want to be the Police Commissioner of Ho-si. Being an old man, you are afraid of running about; Well, you may saunter leisurely in the Commandant's quarters. You need a small salary because you indulge in wine; The government will leave you to your mad songs. The thought of returning to the home hills is ended! Turn around and say good-by to the wind.

Tu Fu probably left Ch'ang-an soon after the appointment was settled. "Five Hundred Words from Ch'ang-an to Fêng-hsien" [LIX] was written after his arrival in Fêng-hsien but before he heard of An Lu-shan's rebellion, which started in Fan-yang (Peiping at present) on December 16, 755. The news of the rebellion probably did not reach our poet in Fêng-hsien any sooner than it did the emperor in the Hua-ch'ing Palace on December 22. Judging by the pessimism in Tu Fu's long poem, we need not doubt that he was expecting the outbreak imminently.

LIX FIVE HUNDRED WORDS FROM CH'ANG-AN TO FÊNG-HSIEN

From Tu-ling, there is a poor and obscure man; The older he grows, the more impractical he becomes, Until he is foolish enough to wish To serve his country as did the best men of the past. The only result has been disappointment; Though white-haired, he has to stand hardship. Still he persists in the face of frustration, Not until he lies in his coffin, will he give up. He worries about the people the year round,

He sighs, and his heart burns with anxiety. Though his old school-mates may laugh at him, He continues to pour out songs, sad and passionate. He has not forgotten the dream of sailing away on the river and the sea To while away days and months, easy and without care. Simply because he lives under an extraordinary prince, He loathes the thought of cutting himself off permanently. He knows there is already enough building material: No new wood is needed for the edifice of government. But that the sunflower turns to follow the sun Is its nature which it cannot help. Yet he reminds himself of the tiny ants: Each will seek its own hole. Why then should an ant emulate the giant whale And wish to float on the great waves? From this he has come to understand the principles of life, And is only shy of imploring others to help. Failure after failure continues to the present, And he will have to contend with ending in the dust— Regretting that he had not simulated the best hermits Who could not be made to leave their hermitage. Let him drink to soothe himself, Let him sing to break the spell of sadness.

Toward the end of the year the grasses are dead, A fierce wind tears the high ridges. The thoroughfare from the capital is darkest When I, a traveler, set out at midnight. Biting frost snaps the girdle on my clothes, With stiff fingers, I cannot tie another knot. By dawn I pass the Li Hills; I know His Majesty is reposing in the Hua-ch'ing Palace. Here the banners of Mars fill the cold air; The troops tramping over the hills have worn the rocks smooth. A dense mist rises above the jasper-green pools. The Imperial guards rub elbows one with another. Here His Majesty entertains his ministers, And music echoes in the ravines. Only the high dignitaries may bathe here, The humble people have no share in the feastings. But the silk distributed in the Imperial harem Was woven by poor women; The officers beat their husbands To extort the tribute for the Court. His Majesty's lavish gifts Were meant to benefit the country and the people. It is the ministers who have ignored vital principles of government And not His Majesty who causes the waste. Among the many talented men that fill the Court, The benevolent ones may well take fright. And we hear too that the golden platters of the palace Have all gone to the houses of the royally related. In the central halls there are fair goddesses; An air of perfume moves with each charming figure. They clothe their guests with warm furs of sable, Entertain them with the finest music of pipe and string, Feed them with the broth of the camel's pad, With pungent tangerines, and oranges ripened in frost. Behind the red-lacquered gates, wine is left to sour, meat to rot. Outside these gates lie the bones of the frozen and the starved. The flourishing and the withered are just a foot apart—It rends my heart to ponder on it.

I turn north to where the Ching and the Wei meet, And find that the ferry has changed again to another spot. Many torrents pour down from the west. The further I look, the higher the waters seem to be. They may have come from the K'ung-t'ung regions; Might they not have destroyed the Hill of Heaven's Pillars? Fortunately a bridge still stands, Though a loud cracking rises from its infirm supports. Travelers hold hands and crawl over laboriously; I almost curse the river for being so wide.

I have left my good wife in a strange district, For disastrous times have broken up our household of ten. I cannot leave them any longer without care, So I have come to share hunger and thirst. Wails rise when I enter the door; I am told my infant boy has died of hunger. Why should I suppress a natural grief When even the neighbors in the village weep? I am ashamed of being a father, so poor and useless That a little son had to die for the lack of food. And I hardly knew that the good harvest of the autumn Had been of no help in a crisis of poverty!

I am one of the privileged, free from taxation And exempt from draft. If my lot is so bitter, That of a common man must be worse. When I think of those whose property has been seized, And of those recruited to garrison the far frontiers, My anxiety rises like a flood to inundate even the Southern Mountains, With mad swells utterly impossible to abate.

"The rebellion of the eastern Tatars has not come to an end."

CHAPTER SIX

The rebellion of An Lu-shan began on December 16, 755. An's pretext was to lead a punitive expedition against Prime Minister Yang Kuo-chung in Ch'ang-an. The rebel forces, said to number 200,000, started from Fan-yang southward; and all of the prefectures and districts of the Ho-pei Department that lay in their path surrendered with no resistance.

The Brilliant Emperor was at the time in the Hua-ch'ing Palace east of the capital and did not receive definite news of the rebellion until December 22. Two days later, Governor General Fêng Ch'ang-ch'ing of An-hsi proceeded under imperial command from Ch'ang-an to the Eastern Capital, Lo-yang, to plan for blocking the rebels' approach. In a few days' time, the clubfooted Fêng recruited 60,000 men for the defense of Lo-yang, and destroyed Ho-yang Bridge some twenty-seven miles to the east, in order to cut off An's approach from the north, across the Yellow River from Ho-nei.

On December 28, the Emperor returned to Ch'ang-an, had An Lu-shan's son An Ch'ing-tsung executed, and ordered An Ch'ing-tsung's bride, a princess of the imperial family, to commit suicide. An Lu-shan's brother, Governor General An Ssŭ-shun of Shuo-fang, was called to the capital and given a nominal position. The command thus vacated was given to a subordinate general, Kuo Tsŭ-i, who was later to become the most important defender of the dynasty. A Chang Chieh-jan was appointed governor general of Ho-nan in charge of some thirteen prefectures beginning with Ch'ên-liu. Thus began the practice of having governor generalships in the interior, and as time went on, the whole empire was covered with them. On December 29, the veteran General Kao Hsien-chih was given command of another army to be recruited with special grants from the emperor's private treasury. On January 7, 756, Kao led this hastily formed and poorly disciplined army of 50,000 eastward. This army was to be stationed at Shan-chün, sixty-seven miles east of T'ung-kuan, and thus to block the road to the capital.

In the meantime, An Lu-shan, moving from Fan-yang southwestward (somewhat along the route of the present Peiping–Hankow Railroad), came on January 8, 756, to Ling-ch'ang, where he crossed the Yellow River. By January 12, he had occupied Ch'ên-liu and, to avenge the death of his son, had executed Governor General Chang Chieh-jan and massacred about ten thousand of the surrendered officers and men. From Ch'ên-liu, he led his forces westward, and on January 18 he took and sacked the Eastern Capital. General Fêng Ch'ang-ch'ing led the remnants of his routed army to Shan-chün, where he met and persuaded General Kao to abandon the defense and to retreat to T'ung-kuan.

Tu Fu was at this time still visiting his wife and children, who were temporarily living in Fêng-hsien. "Frontier Duties" (a second series of five poems) were probably written after he had met an old cavalry officer who, many years previously, had been recruited in Lo-yang to join An Lu-shan's army in the Northeast, and who had now deserted while the rebellious army was marching toward the Eastern Capital. We shall translate three of these poems.

LX FRONTIER DUTIES (SECOND SERIES, FIVE POEMS)

2

In the morning we report at the East Gate barracks; In the late afternoon, we march over the Ho-yang Bridge. The setting sun glows on our huge banners; The wind whistles and the horses neigh. Ten thousand tents are spread on the level sand; We rest with our company and our squad.

A bright moon hangs in the center of the sky. The orders are strict, the night quiet. A few notes of the bugle sound; Even the proudest among us are subdued, sad. "Who is our general?" one asks, "Surely you know of the most powerful man," answers another.

LXI   4

Victories are reported one after another. The border is now quiet and will give us no worry. Fan-yang is the place for heroes Who beat the

*drums and play upon pipes. Countless ships come by way of the Yellow
Sea, Bringing the best rice from the distant Southeast. The finest silks
from the valleys of the Han and the Yangtze Adorn the bodies of foot-
men here. The Governor General's rank has been raised so high, That
he now proudly scorns the Imperial Capital. None at the frontier dares
to whisper any criticism; The critic will be executed on the thoroughfare.*

LXII   5

*I come from a good family, And have served in several armies. The
general's haughty ambition has distressed me more and more; Any
promotion for me is nothing. Having served on galloping horses for
twenty years, I shall not become a traitor to His Majesty. I can see the
cavalries of Fan-yang on march Will soon cover Lo-yang with dust.
I desert at midnight by a side road To return only to an empty village.
Fortunate am I to have escaped an odious name; But I am a poor old
man with neither son nor grandson.*

At T'ung-kuan, the two chief commanders, Korean Kao and clubfooted Fêng, coöperatively did their best to strengthen the defense of
this gateway to the capital. But the Inspector of the Army, General Pien
Ling-ch'êng, a eunuch, presented to the emperor complaints of corruption and incompetency against the two generals. The emperor authorized the eunuch to have the two executed on January 24, and the
semi-invalid General Ko-shu Han was appointed to take over the command at T'ung-kuan. The rebel An Lu-shan, at this point, should have
taken advantage of the poor morale of the imperial defense and thrown
his whole force against T'ung-kuan. But having entered the Eastern
Capital, he made haste to proclaim himself an emperor, and on February 5, the New Year's Day of the solar-lunar calendar, declared himself Emperor of the Yen Dynasty, and proceeded to appoint high dignitaries of state.

Moreover, shortly after An left the Northeast, some trouble had
arisen at his rear. Prefect Yen Kao-ch'ing of Ch'ang-shan, who had surrendered the prefecture to An, started to organize with his younger
cousin, Prefect Yen Chên-ch'ing of P'ing-yüan, a loyal revival. By
January 28, after having killed or captured a number of An's subordinate generals, they had rallied seventeen out of the twenty-three prefectures of the Ho-pei Department for the loyal cause and against the rebellion. Ch'ang-shan was especially important for it commanded T'u-
mên, a narrow pass through the T'ai-hêng Mountains, which was to
admit the loyal armies from the west. Since An could ill afford to have
his rear so threatened, he dispatched his ablest general, Shih Ssŭ-ming,
eastward to subdue the trouble. He left his subordinate general, Ts'ui

Ch'ien-yu, at Shan-chün to conduct the expedition westward against T'ung-kuan and Ch'ang-an.

The rebel Shih captured Ch'ang-shan on February 12 and the loyal Prefect Yen Kao-ch'ing was sent to Lo-yang to be hacked to death. But before Shih had recovered for the rebellion many of the northeastern prefectures, the most important defender of the T'ang cause, Kuo Tzǔ-i had recommended to the court that one of his subordinate generals, Li Kuang-pi, be appointed governor general of Ho-tung and sent with 10,000 soldiers from Shuo-fang on an expedition against Ho-pei. On March 20, Li Kuang-pi recovered Ch'ang-shan again. When Shih turned around to attack Li, a war of attrition, which lasted many weeks, began. On May 12, Kuo Tzǔ-i came through the T'u-mên Pass and joined forces with Li at Ch'ang-shan. The infantry and cavalry under their command were said to total over 100,000 Chinese and Turkish soldiers. After a number of skirmishes, they managed on July 1 to inflict a devastating defeat upon Shih in the eastern neighborhood of Ch'ang-shan. It was said that 40,000 of the rebels were decapitated in the battle, and over 1,000 were captured.

Moreover, a number of the Ho-pei prefectures killed the rebel appointees and rallied to the royal cause. In the meantime such men as Yen Chên-ch'ing in P'ing-yüan; Ho-lan Chin-ming in Pei-hai; the Prince of Wu, Li Chih, in Tung-p'ing; Hsü Yüan in Sui-yang; Lai T'ien, nicknamed the Iron-chewer, in Ying-ch'uan; and Lu Hsiung in Nan-yang blocked the rebels from advancing further to the east, southeast, or south. An Lu-shan, still in Lo-yang, was reported to be worried. He rebuked the scholars who, impatient of waiting for their chances of advancement under the imperial government, had incited him to rebel. "For several years, you have advised my rebellion, which you believed to be absolutely certain of success. Now they have defended T'ung-kuan, and for several months we have not been able to advance farther west. Our return route to the northeast is already cut off, and the imperial armies surround us on all sides. We hold only a few prefectures, Ch'ên-liu, Jung-yang, et cetera. Where is your absolute certainty about success?" This speech might have been put by the narrator into the mouth of the rebel. It does, however, describe well the military situation at the moment; hence its inclusion in the conscientious and, on the whole, reliable *T'ung chien* (Mirror of History, 1084) which we generally follow on the political and military events of the period covered by Tu Fu's poems.

The strategy of Kuo Tzǔ-i and Li Kuang-pi was to have Ko-shu Han's armies merely defend the natural barrier at T'ung-kuan, without giving battle to the rebels, while their own armies would attempt to occupy Fan-yang. When the officers and men under An Lu-shan realized that their homes and families were at the mercy of the imperial forces, they would crumble away from the chief rebel, and the whole rebellion would come to an end.

Unfortunately, a good deal of jealousy and suspicion had developed between General Ko-shu Han and Prime Minister Yang Kuo-chung, who complained to the emperor about Ko-shu's cowardice in facing fewer than 4,000 old and tired rebels in Shan-chün. Not knowing this appearance of weakness to be feigned by the rebel general, the emperor sent one eunuch after another to urge Ko-shu to fight. On July 4 Ko-shu led his forces out of the T'ung-kuan Pass toward the east. On July 9 they had battle with the rebel forces, led by Ts'ui Ch'ien-yu, west of Ling-pao (twenty-five miles southwest of Shan-chün). Taking advantage of the east wind, the rebels burned straw to envelop in smoke the imperial forces, which, when confused, were routed. Of the 180,000 loyal troops only 8,000 survived to return to T'ung-kuan. On the following day, Ts'ui Ch'ien-yu captured T'ung-kuan and the great General Ko-shu Han was delivered as a captive to Lo-yang.

Between T'ung-kuan and Ch'ang-an there were ten beacon fires— one for every ten miles—which were lighted in the morning and the evening. On the evening of July 10, the beacon fires failed to be lighted, and the emperor was afraid. On July 14, at dawn, the emperor left the capital by a west gate of the palace park, accompanied, apart from a number of eunuchs and palace servants, by the imperial concubine Yang Kuei-fei; her three sisters; a number of the princes and princesses; Ministers Yang Kuo-chung and Wei Chien-su; Supreme Censor Wei Fang-chin, who was to serve as Commissioner of Provisions during the trip; and General Ch'ên Hsüan-li, in command of the palace-guard armies. The departure was quietly conducted, and the members of the imperial family who lived outside of the imperial palaces were simply abandoned. When the officials came as usual to the front of the palace for the court audience, they found at first everything in order. Then the palace gate was opened, and the women stampeded out with the news. Bedlam broke out in the city. Looting did not subside until Prefect Ts'ui Kuang-yüan of Ching-chao and the obnoxious eunuch General Pien, now in charge of palace keys, had ordered the execution of several looters. Prefect Ts'ui sent his son to Lo-yang to present his respects to the rebel emperor, and Pien also sent the palace keys to An Lu-shan.

By noon, the emperor and his fleeing party had traveled about twelve miles west of the capital. They were hungry. Prime Minister Yang Kuo-chung bought a few sesame-seed cakes to feed the emperor. The common people of the countryside brought some coarse cereal, cooked with a mixture of wheat and beans, and the grandchildren of the emperor grabbed the food with their hands. The supply was exhausted soon, but their hunger was not satisfied. The onlookers all wept, and the emperor wept too. *T'ung chien* tells us that an old man came forward to say, "An Lu-shan long ago planned to rebel, but Your Majesty usually killed those who came to the capital to inform you of his evil designs. . . . The ministers of Your Majesty's government were all afraid to speak the truth. They had to flatter you in order to keep their position. The result was that Your Majesty knew nothing of what was happening beyond the palace gates. I have long anticipated today, but had no means to bring to the attention of Your Majesty the worries of my humble and loyal heart. Had the country not been visited with this disaster, how could I have the opportunity of seeing Your Majesty and of uttering these words?" "It all came from my own stupidity," apologized the emperor. "I am exceedingly sorry, and I am afraid that my repentance is now too late."

The following morning, July 15, the imperial party reached Ma-wei Post Station, about thirty-eight miles west of the capital. The soldiers were tired and angry. It happened that about two dozen Tibetan messengers surrounded Prime Minister Yang Kuo-chung to demand food. Some of the soldiers, noticing the group, shouted that Yang was plotting rebellion with the Tibetans. They discharged their arrows at him, and before he could run into the station building, they caught and murdered him, chopping his body to pieces and spiking his head on top of a spear. They also killed his son Yang Hsüan, the Lady of Han, and the Lady of Ch'in. When Censor Wei Fang-chin advanced to restrain them, they killed him too. Hearing of the disturbance, Wei Chien-su rushed out of the station building to investigate. The soldiers struck him on the head, causing him to bleed miserably. Fortunately, some other soldiers shouted, "Do not injure Minister Wei," and then rescued him.

The emperor stalked out of the station building, leaning on his cane, to order the soldiers to return to their lines. They stood sullenly silent. The commander of the palace guard, General Ch'ên, said, "Since Yang Kuo-chung was guilty of treason, Yang Kuei-fei is no longer worthy of being a companion of Your Majesty. Will Your Majesty please give her up and have her executed?" "Let me handle this myself," answered the emperor. Reëntering the station, he stood stooping over his cane, his head bowed, for a long while. Wei Chien-su's son, Wei O, finally interrupted him: "Your Majesty, this is a critical moment. It will not be wise to court the anger of the mob. Your Majesty had better make a decision quickly." "She is innocent," said the emperor. "Having killed her cousin Yang Kuo-chung, the officers and men would never feel at ease if she remained at Your Majesty's side," said Eunuch Kao Li-shih. "Your Majesty should know that Your Majesty will be safe only when the officers and men feel that they are safe."

The emperor then allowed Kao Li-shih to lead his pretty concubine to the Buddhist oratory in the station and to strangle her to death. Her corpse was carried to the courtyard, where Ch'ên Hsüan-li and a few other officers were called to view it. They shouted, "Long live His Majesty!" and were satisfied. The remaining members of the Yang family—Yang Kuo-chung's wife, formerly a prostitute in Shu; the younger son, Yang Hsi; the Lady of Kuo; and her son—all fled westward to the District of Ch'ên-ts'ang, where Magistrate Hsüeh Ching-hsien had them arrested and executed.

Leaving Ma-wei Station for Shu-chün on the morning of July 16, the imperial party were met by a crowd of people who demanded to know why His Majesty should run away and abandon the people to the mercy of the rebels. As the emperor went ahead, he had his son, the crown prince, return to say a few comforting words to the people. The crowd grew to be several thousands, and they wanted the crown prince to remain and be their sovereign. Two sons of the crown prince, Li Ch'u, Prince of Kuang-p'ing, and Li Tan, Prince of Chien-ning, and a eunuch who was soon to be known as Li Fu-kuo urged the prince to follow the peoples' desire. Their argument was that true filial piety demanded not companionship with the imperial father in exile but work for the recovery of the empire. It was thought that by recalling Generals Kuo Tzǔ-i and Li Kuang-pi from Ho-pei, and by marshaling the troops of the northwestern frontiers, the chances were still good for the recovery of the two capitals. When the Emperor Brilliant heard of this, he sent his son 2,000 imperial guardsmen and a number of horses, together with the women of the crown prince's palace. He wanted, as well, to abdicate the supreme authority in favor of the crown prince; who, however, refused to accept it. After making these arrangements for his son, the emperor hastened sixty-five miles westward to Fu-fêng, thence thirty-eight miles southwestward to the San-kuan Pass, which he reached on July 21. From there it was some 654 miles along the main post road to Shu-chün, where the emperor arrived on August 28.

The crown prince's party turned northward from Ma-wei. They traveled all night to Hsin-p'ing, a distance of about one hundred miles, and most of the guards and equipment were lost during the hurried journey. On July 18, he reached An-ting, sixty miles northwest of Hsin-p'ing along the southern shore of the Ching River, where he met two fleeing prefects, whom he executed. On July 20, he reached P'ing-liang, 107 miles further to the northwest. Here he stayed several days to add a few hundred more men to his troops and to requisition several tens of thousands of the horses in the imperial stud in the neighborhood. While the crown prince waited, Tu Hung-chien, who was provisional officer in charge of the duties of the governor general of Shuo-fang at Ling-wu, sent a delegation to him to urge that he come to Ling-wu. Superior Censor P'ei Mien happened also to be in P'ing-liang, and he too advised the choice of Ling-wu as the place to organize for a revival of the imperial fortunes. On August 9, the crown prince arrived in

Ling-wu, which was 167 miles north of P'ing-liang and some 417 miles northwest of Ch'ang-an. Here he was persuaded to ascend the throne on August 12 and had his father declared emperor emeritus. Thus Crown Prince Li Hêng, the third son of the Emperor Brilliant, became, at the age of exactly 44 years and 296 days, the seventh emperor of the T'ang Dynasty, known posthumously as Emperor Su-tsung.

A new reign brought about, of course, a new crop of appointments. But, for our purpose, only the names that figured rather significantly in Tu Fu's writings need be noted. Tu Hung-chien and P'ei Mien were appointed the highest ministers of state. Hsüeh Ching-hsien, because of his valiant defense of the prefecture against rebels and bandits, was made Prefect of Fu-fêng, which on August 27 was renamed Fêng-hsiang. Prefect Hsüeh's main contribution was in keeping the San-kuan Pass open, which kept communication between Shu-chün and Ling-wu possible and which, moreover, allowed economic support from the Yangtze, Huai, and Han valleys to reach the exile court.

Among the men in the service of the new emperor, Li Pi was the most extraordinary. He had been the emperor's precocious playmate when they were both boys. Later he became a hermit, mainly to allay the jealousy and suspicion of Yang Kuo-chung, who might not like the crown prince to have so brilliant and resourceful a friend. Now, in response to summons, he had come out of hermitage to be the emperor's closest advisor on all matters, private and public, civil and military. Frequently they slept in the same bedroom. Frequently they went out together, the yellow-robed emperor and the white-robed hermit, their two horses abreast. With the humorous but irrefutable argument that to be His Majesty's guest was a higher honor than to be His Majesty's servant, the hermit had stoutly refused any appointment, even the premiership. When the extreme contrast of the colors—the supreme rank and the complete absence of rank—had become a frequent subject of whispered comments, the emperor had a better argument for the hermit. Might not Li's refusal be deemed a reflection upon the ambition for advancement among officers and men? The hermit was at last obliged to don the purple robe—permissible only to officials from the twenty-fifth step up. He was then made the chief administrator of the supreme general headquarters of the generalissimo, the emperor's eldest son, the Prince of Kuang-p'ing. The hermit was prevailed upon to accept the ranking robe and the pompous official title on the emperor's promise that he would be allowed to return to private life when the war was over. As we shall see later, he saw to it that that promise was fulfilled. He was probably not one of the close friends of our poet Tu Fu, but he was one of the few men of the time whom our poet greatly admired. This is not difficult to understand, because, if we recall "Poetry Contest after Dinner at the Tso Villa" [1], Li Pi's career resembled very much that

97

of Fan Li, who sailed away forever after having helped his prince to recover his kingdom.

If Li Pi might be regarded as the most important figure in the reorganization of the available human and material resources to save the dynasty from its enemies, the second and third places of honor might be given to two generals. Kuo Tzŭ-i and Li Kuang-pi, it may be recalled, were already fighting in the east. Hearing about the fall of T'ung-kuan, they withdrew from Ho-pei through the T'u-mên Pass. By August 30, they too had arrived to strengthen the morale in Ling-wu with 50,000 additional men. The winningly coöperative Kuo Tzŭ-i was now made the Minister of Defense and, concurrently, Prefect of Ling-wu; and the surprisingly resourceful Li Kuang-pi was appointed Minister of Economics and, concurrently, Acting Governor of the Northern Capital (T'ai-yüan), and was sent with 5,000 men to block the advance of the enemy through the northern route.

The recent happenings in Ling-wu were of course still unknown to the Emperor Brilliant. While he was on his way to Shu-chün, Vice-Minister of Justice Fang Kuan had hastened to join his fleeing party at P'u-an. Disappointed by the fact that even his favorite son-in-law Chang Chi did not come to join him, the Emperor Brilliant was very pleased with Fang and immediately made him a state minister. On Fang's advice, the Brilliant Emperor issued on August 15 a proclamation naming the crown prince governor general of Shuo-fang, Ho-tung, Ho-pei, and P'ing-lu and the generalissimo of all armed forces, and naming several of his other sons as governors general of other areas. It was said that when the rebel An Lu-shan read this edict, he sighed that he would never be able to conquer the whole empire. The idea was, of course, that princes of the blood were more apt than other officials to uphold the dynasty by fighting the rebellion to the bitter end.

When the messenger from Ling-wu finally reached Shu-chün on September 10 with the news of the crown prince's taking the throne, the Emperor Brilliant was said to be very pleased. Forthwith, he declared himself emperor emeritus, and two days later dispatched a delegation headed by Wei Chien-su and Fang Kuan to convey the Register of Succession and the Imperial Seal to Ling-wu.

In Ling-wu, the new emperor was maturing plans for offensive movement. He sent Kuo Tzŭ-i to subdue the trouble-making Turkish tribes north of the Yellow River in what is our present central Sui-yüan. He dispatched a prince to the Uighurs to request help. He even wanted some Ferghanian troops to come east with the armies from An-hsi. Li Pi suggested that the emperor move to P'êng-yüan to wait for the coming of troops from the Northwest and from there proceed to Fêng-hsiang, which would make a good base of operations. On October 15, the emperor left Ling-wu. Along the way he met the officious executioner, the eunuch General Pien, who had run away from the rebels; the emperor forthwith had him executed. On October 23, the emperor reached Shun-hua, where he met Wei Chien-su and Fang Kuan, on their mission from the emperor emeritus in Shu-chün. He had never thought much of Wei, because Wei had associated rather closely with Yang Kuo-chung. Of Fang Kuan's fine reputation, he had long heard, and he was now well-impressed with Fang's knowledge and eloquence. He proceeded to place great confidence in Fang, and the other state ministers would generally let Fang take the lead in all important matters of government. On October 30, the exile court came to P'êng-yüan, and here they were to stay for several months.

After the fall of T'ung-kuan, An Lu-shan sent an army under Sun Hsiao-chê to occupy Ch'ang-an. Sun staged a reign of terror. Three days were given to a general search of the valuables of the imperial household. It was equivalent to a general pillage of the capital and the neighborhood. Much of the loot was forwarded to An in Lo-yang. The families of those who followed the fleeing court were all put to the sword; not even the infants were spared. On orders from An, the relatives of the Brilliant Emperor were not only killed but also their hearts were scooped out and offered in sacrifice to the spirit of An Ch'ing-tsung. The partisans of Yang Kuo-chung and Kao Li-shih had to suffer death by having the cranium separated from the rest of the skull by an iron claw. More than a hundred persons thus perished either to appease the anger of the rebel chief or to avenge the death of his son.

Sun rounded up the remnant officials, eunuchs, palace women, and entertainers and delivered them to Lo-yang, several hundreds at a time. An compelled many of these to enter his service, and in imitation of the Brilliant Emperor's brilliant court, he held feasting parties and gaudy shows with the musicians, dancers, the equipment, the horses, elephants, and rhinoceroses all sent from Ch'ang-an.

While the rebel chief was thus giving himself to pleasure in the Eastern Capital, the rebel officers were not attending to their duties of war in the Western Capital. The people of Ch'ang-an were hoping daily that the crown prince might come with imperial armies to recapture the capital. Whenever dust rose in the north, there would be rumors that the imperial forces had arrived. Many of the brave among the people organized bands to harass the rebels. A Turkish force of some 5,000 men that had supported An rebelled against him on August 22 and departed from Ch'ang-an toward the north with 2,000 horses. As a result of the subsequent disturbances in the Western Capital, Ts'ui Kuang-yüan, who was then serving under the rebels as Prefect of Ching-chao, was able to escape and arrived in Ling-wu with a number of other officials on August 27. The Turkish force returned to the Ordos region—where the Yellow River loops—to incite the other Turkish tribes to attack Shuo-fang. Though Kuo Tzŭ-i scored some victories over them, it was not until December 7 that Kuo was able, with the help of some Uighur troops, to defeat and pacify them completely.

Shortly before the defense of T'ung-kuan was smashed in July, our poet Tu Fu was visiting the District of Po-shui, about ten miles northwest of Fêng-hsien. He was distressed because the military activities had closed the roads in the eastern neighborhood of Ch'ang-an to civilian travel. It would seem that all through the first half of 756 he was unable to return to Ch'ang-an. After the capital's fall his problems would be where to put his family and how to reach the exile court. In the collection of his existent poems, there is none that was written at that time. From later poems we know that he finally settled his wife and children in the Ch'iang Village in the District of San-ch'uan of the Prefecture of Lo-chiao—still popularly known as Fu-chou. The distance between Po-shui and San-ch'uan was about 133 miles. But we have only a very vague idea when he and his family might have left Po-shui.

The first part of their journey is reminiscently described in "P'êng-ya" [LXXXII], written in Fêng-hsiang in the fall of 757 and addressed to a Sun Tsai of T'ung-chia Marsh. Trudging two miles or so a day through thunderstorm and mud, in hunger and fatigue, the Tu family had evidently taken a hilly side road to P'êng-ya, about twenty miles northeast of Po-shui, to avoid falling into the hands of the roving bands of rebels, whom Tu Fu likened to tigers and wolves. T'ung-chia Marsh, still unidentified, was probably a village near P'êng-ya, and Sun Tsai was the hospitable host who had fed and sheltered the Tu family for a night and had sworn our poet to a secret—possibly a cache of arms and some plans for defending the village if attacked. Two items mentioned in the poem may be taken as clues to the time of the flight of the Tu family: the moon over the hills of Po-shui and the intention of our poet to proceed to the Lu-tzŭ Pass. The Lu-tzŭ Pass was 143 miles northwest of San-ch'uan, and it is possible, as some commentators believe, that our poet had intended to reach the exile court in Ling-wu by detouring through that pass far away from areas in the grip of war. If this guess is correct, the Tu family might have departed from Po-shui shortly after hearing the news of the new emperor's court in Ling-wu, and that would be shortly after the full moon at the middle of August.

On the other hand, since the poem mentions sour plums on the roadside trees, I am inclined to think that the flight took place shortly after the middle of July. Tu Fu's intention of proceeding to the Lu-tzŭ Pass might be merely to make a long detour—in order to avoid meeting the rebels—in search of the fleeing court.

At any rate, he probably did not tarry long in San-ch'uan before setting out to join the exile court. We next find him, however, in Ch'ang-an under the rebels. Obviously, he could not have gone there voluntarily. The supposition is that he unexpectedly met a rebel band along the way, was captured, and brought to Ch'ang-an. They might have robbed him and then used him as a beast of burden to carry bundles of loot. Even if they discovered that he was a poet and an official, neither his fame nor his rank was sufficiently high to inspire respect. This would explain why he was let alone in the capital and was not delivered to An Lu-shan in Lo-yang.

"Moonlight Night" [LXIII] might indeed have been written in Ch'ang-an on the full-moon night of the midautumn festival day, September 13, 756. Our poet was of course thinking of his wife and children in San-ch'uan. "Alas! A Prince" [LXIV] describes the plight of a young member of the imperial clan, who had been hiding from the rebels for about a hundred days. The poem must have been written toward the close of October.

LXIII MOONLIGHT NIGHT

The same moon is above Fu-chou tonight; From the open window she will be watching it alone, The poor children are too little To be able to remember Ch'ang-an. Her perfumed hair will be dampened by the dew, The air may be too chilly on her delicate arms. When can we both lean by the wind-blown curtains And see the tears dry on each other's face?

LXIV ALAS! A PRINCE

A white-headed raven, I was told, from the Ch'ang-an city wall Flew at night to the west gate of the palace park to announce disaster. Then it rapped upon the roof of each big mansion; And the high dignitaries too fled from the Tatars. The strongest whips were broken, the best horses dead; The family could not be kept together in flight.

With precious jewels hidden under his clothing, A pitiable young prince weeps here by the roadside. He will not tell me his name; He says only that he is unhappy and wants to be a slave. For a hundred days he has been hiding among thorny bushes; His body is covered with scratches. Every descendant of our first emperor has a distinguished face, One can easily tell him apart from an ordinary youth.

"Just now royalty is humbled and monstrosity rampant, Do take good care of yourself, O Prince. I dare not talk long on this busy road; I can linger but a moment with you. Last night the east wind carried a bloody stench, The camels from the east almost filled the Capital. Our Shuo-fang troops, well-known for strength and skill, Were invincible in the past, but are now useless. I have just heard the Emperor has given the throne to the Crown Prince. His Majesty has won the support of chief-

tains of the Uighurs in the North. They slashed their faces to swear they will avenge our wrongs. Say not a word, for there are spies. Do be careful, O my poor prince! There is hope, there is always hope."

In P'êng-yüan, because of the misrepresentations of a newly-arrived official, the emperor's attitude toward Minister Fang Kuan suddenly cooled. Fang had a wide circle of friends in various parts of the empire; was Fang not trying to build up a political clique? Fang had advised the emperor emeritus to appoint various princes as governors general; was Fang not endeavoring to ingratiate himself with every possible heir to the throne? Thus warned, the emperor became very suspicious of Fang. To make the situation worse, Fang volunteered to lead an army to recover the capital and employed as strategists a number of scholars inexperienced in military affairs. When the battle took place on November 17, at Ch'ên-t'ao, a short distance west of Ch'ang-an, Fang's antiquarian strategy of using oxcarts proved disastrous. The casualties were over 40,000. Two days later Fang fought again, the rebels were again victorious, and the Emperor had good reason to be angry with Fang. Were it not for Li Pi, who rushed to his rescue, Fang would certainly have been dismissed, if not punished. Our poet's two poems, "The Tragedy of Ch'ên-t'ao" [LXV] and "The Tragedy of Ch'ing-fan" [LXVI] were written in Ch'ang-an when he heard of the defeat of the imperial army. He had, of course, no knowledge of what was happening in P'êng-yüan. "Snow" [LXVII] must have been written in the same winter, not long after these battles. In it, Tu Fu bemoaned the lack of news from various prefectures.

LXV   THE TRAGEDY OF CH'ÊN-T'AO

The blood of youths from the good homes of ten prefectures is now Mixed in the Ch'ên-t'ao marshes with the mud of early winter. The sky is clear, and there is no sound of battle on the wide fields, For the forty thousand volunteers perished on the same day. The Tatars are now returning and are cleaning their arrows. They are singing their barbarous songs and drinking in the market places. The people of the Capital still turn their weeping faces to the north; Day and night they hope the Imperial armies will again come.

LXVI   THE TRAGEDY OF CH'ING-FAN

Our army camped by the east gate at Ch'ing-fan: Excellent plan to pass the winter near the T'ai-po Hills. But the yellow-turbaned Tatars pressed daily westward, With a few mounted archers they challenged our men to battle. Now snow covers the hills, ice the river, and desolation the fields. Black is the smoke left over the camps, and white are the bones of our dead. Oh! had it been possible to send a message to our officers To tell them to keep patience and wait until next year!

LXVII SNOW

The countless newly dead may lament the battles; As an old man, I shall alone mumble my sadness. The whirling wind forces the snow into a mad dance, The confused clouds press down in the dusk. Of what use is the drinking ladle when there is not a drop in the winepot? The ashes look red only because I imagine the stove is burning. Not a word from the several prefectures! Preposterous! Preposterous!

When some news did come, it was bad. By the end of 756, the rebel Shih Ssŭ-ming had undone most of the work of the loyalists in the East. The entire Ho-pei Department fell once more to the rebels. Even the great patriot Yen Chên-ch'ing, the man most responsible for the loyal gains in the area, had to flee. Even the prefectures of Lu-chün, Tung-p'ing, and Tsi-yin—all in the Department of Ho-nan—were lost. The two poems "News about My Brothers" [LXVIII-LXIX] express our poet's solicitude for Tu Ying and his other brothers, who were probably refugees in the District of P'ing-yin of the Prefecture of Tung-p'ing.

LXVIII NEWS ABOUT MY BROTHERS (TWO POEMS)

I

Recent news from far-off P'ing-yin Says my poor brothers are safe. They fled a long distance To find food in a small village. But there the fires of battle have started anew; My weeping means new tears on the old traces, Since I am growing old, I do not know How many of you I shall ever see again.

LXIX   2

You are weak and have no means of coming to me; I am in trouble and can hardly hope to go to you. O singing birds, these are no true good tidings! And with poetry, I can only confess my failure as a brother. What right have I to live and to see people? These worries alone might wear out months and years! Once there were thirty of us in the two capitals! All alive now? The chances are slender.

After his successes in Ho-pei and Ho-nan, Shih Ssŭ-ming moved his victorious army westward to attack T'ai-yüan. Another rebel general, Kao Hsiu-yen, marched from Ta-t'ung to join him in beseiging the Northern Capital. The intention was clear. After the reduction of that strong city, defended by Li Kuang-pi, they would march farther west to the Ordos region, then turn southward to enter the Kuan-nei Department by the Lu-tzŭ Pass. Not only would P'êng-yüan and the exile court be threatened in the rear, but also Lo-chiao Prefecture and our poet's family would be exposed. "Block the Lu-tzŭ Pass!" [LXX] shows that Tu Fu was seriously alarmed. Being in Ch'ang-an under the rebels, he did not know that Li Kuang-pi had defended T'ai-yüan well, and that Kuo Tzŭ-i not only had the Ordos region well in hand, but also had established his headquarters in Lo-chiao itself.

LXX BLOCK THE LU-TZŬ PASS!

How far are the Five Cities? They are just beyond the river. Our frontier troops are all on the expedition eastward; These cities are deserted and overgrown with brambles. Shih Ssŭ-ming has left behind Huai and Wei, And will march with Kao Hsiu-yen continuously westward.

They will approach Kuan-nei through the desert, They will not come through the passes between the two capitals. Yen-chou is the north gate of territories west of the Yellow River; The strategic pass can be relied upon. How can we get ten thousand men To march quickly to block the Lu-tzŭ Pass.

Let us remember that in the Fu-fêng Prefecture the Honorable Mr. Hsüeh, By flank attack, has suppressed the rebels in the hills. Recently I heard that the various unruly bands Retreated a hundred miles on his account. To use the Lu-tzŭ Pass to repulse the two rebels Has a significance similar to this. Who can go quickly to tell this to His Majesty? The Tatars march with a ghastly speed.

"Sent on New Year's Day to My Younger Sister, Mrs. Wei" [LXXI] was written on January 25, 757, the New Year's Day of the solar-lunar calendar. Tu Fu's half-sister, the widowed Mrs. Wei, was then in the Prefecture of Chung-li of the Huai-nan Department, over seven hundred miles southeast of Ch'ang-an. Among the poems Tu Fu wrote in the spring of 757 are "Look at Spring!" [LXXII], "Remembering My Little Son" [LXXIII], and "A Thought" [LXXIV]—all poems of homesickness. I am inclined to think that when our poet left his family in San-ch'uan, Mrs. Tu Fu was expecting a baby. Were both the mother and the baby doing well? Was it a boy or a girl? That was probably why he felt a letter from the family would be worth a fabulous fortune. He had lost an infant son in 755. The remaining son, Pony Boy, would be more than precious. Judging by what was said of his precocity, Pony Boy might be already in his fifth year.

LXXI SENT ON NEW YEAR'S DAY TO MY YOUNGER SISTER, MRS. WEI

I heard only recently that my younger sister of the Wei family Had gone to Chung-li, which was still safe from the rebels. There you follow your father-in-law, prefect of that place, Here I am in the Capital lamenting that the Court is gone. Here in Ching-chao I note the northern stars turn to indicate spring; There in the Huai valley you see trees blossom in the southern breeze. It is no longer possible to see the usual congratu-latory messengers arriving; That has brought tears to my face.

LXXII LOOK AT SPRING!

The nation is shattered. Only the landscape remains. Spring in the city? Yes, unpruned trees and overgrown weeds. Flowers are watered with tears of discouragement, Birds sing heartbreaking songs of separation.

Beacon fires of battle have been burning for months. A letter from home would be worth a fabulous fortune! As I scratch my scanty white hair, more falls; It is almost too thin to hold a hairpin.

LXXIII REMEMBERING MY LITTLE SON

It is spring, Pony Boy, and we are still apart. You may be singing now with the orioles in the warm sunshine. I am startled by how fast one season displaces another; Who now acclaims your growing cleverness?

My thoughts go to the running gully by the lonely mountain path, To the rough wooden gate in the village of ancient trees. I think I see him; I try not to doze While leaning on the balustrade and warming my back in the sun.

LXXIV A THOUGHT

"Pony Boy is good boy"—One of the first things he learned to say year before last. He soon learned to ask and repeat the guests' names, And could even recite some of my lines. This troubled world has been too hard on his tender years, In a poor home, everything depends on a good mother.

Vanished is the hope of living in retirement with my family. Even receiving a letter from home is now uncertain. The universe is filled with the banners of armies, Everywhere one is saddened by the bugles of war. If I can ever return to be with them, all alive, I'll be grateful, no matter how long it may take.

From "Lamentation by the River" [LXXV], we may gather that Tu Fu had come into the walled city of Ch'ang-an from Shao-ling in the south-eastern suburb. That he was able to move about the city, making an overnight visit to "Abbot Tsan's Cell in the Ta-yün Monastery" [LXXVI], which was near the West Market in the city, shows that he was not under the surveillance of the rebels.

Perhaps the surveillance was relaxed only after the gruesome happen-ings in the Eastern Capital. The rebel emperor, An Lu-shan, misbehaved himself so unreasonably that he was implacably hated by his son, An Ch'ing-hsü; his advisor, Yen Chuang; and his attendant eunuch, Li the

Pig—all of whom conspired to murder him. Li the Pig climbed to An Lu-shan's bed at night and with a sword slashed his enormous belly backward and forward until—though the doomed rebel continued to shake and yell—his intestines flowed to the floor. The conspirators then wrapped his corpse in a rug and buried it in the palace. This happened a day or two before January 30, 757. Though An Ch'ing-hsü succeeded to the sham throne, the morale of the counterfeit court must have been badly affected. Tu Fu alluded to these events in "A Happy Meeting with Professor Chêng at the Imperial Son-in-law Chêng's Tower . . ." [LXXVII], in which he says that the death of the wretched traitor (Tung Cho) had enabled the loyal servant (Su Wu) to return. Tung Cho, who usurped imperial powers, was murdered A.D. 192 by an adopted son, and a lighted wick was placed in his navel to burn the fat in his big belly— a clever and apt allusion to the rebel An. Su Wu returned to the Han court in 81 B.C. after being detained by the northern barbarians for nineteen years, during which period he continued to show that he was an officer of Han. An Lu-shan had appointed Professor Chêng as Chief of the Bureau of Navigation and Irrigation (twentieth step); Chêng pretended to be crazed and begged to act as a market manager (second step). He even despatched a secret memorial to the new emperor in Ling-wu. By comparing Chêng's presence in Ch'ang-an to Su Wu's returning to the Han court, Tu Fu was saying that Chêng was already halfway from Lo-yang to Emperor Su-tsung's exile court.

LXXV LAMENTATION BY THE RIVER

I am an old rustic from Shao-ling who cries hard but not loud, For I want to attract no attention as I stroll by the Meandering River in the spring sun. The thousand gates of the palaces on the riverside are all locked. For whom then shall these slender willows and tender rushes put on their green?

When the rainbow banners used to descend upon the South Park, The whole park burst into color. The first lady from the Chao-yang Palace Accompanied His Majesty in his carriage. Before it rode lady courtiers, each with bow and arrows, On white horses champing restlessly at golden bits. A lady bent to face the sky and dispatched an arrow to the clouds—The one shot dropped a pair of birds in flight.

Those shining eyes and sparkling teeth, where are they now? Even the wandering ghost is stained with blood and can never come back. The clear Wei flows far to the east, the road through the Sword Cliffs runs deep into the west. One is gone, the other remains, and they can no longer communicate. Any person with a heart will shed tears enough to wet his shirt; But you, grass and flowers by the river, are you always heartless? At dusk, the Tatar cavalry are filling the city with dust, I want to hasten south of the city, but I turn to gaze expectantly to the north.

LXXVI ABBOT TSAN'S CELL IN THE TA-YÜN MONASTERY

A lamp flickers with my sleeplessness, The delicate scent of burning incense clears my senses. The lofty hall is especially awesome in the depth of night; The tinkling of the eave-bells tells me there is wind.

Darkness in the temple yard has shut off all spring colors; But the fragrance of unseen blossoms floats in the quiet enclosure. The Jade String stars are sinking; only a few are left above the roof, Where the iron phoenix driven by wind seems ready to fly.

Soon the chant of Buddhist litanies will rise in the cloisters, I had better stay in bed to hear out the last bells, For on the bright morrow I shall be tramping the plowed fields, And I dread the thought of flying dust and brown sands.

LXXVII A HAPPY MEETING WITH PROFESSOR CHÊNG AT THE IMPERIAL SON-IN-LAW CHÊNG'S TOWER; WE DRINK TOGETHER

Dare we say that we are both alive in this war? Extraordinary it is that we can now drink together. The wretched rebel has met his retribution like Tung Cho; The loyal servant of the Court is returning like Su Wu.

Your distress on account of the rebels has whitened your hair; Your anxiety for the Court has burned your heart almost to ashes. Since we parted, both of us have nearly met death, And now suddenly we show ourselves on this tower. Again we shall hear the music from the instruments of the Imperial son-in-law, Once more we find ourselves in the residence of your cousin. They are keeping us to dance here in the spring night, Though we cannot hold back our tears, it would be safer to tarry a while.

We need not doubt that both Chêng Ch'ien and Tu Fu wanted to join the exile court of Emperor Su-tsung. We do not know, however, why Chêng did not slip away from Ch'ang-an as Tu Fu finally managed to do. Perhaps it was because of illness, or because, as a prominent and renowned man, he would have greater difficulty in getting away unrecognized. The failure, at any rate, was to get him into trouble later. It may be interesting to observe here how the rebellion and war affected in varying ways the careers of Tu Fu and his intimate friends, Chêng Ch'ien, Su Yü, Li Po, and Kao Shih, all men of extraordinary literary attainments. Chêng had the stigma of a treasonable appointment, had failed to reach the new emperor before the capital was recovered, and as a punishment, had to end his life in exile. Su, however, on the pretense of illness, absolutely refused to accept any title conferred by An Lu-shan. Though he did not leave Lo-yang until after its recapture by the imperial armies, he was promoted as a reward for his loyalty.

Kao Shih's success and Li Po's misfortune had to do with a short-lived side revolt. As a result of the Brilliant Emperor's appointment of his several sons to various governor generalships, his sixteenth son, Li Lin, the Prince of Yung, became the powerful governor general of four departmental areas combined and established his general headquarters at Chiang-ling. Influenced by mischievous advisors, he decided to carve out an empire for himself. On January 19, 757, he led his forces down the Yangtze, intending to conquer the Southeast. On the way, he summoned Li Po, who was pressed into his service. Li's friend Kao Shih—who had assisted Ko-shu Han at T'ung-kuan, had rushed to follow the fleeing Brilliant Emperor into Shu, had later come to the exile court at P'êng-yüan, and had been known to have warned the Brilliant Emperor against the unreliable prince—was made the governor general of Huai-nan and was directed to assist other appointees in blocking the rebellious prince. Thus, two poets and friends were in opposite camps. By March 14, 757, the forces of the disobedient prince had collapsed in the neighborhood of Chin-ling, and he had been killed. Li Po landed in prison in Hsün-yang, hoping in vain that his friend Kao might help to get him out. Though Li was later released by Superior Censor Sung Jo-ssŭ, who interceded for him with the court, he was exiled to Yeh-lang in the autumn of 758 and was not pardoned and permitted to return until the spring of 759.

When Tu Fu succeeded in slipping out of the western suburb of Ch'ang-an, the exile court was no longer in P'êng-yüan but in Fêng-hsiang, where the emperor had arrived on March 4, 757. Fêng-hsiang was 103 miles west of Ch'ang-an; during the first half of his journey there our fleeing poet was still in the territory of the rebels. "Let Me Tell What Is Troubling Me" [LXXVIII], one of the most touching and masterly of Tu Fu's poems, was written in Fêng-hsiang in the later part of the summer and tells us that he had escaped earlier in the season and that upon arrival at the exile court he was made a Reminder. I am inclined to think that he made his journey, on foot, sometime between May 5 and May 28, dates of two important battles. Kuo Tzŭ-i as the vice-generalissimo of the imperial armies was on his way to Fêng-hsiang, gave the rebel cavalries a severe beating about forty miles northeast of Ch'ang-an on May 5, but was in turn badly defeated northwest of Ch'ang-an on May 28. It was perhaps during the interval, while the rebel garrisons in the western suburb were too busy watching the approaches from the north, that our poet was able to escape to the west. If my hypothesis about the time is correct, Tu Fu was probably appointed a reminder before June 1. On June 1, the emperor relieved Fang Kuan of his seat in the State Council, the charge being that Fang had frequently listened to the music of a lute player who was said to have taken bribes. Reminder Tu Fu, taking seriously the title and duties of his office, proceeded to remind His Majesty that, according to the best tradition, a state minister should not be dismissed on such a petty offense; he did not know, and perhaps did not even care, that His Majesty's dislike of the state minister went much deeper. How dare this new reminder interfere with the imperial prerogative of employment? Is it not an evidence of a clique? His Majesty ordered Tu Fu to be placed under arrest and to be tried by Supreme Censor Wei Chih, Minister Yen Chên-ch'ing of the Ministry of Justice, and Chief Justice Ts'ui Kuang-yüan of the Supreme Court.

Tu Fu would have to pay the extreme penalty of death if his offense was judged sufficiently serious. Fortunately, State Minister Chang Hao advised the emperor to be magnanimous, and Supreme Censor Wei reported that though Tu Fu was too free with his words, his intention was only to do his duty. On June 21 the emperor authorized Minister Chang to announce his pardon, and our poet was set free. In a memorial expressing gratitude, he persisted in saying a few good words for Fang Kuan, and congratulated the empire for having an emperor magnanimous enough to tolerate a recklessly frank servant like himself! In this memorial, we note that his rank corresponded to the ninth step up the ladder of officialdom, though the office of reminder was graded on the sixth.

We need not imagine that Tu Fu's precarious experience with saying too much could teach him silence. On July 2 he memorialized the throne to recommend the appointment of Ts'ên Shên as a Mender at court—another advisory office. There were probably many more memorials that have not been preserved. Among the poems he wrote during his short residence in Fêng-hsiang are a number addressed to friends upon their departure to various appointments—for the most part urging them to fulfill their duty to the government and the people. But in "The Moon" [LXXIX] our poet was obviously talking about something entirely different. In legendary and poetic literature certain shadows in the moon were thought to represent a toad, which was originally a fugitive woman, and a rabbit, which with mortar and pestle was pounding medicinal herbs. But Tu speaks of the toad and the rabbit with cryptic disapproval. Among the various interpretations, the most plausible one seems to be that by the toad obscuring the disc of light Tu Fu meant the emperor's concubine, who later became Empress Chang, and that by the rabbit concocting bitter medicine he meant Eunuch Li Fu-kuo. The lady and the eunuch conspired together to fill the emperor's ears with calumnies against some of the best persons at court. In a flash of anger, the emperor ordered his third son, a brilliant and devoted prince, to commit suicide. Even the emperor's eldest son, the Prince of Kuang-p'ing, and the emperor's closest friend, Li Pi, became apprehensive and had to be circumspect.

"Presented to Assistant Chancellor Yen Wu" [LXXX] was probably Tu Fu's first poem to young Yen, who, as we shall see, had a good deal to do with a later period of our poet's life. Reminders and Chancellors both belonged to the Chancellory Division. An assistant chancellor was ranked on the twentieth step of the official ladder and was, therefore, quite superior to a reminder. The duties of an assistant chancellor included indicting unjust officers. Hence Yen was likened to an eagle over foxes and rabbits.

"A Letter from Home" [LXXXI] must have been written in the first week of September. Tu Fu had been separated from his family for a year. We must not blame Mrs. Tu Fu for failing to write. She might have sent several letters by friendly travelers, but in time of war only one actually got through. Baby Bear, later known as Tu Tsung-wu, had probably been born late in the autumn of the previous year. After all Tu Fu's worry and the worst of fears, how welcome this letter must have been! And how intense the desire to go to San-ch'uan and be reunited with his family! The emperor, not being too eager for our poet's reminders, was indeed ready to grant him leave of absence.

Continuous rain delayed Tu Fu's departure for about a fortnight. Then it started to clear. Assistant Chancellor Yen Wu of the Chancellory Division, and Assistant Secretary Chia Chih of the Secretarial Division, leading the menders and reminders of the two divisions, gave him a farewell party. The hosts, of course, all wrote poems, and our poet as the guest of honor wrote one too [LXXXIII]. We should mention in passing that Assistant Secretary Chia Chih was one of the foremost literary celebrities of the time and in his official capacity drafted for the emperor most of the documents of appointment. The style was exemplary.

Our poet left Fêng-hsiang on September 18. The northeastward journey to San-ch'uan covered a distance of about 215 miles. A court officer was ordinarily entitled to the use of government horses; but "Going Home on Foot" [LXXXIV] shows that Tu Fu had to walk at least the first seventy-three miles to Hsin-p'ing, still popularly known as Pin-chou, where, we may presume, General Li gave him a horse. When he wrote "Jade Flower Palace" [LXXXV], he had traveled more than two-thirds of the way home. The palace was first built in 646 for Emperor T'ai-tsung, and Tu Fu, with his familiarity with history, could not have been ignorant of the origin of the ruined structure. I am inclined to agree with a twelfth-century commentator that our poet purposely refrained from naming the great imperial ancestor in order to emphasize the theme vanity of vanities, even in the best of royal splendor.

The three poems entitled "Ch'iang Village" [LXXXVI–LXXXVIII] and the poem "The Trip North" [LXXXIX] were written shortly after Tu Fu reached home. We do not know the date of his arrival in Ch'iang Village, but it could hardly be much later than the end of September or the beginning of October. In the latter poem, Tu Fu mentioned the coming of the Uighur army from the Northwest to help the imperial cause. He heard that the force consisted of 5,000 men and 10,000 horses. According to the records, the kaghan of the Uighurs sent his son Yeh-hu (Yabgu) and a general by the name of Ti-tê at the head of more than 4,000 men. They arrived in Fêng-hsiang sometime before October 29 and were liberally feasted by the emperor, who even promised Yeh-hu that in the recovery of the capital the Uighurs might loot and carry away whatever they wanted. On October 29, the Prince of Kuang-p'ing, assisted by Li Pi, led toward the east the Uighurs and other forces from the Western Regions, actually a total of 150,000 men, but said to be 200,000. About half-way to Ch'ang-an they were joined by forces under Vice-Generalissimo Kuo Tzŭ-i. They were ready to assault the Western Capital under the rebels.

LXXVIII   LET ME TELL WHAT IS TROUBLING ME

Since the T'ung-kuan defense collapsed last year, I have been long parted from my wife and children. When the bushes and weeds were full grown this summer, I hid away and escaped westward.

In hempen sandals I appeared before His Majesty; My elbows showed through tattered sleeves. The Court was touched by my returning alive from death; My relatives and friends were shocked at my old and haggard appearance. In tears I accepted the appointment as a Reminder, My sovereign's grace has been too generous upon a lonely refugee. Though it is possible to return to my humble hut for a visit, I cannot bring myself to ask for the additional favor of a leave.

I did write letters to San-ch'uan To find out if my family was still there. Then I heard that disaster struck that community also—Not even chickens or dogs were spared in the massacre. In the leaky thatched hut deep in the hills, Does anyone wait at the door or the window for my return? Among the stumps of the green pines the ground is cold, Perhaps the bones are not yet rotted. How many after all could live through the catastrophe? Dare I hope that the whole household are alive and together? The possibility is like a narrow spot between dangerous precipices and ferocious tigers; My heart sinks whenever I turn my thoughts to it.

Since I sent my last letter, Ten months have passed. Now I rather dread getting news; I wonder if my one small heart can stand the shock.

III

The fortunes of the Dynasty are rising again, I might be allowed to end my days in wine. But what happy association is there, even in drinking, If I were to be just a miserably lonely old man?

LXXIX THE MOON

The heaven above is approaching autumn; The moon begins to shine with extra brightness upon men. I see the disc mirrored in the river, why is the toad not drowned? I see the shadow of the rabbit, pounding bitter herbs, and I suspect he might live forever. Such a picture will only bring more despair to loyal hearts; It will whiten more hairs on weary heads. O Moon, you know war covers the land, Shine not on the camps west of Ch'ang-an; our men are unhappy enough.

LXXX PRESENTED TO ASSISTANT CHANCELLOR YEN WU

Among the high officers who have accompanied His Majesty in Fêng-hsiang, You alone are still of youthful years. The majestic dragon has cloud and rain to support him in his movements; The golden eagle is cruising in autumn's blue skies. Let the foxes and rabbits be afraid. In your residence, you permit me not to stand on ceremony, In the Chancellory Division, our offices are almost communicating. All of the lines of your poems are good, Please let me pass them around.

LXXXI A LETTER FROM HOME

I took the chance of entrusting my message to a passing traveler, Now the reply has come, enclosed in another man's letter from home. Today I really have reliable news: In that unfamiliar territory, they are still living in the same hut. Fortunately, Baby Bear arrived safely, And Pony Boy loves him best of all. A man growing old is apt to take homesickness too hard; These bad times have prevented our frequent reunions; With whitish hairs, I run hither and thither at Court, With only a humble ranking, I wait on the Imperial chariot. Ch'ang-an in the east is still full of rebel demons. Fêng-hsiang in the west is experiencing the beginning of autumn. The wild geese again are passing in the cool wind; With so much autumn rain, fish can be bred almost everywhere. When I think of farming in those lonely hills, I almost want to say, "Let me end my days as a farmer."

LXXXII P'ÊNG-YA

I remember when we started to flee the rebels, We went northward through danger and hardship. In the depth of night, on the road to P'êng-ya, We left Po-shui with the moon shining on the hills.

The whole family traveled long on foot; We felt ashamed whenever we saw someone on the road. Here and there, birds sang in the ravines; We

*met not a single person coming from the opposite direction. The silly
little daughter tried to bite me when she felt hungry; I feared her crying
might attract the attention of tigers and wolves; I held her mouth tight
to my bosom; She wiggled free and wailed the more. My little boy pretended to be smart, Purposely wanting to eat the sour plums on the
roadside tree.*

*Half of the ten days, we encountered thunderstorms; Hand in hand,
we struggled through the mud. We had not only failed to provide ourselves with protection against rain, We also found the road too slippery
and our clothing too thin. Sometimes, after considerable hardship, We
were able to cover only two miles a day. Wild berries were our food,
And low branches our temporary shelter. In the mornings we waded
through water in the rocky gullies; Toward evening we searched the
horizon for smoke that might indicate a lodging.*

*At last, we made a short stop at the T'ung-chia Marsh In preparation
for our journey out of the Lu-tzŭ Pass. Among my friends was Mr. Sun
Tsai, Whose lofty ideals of hospitality reached above the clouds. It was
pitch dark when we arrived. Lamps were lit, and one gate after another
was opened to admit us. The servants brought warm water to bathe
my weary feet; They hung paper banners to recall my shocked, still
wandering soul.*

*His wife and children came out to meet us; Their tears flowed when they
saw our condition. My children were so tired that they had fallen asleep;
They were awakened and given platters of food. "You and I shall swear,"
said Mr. Sun, "That we two shall be brothers eternally." And the hall
where we sat was prepared for us; And we were told to feel completely at
home. In these dangerous times, who has been so ready To confide in
me frankly his innermost plans?*

*A whole year has passed since we separated; The Tatar hordes are still
rampant. How I wish that I might have wings To fly at once to your
presence!*

LXXXIII   AT THE FAREWELL PARTY I LEFT THIS POEM FOR ASSISTANT
           SECRETARY CHIA SHIH, ASSISTANT CHANCELLOR YEN WU, AND
           THE REMINDERS AND THE MENDERS OF THE SECRETARIAL AND
           THE CHANCELLORY DIVISIONS. (WE WERE TO FOLLOW THE
           RHYME WÊN.)

*I have to leave temporarily for my farm and garden, Though I am loath
to depart from my colleagues in time of war. Before I start on the long
journey, I leave this poem to say good-by. There is indeed much sadness;
let us lighten it with wine. This autumn we have often been troubled*

with rain; Today for the first time the weather is clear. On the mountainous road I shall frequently hear martial bugles: How can I bear such tunes everywhere?

LXXXIV GOING HOME ON FOOT: PRESENTED TO HIS EXCELLENCY GENERAL LI AS I PASSED PIN-CHOU ON THE ROAD FROM FÊNG-HSIANG TO FU-CHOU

You meet these dangerous times with youthful vigor, And your statesmanship is solidly grounded in your heroic character. The fortunes of our country have reached such a crisis, Who else but you can surely suppress the rebellion with might?

In Fêng-hsiang most of the officials are grateful to have food—They hardly dare hope for fine clothing or horses. Among the poorest of green-robed courtiers Is a white-haired reminder who is traveling homeward on foot.

Friendship among men has never suffered because of difference in age. Confidence and trust need not be based on the identity of occupations. In the distant hills, my wife and children raise their cries to heaven; Please lend me one of the flying steeds in Your Excellency's stable.

LXXXV JADE FLOWER PALACE

On the bank of the winding gully where the wind of the pines is echoed long, I find gray rats scurrying among heaps of broken tiles. There is no sign to tell which prince's palace it was That now stands in ruins under the sharp precipice. In the damp, dark rooms, blue ghost fires flicker. Outside, by the abandoned road, a melancholy stream pours downhill.

From the millions of leaves real music rises; And the colors of autumn are just turning dreary. Even beautiful women are now brown dirt under those mounds—Withal, much of their beauty was but powder and rouge. Of the entourage of the princely chariot then, The only reminder now is that sculptured stone horse. When unhappiness surges within me, I sit on a grassy spot, I sing, I sob, I wipe my tears with my hands. On the never-ending road of restless humanity, What matters who has how long to live?

LXXXVI CH'IANG VILLAGE (THREE POEMS)

I

From west of the mountainous purple clouds, The sun stretches a leg down to the flat ground. Above the rustic wooden gate, the magpies shout A welcome to the traveler who has returned from afar. My family are surprised to find me still alive; When the shock is over, they busy themselves wiping their tears. The storms of this troubled world have blown many a family apart; That I have returned alive is just a matter of lucky chance. Many neighbors are climbing on top of the walls; Even they cannot suppress their sighs and sobs. When the night deepens, a candle is lit; We look at one another and wonder whether we are not in a dream.

LXXXVII   2

I am living a stolen life in the evening of age; Even homecoming means but little peace and joy. The dear boy keeps close to my knees; He fears that I might again go away. I remember last year we liked to enjoy the breeze; He and I would circle the trees by the pond. Just now the north wind is howling the approach of winter; As I think over our needs, I have at least a hundred worries. Thank God, the harvest has been good; And I can almost see the drippings from the wine press. At least there will be enough to drink, To assuage the memories of frustration.

LXXXVIII   3

The cocks and hens are crowing and clucking in confusion; They are fighting as the guests arrive. After I have driven the fowls up the trees, I hear the knocking on the wooden gate. Several of our elderly villagers Have come to inquire about my health after the long journey. Each brings a present with him, And into our jars we pour their wine, both weak and strong. "Please forgive us for the poor flavor of the brew," they say. "We have no one to raise the grain for a better kind. Since the war has not ceased, All our boys have gone to the eastern front."

Let me sing for you, my elderly friends; I am unworthy of your sympathy, for the times have been harder on you. After singing, I lift my face to heaven and utter a deep sigh; Tears stream from the eyes of everyone present.

LXXXIX   THE TRIP NORTH

In the autumn of the second year of His Majesty's reign, On the propitious first day of the intercalary eighth month, I, Tu Fu, am about to proceed on my journey north And am at a loss how important I should consider my family. These are the times of crisis, None has the right of leisure either at Court or away. I am conscience-stricken at my reception of His Majesty's favors In the decree permitting return to my distant hut. Though I have gone to register my departure at the palace gate, I linger long and apprehensively before leaving it. I have indeed fallen short of the standard of a good reminder, I fear there might still be something of which His Majesty should be reminded. His Majesty truly represents the renaissance of our Dynasty. He rules and plans with dili-

gence and thoroughness. The rebellion of the eastern Tatars has not come to an end; This is what His Majesty's humble servant, Tu Fu, is particularly distressed about. With tears and with nostalgia for the Court in exile, I take the road, still unable to collect my wits. It seems the whole universe is suffering fearsome wounds, When shall we come to the end of our anxiety and disquiet?

Slowly I drag myself across the land; Smoke from cooking fires is rare, and the countryside desolate. Most of those whom I meet are wounded; They groan and they bleed. I turn toward the Fêng-hsiang District, And can still see the banners fluttering in the fading light. Then I begin to climb into the folds of chilly hills, Here and there passing a cavalry camping ground. The plain of Pin-chou sinks deep in the landscape Cleft by the Ching River's torrential flow. The Fierce Tiger now rises ahead: Its roar must have caused the gray cliffs to crack. The wild chrysanthemums of this autumn are beginning to droop. The road over the rocks bears deep tracks of ancient carts. When I rise among the thin clouds, my spirit too is elevated—Here is the place for any quiet pursuit for its own delights. I find the wild berries to be small; They grow among acorns and chestnuts. Some are as red as crystals of cinnabar, Others are as black as lacquer. Heaven has given them rain and dew; Sour or sweet, they are fruits. My thoughts are carried to the scenes of hermitage close to nature and far from the turmoil of men; The more must I regret that the course of my life has been a mistake.

On top of a slope I gaze at the highlands of Fu-chou, At mountain peaks and deep valleys winding in and out. I hurry on to the bank of the river, My servant is still at the edge of the woods. Strange owls hoot among the brown leaves of mulberry trees, Field mice peep from scattered holes. At midnight we pass a battlefield Where the cold moon shines on the white bones. I wonder why an army of a million men at T'ung-kuan Should suddenly be scattered in the past, Why half the inhabitants this side of the Yellow River Should perish as a result.

Even I had the experience of falling into the Tatar dust; And now I return with my hair completely white. More than one year it took me to reach the thatched hut again—To find my wife in clothes with a hundred patches. Her cries when she saw me wailed like a sharp wind through the pines; Her subdued sobs were like a gurgling brook. The boy that has been the jewel of my life, Wears a face paler than snow. He turned his back to me and wept; I saw that his feet were dirty and without shoes or socks.

Before my couch my two little daughters stand In patched robes that barely cover their knees. The waves of the ocean do not match On the

116

embroidered pieces cut from an old dress. The sea monster and the purple phoenix Are inverted on the short skirts. Who can blame an old man for feeling ill at heart? Nausea confines me for several days in bed. Of course, I have some cloth in my bag That may be used to spare my family from the cold. There are also some cosmetics in little packages; And the bedding may be taken out of the luggage. Once more my poor wife's face is glowing; The silly girls are trying to dress their own hair. Imitating their mother, they will play with anything; They smear their hands in the jars of the morning make-up. In a minute, powder and rouge color their cheeks, And the eyebrows are painted askew and too broad. To return alive and be with these children Enables me to forget the hunger and the thirst. They shower me with questions, they pull my beard: Who has the heart to make them stop? When I recall my weary days among the rebels, All this noisy pestering I joyfully accept.

With the new reunion, I may well enjoy some rest; Sooner or later we shall have to discuss the difficulties of livelihood. Even His Majesty is covered with the dust of exile, How long before we hear the war is ended? I lift my head to gaze at heaven and search for a changing sign above; I feel the demonic atmosphere will soon break. A cold wind has come from the northwest, Blowing steadily behind the many Uighur troops. To our just cause their king has decided to give help, And their custom is to rush and smash. They said they would send five thousand men, And would drive before them ten thousand horses. "Of the Uighurs, a small number is to be preferred": That was the brave decision appreciated by all. They can be used like soaring falcons, And the smashing of the enemy will be faster than the flight of an arrow. His Majesty is inclined to rely on them; Much of the discussion has fallen short.

Lo-yang is within reach, We may leave Ch'ang-an's recapture to the last. Let the Imperial armies march deep into the East, Let them wait until they are all in position, then attack. The first blow will open the Tsi valley; Then we shall recover the Northeast. The august heaven is moving toward winter, The right spirit of which is to kill and punish. This year the worst one of the Tatars has perished; We shall enter the month in which the rest of the rebels will be brought to justice. These Tatars will not be able to put off their fate, For the continuity of our Dynasty is not meant to be cut. I remember when the disaster began, Our deeds differed from those of the historic past. Our wicked minister was actually executed; His vile associates were soon scattered. I know indeed that Hsia and Yin dynasties did come to an end; But their emperors did not have the culpable women put to death. No, we shall compare our Dynasty only with those that stumbled and rose again,

*And His Majesty with the two mighty emperors who revived the Chou
and the Han courts. We are very proud of you, O General Ch'ên
Hsüan-li; You used the axe in the spirit of loyalty and fearlessness.
Without you, the whole nation might have to share in the guilt, Because
of you, the Dynasty still stands erect.*

*Oh, quiet now is the Ta-t'ung Hall where Imperial audiences were
held, Deserted now is the entrance to the Po-shou Gate where courtiers
used to meet. The people of Ch'ang-an are longing to welcome the return of Their Majesties To begin a new and better era of the Golden
Court. Indeed, the spirits of the Imperial Ancestors are in the impressive
mausoleums; Seasonal ceremonies of cleanings and offerings shall never
again be omitted. Our great Emperor T'ai-tsung's Empire Has surely a
foundation both broad and solid.*

"Now, at last, countless armies will sweep away the rebellion like wind upon dried leaves."

CHAPTER SEVEN

A decisive battle was fought on November 13, 757, about five miles northwest of the city of Ch'ang-an. The rebel army was routed. The imperial forces were said to have decapitated 60,000 of the enemy's 100,000 men; the rebels fled the capital during the night. When the Uighurs were about to loot the capital city, the Prince of Kuang-p'ing knelt before Yeh-hu to beg for a postponement until after the recapture of the Eastern Capital. Deeply touched by such humility, the barbarian prince readily consented and led his forces at once toward Lo-yang. The Prince of Kuang-p'ing followed after three days in Ch'ang-an.

It is interesting to note how rapidly the report of victory was transmitted. The news reached the emperor in Fêng-hsiang on November 15. He sent a messenger at once to invite the emperor emeritus to return, and the messenger, covering a distance of 692 miles, arrived in Shuchün on November 18! The emperor also summoned Li Pi to come on fast horse from Ch'ang-an. Li's advice was evidently needed on matters relating to the triumphant return of the courts to the capital. On November 16, two edicts were issued from Fêng-hsiang expressing His Majesty's remorseful concern over the long suffering of the people, proclaiming the recovery of the capital, and announcing December 4 as the date of the departure of the court from Fêng-hsiang for Ch'ang-an. When the court did leave on that date, it went, however, without the company of Li Pi. After imploring the emperor never again to bring about a tragedy like the death of the third imperial prince, he bid His Majesty farewell and retired to the Hêng Mountains as a hermit again— very much like Fan Li of the fifth century B.C.

The moving court reached on December 7 an imperial traveling lodge about twelve miles west of Ch'ang-an. Here the emperor received reports of the recapture of the Eastern Capital on December 3—the bogus emperor An Ch'ing-hsü having fled toward Yeh in the east. On December 8, the emperor triumphantly reëntered Ch'ang-an, amidst dancing, cheering, and weeping multitudes that crowded the road for miles.

In the Ch'iang Village of the District of San-ch'uan, Tu Fu heard about the recovery of Ch'ang-an and wrote three poems. Of these, we shall quote the second.

XC THE RECOVERY OF THE CAPITAL (THREE POEMS)

2

I have become accustomed to a declining life, Quiet and lonely, in a remote corner of the world. Now I hear good edicts of remorse and promise Have again come down from the illustrious Court. The great hermit has done well to protect and help the young prince, We shall enter into the cultural heritage left by His Retired Majesty. Fortunate am I to witness His Present Majesty's humility and resolution; I shed tears and lift my head to thank God.

The biographical account of Tu Fu in the *New T'ang History*, compiled in 1060, states that our poet accompanied the emperor on the glorious return to Ch'ang-an. Commentator Ch'ou Chao-ao, in the early years of the eighteenth century, asserted, however, that Tu Fu did nothing of the sort. Ch'ou identified the edicts mentioned in the poem just quoted with those issued shortly after the return of the court and concluded that our poet did not return to the capital until sometime after December 16. It is unfortunate that Ch'ou's argument and conclusion have been followed by practically all subsequent writers. Ch'ou's trouble arose mainly because of his ignorance of the edicts of November 16, the news of which could have easily reached our poet in San-ch'uan in two or three days' time, and there would still be more than a fortnight for him to repair to Fêng-hsiang to join the returning court. Indeed, a number of allusions in some of Tu Fu's subsequent poems would be unintelligible unless we assume that he returned to the capital with the emperor.

No, it will not do to rob Tu Fu of this experience. It would be like writing an admiring account of the experience of our contemporary hero, General Jonathan M. Wainwright, but denying that he was ever on board the "Missouri" in Tōkyō Bay on September 2, 1945. Patriotism was the outstanding fiber in Tu Fu's character. Having suffered so much on its account, he would probably regard the day of its vindication, December 8, 757, as the most unforgettable day of his life. I can imagine how he might have profusely wept for joy at the sight of the cheering and sobbing crowds before the city of Ch'ang-an.

There were other occasions of joyful weeping to follow. Tu Fu also accompanied the emperor in the ceremony of three days of weeping before the ruins of the imperial ancestral temples. The resumption of the morning court audience in a palace hall was witnessed, as our poet said in a later poem [ccxi], with tearful eyes. Then the emperor emeritus arrived from Shu-chün on January 16, 758. The emperor traveled twelve miles out of the capital to meet him. When he caught sight of his father, the emperor took off the imperial yellow robe and donned a princely purple. Then he threw himself on the ground and hugged the emperor emeritus' legs. Both the father and the son wept copiously, and amidst the cheers of spectators, the father insisted on clothing the son in yellow. The following morning, in the procession entering the city, the emperor acted as his father's escort. The emperor emeritus told the cheering crowds that he felt more honored at that moment than he ever had during his long reign. After holding audience in one of the palace halls, to comfort and encourage his faithful servants, he went to weep before the improvised ancestral tablets in another building, and then repaired to live in retirement in the Southern Palace. As one of the attendants of His Majesty in public appearances, Reminder Tu Fu very likely accompanied the emperor on all of the occasions of tearful rejoicing.

From "The La Festival" [xci], which was written on January 26, 758, we may gather that Mrs. Tu Fu, the four children, and possibly a few servants had already joined our poet in the capital. The La was a festival of ancestral worship, in the course of which facial creams and lotions were offered before the family altar as if the departed forebears still needed them for the protection of their skin against the cold weather. The T'ang court was especially generous to the officers who attended His Majesty in public and on almost every festival occasion distributed among them gifts from the palace. Our poet was happy indeed when he wrote the festival poem. Even the unexpectedly early advent of the spring weather seemed to augur peace and prosperity in the making. We may indeed say that the few months following the recovery of Ch'ang-an constituted the happiest period in our poet's life. Alas! The period was short.

XCI THE LA FESTIVAL

In other years the La occurs long before warm weather; This year the thaw has begun with this festival day. The day lilies are whiter than the snow that is gone; The willow shoots have stolen a march on the light

of the spring. I shall arrange for a good drinking party in the evening
Now that the brilliant Court audience is over and I am on my way home
With the facial creams and lotions—tokens of Imperial grace—Dispensed
in jars of silver and bottles of green jade from the heavenly palace.

On January 28, the emperor mounted the Vermilion Phoenix Tower
to proclaim another grand edict. A general pardon was granted to all
offenders except those involved in the rebellion of An Lu-shan and the
families of such renegades as Li Lin-fu, Yang Kuo-chung, and so on.
Posthumous honors were conferred upon loyal officers who had died in
the defense of the dynasty. Families that had lost sons or grandsons in
battle were exempt from corvée labor for two years. All households
might pay only two-thirds of the taxes for the coming year. The Prefecture of Shu-chün was renamed Ch'êng-tu and promoted as the Southern
Capital. Fêng-hsiang was to become the Western Capital, and Ch'ang-an,
the Central Capital. Names of prefectures and titles of offices that had
been changed since 742 were to revert back to those of older usage.
Generous investitures and promotions were given to a long list of
princes, generals, and officials for meritorious services in the cause of
the revival of imperial fortune. Unspecified officials were given certain
advancements in nominal ranking. So far as our poet was concerned, we
may assume that his nominal ranking was promoted to the tenth step.

Since the death of An Lu-shan, the rebel general Shih Ssŭ-ming had
returned to Fan-yang to strengthen his own position in the Northeast.
After An Ch'ing-hsü lost Lo-yang, Shih had begun to appropriate some
of An's forces. Now Shih thought it unwise to hold out against the
rising T'ang power. On February 4, his messenger arrived in Ch'ang-an
offering his surrender. Accepting it, the emperor conferred upon him
the title of a prince and appointed him Governor General of Fan-yang.
Except for the fact that the bogus emperor An Ch'ing-hsü was still en-
trenched in Hsiang-chou (Yeh before the renaming) and its neighborhood, some seven prefectures comprising sixty-odd districts, the rebellion seemed to have come to an end.

On February 11, the scores were settled with the disloyal officers who
had accepted appointments from the rebel An Lu-shan. Several weeks
previously, some three hundred of these had been sent from Lo-yang,
and they were imprisoned together with those rounded up in Ch'ang-an.
The emperor had found a hermit called Chên Tsi, who had braved
death to refuse An's summons. The prisoners were ordered to bow to
Chên Tsi, whose example of steadfastness might awaken in them a
sense of shame. Now after trials and discussions among judges, the sen-
tences were rendered and executed. Twenty-five of the more prominent
disloyal officers paid the penalty of death by decapitation or suicide.
Next came those who received one hundred strokes with a rod. The

lightest punishments were three classes of banishment. There were also some pardons. An interesting case was that of Chang Wan-ch'ing who was made Prefect of Ho-nan by An and who was now pardoned because he was known to have protected the people well.

Among the friends of our poet, Su Yü, Wang Wei, and Chêng Ch'ien had all pretended illness in Lo-yang. Dean Su's illness was probably of such a type that he could refuse any title conferred by An, and thus he was without the shadow of a stain. The emperor made him the secretary of the Bureau of Examinations and concurrently a drafter of edicts. Assistant Chancellor Wang Wei feigned the loss of his voice. He was thus unable to argue against a nominal appointment. Since the stain was only a shadow, he was demoted to be an associate secretary of the First Secretariat in the Crown Prince's Palace (nineteenth step), and thus still kept at court. Professor Chêng's aberration was quite clear, since, for him, the position of a market manager was too ridiculous. It was nevertheless a stain, however slight. Since he had failed to reach the exile court—though he had gone as far as Ch'ang-an—it was never really washed away. His case thus belonged to the category of light punishments, and he was sent to T'ai-chou on the southeastern coast as a Commissioner of Census. Our poet wrote poems for Wang and for Chêng [XCII, XCIII]. Perhaps there was also one for Su, but it is not transmitted in the existent collection.

XCII   PRESENTED TO ASSOCIATE SECRETARY WANG WEI

Mr. Wang's high reputation is of long standing. Recently, he has been deep in trouble. We hear of the arrest of the fine scholar who has returned from among the rebels; We rejoice to know it has not been made a case of literary treason. Your illness was entirely due to your longing for Their Majesties; And for three years, your heart remained as stout as ever. You must have written songs of loyalty in distress, Please read us some of them.

XCIII   MR. CHÊNG CH'IEN HAS BEEN PUNISHED BY BEING SENT TO SERVE AS THE COMMISSIONER OF CENSUS OF THE PREFECTURE OF T'AI-CHOU. I SYMPATHIZE WITH HIS MISFORTUNE OF HAVING FALLEN INTO THE HANDS OF THE REBELS IN HIS OLD AGE, BUT HAVE NOT THE OPPORTUNITY TO SEE HIM OFF PERSONALLY. I SEND THIS POEM TO EXPRESS MY DEEP FEELINGS.

Impractical and unappreciated is Mr. Chêng, whose hair is like white silk fiber; After having some wine, he calls himself just an old painter. It is distressing to know of his severe punishment in far exile Toward the close of his life, at a time when the fortunes of the Dynasty are rising again. Hurriedly, he has already begun his long journey; I came to the farewell party late and had not the chance of seeing him off personally. This is going to be our permanent separation, I fear; The resumption of friendly associations might have to be in the other world.

The offices of the reminders and the menders in the Eastern or Chancellory Division and the Western or Secretarial Division (where the State Council was also situated), on two sides of the palace gates, had a long history. Though the duties were said to be advisory—to remind His Majesty of oversights in government and to mend His Majesty's breaches in statecraft—the appointees were in reality to serve purposes more ornamental than functional. They were to march in the procession to and from the morning court audience and to stand near the emperor in this kind of government by pageantry. Our poet, however, took his advisory duties very seriously. From "Leaving the Eastern Division Late" [xciv] and "Overnight in the Spring at the Eastern Division" [xcv] we can see that he often worked practically the whole day in his office and would sometimes remain overnight, writing a memorial and staying awake to wait for the earliest moment to present it. He would burn his drafts secretly, for he did not want his associates to know their contents—lest they might criticize the emperor for refusing to act on his good counsel. His friend, Mender Ts'ên Shên, wrote Tu Fu a poem whose last two lines were obviously a hint that it would be better to remonstrate less frequently. Our poet's reply [xcvi] seemed purposely to ignore this point. He did not intend to slow down.

Among literary friends, the writing of poems back and forth was a frequent game. As another example, we might quote our poet's "Written in Support of Assistant Secretary Chia Chih's 'Early Audience in the Ta-ming Palace'" [xcvii]. Chia's father had also been assistant secretary; hence the last line of the poem. Chia's original poem and the supporting poems of Wang Wei and Ts'ên Shên are generally printed together with Tu Fu's. We shall omit the other three poems, though they all give magnificent pictures of the morning court audience. We may, however, quote our poet's "Termination of Court Audience at the Tzǔ-ch'ên Hall" [xcviii] and let it suffice for another portrayal of the pageantry.

XCIV   LEAVING THE EASTERN DIVISION LATE

The day watches reported from the clepsydra are still early, When the spring banners are ready for the court procession. After the audience is over, we disperse under the blossoming trees. I return to the official quarters and feel slightly sleepy under the willows. The city wall is damp because the snow on the towers has melted; The clouds above the palaces seem low because the buildings are high. In the absence of my associates, I burn the rough draft of my memorial; When I mount my horse to go home, it is almost time for chickens to roost.

XCV OVERNIGHT IN THE SPRING AT THE EASTERN DIVISION

Flowers disappear under the high wall at dusk; Twittering birds are passing to roost. While the stars are twinkling above the ten thousand households, The moon shines with extra brilliance on the heavenly precincts. Even the turnings of keys in the palace are heard in my sleeplessness, And the wind reminds me of the tinkling jade pendants on the horses ridden to court. I have a memorial to present tomorrow morning. Several times, I wonder how much of the night is gone.

XCVI IN ANSWER TO MENDER TS'ÊN SHÊN

Leaving the beautiful and quiet palace halls and gates, We return to our offices by different routes. You follow the state ministers, I take the road to the east. Here I see the green willow twigs, weak and slender; There you are enjoying the bright, red flowers. You, my friend, have written very fine lines, And are kind to share them with the really white-haired old man.

PRESENTED TO REMINDER TU FU OF THE EASTERN DIVISION BY TS'ÊN SHÊN

At court we march together up the steps of the audience hall; In our offices, we are separated on two sides of the heavenly palace. In the morning, we both follow the imperial insignia; In the evening, each of us brings home some fragrance of royal incense. As my head is growing whiter, I feel sad to see flowers fade; Watching the soaring birds, I remember and admire your lofty service. The holy Court has committed no blunders; I feel I have presented too few memorials.

XCVII WRITTEN IN SUPPORT OF ASSISTANT SECRETARY CHIA CHIH'S "EARLY IMPERIAL AUDIENCE IN THE TA-MING PALACE"

The sound of the fifth watch from the clepsydra hurries the dawn. The peach blossoms blush as if they had drunk too much spring wine. Embroidered dragons move on the banners in the warm sunshine, High above the palace halls, swallows fly in the light breeze. Leaving the audience, you carry the fragrance of incense in your sleeves; Writing poetry, you let sparkling thoughts run rapidly from your pen. Men are wont to call the Secretarial Division the Phoenix Pond, We are proud of two generations of literary phoenixes: first the father, now the son.

XCVIII TERMINATION OF COURT AUDIENCE AT THE TZǓ-CH'ÊN HALL

Outside the inner doors, the two court ladies with flowing purple sleeves Now turn to the throne to lead the imperial procession from the audience chamber. The spring wind blows the circling smoke of the burning incense in the hall. The sun rays flicker through the flowers on the dazzling robes of the thousand officials. The striking of the hour is heard from the clepsydra in the high tower. As an officer standing near, I note His Majesty's joyful countenance. After I leave the palace I return first to the Chancellory Division to the east, And then proceed to the Secretarial Division in the west to wait on the State Ministers.

"Wash the Weapons!" [XCIX] might be said to represent the climax of Tu Fu's elation during this happy period of his life. He was expecting that the rebel An Ch'ing-hsü would soon be destroyed and that the rebellion would be completely ended. He hoped too that good men like Fang Kuan and Chang Hao—comparable to Hsiao Ho and Chang Liang of ancient times—might remain in service, that the worthless upstarts such as Li Fu-kuo might know their own places. He was dreaming that peace might be perpetuated and that weapons could forever be laid aside. Many commentators insist on placing this poem in 759. I believe they are definitely wrong. Several arguments might be advanced from the text; I shall mention only one. The erstwhile Prince of Kuang-p'ing was made the Prince of Ch'êng on April 14, 758, and the Crown Prince on June 29, 758. Since the poem used the title "Prince of Ch'êng," it must have been written between these two dates. I am inclined to think that it was written during the second half of April, since it mentioned that the farmers were waiting for rain in order to begin spring planting.

XCIX WASH THE WEAPONS!

The generals of the renaissance are covering the prefectures of the East; Reports of victories are expected by day and night. It is said that the broad Yellow River has been crossed with ease; The fate of the Tatars will be settled like the splitting of a bamboo pole with the axe. Their last strong city, Yeh, will not require many days to recapture. These achievements have resulted from complete reliance on the Shuo-fang armies. In the capital, the officers all ride on the best war horses; The Uighurs are feasted in the Imperial palaces. While we rejoice in the submission of the Northeast to Imperial authority, It may be well to recall the days of moving the royal insignia back and forth from Ling-wu. Our men for three years have been saddened by the music and songs of war and separation. Now, at last, countless armies will sweep away the rebellion like wind upon dried leaves.

The more the Prince of Ch'êng succeeds, the more cautious he is. The example of General Kuo Tzŭ-i's wisdom is rare now or in the past. General Li Kuang-pi's perception is like a bright mirror. General Wang Ssŭ-li's patriotism is as deep as the autumn sky. These few heroes have been given by Heaven To save the world and to restore it to order.

Officials have no need of abandoning their duties under pretext; The people may live in peace like birds in undisturbed nests, The living spirit of spring accompanies the brilliantly dressed courtiers to the audience hall, Where the fragrant smoke from the burning incense is circling among the flowers of the palace. All through the night the officers work to make ready the Imperial chariot, For as the cock crows, His Majesty wants to pay his filial respect to the Emperor Emeritus.

Many are those who have become powerful merely by following Their Majesties into exile, It seems the whole world is filled with dukes and nobles. Many hardly know how to merit the Imperial grace; Remember it is only your luck; boast not of your bravery. At the Capital another Hsiao Ho has been kept, In the field, another Chang Liang is employed. Mr. Chang has had in his life wide experience with the world. He is nine feet tall, and his beard and eyebrows are impressively dark. He answers the call to service and rises at the most opportune time, He has saved the stumbling Dynasty from falling, so we know his counsels are good. How many are left of those rebels who pretended determination to succeed? Let us rejoice that our Imperial house has entered a revival of glory, like the houses of Han and Chou.

We expect every nation under the sky will send tributes to our Court, Strange articles as propitious signs will arrive, one close to the other. An unknown country may even send the white-jade ring of the old fairy tale; And there may be reports of the discovery of silver urns in the hills. Our great hermit must not again indulge in songs of retirement. Let all men of letters join in the praise of peace and sagacious rule.

Just now the farmers are worried by insufficient rain; The cuckoos everywhere are calling for spring planting. Let our valiant boys return soon from their victories in the Tsi Valley, For their wives south of Ch'ang-an are anxious even in their dreams. Oh, I wish a mighty man would bring down the Heavenly River to wash the weapons, And then put them away, never to be used again, never.

That the rain did soon come, we can infer from "Annoyed" [c], which according to Tu Fu's own note was presented to his friend Pi Yao. The tone of the lines seems to indicate that it was more than rain, poverty, and the lack of a horse that annoyed Tu Fu. Kao Shih had already suffered from Li Fu-kuo's calumnies, had been demoted to a nominal position, and then sent to the Eastern Capital. About this time, Chia Chih was also sent out to be prefect of Ju-chou. Our poet was perhaps already apprehensive of the troubles that the officious upstarts could cause.

C ANNOYED

Annoyed I am. Why annoyed? We live at the two ends of the same lane, you north and I south; Is it not distressing that, as neighbors, We have not caught a glimpse of each other for ten days? Since I returned the official horse to the local government, The road is harder to tread than if strewn with brambles. I am too poor to hire any conveyance, though I am not without feet; I could walk to call on you in the past, but now I cannot. It is not because I hesitate to expose myself, Nor is it that my legs are not strong enough. My superior officers will be angry if they find me walking on foot; That is my difficulty, please understand.

With the morning has come a fierce rain, and the spring wind is mad; In sound sleep, I heard neither the bell nor the drum that call courtiers to audience. My neighbor to the east is willing to lend me his lame donkey; But the mud is so slippery, I dare not ride it to Court. I have sent to have my name placed on the record of leaves of absence. The life of man is indeed overfilled with troubles!

How can I bear the whole day with a longing heart—Longing to hear your poems that always impress me with awe? The first blooms of the magnolia have fallen; You and I are, moreover, no longer young. We have often complained of the high price of wine at the street corner; Otherworldly drinkers can seldom afford the pleasure of an inebriated sleep. Please come now quickly to drink one gallon with me, For I happen to have exactly three hundred copper coins.

Among Tu Fu's poems that can be assigned to the spring of 758 there are four which were written on the banks of the Meandering River in the southeastern corner of the City of Ch'ang-an:

CI RAIN ON THE MEANDERING RIVER

The spring clouds above the city are descending upon the walls of the Imperial Park; From the River Pavilion I see the hue of dusk has subdued the riotous florescence. The rouge on the tree blossoms in the forest is wet with rain; The duckweeds, stretched by wind, float on the water like long belts of green jade. The Imperial chariot is not seen here with the new Dragon and Tiger Guards; The burning of incense in the Hibiscus Halls is in vain. When will His Majesty order the revival of the festal party with generous grants of money, So that I may tipsily doze for a moment among the pretty ladies with painted lutes?

CII DRINKING BY THE MEANDERING RIVER

Outside of the Park, on the bank of the river, I sit and forget to return. I note the reflection of the crystal palaces is slightly blurred. Peach blossoms and willow catkins vie with one another to fall. Brown birds and white birds mingle in their flight. Enough wine provided, I have long ceased to care if all men abandon me. With a poor attendance record at Court, I am really unsuited to this world. The fairyland of retirement is now further away in the dreams of a mundane official. Too late is my regret of not having followed a better course.

CIII MEANDERING RIVER (TWO POEMS)

I

Every fallen petal means so much less of the spring; The wind is carrying away many thousand bits just to sadden me. I shall let my eyes feast upon the flowers still left, And shall not grudge my lips the wine, though I know much of it will be harmful. The kingfishers are nesting on the ruined little buildings by the river, A stone unicorn lies near the high tomb outside the Park. Nature means for everyone to enjoy himself with no loss of time, Why then let such superficial matters as rank and office deter me?

CIV 2

Each day after Court I take my spring clothes to the pawnshop; Each evening I return home from the riverbank drunk. Wine debts I have almost any place I pass; Well, few men ever live up to seventy, anyhow. Butterflies can be seen deep among flowers; Dragonflies flick the surface of the water now and again. O wind and light and time, roll on; Let us not quarrel; let us enjoy life while we can.

Rebellion and war had seriously impoverished the empire. The earlier system of remuneration for official service had been discontinued. Monthly salaries were no longer paid, and officials had to rely on irregular grants. Otherwise, a court officer like Tu Fu should hardly need to pawn his clothes in order to get money for wine. To pawn his spring clothes in the spring is bad enough. And he still owed wine debts! Why had he become so careless? Why did he abandon himself to truancy and drunkenness? What had become of his eagerness in writing and presenting memorials, joy at court attendance, hope for the revival of peace and abundance? Why should he now long for retirement—and even death? Perhaps he has already sensed the approaching end of the emperor's tolerance of a reminder that persisted in reminding. Hence the tone of surprise in "His Majesty's Gift of Clothes on the Midsummer Festival Day" [CV], which was written June 15, 758. He realized of course that he was only one of the many recipients of such gifts. And yet, there was His Majesty's own handwriting of his faithful servant's name on the package containing the clothes of perfect fit. Had

His Majesty awaked to the real issues between those who were wont to flatter and slander and those who stood ready to warn and remonstrate?

If His Majesty had, events would have followed a different course. On June 27, Chang Hao was dismissed from the State Council and sent to be governor at Ching-chou. About a month later a severe blow came down upon Fang Kuan, who, though dismissed from the State Council in June 757, had been retained at court as a high official without portfolio, and who had been, in the grand edict of January 28, 758, advanced to the twenty-seventh ranking step and ennobled as a second-class duke. Now the emperor issued a caustic edict not only blaming Fang for losing battles in the winter of 756 and for keeping a worthless guest (the lute player?) in the summer of 757, but also accusing him of continuous cultivation of empty fame and the promotion of cliquishness in officialdom. His Majesty ordered Fang to be banished to Pin-chou as prefect. Furthermore, His Majesty named President Liu Chih of the Imperial University and Vice-Prefect Yen Wu of Ching-chao as two of Fang's closest partisans and ordered that they should be sent out as the prefects of Lang-chou and Pa-chou respectively. The emperor evidently had made up his mind to drive out of his court all those whom the evil-tongued had induced him to dislike. While this catastrophe was in progress, what could Tu Fu do? According to his poem to Abbot Min in Chiang-ning [CVI], he could get drunk and sleep.

We do not know the exact date of Tu Fu's own banishment. It probably followed closely those of Fang, Liu, and Yen, if it did not occur at the same time. He was sent to Hua-chou, sixty miles east of Ch'ang-an, to be the commissioner of education—a position ranked on the ninth step of the official ladder. Before starting his journey east, he went to the western suburb to say farewell to some of his relatives and friends. Just a little over a year ago he had slipped out of the same Golden Light Gate on his way to Fêng-hsiang. "It Saddens Me to Think of the Past" [CVII] is full of the pathos of one reluctant to leave the position which had cost a great deal to attain.

"To Mêng Yün-ch'ing" [CVIII] contains no securely datable data. It could have been written before or after this time. The commentator of 1226 thought our poet wrote it just before his departure for Hua-chou, which might indeed be so, though we are without confirmation. Mêng, after passing the imperial examinations, served as a collator (fourth step). The Complete Anthology of T'ang Poetry ascribes seventeen poems to him and says that he was a friend of Tu Fu.

"Insufferable Heat in Early Autumn and Too Much Work Piled on My Desk" [CIX] shows that our poet was already in his office in Hua-chou on August 14, 758.

CV HIS MAJESTY'S GIFT OF CLOTHES ON THE MIDSUMMER FESTIVAL
DAY

*So my name too is on the list for the festival gift Of fine clothes tailored
in the Imperial palace. The fine muslin looks unusually soft in the
breeze; The fragrant silk gauze folds up like a thin layer of snow.
I note the label bears His Majesty's handwriting, hardly dry; The
summer heat will vanish once I have these on. How did they guess
my size so accurately? Forever I shall remember my master's fitting
grace.*

CVI TO ABBOT MIN IN CHIANG-NING, THROUGH THE KINDNESS OF
REMINDER HSÜ

*I have not seen Abbot Min for thirty years, With many tears I send this
message now. Can you still do many of the interesting things you did?
To whom do you show the fresh poems in your old age? I imagine
your chess pawns are still moving under the bamboos of the quiet
ravine; I remember the fine kashāya you wore when we went boating
on the lake. I hear you have been telling friends that I am now an
official; Well, it is nothing more than a stupid white head, drunk and
asleep.*

CVII IT SADDENS ME TO THINK OF THE PAST

Last year I left the capital through the Golden Light Gate and took a
side road to return to the temporary court in Fêng-hsiang. Now I am
transferred from the position of a Reminder in the Eastern Division to
that of an associate official in the prefectural government of Hua-chou,
and in order to take my leave from relatives and friends west of the city,
I come out again from this same gate.

*Last year I returned to the Imperial cause by this road, When the Tatars
were numerous in the Western Suburb. Even now I have hardly recovered from the dangerous experience, Perhaps a part of my frightened
soul is still wandering hereabout. Having waited closely upon the
Throne, I am now sent to a great prefecture; This transfer could hardly
have come from His Majesty's own intention. I have no talents and am
growing old; I halt my horse to gaze longingly on the palace precincts.*

CVIII TO MÊNG YÜN-CH'ING

*Such sublime joy will be rare between two white-haired men; Let us
take full advantage of these bright candles and the long watches of the
night. Since it is difficult to expect that we can continue to meet, Let
us not take the present departure too hurriedly. I only dread that the
starry Heavenly River will soon disappear; Neither of us shall refuse
to drain many cups. When the dawn comes, we shall remember our
worldly entanglements, Wipe our tears, and part—east and west.*

131

*Insufferable steaming heat on August fourteenth Makes it impossible
for me to eat even a few bites. I have been worried about scorpions at
night; And now there are even more flies after autumn has begun.
Robed and belted, I am about to scream madly in the office, Especially
when they bring more papers to pile high on my desk. I gaze at the
green pines over narrow gullies in the Southern Mountains; How I
wish I might tread barefooted on packed ice!*

Of course there were many papers. The duties of a commissioner of
education were widespread. He had to look after schools and temples,
examinations, ceremonies, furnishings, et cetera. He had to help the
prefect in drafting memorials and letters. He had to keep the record of
merits, demerits, lengths of service, and leaves of absence of all officials
of the prefecture. Though there were three assistants and six clerks to
help him, the amount of paper work that required his attention could
be immense.

In the existent collection of our poet's prose writings, there are two
pieces that belong to this period. They might have been those that he
was proud of and wanted to transmit to posterity. One of these is the
draft of a memorial for Prefect Kuo, who urges His Majesty to take
early military action against the rebel An Ch'ing-hsü and suggests that
the imperial armies concentrate on attacking the two prefectures east
and west of Hsiang-chou and that this action should be taken before the
time of harvest. It is interesting to observe that though the memorial
specifies the deployments of the various armies, no recommendation is
made of using the forces under Shih Ssŭ-ming to attack An from the
north. Messrs. Kuo and Tu probably already suspected that Shih's surrender was not genuine.

The other text consisted of a series of five questions for examining the
prefectural candidates, three or more of whom might be passed and forwarded to Ch'ang-an to take the imperial examinations. What measures
would the candidates advise to increase the receipts of the government
so that the imperial armies might be sufficiently fed without increasing
the economic burdens upon the people? What would be the candidates'
advice about improving the post-station highway system by the use of
the recent limited grant for procuring horses that are almost unobtain-
able in the open market? What plans can the candidates suggest for the
resumption of river conservancy to make the Wei more navigable for the
grain ships coming to the Central Capital? What revisions in the present
draft laws would the candidates advocate to provide the armies with
enough men without robbing the farms of labor needed to produce
enough food? Since the complete suppression of the remnants of the

rebellion is not far off and a program of rehabilitation will be near at hand, what concrete suggestions would the candidates advance in such matters as currency reform and a new system of granary reserve? Tu Fu emphasized the importance of questions such as these in the following statement: "In the examinations of recent years, the candidates generally have filled their papers with conventional knowledge and have given little attention to political economy. Since literary learning is separately tested in the prose and poetry compositions, it will be well to remember that you are expected to demonstrate in these papers your knowledge of current problems. My only demand is that you try to be practical in your answers."

I imagine that these examination questions did not endear Commissioner of Education Tu Fu to the students of the prefecture. If current-problem papers could be filled in the past with generalities culled from classical literature, why should the examiners now demand real acquaintance with the issues of the day? And who are you, anyway, Tu Fu? You were never too successful with imperial examinations. You were not even successful at court as a reminder. It shows that such knowledge is not wanted by the imperial government. We want to be successful candidates and successful officials. Why should we follow your type of scholarship? If there were such murmurings, it would help to make the duties of a commissioner of education more distasteful to our poet.

Three more of Tu Fu's famous poems very probably were written in the autumn of 758. The two poems, "Dreaming of Li Po" [CX–CXI], have generally been assigned to the autumn of 759. The elder poet was in the autumn of 758 on his way to his place of exile, Yeh-lang. By the spring of 759 he had been pardoned and permitted to return down the Yangtze. Since the first poem refers to him as still in the net of the prosecutors, it must, therefore, have been written before the pardon.

"Double Ninth at Mr. Ts'ui's Farmhouse in Lan-t'ien" [CXII] was written on a visit Tu Fu made to that district, about thirty-three miles west of Hua-chou. The Double Ninth was a festival day, the ninth day of the ninth month of the solar-lunar calendar. In 758 this day occurred on October 15. It was customary to have a party with one's relatives or friends and to climb some height to view the scenery. Popular belief regarded the dogwood leaves worn on such occasions to be a symbol of longevity.

CX DREAMING OF LI PO (TWO POEMS)

I

Grief can be swallowed after separation by death; The absence of a living friend means an anxiety without end. From the malarial regions south of the Yangtze, I have had no news of the exiled Li Po. That you have come into my dreams Shows you know of my longing for you. Was it a soul of the living or of the dead? Across so long a distance, it would be hard to be sure. Through the green maple forest you came; By the dark mountain pass, you turned to go back. But you are now caught in the prosecutor's net. How could you have flown out of it? The setting moon is shining on the beams above my bed; I can almost see your face in the pale light. Where you are, the waters are deep, and the waves mad: Beware! Let not the watery monsters swallow you up.

CXI 2

All day I watch the clouds float And wonder why my wandering friend has not come back. Three successive nights I saw you in my dreams; I know well what you think of our friendship. Each time, before departing, you seemed to hesitate; The road to come was surely difficult. There are frequent storms on the river and lake. What would happen if you lost the paddle and the boat? I saw you scratching your white head outside the gate As if you knew not what to do with life's heavy sorrow. Oh, the flowery Capital is filled with men of success, Only my friend is left to be lonely and sad! Who says that the heavenly law is merciful; Here is an aging man with his freedom lost. A fame that is to last thousands of years Will rise after an unappreciated life is past.

CXII   DOUBLE NINTH AT MR. TS'UI'S FARMHOUSE IN LAN-T'IEN

Autumn brings sadness hard for an aging man to escape; On an impulse, I have come today to share your happiness. I shouldn't let the wind expose my almost bald head; Laughingly I ask a friend near by to secure my hat with his hand. The Blue Water comes from a thousand pouring gullies in the distance; The Jade Hill reaches high to challenge the two cold peaks of the Cloud Tower Mount. How many will be well enough to meet here again next year? With tipsy eyes, I examine the dogwood leaves I am to wear.

The emperor had not at once acted upon the advice contained in Prefect Kuo's memorial drafted by our poet. He probably wanted to await the arrival of some 3,000 Uighur troops to be sent by the kaghan, now the emperor's son-in-law, since the Princess of Ning-kuo, the emperor's youngest daughter, was given him in marriage on August 25. After the Uighur troops had arrived, the emperor ordered on October 27 nine governors general—among them Kuo Tzŭ-i, Li Kuang-pi, Li Ssŭ-yeh, and Ts'ui Kuang-yüan—to make a concerted attack on An Ch'ing-hsü. The deployments were indeed somewhat as suggested in Kuo's memorial. By December 14 both of the neighboring prefectures east and west of Hsiang-chou were occupied by the imperial armies. The delay in starting the campaign was nevertheless an error. An withdrew behind the fortified city walls of Hsiang-chou, and the imperial armies could only lay siege, waiting for the rebels to exhaust their harvested grain. The emperor blundered again in not having appointed a commander-in-chief for his forces. Since the governors general had to confer among themselves, tactical decisions could not be quickly made. Meanwhile, alarmed by repeated defeats, An had sent to beg help from Shih Ssŭ-ming. Shih, having known the imperial treatment of him to be more temporizing than wholehearted, decided to be an open rebel once more. He got some 130,000 men ready and sent 10,000 south to within twenty miles of Hsiang-chou. He himself was to follow soon. The imperial armies had not moved successfully to block him.

The news of these court decisions in Ch'ang-an and military activities in the east could hardly fail to reach the ears of our poet in Hua-chou, since Hua-chou was on the main thoroughfare between the Central Capital and the East. There is, however, no record of his reactions to them. He wrote very few poems in Hua-chou, perhaps because he was too busy with the never diminishing routine documents on his desk. But the day of the winter solstice, December 18, was a holiday. He wrote two poems addressed to the menders and reminders in Ch'ang-an. We quote one [CXIII] of these to show that he was tired of the life in Hua-chou and was longing for the life at court.

Toward the end of the solar-lunar calendar year, which would be about the end of January 759, Tu Fu was sent on business 227 miles eastward to Lo-yang. On the way, he met Mêng Yün-ch'ing east of the city of Hu-ch'êng (sixty-six miles east of Hua-chou) and returned with Mêng to Hu-ch'êng to drink in the home of a friend [CXIV]. It was probably farther along the way that he witnessed the scene described in "Parting of an Aged Couple" [CXV]. The urgent need of replenishing the armies had driven the government to impress even old men into service.

CXIII   AN IMPULSIVE EXPRESSION ON THE DAY OF THE WINTER SOL-
STICE: TO BE SENT TO THE MENDERS AND REMINDERS OF THE
TWO DIVISIONS (TWO POEMS)

I

Last year on this very day, exactly on the third stroke of the fifth watch, We were in the procession to wait upon His Majesty. Do you know, just now amid the burden of work and the distress of spirit I am visualizing the coiling incense smoke in the audience hall? There is no way for me to join you again in pleasant and leisurely associations. Sometimes, in haste to answer office summons, I put on my clothes inside out. Who will ever be able to forget this day of depressing sadness Since both the day and the sadness can now only increase?

*A fierce wind whips up dust to darken the districts along the river; A
traveler can hardly see his own hand. East of the city of Hu-ch'êng, I
happen to open my eyes: There, on a halting horse, I recognize Yün-
ch'ing's face. Had we not Liu Hao for our host, We could not have returned to this grand feast. Mr. Liu is pleased that I have brought a
guest; He lights lamps, brings out wine, and spreads a fine table. "Let
us talk and enjoy this whole night," says he. "Make no reference to the
difficult progress of war!"*

*The stove burns red in the room with the semblance of dawn; The pale
moon gives the papered window the appearance of rippled silk. Not
long ago the universe was turned upside down near Ch'ang-an, Just now,
winter is ending and spring is commencing in Lo-yang's palace halls.
Who could ever have thought that our paths would lead to this same
place? We regret that the hours of the clepsydra are running fast;
Such happy meetings are rare in one's life. When the cocks crow among
the trees in the yard, our parting tears drop like rain.*

CXV   PARTING OF AN AGED COUPLE

*There is still no peace on all sides of the Capital; There can be no rest
for even an aging man. My sons and grandsons have all perished in
battle, What good is it for me alone to live? Throwing away my cane,
I depart by the gate; Even the comrades on the march grieve for me.
Fortunately, I have a few teeth left, But the marrow in my bones is
mostly gone.*

*Once a man has put on the military uniform, He must salute the officer
and obey the order to go. My aging wife lies on the roadside to weep;
The year is late, and her clothing thin. Though I know well we shall
never meet again, I shall still worry about her shuddering cold. Though
she realizes that I cannot return alive, She still urges me to eat plenty
and keep well.*

*The rampart of T'u-mên is hard to break, The ferry across to Hsing-yüan
is known to be difficult. Our predicament is different from the siege of
the city of Yeh; Though I may die, death will not be immediate. Parting
and reunion are matters of human life; One cannot expect consideration
for either age or youth. When I recall the younger days of our married
life, I cannot help lingering a moment for a long sigh.*

The whole world is on a military expedition; Battle fires blaze on every hill. Corpses left in the woods are stinking; Human blood has stained the landscape red. No village is a safer place than another; I may as well leave and cease to hesitate. Leaving forever the thatched hut that has long been our dwelling, I feel despair has broken everything inside of me.

"Within one year, four long trips."

CHAPTER EIGHT

We do not know the nature of Tu Fu's business in the Eastern Capital. A recent guess that he had gone east to advise General Kuo Tzŭ-i may be too bold. Yet, it is a guess that is at least not contradicted by the sources, and something may even be said in favor of it. Since our poet was deeply interested in military affairs and had suggestions to offer, it was not impossible that his mission had something to do with the war. Might not Prefect Kuo of Hua-chou be a relative or kinsman of the great general? If so, it would be entirely permissible to conjecture that he had sent the commissioner of education to Lo-yang, ostensibly on some official pretext, but in reality to advocate such strategical deployments as they both regarded as urgent.

At any rate, "Military Review" [CXVI] shows that Tu Fu was in close touch with the commanding circles. The poem, which might have been intended for circulation among them, voices the need of a supreme command (could not some of the generals memorialize the throne to have General Kuo Tzŭ-i so appointed?) and the urgency of immediately subduing the rebel Shih Ssŭ-ming. It was the failure alike of the court to see such a need and of the field to respond to such an urgency that was to lead the grandiose campaign of the nine governors general into disaster.

Since Yen-shih was very near to Lo-yang, our poet would, of course, want to revisit the old homestead. "Heard about My Brother" [CXVII] concerns Tu Ying, who was still in P'ing-yin. That Tu Ying had control of the family property and had entered officialdom early might explain his having a plurality of wives. The concubine he had left behind in the old homestead could be one for whose company he had ceased to care. With desertion, war, and the interruption of communications, she could hardly be blamed for having run away.

Though we know nothing about the identity of the man or the place in "Presented to Hermit Wei" [cxviii], we may follow the editors who placed the poem in the spring of 759. It fits this period and the neighborhood of Lo-yang perhaps better than another time and another area.

CXVI MILITARY REVIEW

Pei-t'ing has sent these strong men Who will fight like tigers and leopards. Their valor has long been known as invincible; See how tranquil the frontiers are now. But evil spirits have again brought forth the daring rebel, There is need of the appointment of a commander in chief for the present campaign. Keep not vigil under the besieged city of Yeh; Proceed to slay the whale on the unruly waves farther north.

CXVII HEARD ABOUT MY BROTHER

How many have been able to return since the war made A strange place preferable to their own? That I am feeling so bitterly sad now Is because I have long wanted to see you. Your books are still hidden in the walls; Your concubine has already left the house. Only the old dog sympathizes with my grief; With a drooping head, he sits beside my bed.

CXVIII PRESENTED TO HERMIT WEI

In life two friends can meet Almost as rarely as the morning and the evening star. What a happy night this is When we are together under the bright candlelight! How long did youth last? Now our heads are both white. Half of the people we knew are reported dead: We are shocked and feel sick inside. Who could have imagined that it would take two decades For me to come again to this hall of yours? You were not married when we last parted; Now, suddenly, your children stand before me in a line! Beaming, they welcome their father's friend, And inquire whence I have come. Before many of the questions are answered, The children have brought food and wine. Spring leeks are cut in the garden in the night rain, Freshly steamed rice is served with a sprinkling of yellow millet. "This is a rare meeting," says our host, As he pours into two rows of ten big cups. Even ten cups, I can stand; And I do appreciate your unchanging friendship. Tomorrow, with mountains between us, Neither of us knows what will come next.

In Hsiang-chou, the armies of the nine governors general had been besieging the prefectural city for months. By February 1, 759, the rebel Shih Ssŭ-ming had occupied Wei-chou, the neighboring prefecture to the east. Governor General Li Kuang-pi, who saw, as our poet did, the necessity of fighting Shih first, proposed that he and Governor General Kuo Tzŭ-i should move their armies to beleaguer Shih in Wei-chou. Eunuch Yü Ch'ao-ên, the inspector general of the campaign, opposed this move, and it was abandoned. In the meantime, while the invested city of Hsiang-chou was approaching the end of its resources, the morale of the surrounding imperial armies was also declining. Suddenly, on April 7, Shih led 50,000 of his best troops to attack the 600,000 men of the nine imperial armies. While the battle was in progress, a tremendous sandstorm arose. Both the imperial and the rebel forces stampeded. For the imperialists, it meant the end of the campaign. In the army under Kuo Tzŭ-i only 3,000 horses were left of the 10,000; and of the equipment for 100,000 men, hardly anything remained. Kuo's army retreated 193 miles southwestward toward Lo-yang; the officials in the Eastern Capital abandoned their offices; and the people fled from their homes. Fearing that Shih might lead his armies west and there might be a repetition of the disasters of 756, Kuo planned to defend Shan-chou. But as the region was then suffering from a famine, he finally settled in Ho-yang, about twenty-seven miles northeast of Lo-yang, trying to rebuild his army to block the advance of Shih.

For the rebels, the rout of the imperial forces did not mean as much as a respite for the bogus emperor An Ch'ing-hsü—for he was soon executed by Shih Ssŭ-ming—as it did a new era for Shih, who soon declared himself the Emperor of the Great Yen dynasty and renamed the city of Yu-chou Yen-ching.

Whether or not our poet had finished his mission in the Eastern Capital, we may assume that he could transact no more business when the city was emptied of its officials and inhabitants and that he would be hastening homeward to Hua-chou. On the way he wrote several celebrated poems, perhaps intended for circulation among the governors general. Of these we shall quote "The Recruiting Officer at Hsin-an" [cxix], "A Recruiting Officer at Shih-hao" [cxx], and "The Parting of a Newly Wedded Couple" [cxxi]. The District of Hsin-an was about twenty-three miles west of the Eastern Capital. The village of Shih-hao was seventy-three miles farther west.

CXIX THE RECRUITING OFFICER AT HSIN-AN

I travel on the road through Hsin-an, And hear the roaring voices of an army's roll call. The officer of Hsin-an tells me: "In this small district, all men over twenty-two have gone. Last night an order came down from the prefecture, Making us take the boys over seventeen. These boys are short and slight; How can they defend His Majesty's cities?" I notice the stout youths have mothers to see them off, Only the thin boys are lonely and forlorn. In the evening, I watch the clear water run eastward; I still hear the sound of weeping in the green hills. O mothers, stop those

streaming tears, More weeping will only wither your eyes. Though your
eyes are dried to the bone, Neither heaven nor earth will do anything for
you. Our armies were besieging the city of Yeh, We expected its fall
almost any time. Who could have foreseen that the rebels would be so
unpredictable, And that our forces would return in scattered battalions?
They are now by the old rampart to defend the provisions; They are in
the neighborhood of the Eastern Capital to train new soldiers. Trenches
are dug, but not deep enough to reach water, And the work of pasturing
horses is not too hard. Moreover, the royal armies are good armies; The
soldiers are clearly well fed and provided. Seeing your sons off, you need
not cry your hearts out; General Kuo Tzŭ-i treats his men like his own
children.

CXX A RECRUITING OFFICER AT SHIH-HAO

In the evening, I found a lodging place at Shih-hao Village. A recruiting
officer came to take men at night. My old host scaled the wall and fled;
His old wife went to answer the gate. The officer was raging; The old
woman cried bitterly. I listened to what she said: "My three sons went to
the camp at Yeh; A letter came from one of the boys, Telling of the
death of his two brothers in battle. The dead ones are forever gone. How
long can the living one last? There are no more men now in the household Except a suckling grandson. His mother has stayed here because
of the son—She hasn't a whole skirt to put on. Though I am an old
woman and have not much strength, I will go with you, officer, this
very night. Let me answer the urgent call from Ho-yang; I can at least
cook meals for our men." Voices of talking ceased late in the night, I
seemed to hear only subdued sobbing. At dawn, I resumed my journey;
Only the old man waved farewell.

CXXI THE PARTING OF A NEWLY WEDDED COUPLE

A dodder, clinging to a flax plant, Hasn't a firm hold for long. To marry
a girl to a soldier Is worse than casting her away on the roadside. With
my hair knotted, I am indeed your wife; But our nuptial bed has hardly
been warmed. Married in the evening and parting on the morrow, Is it
not too soon and hurried? I know you do not have far to go, For you are
only to defend the front at Ho-yang. But since our marriage is not con-
summated, How am I to appear as a daughter-in-law? My parents
brought me up, And kept me day and night in the house. When they
gave me away to be married, They did not expect me to be more lone-
some than a dog or a hen. You are now going to the neighborhood of
death, My heart is sinking deep in pain. If I insist on going with you,
I might only make the situation worse. You had better forget about your
bride, And give yourself to the duties of war. The presence of women in
the camp Would hardly enhance the martial spirit.

I am a daughter from a poor family; It has taken me long to make these silk clothes. These I shall no longer wear, And I am washing the powder and rouge off my face. Do you see those birds in flight above? Big or small, they are flying in pairs. Our human world has gone awry; Only longing to be together is allowed you and me.

Commissioner of Education Tu Fu should have been back in Hua-chou for some time before he wrote in midsummer "Sigh on a Summer Night" [cxxii]. He had already begun to think of abandoning his official career. When he wrote "Day after the Beginning of Autumn" [cxxiii], probably on August 5, his mind was practically made up. All biographical accounts of Tu Fu state that he gave up his position in Hua-chou because of famine in the area. This I am inclined to doubt. Though we know of famine during the spring farther east and though we have one of Tu Fu's poems in which he deplores the insufficiency of rain in the summer, we are unable to find any express evidence of famine in his neighborhood in the autumn. Even granting that there was, we should not forget that since the local government collected taxes justly or unjustly in kind, the prefectural officials and their families were not likely to be those first to suffer from the scarcity of food.

I should say that it was rather the accumulated sense of the futility of service that at last led Tu Fu to abandon his official employment. What he called "senseless tasks" might include not only the multitudinous routine papers that failed to diminish, but also the apparently practical advice that failed to be followed, as well as the magnificently prepared examination questions that failed to be appreciated. Since the time was approaching for another examination of the prefectural candidates, he probably thought it timely to leave before having to submit to the temptation to follow the rut of the more popular commissioners of education.

From Hua-chou westward to Ch'in-chou, Tu Fu's next place of sojournment, was a journey of 327 miles. Even traveling slowly with a family between the two places should not require more than a fortnight. "Thinking of My Brothers on a Moonlight Night" [cxxiv] was written toward the end of the journey. The poem mentions the White Dew Season, which was one of the twenty-four subdivisions of the solar-lunar calendar year and which during the eighth century would begin about September 5 of the Julian calendar. This date shows that the Tu family probably left Hua-chou in the latter part of August. We do not know what sort of arrangement our poet made with the government—possibly an indefinite leave of absence. Health was generally a convenient pretext. At any rate, it has usually been easier for one to give up employment than to obtain it.

"Swallows on Their Return Flight to the South" [cxxv] might have been written in the same September before Tu Fu reached Ch'in-chou.

We may observe that our poet was again longing for the court and his master, though he had so recently given up his official career. Just as a swallow would want the old nest to remain intact, so Tu Fu hoped that the dynasty might stand despite such enemies within and without as Li Fu-kuo and Shih Ssŭ-ming.

CXXII SIGH ON A SUMMER NIGHT

The endless sun seems never to set! The steaming heat is poisoning me. Where can I get some long-drawn wind, And let it blow and blow on my clothes!

The clear sky then hangs out a bright moon, Pouring thin rays through the thick forest. The night is too short in June. I open all the windows to the light breeze. Everything is visible in the luminous air Where tiny insects are fluttering their wings. For all creatures, big or small, To seek comfort is but natural: I am thinking of our men who bear arms To defend the frontier for the whole year. Talking in vain of a bath, They bear the heat, and look morosely at each other. They beat copper pans the night long to keep the watch—And noises loud enough to be heard afar are hardly cooling. Though the reward be green or even purple robes of high rank, How does it compare with an early return home?

A few melancholy notes of the bugle sound from the north city wall, A few cranes are calling and flying. A new weariness rises in me. Oh, how I long for peace!

CXXIII DAY AFTER THE BEGINNING OF AUTUMN

Time makes no allowances. One season succeeded another last night. The dark cicadas are buzzing ceaselessly; The autumn swallows are like flitting guests. Independence has always been the desire of my life; And now I am sadly approaching fifty. To continue or to leave an official career, I am free to choose. Why then allow myself to be further burdened with senseless tasks?

CXXIV THINKING OF MY BROTHERS ON A MOONLIGHT NIGHT

The watch-tower drum has sounded to close the road to traveling, I hear a lone wild goose's cry in the autumn skies of the frontier. The White Dew Season begins tonight; The moon is not as bright as I used to see it at home. Brothers I have, but they are all scattered. There is no home where I can inquire if they are alive. Their letters will never reach me now; Moreover, the war that separates us is not ended.

CXXV SWALLOWS ON THEIR RETURN FLIGHT TO THE SOUTH

Are they leaving merely to escape frost and snow? But they could hardly have many companions in the North. The four seasons are well ordered,

Every September these birds naturally return to the South. Will they ever come back with the colors of the spring? Should not the little ones be warned and afraid? "If the old nest is not destroyed," they seem to say, "We shall return to fly near the master."

Though our poet stayed in Ch'in-chou only about a month and a half, he wrote many poems. He had come to this frontier city probably because some relatives and friends had chosen, for one reason or another, to settle there for a time at least. There is no evidence that he had any employment. He probably spent his time in resting, visiting friends, and writing poetry. "An Event" [cxxvi] might have been written shortly after September 18, when the Princess of Ning-kuo, having refused to be buried alive with her dead husband, the Uighur kaghan, returned to Ch'ang-an. Tu Fu emphasized the fact that even the Uighurs were defeated in the Hsiang-chou battle of April 7, to show the folly of relying on barbarian troops to clear the country of rebels. The rebel army at this time was moving toward the Eastern Capital, which fell to them on October 22.

The collection of twenty "Miscellaneous Poems of Ch'in-chou" very likely were not written all at once. The second of these [cxxvii] describes the temple north of the city on the site of the palace of the first-century war lord, Wei Hsiao. The Tu family might have been temporarily lodged there while looking for a more suitable place to settle. Tu Tso, who had a home in the Lu-hun Hills near Lo-yang, and who was a distant cousin of our poet, though Tu Fu regarded him as a nephew, was now living in the Tung-k'o Village some seventeen miles southeast of Ch'in-chou. "Shown to Cousin Tu Tso" [cxxx], "Three Poems Sent to Tu Tso after He Has Returned to the Hills" [cxxxi–cxxxiii], and the sixteenth of "Miscellaneous Poems" [cxxix] seem to show that the elder and younger cousins had visited back and forth with each other and that our poet was very much tempted to settle down in Tung-k'o permanently.

This desire, however, was not realized. Tu Fu found that his old friend Abbot Tsan of the Ta-yün Monastery in Ch'ang-an, who, having been driven out of the capital—perhaps also on suspicion of being a partisan of Fang Kuan—was settled near the Hsi-chih Village also in the neighborhood. Therefore, Tu Fu decided that he wanted to buy some land and build a hut near Abbot Tsan. Nor did this plan materialize, because our poet changed his mind and wanted to go to T'ung-ku in Ch'êng-chou. He wrote several poems to Abbot Tsan, but we shall quote only one [cxxxv]. Among the other friends of Tu Fu's in Ch'in-chou was Hermit Juan Fang, who supplied our poet with shallots [cxxxiv].

"The Fair Lady" [cxxxvi] has been interpreted by some commentators as an allegorical description of a loyal minister unjustly exiled by the court. It is, however, difficult to make the details fit such an interpretation. I am inclined to the view of those who believe that there might really have been such a lady in the neighborhood of Ch'in-chou. If so, she might have been a friend of the Tu family. This lady remains nameless, as does the subject of "Seeing a Friend off on a Long Journey" [CXLVIII]. Nor, in the seventh of the "Miscellaneous Poems [CXXVIII], do we know the name of the ambassador—obviously one of our poet's friends—sent on a mission to the Tibetans. Since the outbreak of the An Lu-shan rebellion, the Tibetans had taken advantage of the internal trouble of the empire to harass the frontiers frequently. The emperor was naturally anxious to reach an understanding with the Tibetan sgam-po. But as we shall see in subsequent chapters, the efforts of the embassies were mostly in vain.

Being a person who attached great value to friendship, our poet would naturally write poems about or to friends far away—for instance, "Twenty Rhymes Sent to Li Po" [CXXXVII], "Thinking of Li Po" [CXXXVIII] and "Thinking of Chêng Ch'ien" [CXXXIX]. Tu Fu had received word from Chêng in T'ai-chou but no word from Li in the neighborhood of Lake Tung-t'ing, near the river Mi-lo, where early in the third century B.C. the great poet Ch'ü Yüan had drowned himself because his loyalty had suffered calumny. We shall not quote the long poem to Kao Shih, who was appointed prefect of P'êng-chou in June, and Ts'ên Shên, who was sent out of the Central Capital to be associate prefect of Kuo-chou. In this poem, it should be mentioned, our poet stated that he was suffering intermittent fever from malaria and that the malady had attacked him for three successive years.

A longer poem to two friends, "Fifty Rhymes Sent to Mr. Chia Chih, Assistant Prefect of Yo-chou, and Mr. Yen Wu, Prefect of Pa-chou" [CXL] recalls quite a bit of the history of the preceding years. Toward the close of the poem, our poet refers to himself in an extremely depressing tone. The disappointment and disillusionment with his own official record are real enough. That he communicates such sadness to his friends Chia and Yen is purposeful. They must have taken their own banishment very hard, and Tu Fu wants them to be somewhat comforted in the realization that they are much less unfortunate than he. He wants them to refrain from airing their angered feelings in writing, lest it be used by the calumniators against the chances of their return to the court.

When the armies of the nine governors general were routed in the spring, Chia had run away from his post in Ju-chou, and, in punishment, he was demoted and sent to Yo-chou. In the title of the poem his name was given precedence over Yen's because he was the elder man though his official rank was then lower. Our poet compared Chia to Chia I of the second century B.C. and Yen to Yen Kuang of the first century of the Christian era mainly because of the identity of the family names. Chia I, though highly esteemed by the emperor for his scholarship, was banished to a lower post in Ch'ang-sha, which was near the Yo-chou of T'ang. Yen Kuang, an early friend of the emperor, had visited the court, slept with the emperor in the same bed, and then withdrew to his retirement as a fisherman.

Of the many Ch'in-chou poems on scenic subjects, we may choose "The Heavenly River" [cxli], which describes the Milky Way; "The Waxing Crescent Moon" [cxlii]; and "A View of the Wild Plain" [cxliii]. There are also a number of poems on such minor subjects as "Washing and Pounding Clothes" [cxliv], "The Cricket" [cxlv], and "The Firefly" [cxlvi]. Commentators are wont to read into poems of this type some hidden thoughts of the poet. Only the last is quite clear—the firefly is Eunuch Li Fu-kuo. The three poems under "Miscellaneous Feelings" deal mainly with the need for good men in government service; and in the second poem [cxlvii] Tu Fu expresses sympathy for the aged and weak among the barbarians of Ma-i. Ma-i was one of the numerous prefectures especially created to accommodate the barbarians who had submitted to the T'ang authority. In 759 it was still situated in the hills immediately south of Ch'in-chou, but was moved elsewhere after 762.

CXXVI AN EVENT

We hear that even the Uighurs were defeated; So the marriage alliance did not turn out to be advantageous. We pity the princess of our august Court Who is barely able to cross the river and return alive. In these dreary autumn days, she no longer dresses her hair in a chignon And has grown so thin that her fine clothes hang loose about her. The hordes of rebels are still demanding battle. Amazing, so many of our hopes have come to nought.

CXXVII MISCELLANEOUS POEMS OF CH'IN-CHOU

2

The temple north of the city of Ch'in-chou Is said to have been the palace of Wei Hsiao. Moss has covered the old stone archway, The painted hall is now dilapidated, abandoned, and empty. A bright moon shines on the drooping leaves laden with dew; A few patches of clouds race the wind across the river. O Clear Wei, why are you so heartless? Do you have to flow east when I am sad?

CXXVIII 7

A chaotic pile of countless mountains Overawing a lonely city in the valley! I feel no wind, but the clouds are moving over the ramparts. It is not yet night, but the moon is already above the pass. Why has the embassy been delayed in returning? Could they have awaited a chance to execute the T'u-fan chief? Every time I look through the smoke and dust to the west, My anxiety must make me look even older than I am.

CXXIX   16

The beautiful rocky valley of Tung-k'o Surpasses comparison with any valley of the other hills. Birds in pairs fly toward the setting sun; A single puff of cloud floats in the clear sky. The inaccessibility of the region is the boast of the rustics here. In the landscape, water and bamboo are evenly divided. Here I want to live the rest of my life, gathering medicinal herbs, Though I have not yet said a word to the children.

CXXX   SHOWN TO COUSIN TU TSO (TU TSO'S THATCHED HALL IS IN THE TUNG-K'O RAVINE)

I suffer much illness as the autumn wind is taking leaves off the trees; Your coming has brought me considerable comfort. After you described the fine surroundings of your thatched house, My only wish has been to sleep in that forest of bamboo. I can visualize how the clouds rise to fill the ravine, And how the hanging cataract sprinkles your hedge. Among my numerous cousins of the younger generation, I have always known that you are the wisest.

CXXXI   THREE POEMS SENT TO TU TSO AFTER HE HAS RETURNED TO THE HILLS

I

Floating clouds gathered in the hills late in the afternoon; I feared the roads were hidden when you returned. Just before you reached the cold gully, The birds must have roosted in the dark village. When you hastened under the low trees by the farm To enter the small thatched hut of your sojourning family, They should know it was lazy Uncle Tu Fu Who needed your help and kept you long.

CXXXII   2

The millet was harvested early in September, You had promised to share it with me. It must have been ground very fine; I feel it has been somewhat delayed in reaching me. It is hardly necessary to wait for the golden chrysanthemums, The flavor of the millet will go well with the green mallow soup. You know it has long been the old man's favorite food, Just now his mouth waters at the very thought of it.

CXXXIII   3

How many lines of spring-water for your vegetable garden Run like a net down a shaded slope! The sturdy leaves must be thin in autumn;

You probably see more of the flying clouds now. Fragrant caltrops are abundant in the adjacent pond; Dodder vines drape the trees of the forest. I have heard much about the white shallots under frost, Would you send me some more of them?

CXXXIV THIRTY BUNDLES OF SHALLOTS FROM HERMIT JUAN FANG ON AN AUTUMN DAY

Behind the rough wooden gate of my hermit friend, Autumn vegetables grow in the garden surrounding his house. A whole basket of shallots still wet with dew, He has sent, without my even writing to beg for them. Every bundle has the appearance of light-green grass; All of the bulblets have the color of white jade. The stomach of an old man dreads cold, The warming taste of these will surely bring some comfort.

CXXXV OVERNIGHT IN ABBOT TSAN'S ROOM (HE WAS THE ABBOT OF TA-YÜN MONASTERY IN CH'ANG-AN, WAS BANISHED, AND CAME HERE)

How is it that you come to this place When the autumn wind has already turned sharp? Rain has rotted most of the chrysanthemums in the shady court; Frost has overturned half of the lotus-plants in the pool. For you, exile is hardly disagreeable, For you contemplate as usual the complete nothingness of all things. We meet and we pass the night together, It seems the round moon over Ch'in-chou shines especially on our account.

CXXXVI THE FAIR LADY

She is the most beautiful woman of the age, But she lives quietly in a deserted valley. "I come from a good home," says she. "Misfortune has brought me here among the weeds. When rebellion and war broke out east of the passes, All my brothers perished. High ranks availed them nothing; Even their bodies have not been found. The world despises the unfortunate; No affection lasts longer than a candle's flame in the wind. My husband, a fickle man, Has already taken a new woman to his heart. Leaves of mimosa fold together at nightfall; A pair of mandarin ducks never roost apart. My husband wants only to see his new love laugh, He will not listen to his first wife's sobs."

Up in the hills the spring-water is clean, It becomes turbid when it runs on the plain. When her maid returns from selling her pearls, They pull the creepers to mend the thatched hut. She picks a flower, but not to wear in her hair, And she cuts an armful of the never-changing cypress. Though her green sleeves are thin, and the weather is cold, I find her still standing by the tall bamboos, still radiant in the dusk.

CXXXVII TWENTY RHYMES SENT TO LI PO

A number of years ago the famous Ho Chih-chang Called you an immortal banished to this world, Because your prose was composed with the speed of a storm, And your poetry had power enough to move the ghosts. On this account your fame spread far And rose suddenly out of its undeserved obscurity. Then His Majesty showed especial fondness for your works, Which were indeed unrivaled in the world. The Imperial barge sailed late just to wait for you; No other poet could win the embroidered robe with you in the contest. In bright sunshine you rode to see the Emperor in the palace hall; Your admirers thought you were riding high upon the clouds.

A gracious edict permitted your retirement; Then you met me and treated me as if we had long been intimate friends. You were true to your desire for quiet pursuits; You were able to preserve your integrity in both obscurity and prominence. Despite my talkativeness, you liked my bucolic openness. Through your fondness of wine, I saw your greatness. We drank and we danced at night in Pien-chou; We took walks and sang of spring in Yen-chou.

You had great talents, but you wanted no political success. Holding aloof from the world, you lived alone in retirement. Though you were a private individual recognized for unusual ability, You were also a scholar content to remain in extreme poverty. When a hungry man had a few grains of Job's tears, How the slanderers made them into ill-gotten pearls! The climate of the southwestern corner of the empire is hot and unhealthy, And you were exiled there as if you were a wicked rebel! How long can you stave off a visit by the bird of death? I would weep as Confucius did when the propitious unicorn was met with an ill fate.

You were kept by the rebellious prince against your will, How could it be said that so loyal a man had helped the rebellion? You refused his gifts and ran away; This was clear in what you wrote in the Hsün-yang jail. When they were applying strict law to your case, Why was there no one to make the truth known? Now I am just out of my sick bed by the bank of the river, And am singing an old man's feeble song under the autumn moon. Were it not that the Heavenly River is now beyond my reach, I would have sailed on it to make a plea for you.

CXXXVIII THINKING OF LI PO

The cold wind rises above this remote district. Have you no advice for me, my friend? When will the flying wild geese bring me a letter From the river-and-lake region where the autumn waters are high? Literature seldom leads to a life of worldly success; Demons are usually pleased to meet their victims. You had better talk with the ghost of the unjustly used Ch'ü Yüan; Drop a poem into the waters of the Mi-lo for him.

149

CXXXIX THINKING OF CHÊNG CH'IEN

According to news from T'ai-chou, My old friend Chêng Ch'ien is still in exile, Working as a farmer by the gullies deep in the hills, Often lying down too ill to enjoy the clouds blown in from the sea. The world has no regard for a good scholar, Who still has to beg money for wine. I can only gaze at the stars above his region; Is there no way to bring the talented man out of that burial ground?

CXL FIFTY RHYMES SENT TO MR. CHIA CHIH, ASSISTANT PREFECT OF YO-CHOU, AND MR. YEN WU, PREFECT OF PA-CHOU

Yo-chou is within hearing of monkeys' wails, Pa-chou is in the mountains, where only birds can reach; Neither of you, friends, can be happy In these distant places of banishment. The recovery of the Empire resembles just creation, But Imperial grace, like rain, falls unevenly upon different places. So you, another Chia I, are exiled to the neighborhood of Ch'ang-sha, And you, another Yen Kuang, are no longer with the Emperor.

I recall when we three were with the Court at Fêng-hsiang, We stood near the Throne anxious to advise The appointment of able generals to crush the Tatar rebellion And of good envoys to the Uighurs and the Tibetans. This was when the Imperial regalia were incomplete, When our fleet remained useless in the lakes near Ch'ang-an, When all our northeastern cities had fallen, When most of our valiant men were scattered, When the war bugles sounded east and west of the Yellow River, When the chief of demons reigned in the city of Lo-yang.

Though poorly informed, I knew the pretentious rebel would fail; With better knowledge, you predicted for him a wretched end; For he was like the foolish bird trying to fill the sea with pebbles, Or the idiot shooting arrows at heaven.

Then many armies rose to support the Imperial cause; Once the drums sounded, the martial spirit was invincible. Gloom disappeared over Fêng-hsiang; Bright days began for the temporary Court. The rebels were chopped down in Wei-chou like weeds. Their Yu-chou stronghold was about to split like a bamboo pole. Royal armies marched along the eight rivers near Ch'ang-an, And the Imperial chariot returned to the Capital. Even I had then a humble place in His Majesty's entourage; I noted an auspicious atmosphere in all movements. The Imperial guards, with the strength of leopards and tigers, marched in shining armor; The Imperial steeds were impelled with jade-decorated whips. The courtiers knew their usual places in the procession; Even long-stabled horses were aware of their new honors. Snowflakes sprinkled the red-lacquered towers; The evergreen trees merged into the surrounding mist. The officials were sad with the memory of recent experiences; The elders among the population wept for joy at the Court's return.

Amid a bitter wind His Majesty went to weep at the Imperial Temple; But on New Year's Day, the sun shone bright for the Court audience. To us, as courtiers, tribute rice was distributed each month; In spring-time, a special gift of money came from the palace. In the audience halls where the flowers were brighter than brocade, Or in the Imperial gardens where the grass was softer than silk floss, You and I often bowed together to thank His Majesty for gracious favors. Entering or leaving the palace, we were most of the time together. In the evenings, I frequently ate and drank in your grand halls, Sometimes I even slept under your embroidered quilts. We rode with horses abreast, sometimes late at night. Still I got letters from you, enough to fill my pockets.

Whenever I found a vacancy in the government's elevated ranks, I had hoped to see one of you promoted to the post. When you were but a short step from the top, Suddenly, one after the other, you were dropped from the sky like birds with clipped wings.

While I missed my friends in the service of the Court; I was allowed to live in an obscure post. I was willing to die for the stand I took, But His Majesty was lenient because of my age. The students in Hua-chou knew I was poverty-stricken, And thought me too old to teach. If an educator was himself unsuccessful, Why should he be honored merely because of his years? My heart almost breaks when I remember our pleasant times together, New worries arise when I allow my imagination to reach far.

The green of the bamboo supports of Pa Hills' precarious wooden road is faded; The red of the lotus blossoms in Yo-chou's little ponds is bright. Mr. Chia must have written about his lonely indignation; Mr. Yen too must have composed a number of poems. I know these writings represent thoughts sober and timely. It would be safer, however, not to have them widely read, For mischief-makers, like weavers of brocade, are looking for material; The threads might be picked and used on the loom. Let the beach gulls be careful lest their heads be crushed By the cold-hearted vultures that never strike in vain. Whether in a remote place with warm and gloomy miasma, Or in a mountainous region jammed in among rocks and springs, You can better spend your days playing chess, And you can forget the dreary year by drinking wine. Though the position of a prefect is too small for Mr. Yen, And that of an assistant prefect too negligible for Mr. Chia, Yet a high-minded official will manage well even a petty job, Which perhaps can be taken *in the spirit of humble retirement. Leave not, for your talents are too rare to be spared, Though to understand the ways of heaven just now is difficult.*

As for me, I follow the ancient advice which said, "Be gone!" For I know my usefulness is finished. I have taken refuge in remote Ch'in-chou, Since the Yu-chou rebels made another westward push. Though ridiculous for one so much burdened with a family, I am quite willing to be idle and to let time pass. My relatives and friends become fewer and fewer, As the war spreads from one place to another. In this strange area I am rich with sleep and dreams; But even in dreams it has been difficult to see you, my friends. Much illness on top of the inconveniences of a sojourner's life Has made the writing of this long poem hard. You, two friends, are both in magnificent health and strength; Keep your ambition, you will rise again and rise high.

CXLI THE HEAVENLY RIVER

The Heavenly River is slightly blurred during the year, Except in autumn when it is quite clear. Though a few clouds may shadow it for a while, It never fails to shine throughout the night.

The stars that swim therein twinkle over the Central Capital. In company with the moon, it sets behind the border cities. The cowboy and the weaving girl cross it every fall, We never hear that wind or wave troubles them.

CXLII THE WAXING CRESCENT MOON

A crescent has just risen with its delicate light. Since the disc is incomplete, the shadow is lopsided. Barely has it risen above the old rampart Before it disappears behind the edge of floating clouds. The Heavenly River has not changed its color; These lonely frontier hills are already cold. The dew in the yard is frosty And chills the chrysanthemums in the dark.

CXLIII A VIEW OF THE WILD PLAIN

I look at the endless expanse of the limpid autumn; A few layers of mist rise in the horizon. The distant river carries away the clear sky. A lonely city is blurred by the thick smoke from a thousand hearths. The wind tears more leaves from the thinning trees; Behind the hills far away, the sun has just sunk. That single crane is rather late on its return flight; The forest is already full of roosting crows.

CXLIV WASHING AND POUNDING CLOTHES

I know you will never return from the frontiers, But I use the washing stone, because the autumn is here. Time is approaching when you will feel the cold As much as the pain of our long separation. How can I shrink from the toil of laundering When I want these clothes to reach you near the Great Walls? Every ounce of a woman's energy is used with this club; If you listen to the air, you might even hear the pounding.

CXLV   THE CRICKET

The cricket is a tiny creature; Yet its melancholy notes are profoundly touching. Refusing to sing among the roots of the weeds, It has come indoors to be with people—under their bed. A lone wanderer will not be able to withhold his tears; An abandoned wife will not be able to sleep until the morning. Neither the strings nor the pipes Can move us so much as nature's own music.

CXLVI   THE FIREFLY

Remember, you come from among rotted weeds, How dare you fly near the light of the sun? You are not really bright enough to make books legible; You can only make specks on one's spotless clothes. Wind-borne, you can hardly be seen on the other side of the curtain; After the rain, you shimmer at the edge of the forest. When winter comes with severe frost, Scattered and afraid, where can you go?

CXLVII   MISCELLANEOUS FEELINGS (THREE POEMS)

2

I climb the cold hills in late autumn To gaze at the Ma-i Prefecture in the south. The submissive barbarians had been sent east to fight the Tatars; Not one of the able-bodied men is left. The abandoned tents are scattered and desolate; Sad clouds hover above them. The old and the weak weep by the road; All long to hear that armor and weapons might be put to rest. The defeat we suffered in Hsiang-chou Must have left mountains of corpses. All of our generals are already noblemen, Who now can be trusted with the crises of war?

CXLVIII   SEEING A FRIEND OFF ON A LONG JOURNEY

While fighting fills the universe, Why must you go on a long journey? Your relatives and friends weep To see you leave this lonely city on a saddled horse, When the countryside is no longer green, because the year is late, When the frost and snow are clean, because the roads are deserted. Human parting is not new; We understand now why the ancients were sad.

The Tu family's next place of sojourn was the town called Chestnut Station in the District of T'ung-ku of the Prefecture of Ch'êng-chou. From "Leaving Ch'in-chou" [CXLIX], we can gather that they started about the beginning of November, and the route was by way of Han-yüan. From Ch'in-chou southwestward to Han-yüan was a distance of approximately forty-three miles. From Han-yüan, we may presume that they traveled southward seventeen miles to the prefectural city of Ch'êng-chou; thence sixty miles eastward, slightly to the south, to the district city of T'ung-ku; thence seventeen miles eastward to Chestnut Station. To travel a total distance of 137 miles in a mountainous region would probably take a few days. Our poet began the journey with rather a cheerful heart, partly because he had tired of the multiplicity of social obligations in Ch'in-chou, and partly because he had been led to believe that the neighborhood of T'ung-ku would offer warmer weather, finer scenery, and easier living. According to another poem, he had received, from a man he had not met, letters of attractive description and warm welcome.

He should have known better than to trust the words of a stranger—perhaps one eager to sell him a house and some land. The scenery in the neighborhood of T'ung-ku was indeed exquisite, as we can gather from "The Abysmal Pool" [CL]. But as for the weather and the means of livelihood, "The Empty Purse" [CLIII] and several of the "Seven Songs of a Sojourner in T'ung-ku District in 759" [CLIV–CLVII] can testify to the miserable poverty, hunger, and exposure Tu Fu had to suffer. Perhaps the initial expenses of acquiring some property had exhausted all of his savings.

Several of his poems indicate he had to do considerable traveling in the neighborhood, perhaps in search of such loans and literary employments as his scruples would permit him to accept. As if to make it harder for him, his old horse was sick [CLII]. Tu Fu might have written the poem "General Censor Wu Yü's House on the Bank of the River in Liang-tang District" [CLI] on one of the walls of his absent host's house. Liang-tang was twenty-seven miles east of Chestnut Station; and I am inclined to think that Tu Fu might have stopped there overnight; his real destination might have been the prefectural city of Fêng-chou, seventeen miles further to the east and an important center of communications. The poem addressed to the absent Wu Yü contains a contrite confession. Tu Fu blamed himself for not having saved Wu from the unjust banishment to T'an-chou by some effective remonstrance with the emperor. The time referred to was of course during his short service in Fêng-hsiang; and, having miserably failed to save State Minister Fang Kuan from dismissal, he was really in no position to save General Censor Wu Yü from banishment. But he was a man who took his official duties very seriously, and was mercilessly honest about his own shortcomings.

The time of this poem and of the trip to Liang-tang poses a problem. Editors and commentators generally place this poem before our poet's reaching Chestnut Station, because they thought his route from Ch'in-chou to T'ung-ku was by way of Liang-tang. Apart from some other evidence to the contrary, it may be noted that the present poem mentions the fallen red leaves in Liang-tang—quite a contrast to the healthy green leaves in Han-yüan where our poet passed early in November on his way to T'ung-ku and Chestnut Station. His trip to Liang-tang must have been after his arrival in Chestnut Station.

CXLIX LEAVING CH'IN-CHOU

As my strength declines, I have become lazier and more foolish; I have neglected to plan ahead matters of livelihood. I think of a plentiful land only in times of hunger, And of a southern prefecture only during cold weather. Early November in the District of Han-yüan, The weather is like brisk autumn. Leaves have not yet turned yellow or fallen, And the landscape is said to be intriguing. Chestnut Station is a particularly promising name; There are good farming lands on the plain, Plenty of yams for food, And wild honey too is easy to find. Thick bamboo forests provide shoots as vegetable; Clear ponds allow fishing boats. Though it is rather too remote for a sojourning family, It does appeal to my usual adventurous spirit.

Ch'in-chou is on an important thoroughfare; I am really afraid of too complicated human affairs. Superficial social contacts do not suit my nature; Even sight-seeing affords no diversion from my worries. There are no rocks of strange shapes in the mountain ravines; Sandy farms yield only a slight harvest. There is hardly enough consolation for an old man, Clearly I cannot remain here long. The lonely fort has disappeared with the darkening dusk; From the city walls come the cries of ravens. We leave at night by carts. The horses stop to drink fresh water in the ponds by the road. The moon and the stars are crystal clear high above us; Some uncertain mist and clouds are floating here and there. Space within the universe is magnificently great; The way before me is free, long—infinite.

CL THE ABYSMAL POOL

This green gorge is the embodiment of mysteries, Though the super-natural creature bides its time to appear. We know a dragon must crouch deep under the water; His cave is perhaps hidden within the immeasurable depth. With cautious steps we walk along the rocky edge; Turning and twisting, we descend through the bluish haze. Now a great stretch of moving water is before us, And behind us, huge gray rocks stand erect. The end of the solitary path up the precipice is barely visible; The shore-line breaks between two walls of cliffs, Each sharply hewn, straight down to its invisible root, And casting into the shiny pool a shadow unsteady and inverted. The dark area must be a curved inlet near the bottom; The few broken reflections are only ripples of transparency. A lonely cloud pours itself into the deep—With birds flying in its midst. Overhanging creepers appear like curtains; Frost-bitten trees resemble crowded banners. Winding streams bring distant waters to this pool; Tubular caverns carry off its undercurrents.

No man seems ever to have known this exquisite spot; We are doubtless the first to explore it. It is time to return, and I am filled with much regret, For of all outings in my late years, this is the best. This is the hibernating season for the miraculous reptile; His great claws are numb, and he cannot move at will. How I wish I might come here again in the summer And marvel to watch how he rises in a storm!

CLI   GENERAL CENSOR WU YÜ'S HOUSE ON THE BANK OF THE RIVER IN
      LIANG-TANG DISTRICT

The morning smoke over the cold city is thin; The fallen leaves in the mountain ravines are red. A chilly wind comes from hundreds of miles away To blow sharply on your riverside house.

The yellow cranes of Crooked Beach near T'an-chou Must be crying day and night on the open fields. O strict and just General Censor, How long are you to remain in exile at Ch'ang-sha? Even a monkey is exceedingly sad to lose its nest in the woods, And a bird that has barely escaped the arrow is still afraid. You must, of course, have thought of the joy of returning home, But I feel it too bitter to recall how your punishment was brought about.

In the days of the temporary capital in Fêng-hsiang, You and I were both members of the Golden Court. His Majesty had to suffer the dust of seeking refuge; And the eastern suburb was gloomy with the atmosphere of war. Military security required vigilance against enemy spies Who were frequently found to have sneaked into the city. The Tribunal of Censors had the duty of prosecution; But you insisted that every case be thoroughly investigated. You could not bear to see unjust executions; You had the innocent and the guilty separated as white from black. Your superiors only pretended to let you proceed with your course; You were deemed obstructive and were banished as a result. The Court as a whole knew well the truth; But apart from a few suppressed sighs, they kept their mouths shut. For the country, the case was like the exile of Confucius. For you, you knew wisely it was not a personal loss.

At that time, I was unworthily a fiery Reminder, Standing near enough to His Majesty's throne. That I saw the injustice without a protest

Is a regret I shall carry to my grave. Since I started on my long trip, I have been often sad; Leaving this house of yours, I feel now completely lost. I failed to perform a clear duty in your case; My remorse will turn my hair still whiter.

CLII SICK HORSE

Long have I ridden you, Far along the frontier and deep in winter. You have toiled hard in this world all your life; I grieve now over your age and your illness. There are no unusual features in your appearance; But your good temperament and loyal service have been constant. The noble significance of a humble creature Is touching and worthy of a sad chant.

CLIII THE EMPTY PURSE

Green cedar leaves, though bitter, can still be swallowed; The rosy sky at dawn is ample for food. The world will stop at nothing; But my way is the hard way. Without cooking, the frozen well can be undisturbed in the morning. Without bedding, the bed is naturally cold at night. The purse may be shy of complete emptiness; I must leave one copper coin for it to keep.

CLIV SEVEN SONGS OF A SOJOURNER IN T'UNG-KU DISTRICT IN 759

1

A sojourner by the name of Tu Tzŭ-mei With disheveled white hair falling over his ears Has been compelled by hunger to pick acorns for food, In the mountain ravines, in the dusk of a cold winter day. No letters have come from the Central Plains, and I cannot return there; My limbs are frozen, chapped, covered with half-dead skin and flesh. Oh! Just this first song is sufficiently sad: A bitter wind blows on me from high above.

CLV 2

A spade with a long handle of white ash Constitutes my sole means of livelihood. I cannot find the yellow yam with the sprouts hidden under the mountain snow; No stretching of the robe will cover my shivering shins. I have now returned empty-handed, save the spade, To find my family groaning within a cold and ghastly room. Oh! With this second song, my voice begins to rise: It will make the whole neighborhood sad on my account.

CLVI 3

Brothers I have far away from me, Which of you three thin men is the strong one? We have been rolling apart with no chance of reunion,

*For the road is long and darkened with dust of the Tatar rebellion.
I see the wild geese and then the cranes flying eastward; I wish I
could mount one of them to reach your side. Oh! This third song, I
shall sing thrice. If I die here, will you know where to find my bones?*

CLVII   4

*A sister I have in the District of Chung-li, Who is a widow with young
and weak children. The Huai River is long, and the watery monsters
ill-humored; I cannot expect you to come after ten years of separation.
Can I take a boat and sail to see you? I can visualize only arrows in
the air and war banners in your region. Oh! This fourth song shall be
repeated four times, Until the monkeys in the forest will cry on this
clear day.*

"Leaving T'ung-ku District for Ch'êng-tu on December 24, 759"
[CLVIII] shows that the Tu family was moving once more. They had
no real friends in T'ung-ku. Though our poet was reluctant to leave
the fine scenery, poverty drove him to seek better hospitality elsewhere.
The southward trip to Ch'êng-tu, by way of Hsing-chou, Li-chou,
Chien-chou, Mien-chou, and Han-chou, totaled 503 miles. During the
journey Tu Fu wrote about a dozen poems that reveal a magnificent
landscape along the way; "The Wooden Road of the Flying Immortals'
Ridge" [CLIX] is an example. "Ch'êng-tu City [CLX] written at the destination mentioned the waxing crescent moon. Our poet and his family
must have been traveling fast—mostly downhill—in order to reach
Ch'êng-tu before the very end of December.

CLVIII   LEAVING T'UNG-KU DISTRICT FOR THE CITY OF CH'ÊNG-TU ON
DECEMBER 24, 759

*One of the wisest men left an unblackened hearth; The greatest sage
never sat long enough to warm the mat. How can a hungry, inept man
like me Expect to settle peacefully in one place? When I first came to
these hills, I was pleased to have found a remote place for a long rest.
What can I do with worldly cares that have compelled me to make
Within one year, four long trips! I leave this superb region with regret;
With uncertainty, I now begin a long journey afresh. I halt my horse
to have another look at the clouds above the Dragon Pool; I look several times toward the Tiger Cliff. At the turn of the road, several
men have come to bid us farewell; When I take their hands, my tears
again fall, Not necessarily because of deep and old friendship; It is
easy for a poor old man to feel sad. To meet a lazy, clumsy man's long
desire, This is a hermit's ideal spot, But to remain or to leave is alike
difficult; Shamefully, I envy the birds in the forest.*

Above T'u-mên the climb becomes steep; A mere hairbreadth of a path winds up and up. The boards and railings high among the clouds Are firmly propped and supported on the rocks. Thin woods seem to nestle obliquely in countless gullies; Rushing torrents now and then gleam out of misty shadows. A pale sun fades above the narrow ravine, A long wind howls through it. Only after we have halted at the bottom of the valley, Do we realize we have traversed frightening heights. Coming or going, travelers will sit or lie down for a rest; For both men and horses are exhausted.

For every flitting life there is a fixed lot, Hunger or no hunger, can one really escape it? Sighing, I say to my wife and children, "I should not have followed your advice to take this trip."

CLX   CH'ÊNG-TU CITY

Only a late afternoon sun Glimmers on my traveling clothes. I have traversed different landscapes, And suddenly I have reached a distant corner of the land. From now on, I shall meet many new people; I must not think of seeing my home country ever again.

The Great River flows eastward. As endlessly as the days of my wandering. Within the towering city walls stand many mansions; The trees are green even in late winter. This is a great metropolis much talked about; I can hear the music of various instruments—Even such fine surroundings do not relieve a stranger of loneliness; I turn my gaze to the bridges across the streams.

A crow or a sparrow—each can return to its nest at night; For me, the Central Plains are far and difficult to reach. The waxing crescent moon rises to no great heights; The stars compete with one another in flickering lights. Many of the ancients had to content themselves with exile, Why should I alone grieve?

"Is this life to be finished in Shu?"

The period from the beginning of 760 to August 762 covers Tu Fu's first sojourn in Ch'êng-tu, which was the capital of the area known as I-chou until 742 and as Shu-chün until 758, when, to commemorate the flight of the Brilliant Emperor there in 756–757, the region was promoted to be a prefecture of the first class under the name Ch'êng-tu Fu. Until October 30, 760, the city of Ch'êng-tu bore also the honorary name Southern Capital.

During this period of Tu Fu's sojourn, the prefect of Ch'êng-tu was concurrently the governor general of the Western Section of the Chiennan Department, and as such, he had under his supervision some twenty-odd prefectures and more than one hundred districts. When Tu Fu arrived in Ch'êng-tu, the governor general was P'ei Mien, who had served the government in various capacities and was for a few months after Su-tsung's ascension to the throne one of the highest ministers of state. When Tu Fu reached Fêng-hsiang, P'ei was no longer a state minister, but was serving as an executive of the Executive Division. Before and after court audiences in Fêng-hsiang and Ch'angan, the two men must have met frequently. Although there is no evidence of a close friendship, Tu Fu did express a high opinion of P'ei—in a poem on his approach to Ch'êng-tu, he mentioned that the people of Shu might congratulate themselves for having as their governor general a man of P'ei's prestige and statesmanship. We may take it for granted that, after his arrival at the Southern Capital, Tu Fu would call on P'ei as well as a number of other officials whom he had recognized before as relatives or friends.

Social and ethical codes require that a friend coming from afar and in distress should be given assistance, especially if he is a man with an unblemished reputation and still possessing possibilities of a future rise into power and influence. Tu Fu was exactly such a man. Assistance would generally take three forms: gifts of money to relieve his immediate poverty; recommendations for literary jobs which would bring him some income from time to time; an official employment which would give him a regular salary for maintenance. Of these, the last would seem to be the most difficult to manage in Tu Fu's case. Throughout his life there had been a constant conflict between two desires: the desire to withdraw into the mountains and the woods and the desire to serve his country at court. Poverty and the sense of responsibility towards his family had been the main deterrents of the first. Ill health and the sense of duty to give loyal and frank counsel were handicaps to the second. If a position was to be found for him, it would have to be in an advisory capacity, for neither his health nor his temperament was suited to offices with administrative duties, and it was well-known that in 755 he had refused to enter one, and in 759 had abandoned another.

An advisory position would have to depend on how the advices were appreciated. In Tu Fu's biography in the *New T'ang History* it is said, "He loved to discuss the important issues of the world, but his comments were more high-sounding than practical." As we now read his opinions on current issues against a historical background of causes and consequences, we have come to feel that most of them were both ethically and practically sound. With the possible exception of a very few men, it is doubtful, however, that his contemporaries regarded him as a practical man. At any rate, an advisory position with regular salary in a provincial government had also to be recommended to the throne for appointment. Since His Majesty did not want Tu Fu as an advisor, it would be awkward for a governor general to say, "I wish to have him advise me." So, all that Tu Fu might expect from his friends in Ch'êng-tu would be voluntary donations and occasional literary jobs. Immediately after his arrival, he and his family probably lived in the city on the generosity of friends. The donations must have been handsome, for he planned to obtain some land and build a modest house of his own. And he wisely chose a spot that was near enough to the city so that he and his friends could be within reach and yet far enough in the country so that he might enjoy the life of semi-hermitage amidst quiet and beautiful surroundings.

The plain of Ch'êng-tu is an area of about two hundred square miles to the southeast of a range of permanently snow-capped mountains, and it is therefore slightly higher in the north and the west than in the south and the east. More than a thousand years before the time of our poet, engineers had manipulated the course of the north-south running Min River, making it into a network of streams divided at the north, reunited at the south, and irrigating the plain in between. Neither the present city of Ch'êng-tu nor the irrigating streams in the neighborhood are now the same as they were in the days of Tu Fu. In 879 the city was enlarged to a size about four times that of 760, when it covered about one square mile. At present, one stream runs from west to east through the walled city, and another runs from west to east south of the city. In Tu Fu's time both of those rivers ran south of the city, and both had numerous names. The one nearer the walled city was generally called the Inner River, the Brocade River, the Flower Washing Stream, or the Hundred Flower Water. The one further south was known popularly as the Outer River or the Great River.

It was said that several centuries before Tu Fu's time the city was famous for the beautiful brocades made there and offered to the court as tributes. A "brocade officer" was said to have resided in the city. Hence the city was also called the City of the Brocade Officer, or the Brocade City. Since the brocade was washed in the river, it was called the Brocade River. There was a legend that a certain lady took pity on a Buddhist monk who had fallen into a dirty ditch and offered to wash his soiled clothes in the river. When she did so, one hundred flowers miraculously appeared on the water, hence the name Flower Washing Stream or Hundred Flower Water. I am inclined to think that the term "flower" in the names probably referred to the flowers woven in the brocade; the legend of the lady was, of course, of later origin. A bridge across this stream at a short distance south of the city bore the name Several-Thousand-Mile Bridge; the name was said to have originated in the third century when a member of a farewell party said to his departing friend, "Your journey of several thousand miles is to begin at this bridge."

Possibly only two or three miles west and slightly south of this bridge, the Inner River—or Brocade River, Flower Washing Stream, et cetera— veered around a thinly populated village with a few houses. This was the spot where our poet chose to build a thatched hut. According to his poems, his hut was on the northern bank of the river, both west and south of the bridge, and southwest of the city of Ch'êng-tu. Now in the southwestern neighborhood of the very much enlarged city of Ch'êng-tu, we have a temple to the memory of Tu Fu. According to the records, this temple had been repaired a number of times throughout the centuries, and it has been said to trace its origin to the first one erected in 1090 by Lü Ta-fang (the first scholar to make a chronological study of Tu Fu's life) on the original site of our poet's thatched hut. Since Lü's chronological study is not completely accurate and since the earliest date of the erection of the temple is more than three centuries after Tu Fu's time, it is not too likely that Lü accurately determined the site for the memorial temple.

Of Tu Fu's poems that can plausibly be assigned to 760, after his arrival in Ch'êng-tu, "Written in Answer to Prefect Kao Shih" [CLXI] is very likely the earliest. The T'ang histories have erroneously made Kao first the prefect of Shu-chou and then the prefect of P'êng-chou. A comparison of the poems of both Kao Shih and Tu Fu makes it clear that Kao was the prefect of P'êng-chou from the summer of 759 to probably the winter of 760–761, and then was transferred to Shu-chou. While in P'êng-chou early in 760, Kao heard that Tu Fu had come to Ch'êng-tu, which was only thirty-three miles southeast of P'êng-chou. In his poem "To Reminder Tu Fu" Kao stated that he had heard Tu was living in a Buddhist monastery and was deeply concerned with books. He believed that Tu was quite capable of elucidating the Buddhistic sutra and could not only understand the lectures of the abbot but also participate in the discussions. In the last two lines, he asked Tu, "Now that you have finished writing *The Great Mystery*, what are you going to say next?" *The Great Mystery* is a metaphysical treatise by Yang Hsiung (53 B.C.–A.D. 18), still existent. It is difficult to see what the point of Kao's question was, and none of the commentators have ventured to clear the obscurity. Yang was a native of the region and tradition assigned the neighborhood of Ch'êng-tu as the place where the famous book was written. Could the allusion to Yang be only a casual compliment to Tu? Yang was said to have written the famous book at a time of retirement, when the fortunes of the First Han Dynasty were declining because of the employment of unworthy ministers. I am inclined to think that Kao's last two lines were intended to hint that Tu should soon get over his not wanting to serve the government. If this interpretation is correct, then the last two lines in Tu's answering poem might be understood as equivalent to saying that retirement was not really his best choice and that he would be eager to serve the emperor in some literary capacity, as Yang Hsiung had once served in the Han court.

CLXI   WRITTEN IN ANSWER TO PREFECT KAO SHIH

Only a few monks are left in this old monastery, Which has spare rooms to accommodate sojourners. Old friends share with me part of their salary and rice; Neighbors bring me vegetables from their gardens. Only two trees here remind one of those under which Buddha preached; The three carts I brought are for books, not sutras. How dare I write The Great Mystery? *In literature I might aspire to resemble Yang Hsiung.*

Commentators identify the monastery in question with the Thatched Hut Monastery, said to have originated from pre-T'ang days, and situated very near and to the east of the site of Tu Fu's thatched hut. If this identification is correct, we may assume that soon after his arrival in Ch'êng-tu, our poet and his family moved out of the walled city and lodged themselves temporarily in this monastery while they supervised the construction of the new house. "Choice of Domicile" [CLXII] portrays the locality. "Cousin Wang, the Governor General's Staff Officer, Comes out of the City to See Me and to Bring Me Money for the Construction of My Thatched Hut" [CLXIII] was probably written while Tu Fu was still in the monastery, before the house was completed. We do not know how this cousin was related to our poet, but since a half-sister of Tu Fu's father had married into the Wang family, we may guess, in the absence of other clues, that the young man was her son. "Requesting Police Commissioner Wei Pan to Find for Me a Few Pine Tree Saplings for Planting" [CLXIV] is one of several poems of a similar nature, asking for fruit trees, bamboos, earthenware, and so on from various friends. According to "The Hut Is Completed" [CLXV], it was apparently late spring when the Tu family moved into the new house.

CLXII   CHOICE OF DOMICILE

Along the Flower Washing Stream and crossing it to the west, The master has chosen a quiet spot near the river and among the woods. Out of the city, one is relieved of many worldly entanglements; And here is clear water to dissolve a stranger's sadness. Countless dragonflies are playing in the air, up and down, A pair of wild ducks swim and dive together. To the east, a journey of several thousand miles is possible— If one has the inspiration to take a boat downstream.

CLXIII   COUSIN WANG, THE GOVERNOR GENERAL'S STAFF OFFICER, COMES OUT OF THE CITY TO SEE ME AND TO BRING ME MONEY FOR THE CONSTRUCTION OF MY THATCHED HUT

What an unsettled life awaits a stranger! I was just now feeling lonely and sad by the river. You are kind to come and seek an old man, And help him banish his worries this very day. You are solicitous about my attempt to build a thatched hut; You bring me money across fields and bridges. In this strange land, I have only you, my young cousin, Who would not grudge the distance to come and return.

CLXIV   REQUESTING POLICE COMMISSIONER WEI PAN TO FIND FOR ME A FEW PINE TREE SAPLINGS FOR PLANTING

Willows are never so uniquely towering. Is arbutus as permanently healthy and green? I am imagining the widespread shade a thousand years hence. Please find me a few saplings for planting with several inches of sturdy roots.

My hut, with its back to the city, is now finished and roofed with white thatch, You can reach it by the familiar road along the river and across a green countryside. Sallows keep out the sun and sing with their wind-driven leaves. Giant bamboos condense the mist and drip it with dew drops from their branches. The flying rooks, old and young, have stopped for a temporary perch; The chattering swallows have come again and again to choose a spot for nesting. Someone may indeed by mistake liken this to the house of Yang Hsiung. Yang wrote his famous "Apology." I am too lazy to do so.

Although there is no evidence to confirm it, I am inclined to think that Tu Fu did some sight-seeing during the first few months after his arrival in Ch'êng-tu. "The Temple of Chu-ko Liang" [CLXVI] and "The Lute Terrace in Memory of Ssŭ-ma Hsiang-ju" [CLXVII] are poems on places of historical interest, both in the neighborhood of the western suburb of the city of Ch'êng-tu. Chu-ko Liang (181–234), also familiarly known as Chu-ko K'ung-ming and posthumously honored as the Martial Marquis, came out of his hermitage in Nan-yang to serve his prince Liu Pei, the First Ruler of Shu, only after the latter had personally called upon him three times. With amazing scholarship, statesmanship, diplomatic skill, and military ability, he gave himself unreservedly to the house of Liu under both father and son, the First Ruler and the Second Ruler, and made Shu, if not the most apparently formidable, at least the most plausibly legitimate of the three contending kingdoms—the other two being Wei of the Yellow River valley and Wu of the valley of the lower Yangtze. As prime minister and commander-in-chief, he died while on an expedition against Wei. Tu Fu, like many Chinese scholars, doubtless regarded Chu-ko Liang as the greatest hero of the period of the Three Kingdoms (221–265). The complete trust on the part of the First Ruler and the utter loyalty on the part of the prime minister were more than once alluded to by our poet. We would not be far wrong if we imagine that Tu Fu had hoped for some such relationship between his emperor and such men as Li Pi, Fang Kuan, Chang Hao—and perhaps even himself.

The poem on the Lute Terrace was written in a much lighter vein. Ssŭ-ma Hsiang-ju of the first century B.C. was one of the most celebrated literary men of Shu. Suffering from diabetes, he left the Han court and returned to Shu, where he met Wên-chün, a widowed daughter of the wealthy Cho family. Wên-chün was fond of music, and Hsiang-ju wooed her with a lute melody, the song of which concerned a phoenix returning to seek its mate. The girl visited him at night, they eloped to another locality, and later they bought a wineshop; Wên-chün served wine, and Hsiang-ju washed dishes. The Lute Terrace was doubtless a local monument erected by later busybodies to interest sightseers.

CLXVI THE TEMPLE OF CHU-KO LIANG

Where can I find the temple of Prime Minister Chu-ko Liang? I find it among somber cedars outside the City of the Brocade Officer. Green grass between stone steps expresses only its own spring color; Hidden orioles among the leaves are wasting their pretty songs.

Three visits of the good prince were all concerned with saving the world; Two reigns allowed the great minister to unfold his fine statesmanship. That he should die before his last expedition was crowned with victory Has brought tears to the eyes of great men of succeeding generations.

CLXVII THE LUTE TERRACE IN MEMORY OF SSŬ-MA HSIANG-JU

Ssŭ-ma Hsiang-ju, though a sick man, Still fell in love with Cho Wên-chün. Once the wineshop was a joke upon the world; Now forlorn, dusky clouds hover over the Lute Terrace. Are these wild flowers those she used to dress her hair? Is the color of these weeds the same as that of her silken skirt? But the melody of a phoenix returning to seek its mate Is no longer heard in this deathly quietness.

I have selected a dozen poems [CLXVIII–CLXXIX] to illustrate our poet's life in the village by the Hundred Flower Stream from the late spring to the early autumn of 760. Some of these poems can perhaps be assigned to 761 with equal plausibility, though despite all commentators, "On a Boat" [CLXX] must have been written in 760, for by 761 Ch'êng-tu had ceased to be, as referred to in the poem, the Southern Capital.

Though Tu Fu said that he had become a farmer [CLXVIII, CLXX], he was probably only a gentleman-farmer—albeit a very poor gentleman—with some hired hands to help him. He was in poor health [CLXIX, CLXXII, CLXXIII] and, of course, could not work hard. We may recall that in his memorial to the throne in 754 he had mentioned having trouble with his lungs. The symptoms of what was known in ancient times as lung-illness were generally coughing and asthma [CLXXI]. I am inclined to think that Tu Fu, in our modern terminology, suffered from an allergy. Though he did not specify the medicinal herbs he cultivated in his garden, there might have been ephedra among them, which was known to be helpful in giving temporary relief to coughing and asthma. He must have planted his medicinal herbs in considerable abundance, for two of the poems seem to suggest that some of his visitors bought some from him [CLXXII, CLXXIII].

Among those who visited him, Wu Yü [CLXXIX] and Wei Yen [CLXXV] are of special interest. Wu Yü, we may remember, was the absent host to whom Tu Fu had left a self-accusing, confessional poem [CLI] in Liang-tang in 759. We do not know how Wu had left his place of banishment, T'an-chou, or how he came to be in Ch'êng-tu in 760. As he had issued from the city especially to make a call on Tu Fu, we may reasonably guess that he was eager to absolve our poet from any responsibility for his unjust banishment. Tu Fu had met Wei Yen several times, perhaps in the city of Ch'êng-tu, and had seen him painting pictures of pine trees. In one poem to Wei, he playfully mentioned that he would someday bring the artist a long roll of silk for a tall, straight pine—though this he probably never did. Now, before departing from Ch'êng-tu, the artist had come to the newly built thatched hut to bid our poet farewell, and, as a parting gift, had painted on a plastered wall a pair of horses. Tu Fu must have been delighted indeed. Since his youth he had always been fond of horses, horse-riding, and pictures of horses; and Wei Yen was a famed painter, especially good with equine postures.

Tu Fu and his neighbors also visited back and forth with one another. And it is possible that one of these neighbors saw and liked so much the poem on the wall with Wei Yen's horses that he requested our poet to compose and write another on a scroll of landscape painting by Wang Tsai, which he had hanging in his own house [CLXXVI]. Among these neighbors, the one to the north was a man who had been once a district magistrate [CLXXVII]. We do not know his name. One of the neighbors to the south [CLXXVIII] was, according to another poem, a Mr. Chu. His identity is also difficult to determine. It suffices to note the pleasant atmosphere of cordiality and mutual respect, very evident in these poems.

Thus, though poor in health and in worldly possessions, though frustrated in an official career and still worried over the affairs of the troubled state—and though constantly aware of being a stranger in a distant land, depending mainly on the generosity of friends—here our poet, nevertheless, lived with his family among congenial neighbors and occasionally receiving appreciative callers. He was on the whole happy —perhaps happier now than during most of the years since his marriage and having a family of his own. He would, of course, have preferred to be called back to court and to repeat the early days of 758, for his greatest happiness was in being able to serve his country. If he were to remain unemployed, he might have preferred to take his family to the homestead in Yen-shih, as he expressed three years later in a poem of premature rejoicing [CCXXV]. Now, the one was impossible because the emperor would have no more of his remindings. The other was impossible because the rebels were still occupying the Eastern Capital. Under the circumstances Tu Fu was content with, and grateful for, what Ch'êng-tu could offer him. He was one who was able to make a good deal of life out of very little livelihood. The first few months of his sojourn in Ch'êng-tu perhaps illustrate this point more clearly than any other period.

CLXVIII BECOMING A FARMER

In the Brocade Neighborhood, but beyond the smoke and dust of the city, Our village has less than ten households. The small dislike leaves of the water lotus float upon the river. The light flowers from young barley stalks drop upon the field. In this chosen domicile, I shall grow older and older; The affairs of the country recede further and further from me as a farmer. I regret I cannot follow the footsteps of ancient Ko Hung, Who could be an officer and concoct the elixir of life at the same time.

CLXIX THE RIVER VILLAGE

A curve of the clear stream flows around our village; Everything is pleasant in the river village on a long summer day. The swallows on the beams go and come as they please; The gulls on the water flock together in affection. My good wife draws a chessboard on paper, Our small sons hammer needles into fishing hooks. All that a frequently sick man needs is medicine; What more can a humble person ask?

CLXX ON A BOAT

A stranger expecting to stay long in the Southern Capital has become a farmer of the southern fields, Though he frequently sits by the north window and gazes northward with a broken heart. This morning he leads his good wife to sail in a little boat. Together they watch their children bathing in the clear stream under the bright sun. There the butterflies are fluttering together or chasing one another; Here two lotus blossoms on a single stalk make a perfect pair. Ample tea and sugar-cane juice have been brought from the house. Crude earthenware is just as good as jade pots.

CLXXI A GUEST

My difficulty with breathing is an old ailment. My house over the river is a new choice. It offers not only relief from the noisy city life, But also free and fresh air especially good for me. A guest has come to call at my thatched dwelling, I call my son to help me tie my headgear straight. "These are the tender vegetables that I have planted myself. Let me pluck a few for you as a token of friendship."

CLXXII A VISITOR

Few people come to this quiet dwelling in a secluded place, And a sick old man, leaning on a boy, finds it hard to bow. How can my writings

168

be good enough to startle the world, That you should stop your cart
and horses by the riverside? I shall keep such a fine guest to sit with
me the whole day, I shall offer the coarse rice that has always been a
poor scholar's fare. If you despise not such poor meals in the country,
Please come again whenever you like to see my medicinal plants.

CLXXIII GENERAL CENSOR WEI CAME TO SAY GOOD-BY

A guest on a censor's horse Has come to my thatched hut by the riverside. He has come a long distance to leave money for medicine And to
say he regrets the interruption of our literary fellowship.

Amidst waving banners you came to help the governor general. Leaving, you will travel in a chaise with scented brocade curtains. At times
you should remember the sick old man, Do send some letters to this
rustic place.

CLXXIV SECLUSION

I rise late and inquire if there is any chore to perform; Since there
is none, this place is doubly pleasant. The color of the bamboo mixes
with that of the plain; The reflection of my hut shakes in the running
stream.

Let your children grow lazy with no instruction! Let your wife worry
over long poverty! Your whole life is a drunken dream! For a whole
month you have not combed your hair!

CLXXV WRITTEN ON THE WALL BESIDE THE HORSES PAINTED BY
MR. WEI YEN

Mr. Wei, who comes to say good-by before his departure, Knows that
I love his unrivaled painting. Playfully, he takes up a worn writing
brush, And suddenly marvelous horses appear on my eastern wall. One
is grazing and the other neighing. But both are able to pound a
thousand miles with their hoofs. Oh, in these troublesome times, how
can they become real To serve their master in life and in death!

CLXXVI LINES PLAYFULLY WRITTEN ON A LANDSCAPE PAINTING BY
WANG TSAI

Ten days to draw a river, Five days, a rock. You must know that good
work cannot be hurried, In time Wang Tsai will leave you a real painting Of the marvelous K'un-lun Mountain and Fang-hu Island To hang
on the white wall of your lofty building. From Lake Tung-T'ing near
Pa-ling eastward to Japan, The water between red banks seems to
flow into the Heavenly River Through the vapor, the clouds—and flying dragons too are rising. Here the boatmen and the fishermen are

*turning into a harbor, There mountain trees are bending under waves
of wind. This artist excels even the ancients in the painting of distance;
There must be several thousand miles to a foot. I would like to take a
pair of sharp Ping-chou scissors, Cut down and carry away this half
of the Wu-sung River!*

CLXXVII   OUR NORTHERN NEIGHBOR

*You could hardly have left the magistrate's office on account of years.
It is the desire for hermitage that has led you to retirement. With good
coins, you buy wild bamboos; Wearing a white cloth cap, you are con-
spicuous on the riverside. You are no less a connoisseur of wine than
ancient Shan Chien, And no less a poet than the venerable Ho Hsün.
Two celebrities in one come on foot To visit a sick old man in a
humble hut among weeds!*

CLXXVIII   OUR SOUTHERN NEIGHBOR

*The master of our Brocade Neighborhood wears a sharp-cornered black
cap. He reaps taros and chestnuts from his garden and is not entirely
poor. The children are accustomed to welcome a guest with smiling
faces; Even the birds feel at home when they pick food from the hall-
steps.*

*The autumn water is only four or five feet deep, And the rustic boat
is just big enough for two or three persons. The white sand beach and
the green bamboos of the river village are blurry at dusk; A thin new
moon shines on the wooden gate when we part.*

CLXXIX   AUXILIARY SECRETARY FAN MIAO AND GENERAL CENSOR WU
YÜ CAME ESPECIALLY TO CALL. REGRETTING MY LACK OF HOS-
PITALITY, I SEND THEM THIS POEM.

*I went to a nearby neighbor for a short while; Upon returning, I learned
you two gentlemen had left. The secluded household is really guilty of
inhospitality; But my humble self is overwhelmed with the honor of
your visit.*

*A poor home out in the country might appear far to you; Good visitors
to the village are too few. I can perhaps make bold to discuss literature;
Would you not knock on the shabby wooden gate again?*

With the beginning of autumn in 760, Tu Fu was not merely poor,
but poverty-stricken. Perhaps the gifts of money he had received upon
arrival in Ch'êng-tu had run out. On April 1, the imperial court had
appointed Li Jo-yu to take the place of P'ei Mien as prefect and governor general at Ch'êng-tu. This fellow, who later changed his name to
Li Kuo-chên, was an honest man, though a stubborn and hard master,

lacking somewhat in tact and humor. There is no record that our poet
was previously acquainted with him, and he was not likely to be the
type of person capable of appreciating the talent and humor of Tu Fu.
With the departure of P'ei Mien, and probably of most of P'ei's associates as well, our poet could hardly expect more assistance from the city
of Ch'êng-tu. In "A Mad Man" [CLXXX] he worries about starvation and
thinks of possible help from friends in other cities nearby. In "To Be
Sent to the Prefect of P'êng-chou, Kao Shih . . ." [CLXXXI] he actually
asked his friend for relief.

"One Hundred Worries" [CLXXXII] has generally been assigned to the
autumn of 761. But I am inclined to think that Tu Fu's circumstances
were not so desperate in 761 as they were in the autumn of 760. "The
Autumn Gale Tears off My Thatched Roof" [CLXXXIII], one of the most
widely cited poems of Tu Fu, might have been written in 760 or in 761.
I give preference to 760 because Tu Fu's complaint of his loss of sleep
during several years would be more convincing before he had had a year
and a half of late rising and idleness in the secluded life of the river village. If this dating is correct, the autumn gale will illustrate the prover-
bial truth that a calamity generally strikes one at the worst time. The
poem is famous principally because of its last few lines. A sick man without shelter thinking of solving the housing problem for the whole world
is like a dying soldier on the battlefield dreaming of universal peace.
Such poetry is true to the noblest sentiments of humanity.

CLXXX A MAD MAN

*West of the Several-Thousand-Mile Bridge is my thatched hut. The
Hundred Flower Stream can be any hermit's delight. Every green bamboo caressed by the wind is like a coy maiden; Each blossom of the red
lotus bathed by the rain offers a supply of perfume.*

*No letters have come from friends with ample salaries. Ghastly pale are
the faces of my hungry children. A mad man should be light-hearted
before dying in the gutter; He should even laugh at his being the older
the madder.*

CLXXXI TO BE SENT TO MR. KAO SHIH, THE PREFECT OF P'ÊNG-CHOU, THROUGH THE COURTESY OF GENERAL CENSOR TS'UI

*Half of a life is long gone, And now hunger and cold come with autumn.
Please ask the Prefect of P'êng-chou When he will give some help.*

CLXXXII ONE HUNDRED WORRIES

*I remember I was still childlike at fourteen And was running about as
healthy as a brown calf. When the pears and dates were ripe in the court
in September, I would climb the trees a thousand times a day. Now, before long, I shall reach my fiftieth year; I sit or sleep far more than I*

*stand or walk. Though I try to please the people I call upon with pleas-
antries, I never cease to be sadly conscious of one hundred worries about
my livelihood. Returning to the house, I find the rooms as empty as ever.
The good wife recognizes on my face the usual color of disappointment.
The spoiled children never learn to behave before their father; They
shout and cry for not having found food in the kitchen.*

CLXXXIII   THE AUTUMN GALE TEARS OFF MY THATCHED ROOF

*The madly howling wind of a matured autumn in September Has rolled
off the three layers of thatch on my roof. Most of the stalks flew across
the river and dropped along the bank. Some are caught and entangled in
the treetops; Others tumbled along the ground until they sank into the
hollows. The boys of the southern village take advantage of my age and
infirmity To steal my property before my eyes, To carry openly armfuls
of thatch into the bamboo grove; I shout, I protest until my mouth is
dry and my lips are parched; Then I return to the house, I lean on my
staff, and I sigh.*

*Soon, the wind subsides, and the clouds, ink-black, Cover the autumn
sky to hasten the dark night. The cotton quilt after many years' use is as
cold as an iron sheet And is torn inside because our spoiled children
sleep restlessly and kick their feet. The roof leaks over the bed, and there
is no dry spot. The streaming rain streams like flax fibers without a
break. Since the rebellion, I have lost much sleep; Now I wish a quick
end to such a long and drenching night. Would it be possible to build a
huge house with many millions of rooms To give shelter to the poor
scholars of the whole world, who should all be happy Even in a rain-
storm; for the house should be as unshakable as a mountain? Oh, if I
could only see this house suddenly appear before my eyes, Let my hut
be smashed, let me die alone in exposure and I shall die content.*

"Presented to Prefect Kao Shih" [CLXXXIV] was probably written on
the occasion of Kao's making a trip from P'êng-chou to Ch'êng-tu to visit
the governor general who was his immediate superior in the region. Did
Kao respond to our poet's appeal for help? I would imagine that he did,
though the amount of money sent was probably not large. In a memorial to the throne, Kao had stated that the Shu region was crowded with
refugees from the war-torn Central Plains. When Tu Fu called on Kao
in the city to thank him for the gift, Kao probably informed our poet of
the many demands on his generosity and of his regret for not being able
to do as much as friendship had a right to require of him. Such a scene
might have been the background for the last two lines of Tu Fu's poem.
With nothing more to be expected from Kao it became necessary for
Tu Fu to seek aid elsewhere.

"Leaving Ch'êng-tu for the Ch'ing-ch'êng District, I Sent This to

Messrs. T'ao and Wang, Two Vice-Prefects of Ch'êng-tu" [CLXXXV] has been generally assigned to the late autumn of 761. Ch'ing-ch'êng was about fourteen miles north of Shu-chou, which was fifty miles west and slightly south of Ch'êng-tu. By 761 Kao Shih had become prefect of Shu-chou, of which Ch'ing-ch'êng was a subordinate district. If the trip was made in that year, I would imagine that our poet would visit his old friend the prefect first in Shu-chou, instead of going direct to Ch'ing-ch'êng. I would therefore prefer to date this trip in 760.

We do not know whether from the region of Ch'ing-ch'êng, Tu Fu returned first to Ch'êng-tu before starting out again to the southwestern districts. At any rate, "A Second Poem to Magistrate Wang Ch'ien" [CLXXXVI] places him in the winter of 760 in the District of T'ang-hsing. Tu Fu has a piece of prose, an inscriptional text for a hostel built by Wang Ch'ien, Magistrate of T'ang-hsing, dated September 761. The name T'ang-hsing has puzzled commentators considerably, for there were several districts under that name at different times in the T'ang empire. The nearest they could find was a locality about one hundred miles east of Ch'êng-tu, which had a superceded name, T'ang-hsing. Actually, the right district was T'ang-an, which in 757 was renamed T'ang-hsing and which was only about twenty miles southwest of Ch'êng-tu. The date of the inscriptional text need not oblige us to assign to the winter of 761 this second poem to Wang Ch'ien or the first poem which we shall omit. The second poem complained of rain, but the winter of 761, as we shall find soon, was a dry season, with no rain at all in the area under the jurisdiction of the governor general at Ch'êng-tu. Since the district was not far from Ch'êng-tu, Tu Fu could have gone there again in the autumn of 761. Magistrate Wang Ch'ien was probably one of those from whom our poet had received financial assistance.

CLXXXIV PRESENTED TO PREFECT KAO SHIH

Counting the writers of the age, How many can I find like you? The stallion has really covered distance; The eagle is sure to soar above wind and dust. Your departure will be among the brilliant colors of late autumn. Our friendship is dearer as we grow older. It is a rare joy to meet at this remote edge of the Empire. I deeply appreciate your entire frankness toward me.

CLXXXV LEAVING CH'ÊNG-TU FOR THE CH'ING-CH'ÊNG DISTRICT, I
   SEND THIS TO MESSRS. T'AO AND WANG, TWO VICE-PREFECTS
   OF CH'ÊNG-TU

The burden of worldly cares does not spare even an old man; It is poverty that must account for the dreaded fatigue of my trips. I am now going to a strange district with all the feelings of a stranger, And I can not forget you, friends, especially your poetic moods.

The eastern metropolis is circled within clear rivers; The Western Mountains are capped with glaring snow. What trouble can writing be expected to remedy? I would much rather turn back just to enjoy the whims of poetry.

CLXXXVI A SECOND POEM TO MAGISTRATE WANG CH'IEN

The climate is strange in the Southwest; The cold has been mild since winter began. On what night have there been fewer clouds over the river? The rains in Shu seem never to end! You are kind to inquire about my traveling preparations; Could it mean that a poor man's worries are about to be lightened? Did you hear the cries of a passing wild goose? Such cries might be due to the difficulty of finding food.

As a general portrayal of what Tu Fu saw and how he felt in the spring of 761 in Ch'êng-tu, the following twenty-one short, simple, and often pretty poems are quite self-explanatory. That spring was a wet and flowery season.

CLXXXVII PLEASED WITH RAIN ON A SPRING NIGHT

A nice rain knows when to fall—Coming as a natural product of the spring. Following the wind, it smoothly occupies the night And moistens everything with soft and silent blessings. Dark are the clouds above every country road; There is only one light coming from a slowly moving boat. In the morning I shall see many red and wet patches Of full and heavy flowers everywhere in the City of Brocade.

CLXXXVIII A SPRING FRESHET (TWO POEMS)

I

On the night of March sixteenth a spring freshet rises. In the morning, the water almost covers the sandy beach before my gate. You, cormorants and wild ducks, must not be too happy; Don't you see the danger of flood as well as I do?

CLXXXIX 2

The water rises more than two feet in one night: We shall not be able to stand it in a few days. I know there are boats for sale at the wharf near the southern market; I have not enough money to buy one and tie it to my fence.

CXC CORMORANTS

The cormorants have ceased to come to my front gate. Today, they meet me on the beach with suspicious eyes. From now on, you should know of my good-will; You are welcome a hundred times a day.

CXCI WALKING ALONE AND VISITING THE FLOWERS ON THE RIVERSIDE (SEVEN POEMS)

I

The flowers on the riverside are annoying me without end, For I know of no place to tell of their maddening effect. I went to see Hu-ssŭ Jung, my southern neighbor and drinking mate; He has been out drinking for ten days, and I found only an empty bed.

CXCII   2

Flowers in profusion and confusion enwrap the riverside. I walk staggeringly in real awe of the spring. Fortunately I can yet manage with poetry and wine; Please try not to captivate a white-haired man.

CXCIII   3

A few houses stand where the river is deep and the bamboos are still; But too coquettish are these glowing flowers either red or white. I know my way of requiting the good spring: Some good wine to speed life on its course.

CXCIV   4

I see to the east Ch'êng-tu's flowers are covered with smoke; And the lofty Tower of Hundred Blossoms is more to be pitied. Who can afford to go there to drink wine in golden cups And to call the pretty girls to dance before the luxurious mat?

CXCV   5

East of the river, before Abbot Huang's grave, The spring seems to be weary, and the wind weak. A patch of peach blossoms are free for one to pick. Which shall I have, the pink or the red?

CXCVI   6

In Madame Huang's garden, the flowers crowd out the walks; Thousands upon thousands are pressing the branches low. Playful butterflies now and again stay to dance among them, And orioles accompany them with appropriate notes.

CXCVII   7

Think not that I love flowers at the risk of my life, But I fear I shall age faster after the flowers are gone. Clusters are liable to drop too quickly, Let the tiny buds arrange to open more slowly.

1

You can see that the stranger is lost in his sad dreams, Why must you intrude into this river pavilion, O shameless spring! Even if you must have the flowers open so immodestly, You needn't have the orioles sing such passionate songs.

CXCIX   2

I myself planted these peaches and plums, they are not without an owner; The old rustic's walls may be low, but this is still a private home. It is just like the bully of a spring wind To come in the night and break several blossoming branches!

CC   3

Knowing very well my thatched study is small and low, The swallows of the riverside purposely come often, Carrying mud to soil my lute and my books, And driving the flying insects to strike my face.

CCI   4

March is long spent, and much of April has passed: How many springs can an aging man expect to meet? Well, think not of the endless affairs which you cannot control. Enjoy your limited amount of wine while you can.

CCII   5

It is heartbreaking to realize the spring is about to end on the riverside! I halt my stroll to lean on my staff and view the exuberant beach: Mad catkins of willow dancing with the breeze; Fickle blossoms of the peach drifting with the stream.

CCIII   7

Willow catkins, sprinkling the road, spread a white carpet. Lotus leaves, dotting the stream, form a string of coins. A small pheasant hides from view among the bamboo sprouts, While a few tiny ducklings sleep by their mother on the sand.

CCIV   TOO BAD!

Why must flowers fly away so fast? An aging man wants the spring to go slow. Too bad for these happy occasions Not to find me in my youth!

There should be wine to relieve the mind; There is nothing better than poetry to dispatch the mood. The ancient T'ao Ch'ien could understand this, If I had him here with me.

CCV THE SETTING SUN

*When the setting sun is level with the curtain hooks, Spring on the
riverside is at its best. Sweet fragrance issues from gardens on the shore,
And smoke rises on the beach where the boatmen cook their meals.
Twittering sparrows fall from the branch where they fight to roost;
Flying insects swarm the air above my front court. O turbid wine, even
you are a godsend! One sip will dissolve a thousand worries.*

CCVI MAGISTRATE TS'UI COMES

*Spring rain gathers in pools north and south of my hut. Flocks of gulls
are our only every-day callers. The paths strewn with fallen petals have
not been swept to welcome visitors; The rustic gate is for the first time
this year opened for you. The market is far; we cannot offer more than
this plate of food. We are poor; we have only this pot of old home-brew.
Would you like to drink with a good old neighbor of mine? I'll shout
over the fence for him; he will help us finish the wine.*

CCVII EVENING AFTER THE SHOWER

*A sudden wind over the village in the afternoon Carries a passing rain
to sprinkle the fine garden. Now the setting sun is warming the tender
grass; The sparkling river is in view through the screen.*

*These books are in disorder, I can attend to them later. This cup is
empty, I may as well refill it now. I hear there are some comments about
me; As yet no one has blamed me for my secluded life.*

While he was living in Ch'êng-tu, Tu Fu wrote quite a few poems
containing more or less disguised observations on important events of the
country or the court. We shall choose as an illustration only one, a
poem probably written in the summer of 761 and apparently concerned
with an unhappy occurrence that took place in Ch'ang-an on September 3, 760. Li Fu-kuo, the all-powerful eunuch, used a detachment of
five hundred soldiers with drawn swords to compel the imperial father,
the emperor emeritus, to live in the Western instead of the Southern
Palace. Li's excuse was that he wanted to put to an end the retired
Brilliant Emperor's communicating with public officials who might be
tempted to stage a *coup* for his restoration. Historians have explained
Li's extraordinary act as a case of personal revenge, for he was often
slighted by high dignitaries in the retired emperor's entourage, such as
Kao Li-shih and Ch'ên Hsüan-li, who, once their royal master had been
made practically a prisoner in the Western Palace, could easily be sent
into exile. An imperial tragedy of this order was, of course, difficult to
comment upon without running the danger of lese majesty. The local
mythology of Ch'êng-tu, however, ascribed to the cuckoo a royal origin.

Hence Tu Fu's poem "Cuckoo" [ccviii], and the commentators, with few exceptions, are agreed that our poet was worried about the pitiable plight of the royal master to whom he was deeply attached.

CCVIII CUCKOO

Have you not heard of the ancient Emperor of Shu, Who was transformed into a cuckoo resembling an old rook? He was said to leave his young in a strange nest; These have been fed and reared by rooks till now. Although the old respect due a sovereign is nominally kept, He is condemned to a lonely fate, and his children help him not. Thus he has become skilled in fleeing and hiding amidst thick foliage To utter his cries, in May and in June, every day almost. Such bitter cries must have issued from a mouth full of blood; What is the wrong that is impossible to forget? Is it only the injury that is the cause of anger? Is it the ugly feathers that add to the insult? Under the blue sky, there are changes that none can anticipate. When everything goes wrong, is anything impossible? When everything goes wrong, nothing is impossible; Will it be possible for you to remember the throne and the court?

In the month of June in 761 a short rebellion took place in the Eastern Section of the Chien-nan Department when Tuan Tzŭ-chang, the prefect of Tzŭ-chou and vice-governor general of the Eastern Section, attacked the governor general at Mien-chou and then assumed the imperial title. The governor general, a man named Li Huan, fled to Ch'êng-tu to ask help from the Western Section. In Ch'êng-tu, at this time, the governor general was Ts'ui Kuang-yüan, who had replaced Li Jo-yu. Both Ts'ui and Kao Shih, then prefect of Shu-chou, readily gave military assistance, but the real credit of subduing the rebellion belonged to a subordinate general under Ts'ui, Hua Ching-ting. This bit of history is the background of "A Playful Song concerning My Young Friend General Hua Ching-ting" [ccix].

In a twelfth-century book of anecdotes on poets, it is said that Tu Fu boasted that his poetry could cure malaria. His first prescription was the reading of the last two lines of his first poem entitled "The Ch'iang Village" [lxxxvi]. When the malarial fever persisted, our poet's second prescription was the recitation of the poem about Hua Ching-ting, especially the lines on the decapitated head of the rebel. And the patient got well! This is, of course, only a gossipy legend; Tu Fu of all men would know better than to make such a boast. If poetry of any type could cure malaria, Tu Fu himself would not have been a frequent victim of it. The story, however, has been perpetuated in many books, including Professor Herbert A. Giles's *Dictionary of Chinese Biography*.

Our poet was probably quite well acquainted with General Hua Ching-ting. The quatrain "Presented to My Young Friend General

Hua" [ccx] very likely was written in the summer or autumn of 761. The little poem was subtly advisory: a hint that General Hua had better not indulge in so much luxury. This soldier, though brave, was proud, extravagant, and avaricious. He took Mien-chou and looted it thoroughly. Some of his men even chopped off women's hands in order to rob them of their bracelets. When the outrage was reported to the throne, Emperor Su-tsung dispatched an officer to investigate the responsibility. We do not know what happened to Hua as a result. The chief commander, Governor General Ts'ui Kuang-yüan, was so humiliated, angered, and worried that he became ill and finally died in November.

CCIX A PLAYFUL SONG CONCERNING MY YOUNG FRIEND GENERAL HUA CHING-TING

My young friend, the fierce General Hua of Ch'êng-tu, Is known to babes barely able to babble his name. Like a swift falcon issuing from flying flames, The more enemies he encounters, the faster he destroys them. The vice-governor general at Mien-chou dressed himself in the imperial yellow robe. My young friend swept him away and subdued the rebellion in one day. Bringing with him Tuan Tzŭ-chang's head smeared with blood, He threw it before Governor General Ts'ui as a report of his success. His Excellency Li Huan was able to regain his governorship; And people praised my young friend Hua as unrivaled in the world. Since he is unrivaled in the world, Why should His Majesty not call him to recover Lo-yang?

CCX PRESENTED TO MY YOUNG FRIEND GENERAL HUA

"Pipes and strings are played in profusion daily in the City of Brocade, Half of the music is blown to the river, and half rises to the clouds." Such fine melody is fit to be played only in heaven, Who can expect to hear it in this world many times?

In the autumn of 761 our poet must have again made trips to some of the prefectural and district cities near Ch'êng-tu. His visit to the district city of T'ang-hsing, twenty miles to the southwest of Ch'êng-tu, and to the prefectural city of Shu-chou, fifty miles to the west of Ch'êng-tu, can both be confirmed in his writings. It was probably his second visit to T'ang-hsing; he was there the preceding winter, we may recall. This second visit was the occasion of his composing the inscriptional text for the T'ang-hsing hostel, dated September 761. This was of course at the request of Magistrate Wang Ch'ien, who would certainly reward him with a fee—very likely larger in amount than the earlier monetary gift. From T'ang-hsing, Tu Fu probably traveled northwestward to Shu-chou. There he found his friend Prefect Kao Shih had gone to Ch'êng-tu on official business. But some other friends, Kao's official associates, entertained him splendidly on a boat, while they were supervising the construction of a bamboo bridge—to save travelers from wading in the cold water during the approaching winter. Tu Fu stayed in Shu-chou until after the completion of the bridge and the return of Prefect Kao.

It is possible that he also visited other places. He might have gone again to Ch'ing-ch'êng, only fourteen miles north of Shu-chou. Some of his Ch'ing-ch'êng poems could be assigned to the late autumn of 761 as well as that of 760. He might also have visited Han-chou, thirty-three miles north of Ch'êng-tu. His old friend Fang Kuan—transferred from Chin-chou in September 760—was then the prefect of Han-chou. This will have to remain a guess; there is no confirmation in our poet's extant writings.

There is the long autobiographical poem, "Brave Adventures" [CCXI], which speaks of the old, sick stranger by a hermit's stream in a distant region and of the autumn wind blowing in a mournful ravine. It has been generally assigned to 766. The poem contains, however, no hint of the passing of the two emperors; and the text, moreover, violates the taboo of the personal name of the next emperor—Tai-tsung. We must conclude, therefore, that it was written before 762. Since the hermit's stream must be the Hundred Flower Stream, we have only to choose between the two autumns of 760 and 761. The cryptic maxim about the well-earned glory and the severe frost alludes very likely to the banishment of Chang Hao in May and the humiliation of Ts'ui Kuang-yüan in the autumn of 761—both men having earned prominence by meritorious services in the partial restoration of the empire. The poem, then, was written late in the fall of 761, while Tu Fu was staying in some hills not far from Ch'êng-tu. It is unfortunately not possible to ascertain the precise locality.

In the last four lines, the cryptic mention of a modern Fan Li is not difficult to explain: our poet is here speaking of Li Pi. Though the rebel emperor Shih Ssŭ-ming had been murdered by his son Shih Ch'ao-i, the latter had also assumed the imperial title, and was in control of the Eastern Capital as well as much of the territory of the Northeast. Hence Tu Fu thought that Li Pi's task was not really completed and that Li should come out of retirement again.

CCXI BRAVE ADVENTURES

When I was still in my fourteenth year, I ventured into the arena of letters. Literary masters like Ts'ui Shang and Wei Ch'i-hsin Thought I resembled Pan Ku and Yang Hsiung. In my seventh year my thoughts already concerned heroic deeds; My first song was on the phoenix, the harbinger of a sagacious reign. In my ninth year I began to practice calligraphy in big characters; My writings were enough to fill a bag.

I was temperamental and was already fond of wine, Which was needed to soften an uncompromising hatred of wickedness. I detached myself from the smart alecks, And associated only with the experienced gray-heads. Exhilarated by wine, we cast our glances over the universe; All vulgar worldliness dwindled into oblivion.

When I ended my visit in Su-chou and went further east, I had already made preparations for sailing on the sea. And even to this day, I have regretted That I was not able to explore the islands of Japan. In Su-chou the aristocratic culture of three centuries past is barely remembered; The royal graveyard of a thousand years ago was overgrown, Though the rocky cliff still stood obliquely over Sword Pond, And the famous lotus blossoms of Ch'ang-chou were still fragrant. Standing imposingly, north of the Ch'ang Gate, A memorial temple cast its reflection into a curved pool. Each time I entered to pay respect to Wu T'ai-po, who refused the throne, My grateful tears flowed, for we too had a prince of such brotherly love. I should recall too the vigilant King Kou Chien, who used a lance as a pillow; The tireless First Emperor of Ch'in, who even came south and crossed the Chê; The murderous dagger in the belly of a fish, with which Prince Liao was assassinated; And the hidden seal of Chu Mai-ch'ên, which the petty officials respected. The girls of Yüeh-chou were the fairest in the world. The Mirror Lake was cool even in midsummer. I found inexhaustible beauty along the Yen Gorge; Though I had to end the trip, I could not banish it from my thoughts.

I returned to the North by boat, passing the T'ien-mu Hills on the coast, And in the prime of life I was sent up by my home prefecture for examinations. I feared no rival among competing scholars, Nor any difficult questions that might be put to me. Unfortunately, I was failed by the Bureau of Examinations. I went alone to say good-by to the Prefect of Ching-chao. Then I played and roamed in the regions of Ch'i and Chao, Clothed in fine furs and riding fine horses. In the spring, I sang on the Cluster Terraces; In the winter, I hunted among the Green Mounds. I whistled for the falcons in the Purple Oak Forest; I chased the wild animals on the Cloud and Snow Ridge. I let my horse gallop while I dispatched my arrows; Each stretch of the arm brought down a flying stork or crane. The Honorable Su Yü laughed in his saddle And felt he had suddenly a talented young companion.

More than eight years of lively freedom; And then I returned to the West, to Ching-chao. Those who appreciated me were all literary masters; I was invited to pleasant parties by a truly good prince, And I felt perfectly at home in the hospitable princely mansion. I offered my literary pieces to the Imperial palace. The Emperor immediately sent me a

*summons; I met the high dignitaries in their official ostentation. I left
them with no sense of regret; I drank heavily, and it mattered little
whether I was wanted or not. With unemployment came humiliating
poverty: A grayhead at a feast kept dazedly drinking toasts to others. In
the Tu Village, vacancies occurred in the rank of elders; Graveyard
poplars were everywhere in the neighborhood. To me the clan gave an
honored seat, And I was busy daily with funerals and birthdays among
the village families. This was the period when the powerful indulged in
murder and plunder; By turns, they and their families would also perish.
Military horses exhausted the tax grain; For Imperial fighting cocks,
food had to be collected. These were examples of many extravagances;
Warnings could have been obtained from history about a dynasty's rise
or fall.*

*Wind and dust rose in the northeastern corner of the Empire, And the
Imperial chariot started its long journey to Shu. Then two Courts maintained separately Imperial guards, One looked to the other affectionately
across a long distance. In the region of P'ing-liang, the martial spirit was
intense; In Ch'ang-an, the approach of the Imperial army was often
rumored; For like the ancient Yü, the Imperial father gave the reign to
the Imperial son, Who assumed the chief responsibility of suppressing
the rebellion. The new Imperial headquarters now stood in Fu-fêng
Where our forces were to be to the rebels as tigers to wolves. When the
first strike of the powerful claws unfortunately missed, The Tatar warriors became even more rampant. The heavenly army acted for a second
time carelessly; The wounds we sustained were almost beyond cure.*

*I became an official charged with the responsibility of advising the
Throne; My anxiety and indignation rose high. I was angered by the
rebel's burning the Imperial Temples; I was grieved by the suffering of
our population. At this time I had some important advice for my Sovereign, And I persisted to remonstrate before the Throne. When my
Royal Master was in distress, I must, of course, risk my life. Fortunately
His Majesty's just anger did not injure the great cause. His Majesty was
the embodiment of wisdom and benevolence; The Empire was able to
recover a measure of peace. I participated in the ceremony of lamentation before the ashes of the Imperial Temples; With tears in our eyes we
went again to the Court audience in the palace hall.*

*Now I, His Majesty's humble servant, have no longer any part in Court
discussions, I am only an old, sick stranger in a distant region. The sadness of my frustration resembles That of a winged creature that can no
longer fly. The autumn wind is blowing in this mournful ravine; The
unhappy green orchid can offer only faint fragrance. Chieh Chih-t'ui
wanted no reward for having accompanied the master in exile; Ch'ü*

Yüan's fisherman chose to sing of a hermit's stream. Even a well-earned
glory might not last; To the luxuriant plant winter brings the severe
frost. I believe that our modern Fan Li Is by far the ablest and wisest of
our generation. Many rebels are not yet put to justice, I hope that a
great talent like his will be offered in service again.

Hu-ssŭ Jung, Tu Fu's southern neighbor and drinking friend, we
may recall, was mentioned in one of Tu Fu's poems [cxci] in the spring.
The following poem might have been written in the autumn. Like
Hu-ssŭ, Tu Fu probably also depended on writing for livelihood. Unlike
his friend, he probably would not insist on payment.

CCXII   I LEARN THAT HU-SSŬ JUNG HAS NOT RETURNED

My friend has gone to a southern prefecture, To demand payment for
an inscriptional text. You have depended on writing for livelihood; But
you are the poorer for it. Weeds have overgrown the entrance to your
wooden gate; Even the infrequent cooking smoke from your hearth has
ceased. Become not shameless as you grow old. Come back. If you have
no money, you do not have to drink.

T'ang histories mention that after Ts'ui Kuang-yüan's death Kao Shih
was appointed governor general at Ch'êng-tu and that on July 10, 762,
Yen Wu was appointed to the same position but was not able to proceed to Ch'êng-tu on account of a rebellion blocking the way. From
Tu Fu's poems, it becomes evident that these histories are in error. At
the time of Ts'ui's death, Yen Wu was probably governor general of the
Eastern Section of the Chien-nan Department. He was then appointed
concurrently governor general of the Western Section at Ch'êng-tu. He
even called on our poet in the river village early in the spring of 762. It
was customary that when the governor general was changed there would
also be some changes among the officials immediately associated with
him. "Vice-Prefect Hsü Came to Call" [ccxiii] was very likely written
late in the winter of 761–762. Hsü was probably concurrently one of
the chief staff officers in the army under the command of the governor
general.

CCXIII   VICE-PREFECT HSÜ CAME TO CALL

The staff officer and his subordinates came on horses To this solitary and
remote village in the late afternoon sun. The new friendship will give
me much joy; I am ashamed that my talents are undeserving of your
generous gifts. You enjoy the quietness of these tall bamboos; You walk
in the moonlight on the terrace and forget to return. Will you come
again soon to see these buds Burst into plum blossoms to be mirrored in
the stream?

With his friend Yen Wu as the governor general in Ch'êng-tu, Tu Fu would not need to be so frequently destitute as he had been. He was not officially employed, but we need not doubt that he would frequently advise the able governor general. In his small prose collection there is a short memorandum to Yen. Since the previous November there had been no rain or snow for several months and the drought, it was thought, might ruin the spring planting. Our poet advised the governor general to order a speedy adjudication of all criminal cases throughout the prefectures and districts with the hope that all jails in the area might be emptied of prisoners awaiting trial. According to Confucian traditions, heaven's warnings to a government are expressed in the ominous disorders of the elements; Tu Fu was here merely calling the governor general's attention to the usual interpretation of a drought as heaven's disapproval of some maladministration of justice. We do not know whether Yen acted on this advice, but evidently rain at last came and the crop was probably saved.

"Happy Over Rain" [ccxiv] is generally assigned to the spring of 765. Other poems that surely belong to that period show, however, no evidence of drought in Ch'êng-tu. I would assign the poem to 762. I select also two poems from a set of four quatrains [ccxv–ccxvi] and present them here. They have been assigned to 764 or 765. I feel that 761 or 762 should be preferred.

CCXIV HAPPY OVER RAIN

There has been drought in this southern region—months without rain. This morning, clouds rose from the river, Thickened in the sky, And began to sprinkle. Swallows ceased their flights and returned to their nests. Flowers in the forest now share the same freshness of color. At dusk, the sound of rain continues. I should like to hear it late into the night.

CCXV FOUR QUATRAINS

I

Because of growing bamboo sprouts, I have to open the gate west of the hut; South of the village but north of the ditch, there is a new line of pepper plants. When the plums are ripe, I shall share them with old Mr. Chu; When these pines grow tall, I shall write Mr. Juan about them.

CCXVI 3

Two brown orioles sing among shining willows, While a line of white egrets climb the blue skies. This window holds the snow that for a thousand years has capped the Western Mountains. Beyond my gate are anchored the boats that can sail thousands of miles east to Wu.

184

Tu Fu wrote quite a few poems to, for, and on account of Governor General Yen. I shall select only two.

CCXVII A FARMER URGES ME TO STAY AND DRINK: A POEM IN PRAISE OF GOVERNOR GENERAL YEN

I take a walk in the spring breeze To enjoy the willows and the flowers from one village to another. An old farmer, busily preparing for the Spring Festival, Invites me to join him in tasting his new brew. Drunken, he proceeds to boast of the new Governor, A better governor than he has ever seen or heard. Turning his head and pointing to his eldest son, he says, "This boy is an archer, Belonging to the Flying Cavalry Detachment, And we cannot hope for his discharge for a long time. But two days ago he was released to come home Just to help his old and weak father on the farm. From now on, we shall accept any order for service, Die if we must; such a governor we shall never desert. We are going to have a grand Spring Festival, Can you, Honorable Reminder, stay with us? I shall call my wife to bring out the big jar, Let me pour more wine into big cups for you."

I am deeply touched by the joyous atmosphere Which is the natural result of good government. He is confusingly, repetitiously talkative, And the Governor is never for a moment off his tongue. I came out early in the morning, Now it is late afternoon. Long a stranger, I appreciate friendliness And cannot offend an old neighbor. While he is shouting for fruits and chestnuts, I try to rise, but he forces me down by the elbow. Though rather rude in his insistence, There is nothing bad in the intentions of a farmer, however crude. When the moon is out, he still tries to prevent my departure, And is surprised at my saying I have drunk too much wine.

CCXVIII THANKING GOVERNOR GENERAL YEN FOR THE GIFT OF A BOTTLE OF CREAM LIQUEUR MADE BY THE TAOIST PRIEST OF CH'ING-CH'ÊNG HILLS

A bottle of cream liqueur, coming from the clouds of the hills, Represents your generous sharing of fragrance and flavor. It has been sent by a special fast horse to the hermit fisherman Who now tastes it in a clean cup right before the messenger.

In Ch'ang-an, the court was to experience another crisis in the summer of 762. The Brilliant Emperor Emeritus died on May 3 at the age of seventy-seven. His son Emperor Su-tsung was at the time critically ill, and he too died on May 16 at the age of fifty-one. For the father, death was perhaps a welcome liberation from what was practically a lonely imprisonment. For the unfilial son, the end was even sadder. Having connived at Li Fu-kuo's outrageous *coup* against the imperial father,

185

Emperor Su-tsung found himself more and more in the power of the iniquitous eunuch; his remorse only worsened his ill health. His unscrupulous Empress Chang, who since the Ling-wu days had conspired with Eunuch Li in advancing each other's influence and in alienating the emperor's affection and trust from those they disliked, now found the situation unbearable. A few days before May 16, two conspiracies were in rapid progress—Empress Chang and Eunuch Li were trying to destroy each other by force. Eunuch Li, assisted by Eunuch Ch'êng Yüan-chên, led the palace guards, and this faction managed to seize the palace. The dying emperor was left to expire while his attendants scattered and while Empress Chang and her conspirators were arrested and finally executed. Li Fu-kuo then placed on the throne the crown prince, who is known in history as Emperor Tai-tsung.

It was probably soon after the ascension of the new emperor that Yen Wu was summoned from Ch'êng-tu. Tu Fu wrote "Ten Rhymes to Speed His Excellency Yen's Trip to the Court" [ccxix]; I have used the seventeenth line of this poem as the title for this chapter, for it represents the underlying anxiety of our poet's life in Shu. Now that his friend was going to serve the new emperor, Tu Fu's hope of being called to Ch'ang-an was, of course, revived.

CCXIX TEN RHYMES TO SPEED HIS EXCELLENCY YEN'S TRIP TO THE COURT

While we grieve from afar at the passing of Their Two Majesties, A new reign and a new government have begun in the Capital. The world is still full of trouble, Hence an old servant is remembered and called to the Court. Your statesmanship was well-known in the past When you participated in subduing the rebellion. With eagerness you assisted the Court's return to Ch'ang-an; In a leisurely manner, you gave peace to the frontier. Now, borne by enormous wings, a bird flies out of the South To visit the Polar Star at the North. You will again count the drums of the night-watches while awaiting the audience at dawn, Though the orioles will have ceased to sing for spring in the palace.

Though you leave behind excellent plans for military defense; In your absence, worry will seize the people of the Brocade City. You go by the Wooden Road to the brilliant Court; I stay by the river with the white duckweed blossoms. Is this life to be finished in Shu? If not dead, I might have a chance of returning to Ching-chao. If you become a state minister, Be fearless, regardless of danger.

As a matter of fact, the affection and respect between the two friends were such that the old poet accompanied the young statesman as far as Mien-chou, almost a hundred miles to the northeast, just to see him

186

off. At Mien-chou, they were feasted by Prefect Tu Tsi, who, as we remember, was our poet's uncoöperative cousin of 752. In Mien-chou, Yen Wu wrote quite a good poem in reply to Tu Fu's ten rhymes. Toward the end of the poem, Yen seemed to suggest that Tu Fu might prepare for returning to court. This might mean merely to encourage Tu Fu's own hope expressed in the ten rhymes; it might also contain a hint that Yen would watch for an opportune moment at court to recommend Tu Fu's recall. It is rather strange then to note in "Again to Speed His Excellency Yen: Written at the Fêng-tsi Station" [ccxx] the extremely sad tone of forlorn loneliness at the final parting—no hope of the resumption of official career. There was evidently a change in our poet's mood during the interval between the writings of the ten rhymes and of this poem.

Perhaps, in company with Yen during the several days' trip, punctuated with many farewell feasts and with meeting numerous local officials all eager to cultivate Yen's favors, our poet was enough reminded of the usual characteristics of Chinese officialdom—obsequiousness before the influential and an overbearing attitude toward the less successful—enough reminded to realize once more that he himself would never fit. Yen was his friend, liked and respected him. It is doubtful whether even cousin Tu Tsi shared the same esteem. And, among the crowds seeing Yen off at or beyond Fêng-tsi Station there were likely some who even did not know who the white-haired, sickly man was. We might imagine the scene of "A Young Man" [ccxxi] to be on the veranda of the official hostel of the station. Mistaking our poet to be a servant, the son of one of the officials dismounted from a horse, took a seat, and ordered our poet to pour some wine from a silver flask on the table. It has been generally thought that this incident took place in Tu Fu's thatched hut in Ch'êng-tu. But we are not aware of the thatched hut's having a veranda. It is also unlikely that Tu Fu possessed a silver wine flask.

Being a man with humor, Tu Fu probably did not mind the young chap's ignorance and rudeness. We can imagine his acting the part of a hostel servant, getting up, and pouring the wine for the boy. After the boy was gone, he wrote the quatrain with no sense of resentment at all. It was a trivial matter.

"No Recent News of Li Po" [ccxxii] was, however, no trivial matter. In the presence of the poetry-loving Yen Wu, many of the officials naturally would discuss poetry and poets. And they could not have avoided talking about the famous Li Po, who grew up in the K'uang Hills north of Mien-chou. Gossip could be very uncharitable and mean. Perhaps, even Tu Fu could not defend all of the escapades of his friend Li Po. Hence he pleaded for consideration of the elder poet's extraordinary talents. We can imagine how Tu Fu must have been pained at the thought that Li Po was likely to get into more trouble unless he could shut himself off from such an unforgiving world. Little could Tu Fu have foreseen that Li Po had but a few more months to live; toward the close of the year, Li Po died at Tang-t'u on the lower Yangtze.

Here we may pause a moment to remark on the friendship of these two great poets. They met only during two successive autumns. We have more than a dozen of Tu Fu's poems to Li Po, thinking of Li Po, or mentioning Li Po, distributed over a period of almost twenty years. In most of these poems, Tu Fu's high estimate and deep love of Li Po is impressive. We have two of Li Po's poems to Tu Fu at the beginning of their friendship. It is quite evident that Li Po respected the younger poet, and was fond of him. But after these poems, we know of no more. The apparent one-sidedness in the relationship is perhaps rooted in the fact that the two men were very different. Li Po was essentially an escapist. Tu Fu was at heart a reformer. The escapist would naturally take human relationship more lightly than the reformer. The best reformer will not allow his affection to wane simply because it is not requited.

CCXX AGAIN TO SPEED HIS EXCELLENCY YEN: WRITTEN AT THE FÊNG-TSI STATION

Having accompanied you thus far, I now bid you farewell, While these green hills heartlessly let you depart. When shall we again lift our wine cups together, Or walk in the moonlight as we did last night? All prefectures will combine to love you and sing your praise; Under three reigns, you have served in and out of the Court. I shall now return alone to my river village To end quietly my remaining days.

CCXXI A YOUNG MAN

Whose boy is this fair young man coming on a horse, Who dismounts at the veranda and sits on peoples' chairs? He is rather rude, for without announcing his family or name, He points to a silver wine flask and demands a drink.

CCXXII NO RECENT NEWS OF LI PO

It's long since I have seen Mr. Li. His feigned waywardness is truly deplorable. The world would condemn him to death; I say his genius alone is worthy of esteem. With such quick brilliance manifest in a thousand poems, To remain a vagabond just for a cup of wine! Here are the K'uang Hills where he studied when he was young. He may very well come back, now that he is old.

"Is there after all a place for an old man like me?"

CHAPTER TEN

Tu Fu could scarcely have known that his parting words to Yen Wu, "In your absence worry will seize the people of the Brocade City," would turn out to be a bad omen. But shortly after Tu Fu returned from seeing Yen off, rebellion broke out in Ch'êng-tu. The chief rebel was a General Hsü Chih-tao, who on July 31, 762, proceeded to proclaim himself governor general. There was fighting in the city, and the outbreak evidently spread wide and fast, for Yen Wu was marooned on the road and could not proceed to Ch'ang-an until sometime after September.

After the fighting began, Tu Fu fled to Tzŭ-chou, about one hundred miles to the east, then the seat of the Eastern Section—and he fled so precipitously that he did not have time to take his wife and children with him. Why? Most of the commentators have thought that General Hsü Chih-tao was the same young friend Hsü from whom our poet had asked a few fruit-tree saplings for planting in the spring of 760. If a friend had turned rebel, Tu Fu would be wise to flee before getting involved himself. The reasoning is right, though the identification wrong. Kao Shih, in a memorial to the throne, reported that the rebel Hsü had been vice-prefect of Ch'êng-tu. I am inclined to think, therefore, that Hsü Chih-tao was none other than the new vice-prefect Hsü who had come to call on our poet the preceding winter [CCXIII]. Since this man seemed to have considerable esteem for Tu Fu's talents, it became the more imperative for Tu Fu to slip away before he was sent for. After he had returned to his thatched hut almost two years later, he narrated from memory what had happened during the rebellion [CCXLVII]. As to

189

his own flight to Tzŭ-chou, he barely touched on it in "A Song on Our Fellowship: For Vice-Prefect Yen" [CCXXIII]. This vice-prefect belonged to the very prominent and wealthy Yen family of Tzŭ-chou. The purple and the red robes mentioned in the poem were the costume of those ranked on the official ladder not lower than the twenty-fifth and the seventeenth rungs, respectively. Since the beginning of the An Lu-shan rebellion, however, rank without office was lavishly given to men who helped the imperial cause by fighting or by financial contributions.

"Sent to Be Written on the Wall of My Thatched Hut" [CCXXIV] indicates that our poet was solicitous about the welfare of the four little pines after the whole family had left the thatched hut. Did he send for the family and have them join him in Tzŭ-chou, or did he himself return to Ch'êng-tu and leave again with his family? Did the family leave the thatched hut soon after our poet reached Tzŭ-chou or did the removal occur a couple of months after this? These questions are hard to answer. There is a poem in the collection in which Tu Fu says that he was going east at the end of autumn and was not planning to return to the thatched hut. This might be taken to mean that he had returned to Ch'êng-tu and left it again with his family at the end of autumn. I feel, however, that this poem is spurious. In the first place, the rebellion in Ch'êng-tu was put down before the end of autumn. According to one account, Hsü Chih-tao was killed by one of his subordinates, and the rebellion ended on September 5; according to another document, this event occurred on September 15. Even at the later date, a little more than a month of autumn still remained. What need had Tu Fu to flee Ch'êng-tu after peace and order had largely been restored? In the second place, this poem is weak and the allusions used are not apt. The last lines read, "I am willing to be a stranger for a long time and in a far place; But when will my ambition for service ever be realized?" This sentiment is also strange to the thoughts of our poet at this time. For these reasons, I consider the poem not genuine. I would hypothesize rather that shortly after his arrival in Tzŭ-chou our poet made arrangements to send for his wife and children. They might have been accompanied on their journey by Tu Chan, whom we shall soon meet in another poem. The commentators generally have regarded Tu Chan as the youngest of our poet's half-brothers, but he may have been only a young cousin. Most of the commentators have thought that he lived with our poet in Ch'in-chou and Ch'êng-chou as well as in Ch'êng-tu. It might indeed have been so as far as Ch'êng-tu was concerned.

CCXXIII A SONG ON OUR FELLOWSHIP: FOR VICE-PREFECT YEN

When I traveled toward the Eastern Section, Every few steps, I turned my face to the west. Ch'êng-tu would be desolate after the disorder; Could my thatched hut by the Flower Washing Stream still exist?

Among the heroes of Tzŭ-chou, who is the greatest? The Vice-Prefect has long been famous. You seized my arm, you opened the winepots, you gave me drink. Exhilarated by wine, we danced with the swords and roared like dragons. While my black cap was dusted and my gray donkey was fed, Men in purple robes and red robes brought roasts. The candles on bronze supports burned bright as day.

Late in the night, we began to talk heart to heart. It was at dusk that I knocked on your gate; Hardly had I hoped that we could so soon enter an intimate friendship. Nothing seemed to matter then, And my whole life seemed to be filled with never-ending bliss. With such a fine man to inspire my admiration and to give me comfort, The illness that has caused much distress in my long wandering was then lost; What do I care if in the rest of the whole world I can expect only superficial friendships? Alas! I meet you only in my old age; but it is better late than never; Men like you, one can find only among the ancients.

CCXXIV   SENT TO BE WRITTEN ON THE WALL OF MY THATCHED HUT

My temperament is free and easy, And I am much inclined to live close to nature. I am fond of wine and of the sight of bamboos in the wind; I often choose to dwell near a forest and a spring. War and disorder drove me to the riverside in Shu, A spot suited to seeking a cure for my long illness.

At first, we cleared only a sixth of an acre of weeds; Then, gradually, we used some adjacent ground. We began building the hut more than two years ago; Additions did not stop until this year. I hardly dared to put up an elegant structure, But I felt the foundation was firm and the setting good. The terraces and pavilions followed the contours of the land; The whole site was open and spacious along the clear stream. Though I had appreciative friends, Who frequently went out with me in fishing boats, Yet, since war had not ended, We scarcely dared to indulge in songs or in sound sleep. Like the dragon that settled not in one place, Or the brown crane that soared through the skies, The able and wise men since ancient times Have not allowed their freedom to be restricted by environment. I am, however, only a short-sighted and unwise man, How was I to know that I would come to the present plight?

I am now taking my good wife away, And we shall sadly expose ourselves to wind and mist. The whole thing is, of course, not an absolute necessity, But alas! the choice is to follow my interest or to maintain my character unsullied. I still feel concerned about the four little pines Which might easily be enmeshed and suffocated by the weeds. Their stems are still too slender to guarantee sturdy growth; They need to be long pitied by the neighborhood.

We do not know where in Tzŭ-chou Tu Fu and his family lived. His poems of the autumn and winter of 762 are largely concerned with meeting friends, attending social parties, and sight-seeing. Among the friends in Tzŭ-chou, Li Yü, the Prince of Han-chung, a younger brother of the deceased Prince of Ju-yang, was one whom our poet had known rather intimately when he was a guest of the elder prince. The reunion now must have been a happy one. But the half dozen poems Tu Fu wrote to the prince seem to show more of pleasant familiarity than of profound affection. Much of Tu Fu's sight-seeing was done in the winter and in the neighboring districts along the P'ei River, such as Shê-hung and T'ung-ch'üan, twenty and forty-seven miles southeastward from Tzŭ-chou. In some of the poems on sites of historical interest our poet spoke admiringly of the poetry, calligraphy, and painting of several brilliant men at the court in the early years of the century. But in these fields, he and some of his contemporaries had in reality excelled those earlier masters.

While Tu Fu was thus rather uneventfully occupied in Tzŭ-chou and its neighborhood, two of the worst scoundrels of the time—who had contributed so much misfortune to the T'ang government and so much unhappiness to our poet—came to an end. These were of course, internally, Li Fu-kuo, the eunuch whom our poet had likened once to the rabbit in the moon pounding bitter medicine [LXXIX] and another time to the dirty firefly soiling spotless garments [CXLVI], and, externally, Shih Ch'ao-i, the chief of the many rebels that should be put to justice, if we recall the last lines of our poet's long poem of the preceding fall [CCXI]. For Li Fu-kuo, Nemesis acted with jolly speed. As the result of a daring assassination, Eunuch Li was found one early winter morning dead and without his head; a wooden one had to be fitted to the incomplete corpse for burial.

To bring Shih Ch'ao-i to justice turned out to be, unfortunately, a very painful and costly process. The Prince of Yung, the emperor's eldest son, as commander-in-chief of the imperial army went to meet the Uighur kaghan at Shan-chou, where a joint expedition against the rebel emperor Shih was to be organized. His Majesty the Kaghan was angered by the prince's failure to bow and dance at their meetings in accordance with Chinese court etiquette. Though the prince was forgiven because of his youth—he was then twenty—four of his officers were given severe whippings, and two died as a result. The Chinese-Uighur joint expedition was, however, successful. On November 20, 762, Shih's forces were routed north of Lo-yang. The Eastern Capital was recovered; but the Uighurs were so cruel and avaricious in sacking the city and its neighborhood that innocent people died by the tens of thousands, and for months the survivors had only paper for clothing.

As the imperial and Uighur armies moved eastward, most of the rebel generals surrendered and were appointed by the government as governors general of the territories thus recovered. By February 17, 763, the decapitated head of Shih Ch'ao-i reached Ch'ang-an. Thus ended the rebellion started by An Lu-shan on December 16, 755; the Ho-nan (or south of the river) and Ho-pei (or north of the river) departments were now, formally at least, entirely recovered.

We can imagine Tu Fu's joy when the good news reached him in Tzŭ-chou. "Hearing of the Recovery of Ho-nan and Ho-pei by the Imperial Forces" [CCXXV] has a note at the end which says, "My farm and garden are in the Eastern Capital." This refers very likely to the property he left in Yen-shih. He tells in the poem of his desire to start his journey home in the spring and states the route he planned to follow. He would sail down the P'ei River and the lower section of the Western Han River (now known as the Chia-ling River), altogether a distance of about 223 miles, to the District of Pa (now Chungking); thence about 666 miles down the Yangtze, passing through the gorges of the Wu-shan District of the K'uei-chou Prefecture, to Chiang-ling; thence probably overland 150 miles northward to Hsiang-yang; and thence northward 60 miles overland to Nan-yang and another 215 miles to Lo-yang. That he should think of returning to Yen-shih and not Ch'ang-an might be owing to his eagerness for a reunion with his half-brothers, now that the rebellion was ended and they might also be returning to Yen-shih. Since he had left his official position in Hua-chou, it might be awkward for him to appear in Ch'ang-an without a new appointment. That he was hoping for some new appointment at court might be gathered from the poem "The Orange Orchard" [CCXXVI].

Tu Fu did not, however, take the trip to Lo-yang. It might be that further news about the conditions in Lo-yang and vicinity was such as to crush his hopes of a family reunion in Yen-shih—we find out later on that his half-brothers did not return there. It might be that he did not have enough money for the long trip. When he wrote "Two Swallows" [CCXXVII], he was perhaps hoping that by autumn he and his family might leave Tzŭ-chou.

CCXXV HEARING OF THE RECOVERY OF HO-NAN AND HO-PEI BY THE IMPERIAL FORCES

The sudden news of the recovery of Yu-chou reaches Chien-nan, And causes my tears to sprinkle my gown; I turn to see the sorrow vanishing from the faces of my wife and children; I roll up my books at random, for the joy makes me almost mad. I shall sing loudly in broad sunlight and shall not grudge myself wine; We shall take the beautiful spring as companion on our happy journey home. Let us sail at once through the Gorges of Pa and the Gorges of Wu-shan, Let us thence turn toward Hsiang-yang on our way to Lo-yang.

CCXXVI THE ORANGE ORCHARD

Here on the clear river's bank in the sunshine of the spring Stands a seventy-acre orchard with a thousand orange trees. The thick foliage spreads shade darker than dark clouds; The thick blossoms form a covering whiter than white snow. The fruits will follow the tribute-bearing messengers from this frontier country, Who will take them out of the baskets and place them before His Majesty. The orange ripens indeed long after the peach or the plum; It will be offered at last to the Golden Court.

CCXXVII TWO SWALLOWS

A sojourning family at. dinner is startled to see two swallows, Holding mud in their beaks, fly into this hall. We may indeed share our shelter from inclement weather, And pass together the inconstancies of time.

Like us, you will raise little ones amid wind and dust; Like you, we have come from a long distance. You will be leaving next autumn, if the world exists, We too shall hope to leave this strange place.

Though he did not start as he had planned on his homeward journey, Tu Fu did, however, travel from Tzŭ-chou northwestward forty-three miles to Mien-chou and westward seventy miles to Han-chou, all in the spring of 763. We may recall that his friend Fang Kuan had been the prefect of Han-chou since the autumn of 760. But now Fang Kuan had already left for Ch'ang-an and a new prefect had taken his place. Our poet had a feast with Prefect Wang of Han-chou and Prefect Tu of Mien-chou on a boat on the West Pond which had been created by Fang Kuan. "Taking Mr. Fang's Swans from the Pond" [ccxxviii] contains an allusion to Wang Hsi-chih, the famous calligrapher of the fourth century, who exchanged his handwriting for a number of swans. It seems that our poet considered himself a good calligrapher too; and the poem on Fang's swans, I am inclined to think, was perhaps written either on the wall or the pillar of the pavilion near the pond.

CCXXVIII TAKING MR. FANG'S SWANS FROM THE POND

Near State Minister Fang's West Pavilion, a flock of swans, whiter than clouds, Were swimming in the water or sleeping on the sands. Our minister by the Phoenix Pond might inquire about these; Let him know they have gone with the modern Wang Hsi-chih.

When our poet returned to Tzŭ-chou, he was busy again with many social gatherings during the summer. Among the poems he wrote about these are "Two Playfully Romantic Songs: I have Accompanied Prefect Chang of Tzŭ-chou Several Times on Boating Parties with Singing

Girls" [ccxxix–ccxxx]. Prefect Chang I probably took a liking to Tu Fu and included him in many parties. He might also have helped him financially. Tu Fu must have liked the prefect sufficiently in order to venture the personal advice given at the end of the second song. The poem "On the Occasion" [ccxxxi] might not have been written during this particular outing with Chang, for our poet attended many parties at which singing and dancing girls were present. In the whole collection of his poems, this is, however, the only one that is exclusively given to a female entertainer. I include it here to emphasize one aspect of Tu Fu's life. It has been said that a poet's life is generally made up of three W's: wine, women, and words. It is perhaps so with many poets. It was not so with Tu Fu. His three W's were: worry, wine, and words. Though he had a deep appreciation of beauty, including that of beautiful women, there is no evidence that his relations with women ever went beyond the bounds of social propriety. Apart from a number of very affectionate references to his wife, he left no love poems. He was a man chaste and constant alike in his private and in his public life.

CCXXIX TWO PLAYFULLY ROMANTIC SONGS: I HAVE ACCOMPANIED PREFECT CHANG OF TZŬ-CHOU SEVERAL TIMES ON BOATING PARTIES WITH SINGING GIRLS

I

The eminent guests dismount from their horses and are welcomed By the pretty women who crowd the barges near the shore. Their fans are reflected in the clear river while they sing. Their robes sweep the wide beach as they dance. White sleeves float in pairs on the wind; Shining winepots tip and sway with unseen waves. Behold the bright and smiling faces in competition, Each with the coquettish eyes to kindle the flames of youth!

CCXXX 2

Song and dance have brought down the glaring sun; Still the melodies of the flute pierce the darkening sky. Shining eyebrows move as the choruses are repeated; Broad headdresses almost touching form a line. Yonder the horses are standing with their backs to the thousand hills in the dusk; Here our barges return on a stream filled with perfume. My friend, you have a wife waiting at home; Follow not the example of those pairs of wild drakes and ducks.

CCXXXI ON THE OCCASION

You wear a girdle studded with gems. You have armlets strung with pearls. You smile like a flower before our eyes. A shower of brocades will reward your dance.

In the autumn of 763, our poet went to Lang-chou, 117 miles to the east and slightly north of Tzŭ-chou. The purpose of the trip might have been to visit his old friend Fang Kuan, who, while on the way to a new post in Ch'ang-an, fell sick and finally died on September 15 in a Lang-chou monastery. Once in Lang-chou, Tu Fu was probably urged by Prefect Wang to stay. In Tu Fu's prose collection, there is a memorial to the throne which he drafted for Prefect Wang—probably in October, if we judge by the message contained therein. The Tibetans were troublesome in 763. In the summer the emperor had sent Supreme Censor Li Chih-fang as a peace emissary, but the Tibetans detained him and would not allow him to return. Early in the autumn, they started an invasion. By the first part of September, they had taken the whole of Lung-yu Department. Thence they pressed eastward, and by November 11 they had reached the western borders of the Ching-chao Prefecture. Yet the powerful eunuch, General Ch'êng Yüan-chên, did almost nothing to defend the prefecture or to warn the emperor of impending danger. For fear of courting Ch'êng's anger, none of the generals stationed elsewhere dared to come to the rescue of Ch'ang-an. On November 16, the imperial court fled to Shan-chou. Two days later, the Tibetans took Ch'ang-an.

The memorial Tu Fu wrote for Prefect Wang of Lang-chou stated that the Tibetan invaders had taken Lung-yu and were approaching Hsien-yang, and also that they had seized several of the prefectures in the northwestern corner of Chien-nan, including Sung-chou. The purport of the memorial was to suggest that for economic reasons the two sections of the Department of Chien-nan should be united under one governor general, and that for reasons of prestige and strengthening the tie with the imperial court, the governor general should be a prince of the imperial family. In the first part of the suggestion the opinion was similar to that of Kao Shih. The second part voiced again the advice of Fang Kuan, who had long advocated that the best way to curtail the centrifugal tendencies of militarily powerful governor-generalships was to appoint imperial princes to those positions.

Thanks to this memorial, we can approximate the time of the loss of the several prefectures of Chien-nan to the Tibetans. By March 20, 763, Kao Shih had become the governor general at Ch'êng-tu. When the Tibetans seized Lung-yu, Kao attempted to attack them from the south. His efforts were not successful, and the Tibetans took Sung-chou and other prefectures. This probably happened late in September or early in October. Tu Fu wrote several poems on the military situation in Chiennan at this time, one of which is entitled "Emergency" [ccxxxii]. The text has a note which says, "His Excellency Kao Shih is Governor General of the Western Section of Chien-nan." The poem seems to show a sense of disappointment in Kao, who, we may recall, was governor general of Huai-nan in 757 during the suppression of the rebellion of the Prince of Yung. The Jade Rampart Mountains were to the northwest of Ch'êng-tu. Kao's expeditionary forces were probably encamped in the neighborhood of these mountains.

Neither historical records nor Tu Fu's poem inform us of the cause of Kao Shih's failure. Judging by the intimate friendship between them, I am puzzled to note that Tu Fu did not return to Ch'êng-tu while Kao Shih was governor general there. Could it mean that Kao, considering himself an administrative and military genius, was inclined to regard our poet as too idealistic and impractical? Did our poet write Kao some good advice on the campaign and find Kao to be unreceptive? At any rate, the memorial our poet drafted for Prefect Wang of Lang-chou makes it clear that he was of the opinion that for the safety of the Chiennan Department a change in the governor-generalship was imperative.

CCXXXII EMERGENCY

A celebrated genius, once the governor general of Huai-nan, Now commands our armies with exquisite strategy. The declaration of war has indeed resounded among the Jade Rampart Mountains, But will the seige of Sung-chou ever be raised?

Peace through matrimony has proved a stupid plan; Our princess was lost, not to return. Who has now taken our Kokonor? The western barbarians are like falcons, well-fed and soaring.

While in Lang-chou, Tu Fu met some relatives of his, the eleventh maternal uncle and the twenty-fourth maternal uncle. These gentlemen belonged presumably to the Ts'ui or the Lu clan and they were more likely cousins than brothers of our poet's mother or step-mother. The twenty-fourth maternal uncle was on his way to serve as the magistrate of the Ch'ing-ch'êng District; and the eleventh maternal uncle was evidently a poor poet who accompanied his younger brother or cousin, the magistrate, to Ch'ing-ch'êng. Of the several poems dealing with these gentlemen, we shall choose only "In Reply to My Eleventh Maternal Uncle's 'Regret of Departure' at the Party Given by Prefect Wang of Lang-chou" [ccxxxiii].

Tu Fu was certainly still in Lang-chou on November 2, 763. On that day the funeral of Fang Kuan was held, and our poet wrote a beautiful panegyric which is included in his prose collection. He probably left Lang-chou shortly after the funeral, returning to Tzŭ-chou and his family. "Leaving Lang-chou" [ccxxxiv] tell us that it was a sudden letter from the family concerning the illness of his daughter which brought about his hurried return trip.

CCXXXIII IN REPLY TO MY ELEVENTH MATERNAL UNCLE'S "REGRET
OF DEPARTURE" AT THE PARTY GIVEN BY PREFECT WANG
OF LANG-CHOU

*While the countless ravines are filled with the rustle of trees, And the
autumn colors climb high upon the many cliffs, We leave by a boat
from the outskirts of the city To drink our parting cups on the billows
of the river. Such a fine occasion will not last long; Why must our lives
contain so much hurry?*

*Poverty-stricken almost to the bone, Facing brigands as thick as hair,
My maternal uncle is loath to depart, And the honorable prefect presents
him with a warm robe. I see a yellow crane on the sandy beach at dusk;
Even he cries bitterly when he misses his comrade.*

CCXXXIV LEAVING LANG-CHOU

*There may be poisonous snakes ahead and fierce tigers behind; I have
traveled the whole day along the stream without seeing a single village.
The wind over the river is chilly and the clouds are brushing the earth;
The trees in the hills are haggard, and the rain is about to come.*

*I am hurrying home because my daughter is sick and my wife anxious;
Who can stop to count the autumn flowers among the colored rocks?
Three months I have been away from home, and one letter has come.
When can a refugee be relieved of bitter worries?*

"Farewell to Prefect Lu of Ling-chou" [ccxxxv] was probably written in Tzŭ-chou toward the close of the autumn. Tu Fu's solicitude over
the welfare of his country and his people is very apparent in the advice he gave Prefect Lu. The advice was nothing new, but the failure
to be guided by such wisdom has frequently been the bane of Chinese
officialdom.

Tu Fu himself did not remain in Tzŭ-chou long. From "Farewell to
Acting Governor General Chang I and His Associates, for I Am About
to Leave for the Yangtze Valley" [ccxxxvi] we learn that our poet had
engaged or bought a boat. This was probably in Lang-chou, and he
was now taking his family there with plans to sail down the Western
Han River (now the Chia-ling River). "Song of the Peach-Bamboo
Sticks" [ccxxxvii], written as a gift to Chang I, is intended doubtless
to advise Chang to be less ambitious and more contented with his lot.
Before leaving Tzŭ-chou, however, our poet sent his cousin Tu Chan
back to Ch'êng-tu to look after the thatched hut [ccxxxviii]. Tu Fu
probably intended for this young man to stay in Ch'êng-tu to keep the
thatched hut in good condition.

CCXXXV FAREWELL TO PREFECT LU OF LING-CHOU: HE IS ON THE WAY TO HIS PREFECTURE

The Dynasty recently faced many troubles; Hence all high officials were military men. Since the Northeast has again accepted the Imperial command, Literary men have been employed as governors and prefects. Our country has urgent need of good and wise officials, And you are one of those who are now promoted. With the impressive scepter of a prefect You and your entourage are riding through wind and dust. The world has been shattered by war; The people are sick, the treasuries empty. I know you will ensure the complete integrity of your associates And the complete justice of all burdens laid on the population. It is a joy to see such a fine scholar in a high position, Though I realize I shall end my days in humble mud. The autumn is shaking down the leaves; From the banks of the Great River you may perhaps turn your eyes this way.

CCXXXVI FAREWELL TO ACTING GOVERNOR GENERAL CHANG I AND HIS ASSOCIATES, FOR I AM ABOUT TO LEAVE FOR THE YANGTZE VALLEY

Since I came to Chien-nan, Several years have gone by. Not only have my children grown, But I too have become older and more unsightly. I am frequently afraid that my straightforward simplicity Might lead me to trouble through a cup of wine. Recently I have avoided the company of reckless drinkers—I hope my reform is not too late.

When young, I was like a fish leaping in the stream, Now I am like a dog lost from home. Since I have no real attachment to any place I may visit, What difference does it make whether I leave or stay? From friends I meet—half old and half new—I accept parting gifts, whether generous or not. With surprising luck a boat of the Tung-t'ing Lake Has suddenly dropped into my hand.

It is very gracious of Prefect Chang of Tzŭ-chou To spread a feast high above the tall willows. Before the tower, mounted steeds are stationed; Behind the curtains, many guests are gathered; Strong warriors dance and wave the red banners; Such a joyful party is almost immortal. The sun drives westward to hide behind the K'un-lun Mountains. The dusk brings little birds to chirp near the windows.

I have no fear of rough voyage; Nor will the thundering roars of the Three Gorges give me fright. I am worried only about the multitude of brigands; Twice have high officialdom fled for their lives. News from the Central Plains has been interrupted. Is the Golden Court now in safety or not?

I shall probably go south of the Tung-t'ing Lake among the barbarians, And following the advice of Chuang-tzŭ, accept what comes. Or I may follow the clouds for a visit to the Temple of the East God And then set sail toward the Star of the South Pole. I shall send you letters if I can find messengers. If no messengers, I can at least turn my eyes your way.

CCXXXVII   SONG OF THE PEACH-BAMBOO STICKS

The peach-bamboo grows among rocks in the center of a stream; Only with long nurture by the blue waves will it grow tall enough. The stem is like purple jade after the bark is peeled and the root cut; Neither the goddesses nor the nymphs can succeed in keeping it.

The Prefect of Tzŭ-chou displays a bundle—What a marvel in the hall before all the guests! Because of my age and infirmity, he gives me two sticks; I scratch them, and a metallic sound proves their hardness.

I am now about to travel to the Southeast, And shall pass the City of the White Emperor by K'uei-chou on my boat; There in the dark gorges, the ghosts will surely snatch these; Or perhaps I shall have to defend them with swords from watery monsters.

Let me tell each of you, sticks: "O stick, you have been reared plain and straight. Beware of water and of the temptation to transform yourself into a dragon, Lest you might deprive me of your support, And cause my death while I walk on the blue peak above the Tung-t'ing Lake."

Oh! While wind and dust are prevalent and panthers and tigers prey upon men, Where can I go, if I suddenly lose these two sticks?

CCXXXVIII   A POEM FOR MY BROTHER TU CHAN, WHO RETURNS TO MANAGE THE THATCHED HUT

Long wandering must be my fate. You alone have accompanied me. You know all the shortcuts along the streams; And more than once you have returned to the thatched hut. Be sure to count the ducks and geese every evening; And do not forget to shut the wooden gate. The shade of the bamboo grove on the east is too thin; Plant more, even though the year is late.

The poem "Hills of Pa" [ccxxxix] was written either when Tu Fu and his family were traveling between Tzŭ-chou and Lang-chou, or when they were arriving in Lang-chou, or when Tu Fu was traveling with someone in the neighborhood of Lang-chou. By the term "Hills of Pa" our poet usually refers to the mountainous regions which include the Eastern Section of the Chien-nan Department and certain prefectures of the Shan-nan Department, such as Lang-chou and Pa-chou. The precise locality is thus difficult to ascertain. The time of the poem should be approximately January 764, since it was still winter, and the imperial messenger from Shan-chou was imparting news of the precarious situation of the fugitive court. Our poet was obviously worried about the safety of the emperor, and was wishing that every governor would hasten to His Majesty's aid.

In the meantime, the faithful General Kuo Tzŭ-i emerged from semi-retirement to save the dynasty once more. Starting with only a handful of cavalrymen, he gathered the deserting forces to expel the Tibetans from Ch'ang-an. The wicked eunuch Ch'êng Yüan-chên was banished, and the emperor and his court returned to Ch'ang-an on February 2, 764. The news of these events was not likely to reach Lang-chou before the latter part of February or the first part of March. When our poet wrote five poems on "The Grief of Spring," he had not yet learned of the capital's recovery. But he appended a note to the last poem: "Lang-chou is far and not easily accessible; it was only after writing 'The Grief of Spring' that I heard of the recovery of the capital before spring began." Only two of the five poems [CCXL, CCXLI] are given here.

CCXXXIX   HILLS OF PA

We meet an Imperial messenger who says That he comes from Shan-chou, That the brigands are still rampant, And that His Majesty has not returned to the Capital. Even the trees in Shan-chou must feel cold this winter; What agony to gaze across the vast distance to Ch'ang-an! Amid the distress of the wind and the dust, Where are the many ministers?

CCXL   THE GRIEF OF SPRING (FIVE POEMS)

2

The orioles are speaking the language of the new year. Fresh blossoms are covering the old branches. The wind from the clear sky is rolling the curtain; Under the green grass, water is running into the pond. The Imperial armies are far and scattered—All is disorganized and precarious. Long has my hair been white; Teardrops are as usual on my face. It is not that I have no brothers; But what can I do to avoid separation? The spring colors in the Hills of Pa are quiet; But my gaze wanders toward the north.

CCXLI   3

It seems that the sun and the moon are still against each other. And the stars are repeatedly laying sieges. If a just execution is not carried out, How can the present crisis be turned into safety? The atmosphere of war has enveloped the Throne; The Court has fled the Capital. Mist and dust have darkened the Imperial thoroughfare, And elders try in vain to prevent the exodus. Where His Majesty is, there are no armies, And few of the great generals go to pay respect. Many good men are hiding among butchers and fishermen; Why not ride with them and return to the Capital, O King!

Our poet was, of course, thinking of good men like himself who should be employed to advise the emperor how the enemy might be repulsed and a new government organized. A new appointment did indeed come to Tu Fu, probably soon after he learned of the return of the court to Ch'ang-an—some of his friends doubtless had recommended him to the attention of the government. In a note appended to "Sent as a Farewell Message to Prefect Ma of Pa-chou" [CCXLII], he said, "I am at this time appointed as the Commissioner of Education of the Ching-chao Prefecture . . ."

The poem makes it clear that our poet did not want to accept this appointment, and that, instead of going to Ch'ang-an, he was still planning to sail to the region of the Tung-t'ing Lake. The mention of floating clouds was an allusion to Confucius who said that rank and riches were only like floating clouds to him. The appointment was, as a matter of fact, a promotion. The office of the commissioner of education in Ching-chao was ranked two steps higher than that of Hua-chou, which our poet held five years previously. Since he had never liked the earlier office, he was naturally disinclined to accept the new one.

The two poems entitled "I Remember" [CCXLIII–CCXLIV] show, however, that Tu Fu was not ungrateful for the appointment. But he generally considered himself useful only in an advisory capacity on principles and policies, and he was not interested in the routine duties of a local office, even though the appointment might bring him back to Ch'ang-an. In the second of these poems, he contrasted the miserable plight of the country and the people at this time with the peace and prosperity which he had experienced in his youthful years. Rebellion and war had indeed ruined the country. We may recall that in the third chapter the census of 742 gave the figures 8,525,763 for the number of households and 48,909,800 for the population. In 754, the figures were 9,619,254 and 52,880,488 respectively. What were the figures for 764? There were 2,933,125 households and 16,920,386 persons! The terrible shrinkage in the figures for the population was brought about perhaps less by the actual deaths because of the war than by the continuous displacements and the failure of the census to account for the drifting refugees. But more than two-thirds of the people of the whole empire had become homeless. The spectacle was indeed tragic!

CCXLII SENT AS A FAREWELL MESSAGE TO PREFECT MA OF PA-CHOU

Like ancient Ma Yüan, you have a glorious future in store; As for me, my appointment as Commissioner of Education will benefit none. I have a boat long anchored near the sandy beach, And I am thinking of the many floating clouds above the waters of the South. Taking a fishing rod, I shall finally sail far away; And I regret I cannot fly like a bird to make you a visit. I know you are not attracted by the hues of the spring lake, For you are thinking of a glorious ride to an early Court audience.

CCXLIII   I REMEMBER (TWO POEMS)

I

I remember how the last Emperor went to Ling-wu, And how he re-entered Hsien-yang with hundreds of chariots and thousands of cavalry-men, And how he had the proud Uighurs on marvelous horses Drive the eastern Tatars to flee and hide. Our sudden reverses at Yeh were really not so serious as The misdeeds of Eunuch Li Fu-kuo, breaking all moral bounds, Or the displeasures of Empress Chang, sufficient to make the Emperor distracted.

Even now, the present Emperor has to worry and toil With inherited troubles that need correction on every side. I was once an officer in close attendance, And I watched him lead the army with solemn invincibility. Just because a great warrior was kept in semiretirement in Ch'ang-an, All prefectures to the west became vulnerable to the western barbarians, Who came straight away to sit upon the Imperial throne, While our officials fled barefooted with our Sovereign. The Empire now needs men like the ancient Fu Chieh-tzŭ to behead the enemy king; No official appointment need be given an old bookworn like me.

CCXLIV   2

I remember that in the glorious decades, a quarter of a century ago, Even a small district might contain ten thousand households, And the glu-tinous rice was fat and the ordinary rice white, And how they filled up the granaries both public and private! No panthers or tigers paced the roads of the Empire; Distant travelers never worried whether the day was lucky or not. The fine fabrics of Ch'i and Lu could be seen on long lines of merchants' carts; Men plowed the fields; women tended the silk-worms; all were happy at work. Our Brilliant Emperor stayed in his palace to enjoy good music, While the whole world was a solid friend-ship. Then, for over a century, people had no reports of calamities; They had the best law and practiced the best etiquette. Who ever heard of a roll of silk priced at ten thousand coins, Or of people abandoning their farms for bloodshed?

The palaces in Lo-yang were sometime ago reduced to ashes, The temples in Ch'ang-an were only recently rid of foxes and rabbits.

It will hurt only more if we inquire of the experienced elders; They might recount the war and the displacement from the outset. As a humble servant, I can do nothing and am not clever; But I am still remembered and given a rank and a salary by the Court. I hope my Sovereign will rebuild the Empire like the renaissance of Chou, Though I remain ill on the banks of the Western Han and can only weep.

Tu Fu's plan to sail down the Western Han did not become fact. On February 11, 764, Chancellor Yen Wu was appointed governor general of the whole Chien-nan Department. "To Present to His Excellency Yen upon His Arrival" [CCXLV] shows that it was the news of Yen's coming again that brought our poet to cancel his contemplated trip to the south. After a parting ceremony at the grave of Fang Kuan, he took his wife and children overland back to Ch'êng-tu. "Return in the Spring" [CCXLVI], "The Thatched Hut" [CCXLVII], and "Reminding Secretary General Wang of His Promise to Send Money for the Repair of My Thatched Hut" [CCXLVIII] indicate the condition of his old dwelling and his feelings of homecoming.

CCXLV TO PRESENT TO HIS EXCELLENCY YEN UPON HIS ARRIVAL

I rejoice at my friend's return to this distant region; This important department requires just such a talented statesman. Frequently have I marveled at your subordinate generals' earnest expectation, How surprisingly good that it is realized in one year's time! I was about to leave these Hills of Pa amidst the songs of the orioles To proceed to Chiang-ling on a boat that has long been waiting. But I crave to see you because the times are critical and I am old; To whom else am I to confide the deepest aspirations of my life?

CCXLVI RETURN IN THE SPRING

A moss-covered path leads through the bamboos to the river; A border of flowers grows under the wide eaves of the thatched hall. After many months of absence, I have returned at the height of spring. Leaning on my cane, I examine a solitary rock; Carrying the winepot, I come to drink on the sandy beach. While the gulls are swimming quietly in the distance, The swallows here are flying unsteadily in the wind. The ways of the world are indeed full of obstructions; But the span of one's life has also a limit. If I become sober, I can drink again; So long as I am exhilarated, this is home.

CCXLVII THE THATCHED HUT

When I left the thatched hut, The barbarians filled the city of Ch'êng-tu. Now I have returned to the thatched hut, Because Ch'êng-tu is no longer unquiet.

Let me tell from the beginning of the outbreak How the upheaval was sudden and unexpected. After the commanding general left for the Court, Mischievous underlings started to conspire in a strange plot. A white horse was killed at midnight, And they roughly sealed their oath of alliance with its blood. Some went west to commandeer the armies south of Chiung-chou; Some went north to cut off the wooden road near Chien-chou. A few dozen wretched nonenities Assumed responsible positions in important cities. It was only when rivalries arose among them That the Chinese and the barbarians parted company. The western soldiers started a mutiny, And rebel chiefs proceeded to slaughter one another. Who could have foreseen that the internal quarrels among These beasts would end in their mutual destruction?

All good men were angered and grieved, For law and discipline were no longer observed. A plurality of leadership in a single area Was enough to submerge the population in suffering. Among the subordinates who fanned terrorism, There was none that heeded the innocent. They emerged to apply the implements of torture; They retired to enjoy playing music. They ordered massacre as they chatted and laughed; Blood overran the long streets. Even now in a storm you can hear wails and groans From the places where the executioners swung their axes. The women and the horses of the murdered Were forlorn property for the pleasure of the murderers. What had become of the law and order of the empire? The lawlessness was enough to strike fear in a man and make him grieve.

The only thing I could do then was to flee, And for three years I cast a longing eye toward the Southeastern Coast. Bows and arrows darkened the lower Yangtze, It was hard to decide on a visit to the Five Lakes. Since I find it difficult to abandon this place, I have come back to clear the weeds. Entering the gate, I am pleased to see again my four pines; Wearing sandals, I walk through the thin bamboo grove. My old dog is happy at my return; He disappears fawningly under the skirts of my gown. My neighbors are happy at my return; They bought wine and brought me many bottles of it. The great Governor General is happy at my coming; He sends a mounted messenger to inquire my need. Indeed, the whole city seems to be happy at my coming; Visitors and guests over-crowd this village.

The world has not yet found peace; Strong soldiers are to be preferred to useless scholars. But amid the uncertainties of winds and dusts, Is there after all a place for an old man like me? I know well now I am only a parasite; But this frail body is not yet dead. Food and drink for the little balance of life, I know I deserve not; I shall therefore relish even the worst and be content.

*I should be angry with you, Secretary General Wang, For not sending
the money for the repair of my thatched hut. Yesterday you wrote me to
be careful during the rainy spring weather; Could you possibly have
forgotten that the roof would leak?*

Tu Fu was not concerned merely with his own problems of living and
dwelling. "On the Tower" [CCXLIX] was probably written in the city of
Ch'êng-tu on one of his visits to Governor General Yen Wu. Tu Fu was
still concerned about the troubles of the empire, especially the Tibetan
occupation of the Western Mountains and the several prefectures to the
northwest. As he saw from the tower the Temple to the First Ruler of
Shu, he was again reminded of the great minister Chu-ko Liang, upon
whom the Second Ruler of Shu, though a weakling, knew enough to
rely for the protection of the country. Our poet was thinking of his own
time and the need of able men to resist the threat of the Tibetans upon
the empire.

Yen Wu was, in his mind, such a man, and Tu Fu was willing to help
him. Yen, however, had not only ability but also serious faults. Commentators generally have guessed that the poem "The Gift of a Satin-
Brocade Coverlet by Crown Prince's Assistant Secretary Chang" [CCL]
was written really as a warning to Yen. The poem cites the deaths of
Li Ting and Lai T'ien. The latter, a brave warrior, nicknamed The Iron-
chewer, was once governor general of the Eastern Section of the Shan-
nan Department and had rendered distinguished military services to the
empire. He aroused the suspicion of the court by his arrogance and was
ordered to commit suicide in 763. Li Ting was in 761 appointed governor
general of Lung-yu. There is no historical record of his end, and we owe
to Tu Fu the knowledge of his death at Ch'i-yang and its cause. Our
poet dwelt rather emphatically on the dangers of pride and extravagance.
These might indeed have been two of the faults of Yen Wu.

Some writers have described Yen Wu's character unfavorably. It was
said that at the age of seven, angered at his father's preferring the company of a young concubine to that of his mother, he murdered the
younger woman by smashing her head with a hammer, and defended his
crime by rebuking his father.

It was said that when he was a young man, he eloped with the beautiful daughter of an important military officer. Pursued by imperial
officials, he strangled the girl and threw her body in a river in order to
erase the evidence of the elopement. According to the story, it was her
ghost that brought about his sudden death years later.

It was said too that though he owed his early commencement of an
official career to the patronage of Fang Kuan, he was later guilty of

ingratitude by treating old Fang with overbearing discourtesy when Fang, as prefect of Han-chou, was subordinate to him as the supervisory governor general.

It was even said that Yen Wu almost murdered Tu Fu, his father's friend and his own faithful advisor. The story, in slightly varying versions, traced his resentment of our poet to a drunken scene. An intoxicated Tu Fu climbed to Yen's bed, stared at the governor general, and said, "It is surprising that Yen T'ing-chih had such a son." It was a breach of etiquette to mention the father's name before the son, and Yen never forgave Tu Fu. One day he was about to have Tu Fu and Prefect Chang I of Tzŭ-chou both flogged to death. His mother interfered, and our poet was saved. Prefect Chang I alone perished. It was said that this estimable lady lived in constant dread of trouble because of Yen's arrogance, extravagance, and unruly temper. She felt relieved at the governor general's death in 765 when he was only thirty-nine.

How much of these stories about Yen Wu should be believed is a problem. That the wise, fair, and kindly Tu Fu should associate so intimately with such a brutal man is unthinkable. That even after Yen's death Tu Fu still remembered him with admiration, affection, and gratitude has caused most students of Tu Fu to discredit the story of Yen's attempt to kill our poet. When and how Chang I ended is a mystery. The poems Tu Fu wrote to Chang I give us a glimpse of Chang's unstable character. It is not impossible that Yen might have had just cause to rid the empire of a would-be rebel. Among T'ang anecdotes there is a note to the effect that Chang I's family felt an enormous enmity against Yen and did everything they could to damage his reputation. Were the malicious stories about Yen mainly the result of a revengeful effort to smear Yen's memory? On the other hand, it is not difficult to believe that a brilliant young man, rising early into power and success, might have been an easy victim of the temptations of pride and extravagance. One of the duties of a friend is to give needed advice. Tu Fu, in the poem on the brocade coverlet, certainly did so in a clear though indirect and inoffensive manner.

CCXLIX   ON THE TOWER

The flowers near the high tower sadden a visitor's heart; I climb here at a time when the world is seething with trouble. The spring colors of the Brocade River are a gift of creation; The unsteady clouds over the Jade Rampart symbolize the changes of history. The Heavenly Court in the north is at last firm in its place; Let the brigands beyond the Western Mountains cease their invasion. I can sympathize with the inclusion of the Second Ruler in that temple; As the sun goes down, I shall hum one of the songs of Chu-ko Liang.

*My honored guest comes from the Northwest And presents me with a
length of shining brocade. Opening the package, I look upon seething
waves of the sea, And among them a whale with a sweeping tail. Other
marine creatures swim at a distance, Too small for me to name. "For
your cushion," my guest says. "Sit on it to enjoy a glorious feast; Sleep
on it to have a dreamless rest; Display it in the hall, and all demons will
be suppressed."*

*My guest's kindness I do appreciate. But since I am not one of the high-
est ministers, It will not be propitious for me to accept such a gift, And
to use it in such a humble dwelling is hardly appropriate. It is a great
law since the remote past That articles of adornment are graded according to rank. Now, as only a humble old man, I should be satisfied with
plain clothing, even the plainest. Such an exquisite article fit only for
the Imperial palace Will surely bring me trouble if I use it. I am surprised indeed that so many of our important men, In these times of incessant wars, Took advantage of the power in hand To provide themselves with the finest clothing and the best horses. Li Ting perished in
Ch'i-yang Because of his excessive self-conceit. Lai T'ien was ordered to
commit suicide Because his arrogance was a hindrance to military success. Both were said to be immensely rich; No wonder their regrettable
end could not have been avoided.*

*How then can an ordinary old farmer Dare to accept such a generous
gift? Let me roll up this whale-brocade and return it to you, And I shall
then feel myself at ease. Let me dust my coarse mat; please take a seat;
I am really embarrassed to offer you this thin vegetable soup.*

"His Excellency Yen Comes in Midsummer and Brings a Feast to the
Thatched Hut" [ccli] might concern Tu Fu's appointment in 764 as
Yen's military advisor, though most commentators place the poem in 762.
In 762, however, this feast would have occurred only a few weeks after
the deaths of the Brilliant Emperor and Emperor Su-tsung, and it would
have been inappropriate alike for Yen Wu and Tu Fu, both having been
close attendants at court, to indulge in pleasurable feasting open to the
view of the public. The poem fits better with the events of 764, and the
mention of messengers doubtless referred to Yen's repeated efforts to
induce our poet to accept a formal appointment at the general headquarters of the governor general. It might indeed have been the exalted
governor general's visit that finally persuaded Tu Fu to accept the appointment as a military advisor. There is a poem on a military review
which has a note that would date it somewhere between July 4 and

August 1. On its account, biographers of Tu Fu generally placed Tu Fu's beginning of official service with Yen Wu in July. I am, however, inclined to think that it might be in June.

The position of a military advisor at the general headquarters of a department calls for an official ranking at court. In response to a memorial from Yen Wu, the court conferred upon our poet the title of Consultant Auxiliary Secretary of the Ministry of Public Works. This would place Tu Fu on the fourteenth rung of the thirty-step official ladder. Since An Lu-shan's rebellion the old system of salaries and land-grants according to ranking had fallen into disuse. On August 6, 764, the practice began of taxing farms to furnish money for the salaries of officials. We do not know how these salaries were then distributed. But as a consultant, and therefore a rather nominal official, our poet would hardly be entitled to such money. As an official attached to the general headquarters of the governor general, however, he would doubtless receive some remuneration—we know nothing of the amount.

As an official of the fourteenth step, Tu Fu was entitled to wear official robes in green. But he was granted the privilege of wearing the red robe with the red bag containing the silver fish-tally which were the decorative honor of officials from the seventeenth to the twenty-fourth step. This honor was given our poet without a change in his ranking status. It might have come to him in the autumn as a reward for his part in the victories over the Tibetans achieved by Yen Wu, upon whom was conferred the title Duke of Chêng.

As a military advisor, our poet must have given the governor general many memoranda on the expeditions against the Tibetans. There is one in the present prose collection which possibly was written during the early days of Tu Fu's formal connection with the general headquarters. Here our poet said that the failures of the past were economic rather than military. Owing to the corruption of local officials there was insufficient food for the armies. He advocated better treatment and use of the semi-aboriginal chieftains with a view to increasing agricultural production and decreasing the exploitation of the poor by the rich.

Tu Fu's official duties necessitated his staying in the city of Ch'êng-tu a good deal of the time. He probably met the old painter Ts'ao Pa, upon whose work he wrote two poems, in the home of a friend in the city. We shall quote the more famous poem [CCLII] of the two.

The several poems Tu Fu wrote at the general headquarters all contain a tone of sadness. The saddest piece is "Overnight at the General Headquarters" [CCLIII], which portrays our poet muttering alone in the moonlight under the wu-t'ung trees (varyingly identified as *Aleurites cordata* or *Sterculia plantanifolia*). One of the causes of his unhappiness was his consciousness of the jealousy of some of the younger associates in Yen Wu's service. In "Suspect Me Not" [CCLIV] he shows his sensitiveness to the murmurs behind his back. There is another poem which says at the end:

An old man should not feel angry with youths; He should recall Chu-ko Liang's essay on "Peace." A great man lives for immortal fame; It is not for him to remember petty offenses.

Tu Fu went further than forbearance. In his "Twenty Rhymes to Dispel Gloom: Presented to His Excellency Yen" [CCLV] he blamed himself for his age, for his infirmity, and for his failure to achieve harmony among his associates. He begged the governor general to let him spend more of his time in his thatched hut in the country. Probably Governor General Yen did grant him more sick-leaves from office, for we find quite a number of his poems written in the late autumn and the winter, all in the river village. Among these are "It Rains While I Am in the Village" [CCLVI] and "Sleepless Night" [CCLVII]. Freshly washed pines, bamboos, and chrysanthemums could indeed be comforting to the eye; but even they could not relieve the sleepless nights of disappointments, worry and nostalgia.

And, it should also be mentioned, Tu Fu was very much saddened in 764 over the death of some of his closest friends. Both Professor Chêng Ch'ien and Dean Su Yü (renamed Su Yüan-ming since 762), his drinking companions and inspiring mentors of early years, died in this same year—the former having never been recalled from banishment. Tu Fu found that even his southern neighbor and drinking friend, Hu-ssŭ Jung, was no more; in the empty house was only an abandoned coffin-curtain, swinging in the chilly autumn wind. Perhaps, he was too much in a troubled and mournful mood to be able to write a poem of welcome to his half-brother Tu Ying, who came from faraway Ch'i-chou to make him a short visit. Only three affectionate and sad poems exist, all under the title "Farewell to My Brother Tu Ying on His Return to Ch'i-chou"; in one of these [CCLVIII] Tu Fu recalls the whereabouts of some of his scattered relatives. The other two half-brothers he refers to were Tu Fêng and Tu Kuan. They will be mentioned again in the next chapter.

Though spending much of his time in the village, Tu Fu, as a military advisor of the general headquarters, nevertheless had duties to which he had to return now and then. In one of the poems written early in the winter, he describes himself as "an oldish man in a tight military uniform" and as one torn between the urge to serve and the desire to retire. In "Return to the Riverside on January Twenty-eighth: Presented to the Gentlemen of the General Headquarters" [CCLIX], however, he was announcing that since the early arriving spring was so enjoyable, the learned colleagues need not often expect the presence of the white-haired man at the general headquarters. This poem might have been intended to placate the jealousy and suspicion on the part of some of his younger colleagues.

"The Mocking Bird" [CCLX] and "The Spotted Duck" [CCLXI], though generally assigned to other years, seem to fit better this resigned mood of Tu Fu in the spring of 765, while he was in the river village, rarely going, if at all, to the general headquarters. Would the tongue of the mocking bird cease to be active? At any rate, the spotted duck with clear distinction between white and black has resolved not to quack first. It is still not clear whether the outspokenness of the poetic staff-officer concerns poetry or military policies or both. A collection of six quatrains in which Tu Fu undertook to defend master poets of the past against the scoffing of ambitious upstarts, if written in 764 or 765, might indeed have been a cause or a result of the quarrel over poetry and the mockings behind our poet's back.

There was little likelihood that either the mocking or the quacks would cease completely. But, while our poet was busy in the river village, repairing his thatched hut and clearing his garden of weeds, he did have moments of comforting reflection. Here in the hospitable neighborhood and pleasant surroundings he planned to retire with his recently received official honors, for which he was grateful to the governor general who befriended him and to those colleagues who tolerated him. Some of these thoughts are clearly manifest in two [CCLXII–CCLXIII] of the "Five Poems of Springtime in the River Village." The Stone Mirror, alluded to in the first of the two poems, was a locality in the neighborhood of the city of Ch'êng-tu, where a large stone slab was said to be a monument of the grave of a mythological queen. Our poet's allusion hints at the impermanence of human glory.

CCLI HIS EXCELLENCY YEN COMES IN MIDSUMMER AND BRINGS A FEAST TO THE THATCHED HUT

The shining dishes are washed in the temporary kitchen among the bamboos; And the brightly saddled horses are tethered by the flower plots. It is not that I meant to ignore the urgent summons of your messengers, But because I know the great Governor General is tolerant of ceremonial breaches. Now you have come to my humble dwelling in this remote village, In midsummer when the river is deep and the thatched building cool. We will sport with a fishing boat until the sun is gone. What more can an old farmer offer to deserve such friendship?

CCLII ON PAINTING. TO GENERAL TS'AO PA

The General is a descendant of Ts'ao Ts'ao, founder of the Wei Dynasty, Though he is now only a private person of a respectable family. Territorial occupation and heroic exploits are matters of past history, But the brilliant culture has been handed down to this day. The General early

practiced calligraphy after the style of the ancient Madame Wei; His regret is not to have surpassed her pupil, Wang Hsi-chih. Painting and painting, he has forgotten that he is growing old; Prominence and riches are to him but floating clouds.

A quarter of a century ago, he was frequently brought before the Brilliant Emperor; Many a time he was graciously summoned to the Southern Fragrance Hall. The weather-worn portraits of great ministers on the walls of the Super-Cloud Tower Were given a new vividness by the General's retouching brush. You can recognize the state ministers by their high hats. You know the great generals by the huge plumed arrows hanging from their belts. The hair of Marshals Tuan Chih-yüan and Yü-ch'ih Ching-tê shimmers; Their brave faces express thoughts of fierce battle.

The Brilliant Emperor's favorite horse, the Jade Flower Piebald—Which had been differently painted by a host of painters—Was one day brought to stand before the steps of the audience hall. He still suggested the flying wind as he passed the palace gate. At the Imperial command, our General opened a roll of white silk And put his thought and skill to the task of painting. Within moments the true likeness of the Imperial possession appeared To put all horses of all times to shame. Then suddenly the Jade Flower Piebald ascended the throne—Exact duplicates on the throne and before the hall steps! His Majesty smiled and ordered a speedy gift of money; The officers of the Imperial stables were excited and moved.

The General's pupil Han Kan learned early to master the art And could also paint horses with amazing likeness. But Han portrayed more of the flesh than of bones And did not care if this was to the finest steeds an injustice.

The General's skill lies in his grasp of the spirit; When he meets good men, he will also paint portraits. Now that he is among the displaced of the wars, He often seeks models among ordinary travelers. In his distress, he has indeed been frowned upon by the vulgar; For in the whole world there is none so poor as he is now. But he might be reminded of some of the celebrated men of the past Who met frustration every day in their lives.

CCLIII   OVERNIGHT AT THE GENERAL HEADQUARTERS

In the General Headquarters in the city, I spend the night alone, The candle burns low and the clear autumn chills the wu-t'ung trees in the yard. Only the sound of bugles answers my mutterings throughout the night, Who else is watching the delicate color of the moon in the sky?

These unsettled times have continued and word from the home country has stopped; The road through the frontier pass is desolate and travel is hard. For ten years I have endured displacement. Like a bird on a branch, I roost here temporarily with misgivings and with gratitude.

CCLIV   SUSPECT ME NOT

A man accomplishes nothing while his hair grows white. And his teeth are almost all out. The pity of it! I remember when the three *fu* were offered to the Imperial palace, I was startled to find myself instantly famous. The chief officers of the Academy of Talents stood like a surrounding wall In the Hall of the Secretarial Division to watch me write.

In those days, my works could move an emperor; Now I am on a by-path, driven by hunger and thirst—A man in his late years seeking the friendship of youths Who praise him to his face but ridicule him behind his back. Here is a word of apology to all of you, boys of the smart world: "I intend no rivalry. Suspect me not."

CCLV   TWENTY RHYMES TO DISPEL GLOOM: PRESENTED TO HIS EXCEL-
LENCY YEN

The old man with white hair—white as the feathers of the autumn crane—Was once a man with a fishing rod over a shining stream. Since he is suited only to stay in a boat, Why should he ever have come to General Headquarters? I am recorded in the Yellow Register of Service according to law; Even this green robe I owe to you. But my old wife is worried about my rheumatism, And my little daughters frequently ask about my headache. Even on level ground I am liable to stumble and fall, And in the disharmony among colleagues I am often at fault.

Duty requires full use of my feeble strength Better to deserve the friendship of my superior officer, Whose understanding of poetry I have appreciated for many years, Whose glory of military achievements I now have shared, Whose magnanimous forbearance has covered up my clumsiness, Whose thoughtful assistance has answered my needs.

But when I think of the wisteria arbor wet with dew, Or of the cassia blossoms, heavily perfumed, I feel I am a tortoise caught in a fisherman's net, Or a bird that peeps from a cage. The Western Mountains bend about the north of our village; The Southern River curves round the east of my house. The chilly bark of the bamboo is green as usual; The berries of the pepper-plants are red in the new rain. The unused boat might be broken by the heaving waves, The dry cups stand in vain by the empty wine jars. I have to let wild weeds block the paths to my gate And the neighboring boys chop down my trees for fire-wood, Because I have placed myself in bondage, To perform humble acts to repay a friend's trust. And though I thought I knew how to avoid trouble, It does not take me long to realize I have been too careless!

When the vermilion-painted gates are opened in the morning, I come. I do not leave until the bugle sounds at dusk. I have not yet succeeded in reaching my country hut; Nor have I dared to give my humble body a rest. The magpie is shy of the Heavenly River which it cannot bridge; The inferior horse is shamed by the embroidered saddle-cloth which it does not deserve. Let me hope Your Excellency will generously consider my humble nature And grant frequent leaves to enable me to lean against my old wu-t'ung tree.

CCLVI   IT RAINS WHILE I AM IN THE VILLAGE

I have listened to the sound of rain for two nights; High autumn is time to think of preparation for cold weather. Raising my girdle, I gaze at the red string of the fish-tally bag; Opening my trunk, I find the old, worn-out, black fur coat. Sleep will help one to ignore all worldly contentions; The Tibetan brigands are still a threat I cannot forget. The pines and the chrysanthemums are freshly washed; In this thatched hut of my sojourn, I am therefore not without comfort.

CCLVII   SLEEPLESS NIGHT

The chill of the bamboos has invaded my bedroom, While the wild moonlight fills a corner of the front yard. Heavy dews form hanging drops; A few stars flicker now here, now there. Flying in the dark, each firefly has a light for itself. Resting on the water, birds call one to the other. That everything about me is involved in war Is my helpless thought as the clear night wastes away.

CCLVIII   FAREWELL TO MY BROTHER TU YING ON HIS RETURN TO CH'I-CHOU (THREE POEMS)

3

Our aunts are all on the seacoast. Two brothers are also in the East. To find them means passing through war-torn areas; To come here depends on the opening of the road. Be careful in your encounters with warriors in armed territory, As you ride on horseback through the autumn wind. Follow not my example of many tortuous wanderings; I shall be longing to hear of your safe arrival in Ch'i-chou.

CCLIX   RETURN TO THE RIVERSIDE ON JANUARY 28: PRESENTED TO THE GENTLEMEN OF THE GENERAL HEADQUARTERS

My hall in the country stands by a bamboo grove; Beyond the fence the stream runs toward the city. Our home-brew, made last month, still tastes raw. The swimming gulls already report the sound of spring. My neighbors have my permission to cut my herbs; My children are allowed to finger my books. For a white-haired man to busy himself at the General Headquarters Is, I feel deeply, a misuse of life.

CCLX THE MOCKING BIRD

Whence has the mocking bird come? Again and again he proclaims the spring. Such a linguist skilled in every tongue, Can he change his plumage into that of many birds? Hidden among thick flowers, he is rarely seen; From a high branch, he sounds an entirely new note. If after this season, he continues his chatter, I shall know of a slanderer by the master's side.

CCLXI THE SPOTTED DUCK

The spotted duck without a speck of mud Often waddles slowly before the hall steps. "Your peculiar plumage shows your independence; But you manifest a too clear discrimination between white and black. Even if you are not conscious of the jealousy of other breeds; It is hardly wise for you to startle their eyes. You have your share of the feed; Make up your mind not to quack first."

CCLXII FIVE POEMS OF SPRINGTIME IN THE RIVER VILLAGE

3

The bamboos I cultivated have multiplied in greenness; The peach-trees I planted have burst forth in red. The moon that shines on the Stone Mirror touches all human hearts; The wind that blows from the snowy mountains chills all faces. A red-tubed writing brush came with the court appointment; A silver fish-tally was given to an old man. Who could have thought that a man with almost no teeth left Was included in the list of recommendations for official service?

CCLXIII   4

A sick man with a red-stringed bag hanging from his girdle Has come back to rest and to stroll on the purple moss. In the village hut I have plans for my old age; In the General Headquarters I do not deserve a place among the many talented. Sunrays seem to curl as reflected from flying swallows; Leaves of water plants open to make way for diving gulls. My neighbors send me some fish and turtles And inquire if I can often make them a visit.

On May 23, 765, Governor General Yen Wu died in Ch'êng-tu. When the litchi ripened in July, we find Tu Fu in Jung-chou at a feast at which the fruit was served. He and his family had ended their second sojourn in Ch'êng-tu, had sailed down the Great River, and were on their way to the east. It is still an open question whether our poet left Ch'êng-tu before or after Yen Wu's death. In favor of the latter, it might be contended that it should not have taken so long as a month and a number of days to sail down-river 253 miles. On the other hand, Tu Fu might have been ill, and the voyage might have been interrupted part of the way to Jung-chou. In favor of the former, it might be argued that the absence of any writing mourning Yen's death indicates that our poet left Ch'êng-tu before the governor general's death or even his illness. On the other hand, we are not certain if such poems had not actually existed but were lost in transmission.

From Jung-chou, the boat carrying the Tu family sailed slightly north and east down the Yangtze. It should not have taken more than a fortnight for them to reach Chung-chou, where a kinsman of our poet was the prefect. Apart from the hospitality of a feast, this kinsman did little for our poet, who was put up in a temple—perhaps for a few days, for he had time to do some sight-seeing. "The Temple to Yü" [CCLXIV] alluded to the great Emperor Yü (with the doubtful chronology, 2205–2198 B.C.), who was credited with the fashioning of the great rivers to solve the flood problem of China's diluvian age.

The Tu family sailed from Chung-chou to the District of Yün-an, which belonged to the Prefecture of K'uei-chou. "Farewell to the Departing Mr. Ch'ang" [CCLXV] was written early in the winter of 765. Illness detained our poet in Yün-an, not only throughout the autumn but through the winter and almost the entire spring of 766 as well. "January 16, 766" [CCLXVI] shows that, though long sick, Tu Fu was still hoping to go to Ch'ang-an to serve the emperor.

In Yün-an, the family left the boat to live near the foot of the mountain in a dwelling either borrowed or rented. Tu Fu probably wrote "The Sojourner's Dwelling" [CCLXVII] toward the end of the spring. The great general mentioned was Kuo Ying-i, who succeeded Yen Wu as governor general of Chien-nan, quarreled with a subordinate general, Ts'ui Kan; was severely defeated on January 9, 766; fled; and was killed by a partisan of Ts'ui. Then several subordinate generals—Po Mao-lin from Chiung-chou, Yang Tzŭ-lin from Lu-chou, and Li Ch'ang-nao from Chien-chou—all started to fight Ts'ui. The whole Chien-nan Department was affected. On April 10, 766, the imperial court appointed a kinsman of our poet, Tu Hung-chien, as governor general of the Western Section of the Chien-nan Department and concurrently as general commander of all the armed forces in the entire Chien-nan Department and the Western Section of the Shan-nan Department. Our poet, writing probably late in April or early in May, heard that Tu Hung-chien had already started toward Ch'êng-tu. Actually the old, crafty, and cowardly Tu Hung-chien was in no hurry at all and did not reach Ch'êng-tu until August.

216

CCLXIV   THE TEMPLE TO YÜ

In these deserted hills, Yü's temple stands Exposed to the autumn wind and·the slanting rays of the setting sun. In the desolate yard fruits hang from orange and pomelo trees; Dragons and snakes decorate the walls of the old building. I see the gray rocky cliffs wet with the breath of clouds; I hear the river resound with rushing current on the white sands. I learned long ago that he rode on various vehicles To chisel the mountains, to drain the waters, and to fashion the three regions of Pa.

CCLXV   FAREWELL TO THE DEPARTING MR. CH'ANG

Supported on my son's arm, I must also lean on a staff; For I have lain ill during the whole autumn and more. My white hair is rarely washed; My winter robe is now too big and too long. My friend, you are worried that I might die; Your eyes too are filled with tears at this parting. Neither of us knows our future more than these floating duckweeds do theirs. When you write, write fully in closely spaced lines.

CCLXVI   JANUARY 16, 766 (THREE POEMS)

I

I feel this morning the approach of spring in the air, And the river before the city of Yün-an is especially lovely. The cry of a wild-goose: Does it augur a letter from somewhere? I wonder whose boat is being drawn upstream with the tough hawser? Before I let the plum blossoms startle my weary eyes, I should have pepper-wine in readiness to court the favor of distant heaven. To draft documents in the Imperial palace is what I most desire, But with such sick lungs, when can I hope to reach His Majesty's Court?

CCLXVII   THE SOJOURNER'S DWELLING

The hall of the sojourner's dwelling Faces the river and backs up the foot of a mountain. Below the immeasurably steep shore, Dark waves congest, surge, and leap. Looking over the tops of luxuriant trees I see their trunks, slanting or erect among the rocky cracks. I hear the cuckoos cry by day and by night—Crying to sadden the brave souls of bravest men. The gorges spread over a thousand miles; The river gathers the waters of hundreds of streams. Men and beasts share the vast region half and half; With mutually inflicted injuries, they still exist side by side.

The flax of Shu has long ceased to come from the West; The salt from Wu is unloaded at Chiang-ling on its way from the East. Since the Southwest lost its great general, All merchants, of course, have fled. Now the Court has again sent a great commander Who, I hear, has already begun his trip. All commercial navigation, waiting for profitable sailings, May depend on His Excellency's success, perhaps.

I am detained here, having covered only half my way; It is hardly neces-sary to discuss my livelihood. The use of my legs is impaired by long illness in bed, So I go to the little garden and walk with slow steps. I see narrow patches of green grass, And sadly recall the song about the prince who never returned to his homeland. One phoenix has flown away after another; In the evening chattering sparrows alone remain on the fences. Even they remind me of the old country; It is now ten years since I left the deserted village. How many of us, poor birds, will at last return? I fear the northern grove is now unsafe to roost in at dusk.

Oh that I might pour out the waters of the eight oceans To wash clean the entire world! The best ministers are not difficult to employ; They can easily pacify even the beastly barbarians. As a scholar, I have accom-plished nothing in my old age; As His Majesty's servant, I cannot ease my anxiety about the Empire's various corners. So long as there is a pen in my box, I shall take it out whenever emotion moves me to write.

"The old man from Tu-ling marooned in K'uei-chou."

CHAPTER ELEVEN

From Yün-an, the Great River (or the West River, or the Yangtze) runs, on the whole, eastward, about sixty-seven miles to K'uei-chou, and another thirty-odd miles to Wu-shan. Both Yün-an and Wu-shan were districts under the Prefecture of K'uei-chou, which was one of the eight prefectures subject to the jurisdiction of the Ching-nan governor general at Chiang-ling. In the neighborhood of K'uei-chou two mountain gullies, separated by about three miles, run southward into the Great River. The western gully was known as the Nang; the eastern gully is now called the Eastern Nang. Immediately north of the Great River and west of the Eastern Nang a war lord of the first century who called himself the White Emperor had his capital, called the White Emperor City, on a southeastern spur of the mountain known in Tu Fu's time as the Red Cuirass. East of the Eastern Nang, another hill which is now called the Red Cuirass was known in Tu Fu's poetry merely as the Northern Slope, north of the East Village. South of the Great River, the mountains were known as the White Salt.

The water of the Eastern Nang was said to have been used by the White Emperor to irrigate 100,000 *mou* of rice fields of the East Village, less than two miles southeast of the White Emperor City. West of the Nang, several centuries before the time of the White Emperor, there was a city known as Yü-fu, literally, "Fish-return." Tradition had it that breams, swimming upstream and reaching the section of the river below the city, would turn around and go downstream again—hence the name. The Fish-return City later became the city of Hsin-chou and was removed in 576 to the White Emperor City. Thus the White Emperor City became the new Hsin-chou City, which was later enlarged, probably by extensions to the northwest, and was in 619 renamed K'uei-chou. In one of Tu Fu's poems occurs a line: "White Emperor and K'uei-chou, each a different city." Historians generally took this to mean that there were two different cities, one adjacent to the other. Examining Tu Fu's poems closely, I find, however, that he really applied the names, Fish-return, White Emperor, and K'uei-chou to the same place. The line in question was meant perhaps to indicate only a historical difference. In his time, there was but one city, officially known as K'uei-chou, but still popularly known as White Emperor City.

The site of the original Fish-return City was in Tu Fu's time known as Nang-west—probably a group of villages and orchards without city walls. The appellation Nang-west arose doubtless from the fact that the area was west of the Nang; the area east of the Nang was probably called Nang-east, for in one of his poems Tu Fu said, "There are ten thousand households in Nang-east and Nang-west." Thus Nang-east was, like Nang-west, an area of hamlets, orchards, and vegetable gardens. These would spread out from the southern foot of the Red Cuirass to the northern bank of the Great River, and would all be west and slightly north of the rock-built White Emperor City, the seat of the prefectural government of K'uei-chou under the T'ang dynasty.

Sometime between 1004 and 1007, under the Sung dynasty (960–1279), an imperial edict ordered the removal of the prefectural government of K'uei-chou to the Nang-west area, and a new city was built. Thus the K'uei-chou City of T'ang and the K'uei-chou City since Sung times are not the same, and are separated by a distance of a little over two and a half miles. The disappearance of many historical monuments, the removal of sites, and the change of names constitute puzzling difficulties in the way of one trying to reconstruct the geography of Tu Fu's poems written in K'uei-chou and its neighborhood. A recent map of reconstruction which takes the K'uei-chou City since Sung times as the K'uei-chou City of T'ang is, of course, worse than useless. Relying on immovable landmarks in the landscape, Tu Fu's poems, and the geographical works of T'ang and pre-T'ang times, we can, however, make out the general bearings, if not the precise locations. The famous Hesitation Rock stands in the Great River at a point immediately south of the White Emperor City. The visible size of the rock depends on the height of the water. In order to avoid a collision, boatmen must make zig-zag detours around it. Hence the name "Hesitation."

This section of the Yangtze marks the beginning of the Ch'ü-t'ang Gorge downstream. From the neighborhood of Wu-shan begins the Wu Gorge. Ch'ü-t'ang and Wu are two of the Three Gorges famous in

Chinese literature because of their precipitous and curiously formed cliffs, inhabited by crying gibbons, and because of many treacherous rocks and currents in the river. There is no unanimity of opinion as to what the third gorge is. According to one authority, it is the Yellow Cow Gorge, beginning beyond the Wu Gorge and ending in the neighborhood of Hsia-chou (near our present I-ch'ang). Thus the Three Gorges cover a distance of some two hundred miles downstream. According to another source, the third gorge is Bright Moon Gorge, which begins about twenty-seven miles east of Yü-chou (at present, Chungking), and thus it would be west of K'uei-chou. Since Tu Fu's poems mention both the Yellow Cow Gorge and the Moon Gorge, we are not certain what he included when he used the term Three Gorges. Moreover, he seemed to use the names Ch'ü-t'ang Gorge and Wu Gorge indiscriminately. Perhaps even he did not have clear ideas about what the Three Gorges were.

One of the gates in the city wall of White Emperor was probably where the Ch'ü-t'ang Pass was situated, where the traffic up or down the river would have to be cleared with the officials. The area would be also a strategic military spot which separated the regions of Shu to the west, and of Ch'u to the east. The Ch'ü-t'ang Post Station must also have been in the immediate neighborhood.

The southwestern side of the city was on a rock that rose steeply from the Great River. A tall wooden structure perhaps stood on this rock, having a commanding view of a large section of the river and the banks. This was possibly the Hsi-ko (west tall-storied building), with living accommodations for official guests in the upper story, which we shall translate as the West Apartment.

Some piles of boulders in the Great River slightly to the west of the mouth of the Nang constitute what was called the Eight Battle Dispositions of Chu-ko Liang. Less than a mile north of these boulders—therefore in Nang-west—was the ruined site of the Everlasting Peace Palace of the First Ruler of Shu, where, at the time of Tu Fu, only temples to the memory of Chu-ko Liang and his sovereign were left.

To get an over-all view of the area we may visualize the brownish, shining, and raging Great River to be punctuated by two landmarks, the Eight Battle Dispositions to the west near the mouth of the Nang, and the Hesitation Rock to the east, south of the city of K'uei-chou. The areas north of the river are divided by two streams, the Nang and what is now known as the East Nang. From west to east, we have then Nang-west, Nang-east, K'uei-chou or White Emperor City, and finally, across the East Nang, the East Village. In these localities our poet Tu Fu lived for two years—from the late spring of 766 to mid-spring of 768—and wrote more than four hundred poems—more than one-fourth of his extant collection.

A selection of sixty-nine of these poems may perhaps give us a general view of his life and thoughts during this period, which, however, may be divided roughly into three sections: (1) When Tu Fu and his family were living in Nang-east: from the spring to the autumn of 766; (2) when Tu Fu was, for the most part, staying at the West Apartment in K'uei-chou City, leaving his family in Nang-east: from the autumn of 766 to the spring of 767; (3) when Tu Fu owned some property in Nang-west and East Village and moved back and forth between the two places: from the spring of 767 to the spring of 768.

I

From the poem, "Moving to the Prefectural City of K'uei-chou" [CCLXVIII], it is evident that the Tu family left Yün-an by boat for K'uei-chou in the latter part of the spring of 766. In K'uei-chou City, they had perhaps only a temporary dwelling place, either with friends or in an inn. Our poet wrote poems about the city wall and about its highest tower. He joined a feasting party gathered in the hall built on the city wall—said to have been built by the man who enlarged the original White Emperor City.

Tu Fu's stay in the city was, however, very short. Before the spring was over, he and his family had moved to the hilly country northwest of the city. "Piping Water" [CCLXX] yields the information that the place was at a considerable distance from the river and that the inhabitants had to depend on mountain-spring water piped through bamboo tubes. "Entering the House" [CCLXIX] shows that the rising peak of the Red Cuirass was behind or north of the house. The house was obviously in Nang-east.

Being a man very fond of sight-seeing, our poet may have begun to visit the places of attraction in the neighborhood soon after getting settled in Nang-east. Many of the poems on scenic spots and historical sites nearby were probably written within a few months after his arrival in K'uei-chou. Among these, "Temple to Chu-ko Liang" [CCLXXI], "Eight Battle Dispositions" [CCLXXII], and "The Old Cypress" [CCLXXVI] all concern the great statesman of the third century, Chu-ko Liang, and his patriotic service to the First Ruler of Shu—the story of their relation we may recall from an earlier poem [CLXVI] written in Ch'êng-tu. The last two lines of "Eight Battle Dispositions" concern the First Ruler's expedition against the Kingdom of Wu, which Chu-ko Liang was not able to prevent. The disastrous consequence of this mistaken choice between war and diplomacy was that the Kingdom of Shu was not only weakened by defeat but was also precariously placed in having to face, from then on, both an enemy to the north, Wei, and an enemy to the east, Wu.

Some of Tu Fu's poems dealing with the local custom of the K'uei-chou neighborhood were perhaps, like those dealing with places of scenic or historical interest, written during the first part of his stay in the region—before the novelty of impression had been worn off by time. One of these poems, "Faggot-carrying Women" [CCLXXIII], is characteristic of our poet's deep sympathy for the poor and the weak. Worn by work and wretched poverty, these unmarried women were hardly specimens of feminine beauty. But Tu Fu wants his readers to remember that one of the most beautiful women of antiquity, Wang Chao-chün, was a native of a village in the northeastern neighborhood of K'uei-chou City. Wang Chao-chün (or Wang Ch'iang) was the "Bright Concubine" of a Han emperor of the first century B.C. The emperor wanted to pick out the least desirable woman of his large harem to be given to a northern barbarian chieftain in marriage, and so he looked through an album of portraits and chose the Bright Concubine, whose portrait was homely indeed. Upon seeing in person her surpassing beauty, the emperor regretted but could not withdraw the gift to the barbarian; to appease his own anger, he executed the dishonest court-painter who had painted the Bright Concubine so homely merely because she had refused to bribe him. Later, after the death of her barbarian husband, Wang Chao-chün refused to marry his son according to the barbarous custom, and she committed suicide. It was said that the grass on her grave in the northern desert always stayed green. Artists of subsequent centuries generally painted her as an exquisitely beautiful woman riding a Mongolian horse and carrying a loquat-shaped guitar. Some sad melodies and songs were ascribed to her.

Aside from sight-seeing and musing over the strange and interesting patterns of life among the local inhabitants, Tu Fu had, of course, also to attend to the problems of livelihood. From some of his lines, it would seem that he had to go to the city rather often, perhaps to accept temporary literary jobs that would bring fees. He also attempted vegetable gardening; but this was a miserable failure, for K'uei-chou suffered a drought in the summer of 766. Tu Fu wrote poems too on the hot weather. What a subject to write on! The more realistically these poems communicate the idea of heat and thirst, the less they are for refreshing reading. Even after the rain had come in early autumn, and the heat had subsided, his gardening brought no better results. Where he expected some varieties of lettuces only wild portulaca appeared in profusion! He had, however, better success raising chickens. "Hurrying Tsung-wên to Set Up the Chicken Coops" [CCLXXIV] was addressed to his eldest son, Pony Boy of earlier years, who was at this time perhaps thirteen. "The Bound Chickens" [CCLXXV] is one of those poems typical of Tu Fu's sympathy for all creatures in suffering. If, at his time, there had been a Society for the Prevention of Cruelty to Animals, he would very likely have been among the first to join.

CCLXVIII MOVING TO THE PREFECTURAL CITY OF K'UEI-CHOU

After being ill in bed in Yün-an, I have moved to live in White Emperor City. The growing willows are hastening the departure of spring; The river has given our boat clear downstream currents. I hear a good farming season has begun; I know the feeling of birds among these bright hills. Thanks to the great Yü's skill in hewing rocks, We can come to a place where the ground is almost level.

CCLXIX ENTERING THE HOUSE (THREE POEMS)

I

The rising peaks of the Red Cuirass are at our back; We face the abrupt cliffs of the White Salt. Repeated movings of a sojourner are nothing to boast of, Though there is now more spring wine brought by housewarming friends.

The flowers are crowding the bamboos that should be moved elsewhere, The birds peer within as soon as the hanging screen is raised. A man in his declining years dares not feel dissatisfied, When such fine surroundings are pressed upon him.

CCLXX PIPING WATER

K'uei-chou's clouds top the Gorges; There are no wells amid the congestion of rugged rocks. We had to buy water in Yün-an, to the grief of the servants; Now we have moved to Yü-fu, and they can save much labor. Countless bamboos we find west of White Emperor City; The water is led through connected tubes to save us from thirst. Life is hard for one detained in a strange land; A few buckets of water are hardly enough to relieve his many worries.

CCLXXI TEMPLE TO CHU-KO LIANG

The paintings on the walls of the temple are worn; Wild plants have overgrown the empty hills. But one can almost hear his words when he took his last departure from the Second Ruler, Not to retire to Nan-yang, but to die for his country.

CCLXXII EIGHT BATTLE DISPOSITIONS

In achievements, he eclipsed all others of the Three Kingdoms; Hence these Eight Battle Dispositions are associated with his name. That these stones can not turn back the river current Reminds one of his regret in being unable to prevent the expedition against Wu.

CCLXXIII FAGGOT-CARRYING WOMEN

These gray-headed women of K'uei-chou Are still single at forty or fifty. There is even less hope of marriage in these war-troubled times;

They are doomed to a life of bitter tears and long sighs. Local custom makes men sit and women stand; Men manage the home while the women work for its support. Eight or nine women out of ten carry gathered faggots home To sell for money to maintain the household.

A virgin's two-knotted hairdress falling over their shoulders even in old age, They wear wildflowers and mountain leaves fastened by silver hairpins. They spend their strength climbing the heights to the market; They risk their lives to work at the salt wells for profit. Neither ornaments nor cosmetics can cover the traces of tears Brought about by these rocky lands—too barren, too cold, too remote. If one should say that all women of the Wu Mountains are ugly, How is it that the village of Wang Chao-chün is just a short distance north?

CCLXXIV HURRYING TSUNG-WÊN TO SET UP THE CHICKEN COOPS

My frailty makes me dread much of the traveling Which is so pressingly required of me as a sojourner. The meat of black hens is said to be good for rheumatism; Their eggs, except those laid in autumn, are not to be eaten. The chicks that are hatched in the spring Must now, with their mothers, number about fifty. It is useless to guide or control them, They continue to make our house the noisiest on the hillside. They even perch on tables and upset the dishes; The whole day, we hate the sight of their red combs. I instructed the slaves to cut some green bamboos To block the path and keep these fowls from the house. There is a space east of the wall Where some tall palings can be set up.

When I came back to escape the heat of the city I inquired of my son how much of the work had been done. "You should erect a number of coops in the enclosure; Put the fowls in and keep them from jumping out. Plant the palings closely, lest the birds wriggle through And come again to soil my mat with their dirty beaks and claws. Thus I will spare the ants from meeting them; And they themselves will be safe from martens and foxes. You should distribute them among the coops according to age, So they will be of equal strength in case of a fight. The coops, moreover, must be frequently repaired; You should watch closely and make alterations as required. These instructions, you should understand clearly; Carry them out with care, one by one."

These fowls will cry at dawn, rain or shine, They help give some comfort in these troublesome times; Though they are but common birds, They attend their duty with loyalty and constancy. We shall depend on them until the end of the year; Then all care and trouble on their account will disappear like the melting of ice. I do not intend to imitate the old man of Shih-hsiang Who kept on breeding chickens until they covered a whole field.

CCLXXV THE BOUND CHICKENS

My little slave bound the chickens ready for the market; The chickens, resenting the fast binding, cackled and struggled. My family dislikes having the chickens eat the ants. They should know these chickens, when sold, will be boiled. Why should human beings side either with ants or with chickens? I call to the slave to unbind the fowls. "There can be no end to the dispute between chickens and ants," I think, As I lean against our tall building on the hillside and fix my gaze on the cold river.

CCLXXVI THE OLD CYPRESS

Before K'ung-ming's Temple stands an aged cypress With a trunk tanned like bronze and roots as rugged as rock. Rain drips from the cold branches forty yards around; The sky receives the leafy green— two thousand feet of it. A great minister once served a great prince. Their memory is as much Revered as this tree is treasured in the region From the cloudfilled, long Gorges of Wu in the east To the moon- and-snow-whitened mountains in the west.

I remember, on the road to Ch'êng-tu, east of Chin-t'ing, The temple where the statues of K'ung-ming and his prince were enshrined, Where two towering cypresses stood on a ground more ancient—The paint on the buildings had faded, doors and windows were gone. The cypress, I then thought, symbolized K'ung-ming's life: A firm grip on a fine place, a lofty figure with lifting influence. Since Creation succeeded in making it so upright Providence has kept it staunchly supported.

Now I think of the repair of a tottering edifice: The needed timber, heavy as a mountain, too heavy for ten thousand oxen, Has to come from an unflowering tree, the world's marvel, Ready to cut, but too far from where a strong beam is wanted. Alas! I find this tree's solid heart suffers the attack of ants; Let its fragrant shade at least shelter the phoenix. O good men in retirement, murmur not, Remember: greatness makes its use difficult.

2

We may recall from our last chapter the local war in the neighbor- hood of Ch'êng-tu between the rebellious general Ts'ui Kan and sev- eral loyal generals, including a general Po Mao-lin. The governor general and general commander, the old, cowardly, and crafty Tu Hung-chien, appointed by the court to deal with the situation, after deliberate and long delays in reaching the affected area, did succeed in bringing about peace by the simple expedient of having all of the warring generals promoted and given appointments to different areas.

Po Mao-lin now changed his name to Po Chên-chieh and came, probably in the midautumn of 766, to the White Emperor City as the Prefect of K'uei-chou, concurrently Commissioner of Pacification and Military Governor of some five prefectures beginning with K'uei-chou.

Since Governor Po was once a subordinate general under Governor General Yen Wu, he could hardly have failed to know Military Advisor Tu Fu of the General Headquarters at Ch'êng-tu. Now, as the highest and the most powerful official in K'uei-chou, Governor Po undertook to befriend the poor, stranded poet and sojourner. Among Tu Fu's prose pieces there is the text of a memorial which he had drafted for Po, thanking the throne for the K'uei-chou appointment. To a poem written probably in the late autumn of 766, our poet appended a note to the effect, "My host, Governor Po, more than once shared his monthly salary with me." It would seem that Tu Fu was an official guest of and an unofficial secretary to the governor.

It was perhaps the hospitality of Governor Po that extended to the stranded Consultant Auxiliary Secretary of the Ministry of Public Works on the way to the court in Ch'ang-an the long use of some living quarters in the magnificent West Apartment. Tu Fu's first visit to the West Apartment was perhaps even before Governor Po's arrival. "Overnight in the Apartment by the River" [CCLXXVII] was written before he had heard of Tu Hung-chien's peaceful compromise and before he had learned to refer to the place by name. Beginning with midautumn of 766, however, many of his poems were written in the West Apartment, about the West Apartment, or describing views seen from the West Apartment. In these poems there is often a note of loneliness; there is never a reference to the presence of his family with him. It would seem that he did not want to burden the official hospitality with his family. He had left them in the hillside house in suburban Nang-east and would return to them occasionally.

From "Watching the Rain from the West Apartment" [CCLXXVIII], it may be gathered that the upper story of the tall building had a veranda with a vermilion-lacquered balustrade, perhaps running all around the building. It is very likely from this veranda that our poet gazed at the views and listened to the sounds portrayed in some of the poems under the title "Autumn Thoughts" [CCLXXXI–CCLXXXVIII] and in "A Night at the Apartment" [CCXCVI]. The eight poems under "Autumn Thoughts" have been proclaimed by many scholarly critics as Tu Fu's best. A translation may convey, in some measure, our poet's thought and feeling but none of the great artistry of his poetic language.

There are other groups of famous poems which might have also been written in this period and in the West Apartment. Having to attend to only very important documents of the governor, not the routine papers, and not having to teach his own children at home, Tu Fu probably had plenty of free time to give to poetic composition. The set of eight long memorial poems might have taken him weeks, if not months, to draft, revise, and polish. Some of the men so memorialized were among those who had made outstanding contributions to the defense of the empire—to mention one already familiar to us, the resourceful strategist General Li Kuang-pi (died 764). Some were literary men who had been Tu Fu's close friends; and in the case of Professor Chêng and • Dean Su, though Tu Fu had already in 762 written poems of mourning upon receiving news of their death, he now set forth in new elegies at considerable length their personalities, careers, achievements, and their relationships with him. Among the eight men, however, Yen Wu seems to be the only one that combines somewhat the qualities of both categories. Even a cursory reading of the poem in Yen's honor [CCLXXX] should have been sufficient to silence the ugly gossip about the breach of friendship between our poet and his young patron. A careful reading will reveal Tu Fu's high estimate of Governor General Yen's contribution to the security of the southwestern corner of the empire. This point is even more manifest in the concluding poem [CCLXXIX] of another famous group of poems on generals and generalship. When he said there that peace and order in Shu had to depend on Yen's type of generalship, it is quite evident that he was not approving of the work of his own clansman Tu Hung-chien in Ch'êng-tu, who had completely disregarded military discipline.

The five poems "Thoughts on Historical Sites" are also frequently quoted by anthologists. The linguistic rhythm of one of these, on the village of Wang Chao-chün [CCXC], has been widely imitated by later poets throughout the centuries. The story of the Bright Concubine—which we repeated earlier—was a popular item in painting, drama, and music. Why should Tu Fu devote a poem to it? Was he perhaps thinking that her refusal to stoop to unworthy practices and her consequent exile might be said to be essentially similar to the experience of many faithful officials—including himself—banished from the court because of an uncompromising uprightness? From another [CCLXXXIX] of the five poems, it is, however, quite evident that though the subject of the poem was the site of Yü Hsin's home in Chiang-ling, our poet was merely using the story of Yü Hsin's life to tell that of his own. Yü was a literary genius of the sixth century, an official of the Southern Liang court. The Southern Liang dynasty was almost brought to an end by the rebellion of a treacherous Tatar general; and Yü, while on a mission, was detained by the Northern Chou court and never allowed to return to the south. Thus, there are elements similar to An Lu-shan's rebellion and Tu Fu's displacement. But what Tu Fu was really hinting was that to Yü's masterly "Lamentations over the South" may be compared his own poems reminiscent of Ch'ang-an—such as "Autumn Thoughts."

Tu Fu, when he wrote the poem, had not yet been to Chiang-ling, and therefore, had not seen the site of Yü Hsin's early home. It is doubtful too whether he had actually been to the village of Wang Chao-chün. While occupying himself with poetry during the leisurely hours in the comfortable West Apartment, he was simply stringing together several historical sites to link his musings upon his own life and experiences. He was taking a text as a pretext. And this is one of the poetic licenses which he frequently took. Likewise, in "A Parrot" [CCXCIII] and the poems on the white and black eagles [CCXCIV–CCXCV], he was telling more about himself than about the birds. The empire was now teeming with generals, governors, and governors general; each of the more ambitious ones would gather around himself men of literary ability and would have sort of a court of his own. Army Inspector Wang, who requested Tu Fu to compose the poems on the eagles, had come from Chiang-ling where the glamorous Governor General Wei Po-yü had already gathered into his net of hospitality several men of literary distinction, including Tu Fu's old friends Hsüeh Chü and Mêng Yün-ch'ing. Would Tu Fu be interested in entering the wealthy and powerful governor general's service—which could easily put an end to a poet's struggles with poverty? If Wei Po-yü's staff officer Wang had ever hinted such an inquiry, the two poems could serve well as an unequivocal answer. The eagles are meant to soar into the high skies, not to be captured with a net and then tied to the armlet of a falconer. Tu Fu wanted to serve only the Celestial Court, not the purposes of a regional war lord. And even his unofficial and informal service under Governor Po Chên-chieh, whose loyalty to the imperial court he could perhaps trust and whose generosity to him he did certainly appreciate, was after all not to his liking. Tu Fu would compare himself to the shabby-feathered parrot—petted indeed, but it would be better to get out of the cage and be back on a branch of a tree in an imperial park.

These poems on the parrot and the eagles were written perhaps not in the West Apartment, but at a party or in the houses of friends. Of course Tu Fu could not have spent all of his time in the West Apartment. Two of the poems [CCXCI–CCXCII] under the title "Just to Pass the Time" tell about his taking a walk along the riverbank. The second of these mentions his anxiety to reach the East Coast. Perhaps already at this time—late in the autumn of 766—the thought of going to the lower Yangtze valley in search of the lost youngest half-brother, Tu Fêng, had intruded upon his constant desire to start for Ch'ang-an as soon as he was well enough for the long trip. In any event, he would have to pass Chiang-ling, whether his destination was to the north or to the east. Hence, in his farewell poem to Ts'ui I [CCXCVIII], who was going to Hêng-chou and would have to pass Chiang-ling too, he asked Ts'ui to tell his old friends Hsüeh Chü and Mêng Yün-ch'ing that they might expect his arrival sometime in the near future to discuss poetry—that is to say, none of the political affairs of Governor General Wei Po-yü.

But Tu Fu did not make the trip, for his malaria troubled him most of the winter, and he was troubled with a cough as well in the following spring. We find him with his family in the hillside house on December 19, 766. In "Day after Winter Solstice" [ccxcvii], the embroidery threads and ashes in tubes are classical allusions to the lengthening of daylight by the width of a thread each day and to the increase of warmth which renders a certain amount of sedge-ashes light enough to be blown out of some musical tubes. Perhaps, our poet's boys and girls were actually playing with embroidery and some pipe instruments. Otherwise, he was not likely to employ such pedantic artificiality just to say that the day was getting longer and warmer.

April 2, 767, was the Cold Food Festival day, important for ancestral worship and for family reunion. Our poet wrote two poems addressed to his two boys, Tsung-wên and Tsung-wu—the latter being, perhaps, the "Baby Bear" born in the late autumn of 756. In the second [ccc] of these poems, there are items that require elucidation. Tu Fu had three half-brothers, Tu Ying, Tu Kuan, Tu Fêng, and a half-sister, the widowed Mrs. Wei. Earlier in the spring, Tu Fu had heard from Tu Kuan in Chiang-ling and had been expecting Tu Kuan to pay him a visit in K'uei-chou toward the end of April. When he mentioned in the poem his weeping over the thought of Chiang-chou (in the lower Yangtze valley), he was referring to Tu Fêng, who had gone there and had not been heard of again. When he mentioned the lack of letters from Ch'ang-ko—of the Prefecture of Hsü-chou in Ho-nan—he was referring probably to Tu Ying and, possibly, also to Mrs. Wei. The second line of the poem, about the testing of the two boys' filial thoughts on some future occasions, is also vague and has caused considerable speculation among the commentators. The most plausible explanation seems to be that Tu Fu was saying to his boys, "After I am dead, the duties of ancestral worship will fall upon your shoulders, and every Cold Food Festival day will be a test of the extent of your filiality."

He was sick and felt that he was aging fast. And yet, in "Old and Sick" [ccxcix], he took delight in seeing the new outburst of blossoms on the bushes where he had seen flowers fade and drop in the preceding spring, and he felt a new longing for the emperor's gift of two writing brushes which he would be entitled to receive were he in Ch'ang-an at this season. But several months of intermittent attacks of malaria must have worn him down terribly. Getting up late one spring morning in the West Apartment, he was perhaps frightened by his own face in a bronze mirror. That, however, would give him a good excuse. In "Looking into the Mirror: Written to be Presented to His Excellency

Po" [cccɪ], he asked the governor to take pity on his withered appearance. He was begging to be relieved of the duties of the unofficial secretaryship.

Tu Fu had grown to be very fond of the West Apartment. If, however, he was to leave the service of Governor Po, should he continue to enjoy the guest privileges at such fine living quarters? After some slight wavering, he finally decided against it. That the small and noisy hillside house was no longer adequate for her husband, now accustomed to the West Apartment, and that the house was too crowded to accommodate brother-in-law Tu Kuan, soon to arrive, might have been the reasons that persuaded Mrs. Tu Fu to agree to another moving. Our poet's five poems under the title, "Late Spring, to be Written on the Wall of the Newly Rented Thatched Hut in Nang-west," give no description of the new residence. From two [cccɪɪ–cccɪɪɪ] of these, it is evident that his worries are not concerned with cramped livelihood, but with the never-ending wars.

CCLXXVII OVERNIGHT IN THE APARTMENT BY THE RIVER

While the evening here is approaching the mountain paths, I come to this high-up chamber, very close to the Water Gate. Thin clouds rest on the edges of cliffs; A lonely moon turns among the waves.

A line of cranes in flight is silent; A pack of wolves baying over their prey breaks the quiet. I cannot sleep because I am concerned about wars, Because I am powerless to amend the world.

CCLXXVIII WATCHING THE RAIN FROM THE WEST APARTMENT

The rain has entered this upper chamber to dampen the many curtains, And the mountain chill has descended upon the city by the river. The path has to be higher on the sandy beach; More of the sharp rocks will show when the water recedes. The chrysanthemums here are sadly scattered; But the pine forest at a distance shows more freshness. The downpour has wet the red-lacquered balustrade. With countless worries, I stand by a pillar of the veranda.

CCLXXIX GENERALS (FIVE POEMS)

5

The memory of the spring colors of the Brocade River follows one To the Wu Gorge where countless ravines are mourning in the clear autumn. I remember how the late Governor General Yen Wu and I Received the Court messenger on the Nostalgia Terrace. Imperial grace gave His Excellency Yen a generalship thrice; His discipline was so strict that even cups of wine for the staff officers were numbered.

Western Shu is the most strategic section of the Empire; Peace and order will depend on just such extraordinary talent.

CCLXXX IN MEMORIAM: HIS EXCELLENCY YEN WU, THE DUKE OF
CHÊNG, POSTHUMOUSLY HONORED AS THE FIRST EXECUTIVE

The Duke of Chêng's personality was as clean-cut as a crystal of quartz Reflecting the autumn sky over the peaks of Mount Hua. Even when he was but a boy, He was well known for showing a matured wisdom. Indeed the son of a great man Manifested the fine character of his illustrious father. His avowed ambition was to become a great general and a great minister, And he was careful in his choice of friends. In reading, he finished a hundred rolls in a flash; In writing, he amazed everyone whenever he used the pen. It was hardly on the strength of the family that he rose from one post to another; And, at the risk of losing his position, he remonstrated against wicked officials.

At a time when the Court still continued its solemn ceremonies, The Tatar cavalry suddenly overran the country. From the Northwest, our hero hastened by post chaise And inquired of all he met what had become of the great ministers of the government. None could tell where the Court had fled; He wiped his tears and rode on in the bitter wind. It was on the wooden road near Chien-chou that he received the Brilliant Emperor's command To call on the Emperor Su-tsung at Ling-wu, Where Court audiences were held without the usual paraphernalia, And one saw only the fluttering banners of the sandy frontiers. Few messengers traveled between the two Courts separated by a vast distance; Only the sound of bugles and drums manifested the Imperial determination to restore the Empire.

Our hero was among the stout-hearted, fearless of death; He was among the loyal officers, unwilling to be inactive. He shared in the quiet refashioning of a government comparable to that at the beginning of the Dynasty; And he supported wholeheartedly the dispatch of expeditionary armies from Fêng-hsiang. Then the four corners of the Empire were moved, And the two capitals one after the other were recovered. Beef and wine were twice offered at the western suburb to welcome the return of Their Majesties; The destroyed Imperial temples were rebuilt and stood in brilliant colors. But history shows that the best advisors at court never could enjoy permanent confidence, Nor could the ablest defenders of the Empire remain at the glorious work. Our hero was four times head of capital prefectures; Three times he commanded the armed forces of Ch'êng-tu.

But now only the green willows of Ching-chao might remind one of the famous prefect. In the halls of the Executive Division, the steps of

232

the outspoken minister are heard no more. Before the Tribunal of Censors, the crows will perch on the trees day and night, But no longer will a great Censor on a white horse come again.

In Shu our hero was as much loved as Chu-ko Liang by the people; And like the educator, Prefect Wên Wêng of Han, he too exerted a great cultural influence. Because he was in Chien-nan, even the snowy mountains became treasured. After he left, these mountains became valueless and were soon lost. He had brilliant men of letters in his secretariat, And invited loyal friends to be his advisors on military affairs. Peace was restored in the suburbs of Ch'êng-tu; Hotels were opened to accommodate his guests. In the halls, maps were studied; In the camps, music was played. There was plenty of Ch'êng-tu wine; But with the affairs of the state on his mind, he drank only sparingly.

At times he came to the Brocade River to watch the fishing; He never failed to learn about the life of the people on such outings. His hope was to destroy the power of the troublesome Tibetans, And to enable the people to live in the enjoyment of plenty—Thereby to repay the grace of the Sovereign, And to set an inspiring example of statesmanship. His loyal purpose was indeed a shining star; But an incurable sickness wore him down heavily.

Well, Yen Hui, the best disciple of Confucius, died young; Chia I, the finest servant of early Han, died without fulfilling his loyal ambition. I can visualize the coffin with mourning banners on a boat, Sailing east out of Shu and then turning north from Ch'u. I was not able to be present at his burial ceremony; I could only gaze with sorrow in the direction of his grave. An old aide of his, one whom he befriended, am I; I am hardly worthy of the official decorations which came from his recommendations.

CCLXXXI AUTUMN THOUGHTS (EIGHT POEMS)

I

While the crystals of dew are chiseling the forest of maples, A somber atmosphere has developed within the Wu Gorge through the Wu Mountains. The waves of the river swell with the mirrored sky; The storm clouds over the Pass descend upon the darkening ground.

The sight of chrysanthemums again loosens the tears of past memories; To a lonely detained boat I vainly attach my hope of going home. Everywhere people are busy preparing their winter clothing; How heavily they pound the laundry mallets in White Emperor City at sunset!

CCLXXXII   2

After the setting sun has left the solitary City of K'uei-chou, I turn toward the Dipper and gaze in the direction of the Capital. True to the old song, my tears drop as the gibbons cry; Contrary to the legend, the midautumn Heavenly River is not navigable for a returning voyager.

Incense-burners in the painted halls of the Executive Division can hardly be seen from the sick bed; Only the weird sound of bugles can be heard from behind the white-washed parapets of the city towers. Behold! The moon that lit the ivy-clad, rocky cliff Is now shining on the reed poppi on the beach!

CCLXXXIII   3

The early morning sun is soft upon the hilly city of a thousand homes; I sit each day in the purplish reflection on the veranda high above the river. The fishermen who have been out all night are slowly returning; The swallows that should have gone in the autumn are still leisurely flying.

My official career as a Reminder was cut short because of my remonstrance with the Throne. The duties of a Commissioner of Education were hardly to my taste. Most of my schoolmates are now in prominence; I can imagine their fine raiment and fast horses in the neighborhood of Ch'ang-an.

CCLXXXIV   4

It has been said that Ch'ang-an is like a chessboard; But the games have been too sadly played for a hundred years. New masters are now living in the mansions of princes and dukes; Neither the civil nor the military service is like that of old.

Straight north, beyond the mountain passes, one hears the sound of the gong and the drums. To the west, one meets horses and chaises with war's urgent dispatches. Here by the cold river, where the fish and the dragons are quiet in the autumn, One can live peacefully and think of the old country.

CCLXXXV   5

The P'êng-lai Palace faces the Southern Mountains; The golden pillars to catch the night dews rise into the sky. Looking to the west, one recalls the descent of the Fairy Queen Mother upon the Jasper Lake; Looking to the east, one remembers the coming of Lao-tzǔ, preceded by a purple mist filling the Han-ku Pass.

When the pheasant-tail screens are removed—like the opening of clouds —before the throne, One recognizes His Majesty's countenance above

the embroidered robe with the dragon-scales shining in the sun. A nap
by the hermit's stream. One wakes up to realize the lateness of time;
How many more times can he march in the procession through the
palace gate to the Court audience?

CCLXXXVI   6

From the mouth of the Ch'ü-t'ang Gorge to the banks of the Meandering River, A thousand miles of wind and mist share the same autumn.
From the Flower Tower through the Imperial Passageway came royal
splendor To the small Hibiscus Park, where anxious news of battle
fronts was also brought.

Yellow cranes circled the palace decorated with pearl screens and painted
pillars; White gulls arose from the Imperial barges with ivory-like masts
and colored silken cords. One recalls with pity such a gay site of songs
and dances, In a region which since ancient times has been the capital
of emperors and kings.

CCLXXXVII   7

The K'un-ming Lake owes its water to the engineering of Han; One
can visualize the brilliant banners of Emperor Wu before one's eyes.
The statue of the weaving maid at her loom must look sad on a romantic moon-lit night; The bodies of the stone whales seem to move in the
autumn wind.

Wild-rice grains floating on the waves suggest the shadows of sinking
clouds; Lotus blossoms chilled by the dew have dropped much of their
red. Now only a bird can fly to these scenes through the Pass that
reaches so high. I am merely a fisherman lost among the rivers and
lakes, finding no place to land.

CCLXXXVIII   8

It was a long and winding road to the K'un-wu Park by the Yü-su
River, Where the shadow of the Purple Tower Peak fell into Lake
Mei Pei. On the stalks of the fragrant glutinous-rice a few grains were
left by the parrots; A branch of the green wu-t'ung tree was said to be
worn by a perching phoenix.

Pretty women picked up shining feathers and presented them as a
spring gift; Immortal companions sailed in the boat late into the evening.
With a colorful pen, I once portrayed that atmosphere; Now, with a
drooping white head, I scarcely dare to sing of my hope to visit the
place again.

CCLXXXIX THOUGHTS ON HISTORICAL SITES (FIVE POEMS)

I

Displacement began with the dust and storm of the Northeast; Exile has extended to the southwestern corner of the Empire. Days and months waste away among the buildings and terraces of the Three Gorges; Mountains and clouds have to be shared with people wearing the alien costume of the Five Streams.

The filthy Tatar at last turned disloyal to his sovereign; A literary sojourner, lamenting his times, could not return to his homeland. Like Yü Hsin's, my life is also one of the saddest; In the evening of my life, my poetry, too, seems to be acceptable to the people of the River Pass.

CCXC 3

Amid the many mountains and countless gullies that spread toward Chiang-ling, Still stands the village where the Bright Concubine was born. Once she left the purple palace, only an expanse of desert stretched before her, Where now a grass-covered grave, forever green, remains to face the yellowish dusk.

In many paintings, I have seen her face bright with the colors of spring; I can visualize the ghost with tinkling pendants returning in the moonlight to her early home. For centuries, alien tunes have been played on the loquat-shaped guitar; The wrongs she suffered are clear in every line of the songs.

CCXCI JUST TO PASS THE TIME (TWELVE POEMS)

I

Thatched-roofed apartments are scattered behind rough wooden gates. Rain drops have begun to sprinkle the rolling waves of the darkened river. A mountain bird is still leading its young to feed on some red berries, Though a native girl hastily accepts money and leaves some white fish with me.

CCXCII 2

A foreign merchant about to depart down-river toward Yang-chou Tells me of his memory of climbing the upper chambers of Hsi-ling Station. "Will you please find out the price of rice south of the Huai?" I ask. "Though old, I am eager to travel to the East."

CCXCIII A PARROT

The parrot seems to be sad; Perhaps it is wise enough to remember its separation from its kin. The green feathers are now a bit shabby; Still the red beak betrays too much knowledge.

While you vainly wait for the day when the cage will be opened, The branch on which you used to perch has rotted away. Men pet you, and also harm you. What is the use of being a rare bird?

CCXCIV TWO EAGLES

> I met Army Inspector Wang, who spoke of two eagles, one white and one black, in the mountains nearby. Hunters had long tried to capture them with nets, but were not successful. Wang believed that these were no ordinary eagles and feared that by the end of winter and the arrival of spring they might suddenly fly away to avoid the warmth, and he would no longer be able to see such mighty birds, which appeared to long intensely for autumn. He requested me to write these two poems.

I

Throughout the clear autumn, he stands like a piece of white jade or flies like a piece of white cloud; He has no thought of preserving his fine feathers, but will soar far and wide. Let the hunters on the prairie exhaust their tactics without success; What has he to do with those who try to capture him with nets? He knows himself always to be a hunter without equal. Since he never fails on high, how could he submit to being shamefully tied to a falconer's armlet? The roc that covers a part of the bright sky may well avoid this eagle. As for the small rabbits hidden in holes, they need not worry.

CCXCV   2

I hardly believe there is such a black eagle in the world; Perhaps he has come from the North Pole across the arctic seas. Imagine how he stretched his wings to ride the wind over the Purple Frontier Hills, And how he scarcely rested a night on the Sun Terrace in the Wu Mountains. Now, the hunters with nets will display their cleverness without success; Later, the spring geese must fear him as they fly north. With the ability to cover countless miles of the chilly sky in one day, And with such golden eyes and white claws, he is certainly no ordinary bird.

CCXCVI A NIGHT AT THE APARTMENT

Light and dark compete to shorten the day toward the close of the year. Snow has stopped, and we have a clear cold night in this remote corner of the world. The drums and bugles of the fifth watch before dawn sound especially impassioned, While the stars in the Heavenly River above the Three Gorges are twinkling.

Some people are crying for the war-dead—I wonder in how many homes? I hear too the native songs of the early rising fishermen and woodcutters. Both the loyal Chu-ko Liang and the unsubmissive White Emperor ended in graves under the yellow earth. It does not matter that I am lonely—that even letters have ceased to come.

CCXCVII DAY AFTER WINTER SOLSTICE

Heaven's time and man's calendar have daily rushed Toward the winter solstice, after which the sun grows and spring returns, Slender threads of five colors—like the sun's slanting rays—will enter the embroidery one by one, And the light sedge-ash will be blown from the six musical tubes.

The riverside has chosen to wait another month before displaying the willow leaves, But these hills must intend to sweep away the chill and let out the plum blossoms. Nature and season remain the same, but the country is different; I call my son to bring me a cup of wine and let me drain it.

CCXCVIII FAREWELL TO TS'UI I: PLEASE SHOW THIS POEM TO HSÜEH CHÜ AND MÊNG YÜN-CH'ING

A wise man will not wish to make a needless move; But it is difficult to refuse the call of a faithful friend. Is it really worth while to undergo self-discipline and hardship for so long Just to keep one's self uncontaminated by the world? I have heard by day and by night your expressions of solicitude for our Sovereign; Now that you have a chance to rise and fly, you must hasten to save the country. You will pass Ching-chou and meet Hsüeh Chü and Mêng Yün-ch'ing; Please tell them I want to discuss poetry with them.

CCXCIX OLD AND SICK

In these Wu Mountains, I am old and sick, And detained among the sojourners in Ch'u. Though only a few packages of old medicine are now left, Flowers have burst forth again on last year's bushes. The rain last night must have soaked the sandy beach; The wind this spring is against the current of the stream. I should have been in Ch'ang-an to receive the customary gift of two writing-brushes from the palace, But I am still a thistledown in the wind.

CCC AGAIN TO SHOW MY TWO BOYS

My aging is especially manifest at such an important festival; Your filial thoughts will be tested on some future occasions. My drifting life has witnessed many changes; My sorrows have multiplied with the years.

No letter has come from Ch'ang-ko; The thought of Chiang-chou only brings ceaseless tears. We should have a family reunion; of course, I think of my brothers and my sister; If only we, all white-haired, could walk, sit, and sing together!

238

CCCI LOOKING INTO THE MIRROR: WRITTEN TO BE PRESENTED TO HIS
EXCELLENCY PO

My heart is always where the Wei flows west of the T'ung Kuan Pass
And the Southern Mountains rise to the sun. But my spirit was crushed
and my tears were exhausted By the experience with the Tatars and
the thoughts of the Tibetans there. Now I rise too late to be of any
official service; I move too slowly to be with the immortal company;
Such a withered apparition in the mirror—Will not my good friend
give pity?

CCCII LATE SPRING: TO BE WRITTEN ON THE WALL OF THE NEWLY
RENTED THATCHED HUT IN NANG-WEST (FIVE POEMS)

I

A sojourner in the Three Gorges, who has been sighing long, Is to
meet the late spring once more. The mocking bird is about to be silent;
The profusion of flowers will not endure. The clouds are thin above
these spacious valleys; The waves are rough in the late sunlight on the
river. How can wars be ended? This is my bitter worry. Nothing else.

CCCIII 5

I want to present a plan to save the country; But I am only a minor
officer of the Executive Division, and an aging one. So long as these
beastly wars do not come to an end, In vain can I hope to join the
flock of ducks and egrets of the Court. When the times are precarious,
human relations are strained; When the wind blows in the wrong direc-
tion, a bird grieves. After the sad sight of the setting sun over the
river, I weep till midnight, and my couch is wet with my tears.

3

Tu Fu's fear of wars sprang mainly from his view of the rapid spread
of local war-lordism which foments civil wars and invites foreign invasions. Among the many governors general that swarmed the country, he
considered those of the northeast to be the very worst. Most of them are
quondam bandits and rebels, and their semi-independent attitude toward
the court in Ch'ang-an forebodes nothing healthy for the empire.

Tu Fu had, however, a very brief and temporary respite from these
worries toward the end of the spring in 767. In one poem [CCCIV] of
the series under the caption "I Hear that the Governors General of
the Northeast Are Going to Ch'ang-an to Pay Court, and I Write
these Twelve Short Poems for Joy," he states that he had gotten the good
news from the noisy rhymes and gossip on the street. In the other pieces,
he reviewed history, he projected hope, and he bemoaned his own inability, on account of illness, to start at once for Ch'ang-an. In the con-

cluding piece [cccv], he gave the chief credit for the restoration of imperial authority to Kuo Tzŭ-i, who, though not a member of the imperial clan, had been made the Prince of Fên-yang. And Tu Fu was quite correct in his estimate of the great soldier, for despite his military successes, his power and prestige, Kuo was ever loyal and obedient to the court. Typical of him is a little incident in his own family. One of his sons had married a daughter of the emperor. The young couple quarreled one morning. "Do not try to bully me simply because your father is an emperor," said the boy; "my father did not want to be an emperor, because he set no high value on the throne." The princess felt so outraged that she rushed to the palace to complain to her father, who, however, told her that the boy had spoken the truth and ordered her to return to her husband. Kuo Tzŭ-i locked up his boy and went at once to the emperor to request punishment for both himself and his son. "We must not take such childish quarrels seriously," laughed the emperor.

The news about the war lords' change of heart would be good indeed, if only true. We do not know how long it took Tu Fu to find out that such happy rumors were as usual premature. At any rate, before the end of spring he had bought property in Nang-west and in East Village; he had acted as if he were in no hurry to leave the K'uei-chou area. And, if the "Two Quatrains" [cccvi–cccvii] were written at this time, he was not planning to return to the north in the year 767.

The money for the purchase of property might have come from Governor Po Chên-chieh, for it was customary for a prosperous official to make a gift to an esteemed friend leaving his service. The donation might have been rather handsome; for, even if Tu Fu had kept little of it for traveling expenses in the indefinite future, the property he purchased must have cost considerable. In Nang-west, he bought the house he had been renting, a spacious old hall south of it, a small flower garden next to the house, and a six-acre orchard immediately north of the house, containing a magnificent orange grove. In East Village, he acquired some rice farms and a house commanding a good view of the Great River to the south.

Thus Tu Fu became a gentleman farmer, much more in earnest than he ever had been. We find him directing his slaves, servants, and hired agents; chopping wood, mending fences, plowing the fields, planting, weeding, irrigating, and harvesting. We find him moving between Nang-west and East Village, and occasionally going to the walled city of K'uei-chou for such social functions as he could not very well refuse to attend. Though such titles as "In the Autumn I Sent My Agent, Chang Wang, to Supervise the Weeding on the Rice Farms in East Village . . ." [cccviii], "Moving from My Nang-west House to Stay Temporarily in the Thatched Hut in East Village" [cccxvi–cccxvii], and "Returning to East Village after a Short Trip to White Emperor City" [cccxxvi], and so forth, make it quite clear where our poet was when the poems were written, most of the poems leave us to guess about the locality through some topographical or narrative clues among the lines; and with many we are not able to guess at all about the precise place.

Thus, "Autumn Fields" [cccxiii–cccxiv] could be assigned to Nangwest, because date-trees are implied, and because another poem mentions giving the south hall to house a young relative, Mr. Wu, and still another [cccxxiii] requests Mr. Wu not to forbid a poor neighboring woman from plucking the dates off the trees before the hall. "Small Garden" [cccxxvii] belongs obviously to Nang-west, because the nearness to the Nang is implied. Then, "Moon on the Night of September 14" [cccxxii], because of the mention of some citrus trees, would have been written in our poet's "north house" in Nang-west—the south hall being then lent to Mr. Wu. On October 5, there was a poem inviting Mr. Wu to come to the north house again for the Double Ninth festival the following day. Then, the high terrace mentioned in "Climbing on Double Ninth" [cccxxv] would appear to be in Nang-west near the river. This poem alludes to the recent abandonment of the wine cup. About a week later, Tu Fu said in a poem about a party that he would watch and enjoy seeing his friends drink. Perhaps he was at this time following some advice to try temperance for the sake of health.

Though Tu Fu was in Nang-west on the night of September 14, he was in East Village the preceding evening, and in "Moon on the Night of September 13" [cccxxi], he was able to hear the sound of a flute from the city of K'uei-chou. Likewise, "Moon on the Night of September 12" [cccxx] seems to have been written in the East Village, because the title really covers two poems, and the second one paints the moon as barely above the White Emperor City. Indeed, the city may be used as a criterion for assigning also to the East Village "The Morning View" [cccxviii], "Cloudy Again" [cccxxxiii], and "Thoughts and Feelings" [cccxxxiii–cccxxxiv]. The two poems under "Thought and Feelings" represent Tu Fu's low-spirited moments of frustration, moments of doubt about the efficacy of the Confucian emphasis on the reform and betterment of institutions, moments of disgust with his having to practice competitive economy and selfish hoarding, moments of his seeking refuge in philosophical Taoism.

Perhaps to the East Village also may be assigned the poem under the rather colorless title, "Just a Note" [cccxxiv], which represents Tu Fu's comprehensive view of the history of poetry in China and his modest estimate of his own place in it. He mentions dividing his time between agriculture and poetry. The former refers very probably to the harvesting of rice crops. By the latter, he means not only the writing of poems, but also the repeated study of the poetry of ancient masters: the bards of Ch'u at the beginning of the third century B.C.; the many writers of the Han period (206 B.C.–A.D. 220), with special devotion to those of the Confucian school (for instance, Yang Hsiung, 53 B.C.–A.D. 18); the father Ts'ao Ts'ao (155–220) and the son Ts'ao Chih (192–232) of the royal house of Wei; and the numerous poets of the Chin (265–420) and subsequent periods. It may be noted that, in his appraisal of immortal literature, our poet emphasizes character in literary expression. I use the first line of this poem of his on the title page of the present book.

Agriculture was not the only distraction from poetry, for social invitations from the city of K'uei-chou would now and then take Tu Fu away from both. The scene of the poem on the Sword Pantomime dance [cccxxx] was of course in the city, though Tu Fu probably wrote the poem after he had walked home to East Village. Likewise, the drinking party that preceded his fall from a horse [cccxxviii] took place in the city; but since the horse was headed east, we may assume that the East Village was his destination, and that he wrote the masterly poem of humor and pathos there. Perhaps he was well enough toward the end of autumn to relax his new abstinence from wine when coaxed by his drinking friends.

It is difficult to choose between Nang-west and East Village for such poems as "Returning Home at Night" [cccxxxi] and "Deaf" [cccxxix]. The tigers in "Returning Home at Night" might be figuratively some bullies met on the road. Or, it could have been wine that caused Tu Fu to see tigers on the road and two wicks on a candle. We might imagine that he was walking home to East Village after a late party. On the other hand, he might have taken a boat from the city gate to Nang-west and would have to walk a short distance to his north house. As for "Deaf," the scene described would seem to apply equally well to Nang-west or East Village. We might be tempted to think that Tu Fu's falling from a horse might have been the cause of the deafness of his left ear. But, he said that he had been deaf for a month before seeing the yellow leaves fall. It would seem that his partial deafness might have begun with that illness in the autumn that brought him to his temporary abstinence from wine.

On the whole, however, his health and his economic situation both seemed better during the second half of 767 than they were during 766. Since he was feeling better, he would think once more of leaving K'uei-chou. Perhaps the visit of Tu Kuan during the summer might also have had something to do with such thoughts. Presumably the two brothers would discuss plans for the family reunion and for the use of the property left in Yen-chih and Ch'ang-an. In "Watching Fireflies" [cccix], our poet indicated that he hoped to be back home in the north by the autumn of 768. We know from one [cccx] of the two poems on "My

Brother Tu Kuan Returns to Lan-t'ien for His Wife" that Tu Fu was planning to sail down the Great River in September 767, and that he wanted Tu Kuan to meet him in Tang-yang, where the two brothers would have a good drink on the Tower of Wang Ts'an. In "Again" [cccxi], which is another poem attached to "Rain at Night," and in "Autumn Clearness" [cccxii], it is evident that the plan for departure was postponed until winter, and this might have been on account of Tu Kuan's delay in Lan-t'ien. The poems under the title, "For More Than Three Years I Have Had No News of My Fifth Brother Tu Fêng . . ." were probably written late in the autumn; and in the second [cccxix] of these, the departure was further postponed to the spring of 768, and instead of planning to go northward to Ch'ang-an, our poet was thinking of sailing to the East Coast in search of the lost brother. The change in destination was perhaps due to disturbing news from Ch'ang-an. In the middle of September, the Tibetans attacked Ling-wu, and Ch'ang-an was placed under martial law until the end of October.

With better news, however, Ch'ang-an was again uppermost in Tu Fu's thoughts. The Chinese New Year's Day occurred on January 24, 768. On that day, he wrote five poems under the title "Happy to Learn of the General Retreat of the Rebels and the Tibetans," and in the concluding poem [cccxxxvi], he even thought universal peace had at last miraculously been achieved. As a matter of fact, a few days before that he had already heard from Tu Kuan, and in "I Receive Another Letter from Tu Kuan . . . and I Decide to Leave K'uei-chou about the Middle of February" [cccxxxv], our poet intimated once more that he would be going to Ch'ang-an.

"About to Depart from the Wu Gorge, I Present the Six-Acre Nangwest Orchard to Nan Ch'ing-hsiung" [cccxxxvii] was written on the day scheduled for the sailing of the Tu family from K'uei-chou—possibly February 22, 768. Who was this Nan Ch'ing-hsiung to whom Tu Fu made this generous gift? His name is not attested elsewhere. Could he be simply one of the working men, fishing and cutting wood, whose friendship Tu Fu preferred to that of the sophisticated and competitive officialdom? What did Tu Fu do with the rest of his property in Nangwest and East Village? We do not know. It might have been sold, or also given away.

CCCIV   I HEAR THAT THE GOVERNORS GENERAL OF THE NORTHEAST
ARE GOING TO CH'ANG-AN TO PAY COURT, AND I WRITE THESE
TWELVE SHORT POEMS FOR JOY

3

The noisy rhymes and gossip on the street Are telling that all generals of the Northeast are going to pay court. From now on, the Throne and the world are both right; But a stranger by the Great River feels doubly homesick.

CCCV   12

For a dozen years, the battlefields had been multiplying; Now the celestial authority is respected and punitive expeditions are no longer needed. God has blessed this great Dynasty with the rulers for the renaissance And the Prince of Fên-yang, meriting the investiture by work, not by birth.

CCCVI   TWO QUATRAINS

I

The river and the hills are beautiful in the lingering sunlight; The flowers and the herbs are fragrant in the spring wind. The swallows are flying with soft mud in their beaks, While the ducks still slumber on the warm sandy beach.

CCCVII   2

The gulls look whiter against the blue river, And the flowers glow against the green of the hills. This spring too will soon be gone: In which year will occur the days of my home-coming?

CCCVIII   IN THE AUTUMN I SENT MY AGENT, CHANG WANG, TO SUPER-
          VISE THE WEEDING ON THE RICE FARMS IN EAST VILLAGE.
          THE WORK IS NEARLY FINISHED, AND EARLY THIS MORNING
          I SENT MY WOMAN SLAVE, A-CHI, AND MY BOY SERVANT,
          A-TUAN, TO INQUIRE ABOUT IT.

The rain must now be plentiful in East Village; I am eagerly awaiting the fragrant smell of the rice. Since Heaven's grace is impartial, Reeds and tares will also grow. Men consider these plants unwelcome, For they might spoil the work of farming. Therefore, no efforts will be spared To pull up the weeds and throw them on the riverbank. The grain is for the sustenance of life; It can hardly be neglected even by a sojourner.

These farms in the spring received the necessary attention, And were thoroughly plowed according to rule. The water buffaloes were strong and easy to use; We drove them abreast over all the fields. Rich stalks have begun to bear, While the rain water forms square pools in the field. Everything that grows will surely spring up in confusion; This matter will require careful and constant vigilance. It is not that I had failed to appoint a supervisor To guide the workers with systematic directions. But in this warm southern climate, While I am waiting for the slight frost of the harvest season, I am still afraid that the keeper might be careless And not do his best. So I am sending the maid and the servant To convey a message over the high ridges. After the harvest, we shall give away much of what we have gathered; It is not for my granary alone. This is not meant to court the praise of the good neighborhood; I am very much moved by the hardship of these troublesome times.

When the north wind blows on the dried sedge And the crickets are chirping near the main hall, We shall gradually come to the rest and freedom from farm labor, And shall at last ease much of the grief and some of the groans.

CCCIX WATCHING FIREFLIES

In the autumn night the fireflies of the Wu Mountains flutter Through the loose screen to light on my clothes. Inside my study, I feel as if the lute and the books were suddenly cold; Outside the house the fireflies seem to confuse the few stars beyond the eaves. They circle around the well, each to reflect a mate in the deep; They pass by the flowers, now and then to light a flash of color in the dark. Let the white-headed old man in obscurity and sadness watch your prognostics: By this time next year, shall I or shall I not be able to return home?

CCCX MY BROTHER TU KUAN RETURNS TO LAN-T'IEN FOR HIS WIFE
(TWO POEMS)

2

If you recall the sad parting here in K'uei-chou, You will not tarry long there in Lan-t'ien. I can visualize your clothing moistened with white dew, As you ride early on a saddled horse in the clear autumn. On the swift streams through the gorges, I shall set sail in September. Then the two of us shall have a good drink, Perhaps on the Tower of Wang Ts'an.

CCCXI AGAIN (ON THE NIGHT RAIN)

I have been hoping to tread on the early snow, And to proceed on horse-back from Chiang-ling to Ch'ang-an. Now I very much fear that these Wu Mountain rains Will surely spoil the rest of my autumn in K'uei-chou. The courtiers will appear with shining jade pendants; His Majesty will wear a brilliant white fur. My colleagues will all attend the early audience; Why should I be long detained here?

CCCXII AUTUMN CLEARNESS

The trouble with my lungs is somewhat relieved at the height of autumn; I can even comb my white hair myself. I am indeed tired of increasing or decreasing the dosage of medicine; I realize sadly that for days the gateway and the yard have not been swept. Now leaning on a staff, I can return the bows of visitors; Composing verses about the lovely bamboos, I send my sons to inscribe them on the stalks. By early winter, the river will be calm; A light boat will take me wherever I want to go.

CCCXIII AUTUMN FIELDS (FIVE POEMS)

I

The autumn fields become each day more untidy, While the chilly river continues to shake the blue sky. I have moored my boat in the aboriginal section of Shu; I have made my abode in one of the villages of Ch'u. When the dates are ripe, I shall allow whoever wishes to pick them; When the sunflowers are withered, I shall hoe them down myself. This platter of food is more than enough for an old man; I shall share a portion of it with the fish in the stream.

CCCXIV 2

If one can readily understand the urge of all living creatures, One will find it difficult to violate a single item of nature. The fish are happiest in the depth of water; The birds like to return to the thick forest. As an old man, I should be content with poverty and sickness. Prosperity and prominence might not bring all that is good. So long as such autumn weather allows me to sit up or walk; I shall gratefully eat the coarsest food for a poor recluse.

CCCXV 3

What I have learned of propriety and music should be helpful with my shortcomings; Such beautiful hills and wood should give me feelings, joyful and enduring. Shaking my head at the thought of official life, I feel my loose hat become tilted; Reading the writings on the bamboos, I enjoy the warm sunshine on my back. The wind has felled many pine cones which I shall gather; The weather is growing cold, and I shall collect the honey from the beehives. Here and there, only a few red flowers are left; In my sandals I approach their faint fragrance.

CCCXVI MOVING FROM MY NANG-WEST HOUSE TO STAY TEMPORARILY IN THE THATCHED HUT IN EAST VILLAGE (FOUR POEMS)

I

North of the precipitous cliffs of the White Salt Mountains, East of the ancient city on a spur of the Red Cuirass, We have a level site bordered by a calm stream And walled around by hills of almost equal highness. Haze and frost reduce the brilliance and warmth of the sun on the fields; Rice is ready for harvest, and one can smell the crop in the winds. Social life keeps one as busy as a spinning thistledown; For a while, I shall just stay with these cassia plants.

CCCXVII 2

Whether in East Village or in Nang-west, We live close by the same kind of clear stream. Coming or going, we have thatched huts in both places; I now stay a while to attend to my rice farms. The noisy market there is better suited to profit-making; Through the secluded forest here, one can hardly find a path. Let visitors try to seek conversation with a feeble old man, Many of them will become lost on the way and give up the effort.

CCCXVIII THE MORNING VIEW

As the sound of the fifth watch vanishes from the White Emperor City; The colors of the morning become clear over the Sun Terrace Mount. Though the sun has risen to shine upon the cold lofty peaks, The thick clouds along the folding ridges are still asleep. The sails on the river are hidden because our ground is low; The faint rustle of leaves can be heard in the clearness. A pair of wild deer stand at a distance from my rough gate; They and I should really become friends.

CCCXIX FOR MORE THAN THREE YEARS I HAVE HAD NO NEWS OF MY FIFTH BROTHER TU FÊNG, WHO WAS ALONE NEAR THE EAST-ERN COAST

I heard you were in a monastery in the hills Either in Hang-chou or in Yüeh-chou. The days of our separation are filled with war and disturbance; My thought of you has occupied this whole clear autumn. My body is among the crying gibbons of the K'uei-chou woods, But my soul is floating out to alight on the mirage-tower of the Eastern Sea. Next year, I shall sail down the spring stream, Going east as far as the white clouds can go, in search of you.

CCCXX MOON ON THE NIGHT OF SEPTEMBER 12 (TWO POEMS)

I

Behold, this is a bright mirror that has flown into the sky; And the mention of the big sword in the song is enough to shatter my homesick heart! Like a whirling thistledown, I have been blown far enough; But it is as difficult to reach heavenly Ch'ang-an as to grasp the cassia in the moon. The illuminated river is nearly as white as snow; Even the roosting birds can be seen in the woods. As I gaze now at the pale rabbit in the great disc, I can almost count every hair on his back.

CCCXXI MOON ON THE NIGHT OF SEPTEMBER 13

I am to witness again the munificence of silvery rays, Each declaring the glorious autumn of sparkling dew. Though these frontier mountains reach far across the earth, The Heavenly River seems to flow near humanity. Some homeward-bound woodcutters are singing beyond the ravines; A few melancholy notes of the flute rise from the lonely city. The boys of K'uei-chou seem never to sleep! At midnight those boats are still moving.

247

CCCXXII MOON ON THE NIGHT OF SEPTEMBER 14

Tonight the autumn moon is still round, And I am a lonely aging figure in the riverside village. I roll up the screen to let the moon shine again on me; I lean on my staff to walk, and the moon follows me. The piercing light stirs the dragons under water; The restless radiance disturbs the roosting birds in the wood. By my thatch-roofed study grow tangerine and pomelo trees; On these, I note the dews particularly fresh and brilliant.

CCCXXIII AGAIN PRESENTED TO MR. WU

Please allow your western neighbor to pluck the dates from the trees before the hall; She is a woman, without children and with no means of support. Were it not for dire poverty, she would hardly have come for these fruits; And to save her from embarrassment, we have to be especially kind. She is of course needlessly afraid of a stranger from a distance; But even to erect a fence would be to take the matter too seriously. I recall her complaints of the taxation that has made her poor to the bone; The burdens of war on such persons! It makes me shed bitter tears.

CCCXXIV JUST A NOTE

True literature lasts a thousand ages: An inch of conscience can measure its truth. Writers naturally belong to different classes; But fame seldom rests on mere chance. It was long after the bard of ancient Ch'u had passed into history, That the Han masters rose in poetry. They were the vanguard that took the fortress by storm; Those who inherited it decorated and beautified it. Later writers received many examples from the past. Each age clearly added something new.

The greatest models, of course, are of the Confucian school: To them I have applied myself tirelessly since my youth. I have, moreover, long been delighted by the brilliance of the Chin writers, And have often regretted not having grasped the peculiar wonders of the Ts'ao family of Wei—Each of the Chin writers was like a fast horse, The Ts'ao family, father and son, were thoroughbreds. I have erected for myself only a scaffolding; I still lack a complete structure. At random have I ventured the judgment of a nonentity Weakly transmitted in cryptic messages of doubtful elegance.

Much of my poetry is merely for self-consolation During my long illness and frequent displacements. I am ashamed of not having served my country with wise counsel, And of having to seek shelter, like a bird seeking a branch. I am with wasps and scorpions in the dust and on the sands; I am near the dragons and crocodiles of the river gorges. Alas! Peace and prosperity sink further and further into the past; Rebellions, invasions, and wars follow one after another. In Ch'ang-an, the Majestic Court had to admit brigands and rebels; In K'uei-chou, I live among barbarians with strange customs and boisterous manners. I know many good men hiding away, buried under ground like sharp and shining swords, Like powerful dragons submerged and unseen under dark ponds.

While in Ch'êng-tu and Chiang-ling we have general headquarters for governors general, While armed men are counted by the thousands, Yet in the south, the authority of the Government is challenged in Nan-hai. In the north, the people of Ching-chao flee from the Tibetans. Untrue to popular belief, The cries of crows and magpies have brought me no letters; The howlings of wild beasts are truly hard to endure. I mete my time between poetry and agriculture; I have to fashion my livelihood after the mode of this region.

Since the White Tower of the Southern Mountains is beyond my vision, And the autumn waters of the Imperial lakes appear dim in memory, No longer do I venture on magnificent lines of versification; I sing only of separation when melancholy rises.

CCCXXV CLIMBING ON DOUBLE NINTH

The wind storms across the sky and brings the gibbons' bitter wails— Clear river, white sands, birds wheeling, Trees everywhere with silently falling leaves, Endless is the Yangtze with its rolling currents. I am so many times a stranger in a distant land during the autumn; With an illness that has spoiled my whole life, I climb alone to this high terrace. My difficulties and regrets exceed the number of white hairs on my head; Too bad I can not drown them in the wine cup I have so recently abandoned!

CCCXXVI RETURNING TO EAST VILLAGE AFTER A SHORT TRIP TO WHITE EMPEROR CITY

I am returning again to the farms, For the work of harvesting is not finished. In preparing a threshing-floor, no ants should be destroyed; In gathering the crops, sufficient gleanings should be left to the village boys.

Every pounding pestle will be a gleaming white; After the husking, the grains glow faintly red. More food might improve an old man's health; A full granary consoles even a man with no permanent home.

CCCXXVII SMALL GARDEN

The lands watered by the streams of the Wu Gorge Belong primarily to the people of Ch'u. As a sick sojourner, I have remained here to cultivate medicinal herbs; Late last spring, I bought this place because of the flowers. Fruits are now dropped by the autumn wind in the yard; The rain upon the banks of the Nang has washed away the sands. I shall follow local custom in preparations for the winter; Let this poem record that I expect good luck!

CCCXXVIII   DRUNK, I FELL FROM HORSEBACK. SOME FRIENDS CAME TO SEE ME, BRINGING WINE

As an old familiar guest of the great governor, I left the wine cup to sing and to dance with the golden lance. Suddenly remembering the exploits of my youth, I mounted a horse And had its springing hoofs pounding rapidly upon the Ch'ü-t'ang rocks.

Outside the gate of the White Emperor City, both the river and the clouds were below us; Almost perpendicularly down we went, some twenty-seven hundred feet. The white battlements of the city wall passed the purple bridle like lightning; And we were speeding east toward the level ridge beyond the sky-capping cliff. The riverside village and the rustic hills all rushed into view As I eased the rein and the whip, and galloped over the reddish path.

The white-haired man always wanted to surprise his many friends By showing that he could still ride and shoot as he did in his younger days. How was I to know while I felt we had enough of the jolly speed, The good horse, red sweat on his body and white foam on his mouth, did not share the same thought? Just one inadvertent stumble ended in considerable hurt; Surely in life, to follow an impulse as guide is to have disgrace as a result. Indeed I have much to worry me while I lie in bed, Besides my declining years and the usual infirmities.

Now that friends and acquaintances have come to inquire, I must shamefacedly rise, Supported by the servants and still leaning on a stick. When I finished my story, my friends burst into laughter. They took me to the curve of the clear stream and chose a clean spot. Once more wine and meat piled up like a mountain For a feast that began with music from the weird string and the impassioned pipe. All pointing to the west, they said the sun would not wait And shouted for everyone to drain the cup.

But why is it necessary, my friends, to ride thither to give me comfort? Do you not know that Chi K'ang, the author of Good Health, suffered execution at last?

CCCXXIX   DEAF

I feel almost as old as the ancient philosopher with a pheasant-feather cap And as useless to the world as the legendary hermit in a deer-skin coat. I wonder how soon my eyes will go blind, Now that for a month

*one of my ears has become deaf. The gibbon may cry, but I shall be
spared autumn tears; The sparrows may chirp, but they will not make
me melancholy in the evening. I was startled to see yellow leaves falling
from the trees on the hills; I called my son and asked, "Did you hear
the north wind blow?"*

CCCXXX A POEM ON SEEING THE SWORD PANTOMIME DANCE OF THE
PUPIL OF MADAME KUNG-SUN FIRST

On November 15, 767, at the house of Yüan Ch'ih, Vice-Prefect of
K'uei-chou, I saw Madame Li Twelfth from Lin-ying perform the
Sword Pantomime Dance. Marveling at her nimbleness, I inquired
who her teacher was. "I am a pupil of Madame Kung-sun First,"
she said. I remember when I was still a child in 715, I saw
Madame Kung-sun First giving the Sword Pantomime and the
Felt-Cap Pantomime dances in Yen-ch'êng. The freedom and the
strength were superb. During the early years of the Brilliant Emperor's reign, among all the dancers, whether of the two Imperial
schools—Spring Court and Pear Garden—or of those admitted occasionally to the Palace, Kung-sun was the only one skilled in this
dance. The fading of her beauty and prominence must have par-
alleled the appearing of the white hairs on my head. Even her
pupil is now no longer a woman with a youthful face. Having confirmed the transmission of the art, I knew for certain that the ges-
tures of the two ladies were identical. Moved by the thought of
passing events, I have written this poem on the Sword Pantomime
Dance. Formerly, Chang Hsü of Wu District, well known for skill
in cursive calligraphy, saw frequently in Yeh District the West
River Pantomime and the Sword Pantomime dances of Madame
Kung-sun First, and from then on his cursive calligraphy made
rapid progress. In Chang's calligraphy, the impassioned strength
and rhythm are exactly those in Kung-sun's dances.

*In former days, there was a beautiful woman, Madame Kung-sun,
Whose performance of the Sword Pantomime Dance was everywhere
applauded. Spectators, massed mountain-high, all bore a breathless countenance, For they felt as if heaven struggled against earth. She bent
back: you saw nine falling suns shot down by the fabulous I; She leaped:
you beheld gods astride flying dragons in the clouds. She advanced: you
awaited the thunder and lightning from a gathering storm of anger and
fury; She stopped: you contemplated the mellowed light over a vast sea.*

*Her rosy-lipped beauty and the charm of her sparkling sleeves soon
were heard of no more. In her later years, her great art is displayed
only by her pupil. The fair lady of Lin-ying is now in the White
Emperor City, Giving a spirited performance of this exquisite dance
accompanied by song. Having learned from her the source of her skill,
I muse over times and events, and feel increasingly sad.*

*The Brilliant Emperor had eight thousand ladies-in-waiting; Madame
Kung-sun was from the beginning supreme in the Sword Pantomime
Dance. Fifty-odd years have passed quickly, like the turning of a palm;*

*Stormy waves of war have wrapped our royal house in gloom. The
pupils of Pear Garden scattered like the disappearing mist; Now the
fading beauty of the courtesan shines alone in the cold sunlight.*

*The trees south of the Imperial mausoleum on Golden Grain Hill are
fully grown; The grass in the stone city by the Ch'ü-t'ang Gorge is
withered. The brilliant feast, the music, and the songs have ended.
After the climax of pleasure, come melancholy and the moon in the east.
I am an old man who does not know where he is going, Who has pro-
pelled his unwilling limbs too fast in the deserted hills.*

CCCXXXI RETURNING HOME AT NIGHT

*Returning home at midnight, I slip by tigers; The hills are dark, and
the people at home are asleep. To the north the Dippers hang low
above the river; Straight overhead I recognize Venus, shining volu-
minously. I hold a candle in the yard, I am annoyed at seeing two
burning wicks. I listen for the crying gibbons of the gorge, I am
surprised to hear only one. Though white-headed and old, I dance
and sing. Leaning on my stick, I refuse to sleep. But what of it?*

CCCXXXII CLOUDY AGAIN

*Winter is made of an accumulation of inclement weather; Yesterday,
it cleared only in the evening, and today is again dark. Thistledown
from afar is wafted past us. A banner on a pole over the city wall is
blown straight in the wind. The yellow sands are running away, as
the river waves shake the shore; Black rhinoceroses must be howling
from the hills buried under clouds and snow. Do you not know the
old man from Tu-ling marooned in K'uei-chou Is a man with half his
teeth gone and his left ear deaf?*

CCCXXXIII THOUGHTS AND FEELINGS (TWO POEMS)

I

*The world is made of toiling creatures: Where, or in what strange cus-
toms, matters not. All are gradually led into competition; Gradually
they will feel the pressure of the bondage. Ah, if there were no prominence, obscurity would bring no grief; If there were no rich, the poor
could be content. Eternity is only one corpse: The neighborhood takes
turns to weep.*

*Since I came to the Wu Gorge, Three years went like a burning candle
in a whirlwind. For my health, I accept the interruption of my journey;
With humor, I face both honor and insult. A Court rank reaches me
in the evening of life; Husked rice still constitutes my daily food. I live
in a thatched hut east of the stone city; I gather medicinal herbs in the*

northern ravines of the hills. Since my attention is given to the roots
under frost or snow, To seize the luxuriant branches and leaves is needless.

This has nothing to do with any purposely laid plan; and to seek peace
in solitude has been with me a matter of habit. A wise man is as straight
as a taut bowstring; A wicked man is as crooked as a hook. Whether
straight or crooked I shall not inquire; I shall warm my back in the sun
and wait to meet the herdsmen and the cutters of wood.

CCCXXXIV   2

I sit on the southern veranda late at night, With the moonbeams
bright on my knees. A sudden gust seems to have upturned the
Heavenly River; A streak of sunshine is already on the house-top.
Various creatures, each having had a sleep, Will now fly or crawl in
pairs or in groups. I too shall drive my sons To work and to hoard with
a selfish purpose.

In cold weather, travelers are few; Toward the close of the year, time
moves fast. The world is like a swarm of devouring insects, Because
men have been hit with the passion for success. Long, long ago, before
history began, Having filled his belly, a man puts every ambition to
a stop. Why should education and government arise To ensnare humanity in an inescapable net?

The first criminal was the man who drilled wood to produce fire; Graver
perils were created by the historian presuming to record what was
honorable and what was not. You see the lighting of lamps and candles Will attract hundreds of flying moths. Let one's spirit soar beyond
the universe; He will see above and below just one stillness. To understand the ultimate unity of coming and going—of life and death, Is that
not exactly the secret of immortality?

CCCXXXV   I RECEIVE ANOTHER LETTER FROM TU KUAN ABOUT MAK-
ING HIS HOME IN TANG-YANG, AND I DECIDE TO LEAVE
K'UEI-CHOU ABOUT THE MIDDLE OF FEBRUARY

Since your arrival in Chiang-ling, You have written several times to
invite me there To add songs to New Year celebrations And to participate in the joy of the Cold Food Festival. But I depend on others
to navigate the boat, For my frail body still requires the support of a staff.

Let me wait until the constellations turn further around the K'uei-chou
Gorge—Until spring has come to the neighborhood of the Yo-yang
Lake. Then I shall choose a day for starting toward happiness in the
South, And for putting to an end the sighs of never reaching the North.

*We brothers shall be like wild geese flying and singing in close forma-
tion, But also each often holding a reed in the beak—making no noise
to attract the hunters. The scenery of these regions is good, though the
hospitality of the people is thin; The vegetation will revive, after the
hard season is past. Though I am almost too old to be an official at
Court; My hope still is to reach the Imperial Capital at last.*

CCCXXXVI   HAPPY TO LEARN OF THE GENERAL RETREAT OF THE
               REBELS AND THE TIBETANS (FIVE POEMS)

5

*The present spring has filled the world with a joyous spirit, For the
supreme sovereignty is honored north, south, east and west. Who has
brought about this political harmony of the year 768? Long live His
Supreme Mystical Majesty's majestic descendant!*

CCCXXXVII   ABOUT TO DEPART FROM THE WU GORGE, I PRESENT THE
              SIX-ACRE NANG-WEST ORCHARD TO NAN CHʻING-HSIUNG

*I have always been fond of bamboos and mosses, Though, like a floating
duckweed or a flying thistledown, I have no permanent abode. My children have grown while they followed me in long wanderings; Several
times have we left quite pleasant dwellings. Here different flower buds
are competing in varying shades of red; After a while no brocade will
be able to match them in colorfulness. Having gotten a boat for leaving
the gorges, I visit this orchard and recall the work with the hoe. The
noisy orioles are saying that February is two-thirds gone; The painted
fish hawk on the prow of my boat will fly downstream today. I shall
be thinking of plucking the plum blossoms by the snow-covered fence,
Or of watching the willow wands near the pavilion stretch in the wind.
Let me give you this orchard for your permanent possession, And let
me sing of the departure of rustic joys from my life. Even if I should
spend the rest of my life on the Yangtze and the Han, Where else could
I find such good friends among the woodcutters and the fishermen?*

"A solitary boat laden increasingly with melancholy."

CHAPTER TWELVE

Biographers of Tu Fu generally state that our poet sailed away from K'uei-chou in the first month of the Chinese calendar and arrived in Chiang-ling in the third month. Even if the Tu family departed the last day of the first month and arrived the first day of the third month, the interval would be, according to the Julian calendar, February 22 to March 23, 768—and the journey from K'uei-chou to Chiang-ling, though a distance of 253 miles down-river, should not take thirty days. Tu Fu, in a poem describing the navigating skill of Kuei-chou boatmen, once commented on "Departing from the White Emperor City in the morning and arriving at Chiang-ling in the evening . . ." Even combining leisurely travel with sight-seeing, the downstream trip should not have taken more than a week.

The riddle is solved if we realize that the Tu family actually left K'uei-chou later and reached Chiang-ling earlier than these dates. From a misplaced poem we learn that because of a storm the boatmen considered the river too rough for sailing; the boat was thus delayed probably a fortnight or longer. When it reached the neighborhood of Chiang-ling, the moon was approaching the last phase. During the trip, our poet had stopped at Wu-shan for a farewell party and had stayed overnight in a pavilion outside of Hsia-chou. I would guess, therefore, that he arrived in Chiang-ling about the middle of March and that his departure from K'uei-chou was less than a week before that.

Travelers through the gorges from K'uei-chou to Hsia-chou are as a rule breathlessly amazed by the magnificent landscape along the way. Tu Fu wrote only a long poem of eighty-four lines to describe the scenery of the whole trip and to air his sad feelings over his illness and his frustration. This poem is difficult to translate, because its descriptive passages are too terse to be understandable without considerable commentary and because the narrative sections contain allusions that centuries of erudition have not succeeded in clarifying. There is, however, the short poem "Thoughts While Traveling at Night" [cccxxxviii], which may be taken to represent a painting of the spring landscape near Chiang-ling and the summing up of Tu Fu's feelings as a whole.

CCCXXXVIII   THOUGHTS WHILE TRAVELING AT NIGHT

Between two shores of tender grass, in the slight breeze, Glides this lonely high-masted boat. The stars seem to reach down to the fields, flat and wide; The moon seems to be swimming as the Great River flows.

Am I really to achieve an honored name in literature? I ought to give up all hopes of official service because of age and illness. To what shall I compare myself, as I am blown about? Just a beach gull between heaven and earth.

Once Tu Fu had made up his mind to give up the hope of official service, he was no longer in haste to get to Ch'ang-an. In Chiang-ling, he left his boat and took a house. He did not seem to care how much longer he might live, and he took up drinking again. He met his friend Chêng Shên, who was at this time living in retirement in the neighborhood of Chiang-ling. He met also his friend Li Chih-fang (whom we encountered in earlier chapters), who after two years of detention by the Tibetans returned to be promoted to the Ministry of Propriety, and who now had been for several months visiting in Chiang-ling— probably on leave of absence from court. The three friends now met to write poems and to drink in the library of a certain official, Hu. The time was about April 6, 768. It was full moon at night.

CCCXXXIX   AFTER DRINKING IN THE LIBRARY: I URGED MINISTER LI TO DISMOUNT FROM HIS HORSE, AND I SANG THESE LINES UNDER THE MOON

The water of the lake is clear, and the wind of the forest is pure; Do not leave; come down from your horse, and let us finish these pots of wine. I have long decided to let my hair turn as white as the plumage of a wild crane. What do I care if the cocks of the neighborhood are heralding the dawn?

Our poet was in the Chiang-ling area during the rest of the spring, the whole of the summer, and part of the autumn. He had called on

256

his distant cousin Tu Wei, who was then a staff officer with the army under the showy Governor General Wei Po-yü—now elevated to the rank of a prince. Wei would include Tu Fu in some festive parties; but apart from two perfunctory poems for the governor general, our poet seems to have chosen to neglect as far as possible that pompous dignitary. Tu Fu wrote several more poems on drinking and poetry-writing parties in which Chêng Shên or Li Chih-fang or both participated. "Summer Night at Minister Li's Party . . ." [cccxlii] is, in Tu Fu's collection, the only poem of the chain-line pattern, which represents a kind of game quite popular with our poet's contemporaries. In the present case, Tu Fu started off with a pair of lines. Then Li Chih-fang and another guest, Ts'ui Yü, each followed with two lines. The three continued to take turns until they reached a total of sixteen lines. A chain-line poem must present a unity of thought, and the various lines must meet the intricate antithetical requirements in sound values and word meanings. The artifice is what makes the game exciting, but it will not be apparent in the translation.

"The Returning Geese" [cccxl] and "Short Song Presented to Young Inspector Wang" [cccxli] were both written in the spring. We do not know who young Wang was. The poem mentions the Tower of Wang Ts'an which was really the tower on the city wall of Tang-yang, though since the period 1008–1016 the name was given to a building in Chiang-ling. It would seem that our poet had taken an overland trip fifty miles northwestward to Tang-yang. Perhaps, he and his family had gone there to visit Tu Kuan's family, though there is no evidence of such a visit in his existent poems. As to "The Returning Geese," some commentators thought that in it, Tu Fu was quite prophetic about the coming of wars. Traditional thought among Chinese scholars generally interprets unusual phenomena in the natural realm as good or bad omens for human society. Tu Fu was no exception. On December 20, 767, the governor general at Kuang-chou had memorialized the throne that the sudden appearance of flying geese in the Ling-nan Department was a good omen, promising general pacification of the empire. Now our poet heard in the spring of 768 that these geese had left Kuang-chou, and he took the occasion to say, of course, that the omen was to the contrary of peace and was bad.

CCCXL   THE RETURNING GEESE

I hear that the migratory geese of the present spring Have left Kuang-chou for further south. They now depart from the warm sea in the flower season, Though thither they had come to escape the northern snow. This phenomenon is a harbinger of wars; When can a traveler lay his anxiety to rest? In former years these flying birds in the autumn Never went further south than Lake Tung-t'ing.

CCCXLI SHORT SONG PRESENTED TO YOUNG INSPECTOR WANG

Sing not so sadly, as you enjoy the wine and hack the floor with your drawn sword, O Mr. Wang; I can depict your frank and open manner and your rare but frustrated talent. You are like a bay tree shaken by the wind in the sparkling sun, Or a whale leaping between the splitting waves. Please relieve yourself of the sword and stop swinging around. You will find in the West great dignitaries boating on the Brocade Stream, You had better decide at which door you are to present yourself. Here in the depth of spring on the Tower of Wang Ts'an, Let me fix my gaze on you and sing of my hope in you. As for me, thank you for your attention, but I am finished!

CCCXLII SUMMER NIGHT AT MINISTER LI'S PARTY IN HONOR OF YÜ-WÊN CH'AO'S DEPARTURE TO SERVE AS MAGISTRATE OF SHIH-SHOU DISTRICT (CHAIN LINES)

Generous is the hospitality of the minister, On the departure of his good nephew to an official post. Let us pour the fragrant wine—never mind spilling it beside the seat; We are drinking in the shadow of the sailboat soon to leave the riverside. Taste a piece of the pheasant, a bird symbolic of the brilliant beginnings of a career. Help yourself to the duck that reminds one of the story of an immortal magistrate.

The shower is about over; the clouds are breaking up. The night is late, and the wicks of the candles are aslant. Our hats are tilted too while we nod and sway in conversation; Let us have some fine paper to record this occasion. We wish you every joy during your trip; Though tipsy now, we will not use these parting moments for a nap. Remember the story of a famous magistrate who had plenty of leisure time; Of course, you will write, for like another, you are still in your youth. It is not common to meet one's own relative away from home; To separate again is naturally sad.

"Boarding the Boat to Leave for Han-yang" [CCCXLIII] was probably written about midautumn, when Tu Fu was planning to sail down-river 190 miles southeastward to Yo-chou; then northeastward 233 miles to Mien-chou; and then, veering into the Han, northwestward 440 miles upstream to Hsiang-yang. The mention of the preparations for war probably concerned the Tibetan invasion which reached Ling-wu by October 7 and brought Ch'ang-an under martial law from October 11 to November 11.

We do not know how far Tu Fu did go on the voyage. "Mourning over Minister Li Chih-fang" [CCCXLIV] shows that he returned to Chiang-ling very soon. It was probably the news of Li's death that brought him back. The life-long friendship between the two men would require that the survivor express himself over the coffin of the departed. Tu Fu did so in two poems.

CCCXLIII BOARDING THE BOAT TO LEAVE FOR HAN-YANG

In the spring, we left this boat for a house; Now the autumn sail is up to hasten the voyagers' return. I do not like to abandon those still growing vegetables in the garden, But I cannot stop now, as the spray of the waves is already on my clothes. Such a floating existence is not good for livelihood; And one's desires must recede as his years advance toward the end.

In the homelands, I know the people are busy with preparations for war; Few letters have come from long distances. The migrating geese from the frontiers have their seasonal gatherings here; The everlasting ravens will fly about the mast the year round. Let me proceed from here to Han-yang and then Hsiang-yang, To find a place of hermitage and to lay all ambitions permanently to rest.

CCCXLIV MOURNING OVER MINISTER LI CHIH-FANG

From the first evidence of your illness to the end of your life, There is hardly a year! Because I must express my affection for you, I have reversed the direction of my boat and have come. Ours is a friendship that lasted from boyhood to old age, Why should death intervene to make us part? What will the storms of my longing for you accomplish, Other than to sprinkle my tears on the already wet grounds of this lake region?

A great man of letters departed too early for literary labors in the other world; His Majesty will never again find so well-suited an ambassador to send abroad. But the historian will not fail to record your diplomatic achievements; Nor will the poets cease to quote the many fine lines you left.

Here at the station, few friends have come: The cobwebs are hanging over your coffin. Your relatives will have to come a long way to Chiangling, Before your soul and your remains can rest near Ch'ang-an, Where people will pass the revered graveyard with gigantic, unpruned trees, And lament the absence of the great minister from Court. The spring grass that we saw together is fading in the autumn wind; Where are you now, O prince of a man?

The news that in the North there were not only preparations for war but also widespread panic because of the Tibetan invasion might easily have brought about another change in our poet's plans. Should the imperial armies fail to check the advancing Tibetans, even Hsiang-yang,

621 miles southeast of Ch'ang-an, might not be a good place for hermitage. But where else could the Tu family go for even a short period? "Moving to Live in Kung-an: Presented to Wei Chün" [cccxlv] shows that, after meeting some difficulties—possibly bandits—the Tu family were generously given temporary shelters by young Wei, a man of means, fond of literature, and not an official. Kung-an was a district under the jurisdiction of Chiang-ling. It was about thirty miles south of Chiang-ling on a branch of the Yangtze.

"Too Long a Sojourner" [cccxlvi] might not really belong to this time and place. It helps, however, to illustrate the final two lines of the poem to Wei Chün. "Wealth maketh many friends; but the poor is separated from his neighbour," is not a new discovery anywhere any time. So long as poor Tu Fu still had the possibility of a place at court, the worldly-wise might show him some generosity for the sake of investment. But now, he was not only poor and in distress, not only old and sick, but also entirely without prospects of prominence, for he had given up all thoughts of official service. His friends, therefore, were limited to those who liked and respected him as a man or a poet. Most of the petty officials he mentioned in the poem were office clerks or retainers in the service of the dignitaries. They had a separate ranking ladder placed below the first rung of that of regular officialdom.

CCCXLV MOVING TO LIVE IN KUNG-AN: PRESENTED TO WEI CHÜN

It is not easy to find a man like you, Mr. Wei, Who really understands my troubles. You have not only a generous heart With sympathy for all, But you also set a high value on character And show a genuine appreciation of literature. Kindred spirits do meet at last like rivers and seas, Or by chance like winds and clouds. My appearance shows the wear by the elements; It is certainly incongruous in such a fine mansion. And yet, while a retiring man laments the fate common to his kind since antiquity, A strong man takes pity upon his wasted years.

Thus I was led out of the mist of the river to the grassy path of your garden Where the sunflowers are nourished in the autumn dew. And this happened after the wolves had entered this district to fight— When my family and I were like wounded birds starving and afraid. You have taken a white-headed man as a companion, And have provided everything to make him feel at home. Recently I have encountered much snobbery and insult, Today I am able to forget it all.

CCCXLVI TOO LONG A SOJOURNER

A sojourner is a strain on friendship; The longer the stay, the thinner the hospitality. I know my withered appearance to be laughable; But petty officials make the most stinging insults. One understands why Wang Ts'an lamented so much having left home And why Chia I

wept so many times in this region. I should, however, pay scant atten-
tion to the little foxes While tigers and wolves roam every road.

"Tsung-wu's Birthday" [CCCXLVII] might have been written late in
the autumn while the Tu family were still the guests of Wei Chün.
If my guess about the date of the boy's birth is correct, his age at this
time would be exactly twelve. In a note appended to "Leaving Kung-an
at Daybreak" [CCCXLVIII] Tu Fu said, "I have rested in this district several months." It would seem that the Tu family had stayed in Kung-an
not only part of the autumn but also most of the winter of 768–769.
In a poem of farewell to a Buddhist monk, he said that he was going
to find a place of hermitage on Mount Lu in Chiang-chou (194 miles
east of Mien-chou), and that while the snow had not melted in
Kung-an, the plum trees must already be blooming in Chiang-chou.
The departure probably took place a few days before the beginning of
spring—in other words, a few days before February 7, 769. In the poem
written on the morning of the actual departure, he did not, however,
mention Chiang-chou again. Was he already doubting whether he
should go as far as Chiang-chou? At any rate, we find Tu Fu soon
at Yo-chou on the eastern shore of Lake Tung-t'ing. Here he wrote
"The Year Is Drawing to a Close" [CCCXLIX] and "Climbing Yo-yang
Tower" [CCCL]. He ascended Yo-yang Tower a second time, and on that
occasion, the grass was growing in the spring mud. He said that he was
about to go farther south. It seems that he and his family had spent
the New Year's Day in Yo-chou.

CCCXLVII TSUNG-WU'S BIRTHDAY

*When did my small son first appear? He was born in the height of
autumn, on this day. Since friends in Chiang-ling made certain comments, His name has often been mentioned with mine. Poetry is the
distinction of our family; It is natural for the world to expect this of
him. He must memorize and understand Selections of Masterpieces;
He should not have such vain interest in pretty clothing. I already feel
exhausted when the feast begins, I can hardly sit erect. Let me have
just a little of the wine that is like liquid sunset, I shall sip it a drop
at a time.*

CCCXLVIII LEAVING KUNG-AN AT DAYBREAK

*The night-watchmen's rattle should have ceased in the north city, For
the morning star has risen in the east. The cocks of our suburban neighborhood will crow as usual, But how long will such colors and activities
of nature last? Our boat will soon disappear from the sight of these
shores; We shall sail along the rivers and lakes with no definite destination. In the twinkling of an eye, everything here will pass into memory;
Only these packages of medicine shall follow me wherever I go.*

CCCXLIX THE YEAR IS DRAWING TO A CLOSE

Too much north wind toward the end of the year Is blowing snow to enwrap Lake Tung-t'ing. The fishing nets are frozen solid; And the Mo-yu fishermen resort to shooting the passing geese with arrows. Last year the army needed rice, and the price went up; This year it came down and the farmers have been hard hit. The proud dignitaries on fine horses are satiated with wine and meat; In the farming huts, the people have no money to buy yarn for their looms. But fish will sell well in this area, not fowls; You should not molest the migratory birds.

I hear, moreover, that boys and girls are being sold into slavery Just to enable the heart-broken parents to pay taxes. In former days, when coins were needed, the government confiscated the counterfeits; Now to mix lead and iron with bronze is permitted in the private mints. It would have been easiest to mould mud as a substitute! It is not right to let bad money continue to drive out the good. Army bugles can be heard from every city wall; When can there be an end to such unhappy music?

CCCL CLIMBING YO-YANG TOWER

For a long time I have heard of Lake Tung-t'ing; Only now have I climbed the Yo-yang Tower. The lands of Ch'u and Wu slide away to the south and east, While the center of the world is day and night afloat.

Not a word has come from my relatives and friends; Old and sick, I rely on only a boat. In the north beyond the distant mountains, there is still no peace; I weep as I lean on the balustrade.

From Yo-chou, Tu Fu sailed on Lake Tung-t'ing southward about forty-three miles to enter the mouth of the Hsiang. About two miles upstream, he spent a night at the White Sand Station and mentioned in a poem the abundant moonlight on the water. Thus, his arrival in the Hu-nan (literally, lake-south) area would be about February 25, 769. Sailing for the most part southward and upstream, he stopped here and there for sightseeing and for feasting and drinking parties given by friends, who, he said, were all sorry to note his aging appearance. Here and there his boat had to stop because the current and the wind were both against it. His poem "North Wind" [CCCLI] has a note to the effect that owing to the south wind his boat had to stop for two days at the Hsin-k'ang Crossing—fifty-three miles from the mouth of the Hsiang and nineteen miles to T'an-chou.

He probably spent only two or three days at T'an-chou. "Yo-lu-shan and Tao-lin Monasteries" [CCCLII] was written about the two famous places a few miles across the river, west of the city. Tangerine Sandbar, mentioned in the poem, was located in the river near T'an-chou; our poet used the term to denote the T'an-chou neighborhood. He wrote this poem on the wall of the Yo-lu-shan Monastery beside a poem by Sung Chih-wên. About half a century later, other scholarly visitors also wrote poems on the wall. They all praised Tu Fu's poem and one of them commended his handwriting as well.

"Stopping for the Night at Hewn Rock Station" [CCCLIII] was written about March 14 at a place about sixty-five miles upstream from T'an-chou. The guests mentioned were probably fellow voyagers picked up and given a free ride for certain distances. They would help to punt the boat upstream. Some of these people might be robbers in disguise, and an inlet of the river was an isolated place. Hence the poem's apprehensive note. "Southward" [CCCLIV] and "Early Sailing" [CCCLV] could also have been written along this section of the river. Forty-nine miles further upstream the boat reached the Evening Sandbar where the banks were high, the current rapid, and the scenery exquisite. By "Ferry Crossing" [CCCLVI], Tu Fu probably meant a locality across the river east of Hêng-shan—the Hsiang River, flowing northward, curves here again toward the east for a few miles. Our poet did not visit the Hêng Mountain in the neighborhood. In another poem, he said that he would do so on the return trip. There is no evidence that he ever did.

We know roughly when Tu Fu arrived in Hêng-chou (186 miles from T'an-chou, fifty miles from Hêng-shan). In the early part of 769, the Prefect of Hêng-chou and, concurrently, governor of Hu-nan was Wei Chih-chin, a friend of our poet. On April 3, the court ordered the transfer of Wei to the prefecture of T'an-chou, which was then made the seat of the provincial government of Hu-nan. Wei died in T'an-chou probably in the summer; for on August 9, the Court ordered Ts'ui Kuan, prefect of Li-chou, be made prefect of T'an-chou and concurrently governor of Hu-nan. In a poem mourning Wei's death, Tu Fu mentioned that illness had delayed his visit to Hêng-chou in response to Wei's invitation, that when he did come south to Hêng-chou, he was surprised to find that the time of their reunion was to be short, and that while he was longing to rejoin Wei in T'an-chou, the news of Wei's death had reached him. From this, it may be surmised that our poet reached Hêng-chou, shortly before Wei's departure for T'an-chou, which would be soon after April 3.

That Tu Fu should remain in Hêng-chou for several months may be explained by an intensification of his illness that required the attention of doctors. The second of his two poems on "My Feelings" [CCCLVII], written probably about the middle of May, shows that he was hoping to become well enough to proceed further south to the Ling-nan coast. Perhaps, when he was sufficiently recovered to travel again, he had changed his plans once more, and turned northward. It was possibly on his return trip from Hêng-chou to T'an-chou that he visited the Temple of Confucius at Hêng-shan and commended the magistrate of the district for having instituted a new school therein.

After arriving in T'an-chou, he probably rented an apartment by the river. Poverty drove him to leave his family there while he took the boat himself to visit some friends in the outlying districts in the hope of finding aid. "Staying on the Boat: Presented to the Gentlemen in the City" [CCCLVIII] seems to fit such a trip from T'an-chou in the summer of 769 better than the generally supposed voyage from Chiang-ling in the preceding summer—when Tu Fu was not using the boat and when his circumstances did not appear to be so restricted. Though Tu Fu did not specify the city in the poem, it was possibly one of the district cities on a small river running west to east near the southern shore of Lake Tung-t'ing. This short trip was apparently not very fruitful; and it was possibly after his return that Tu Fu wrote "Sick in the Riverside Apartment: For the Information of General Censors Ts'ui and Lu" [CCCLIX].

CCCLI NORTH WIND

Spring brings malarial fevers to the South. North wind will disperse the miasmic atmosphere That smothers the setting sun And places the evening in an oven.

When the wind came, it slashed as if to tear away the Hu-nan area, It sounded as if it had sucked up the whole Tung-t'ing Lake. Fishes and dragons trembled under water; Birds and beasts moaned at midnight.

I enjoy the purifying effects of sailing against the oncoming waves And abandoning my severe melancholy to the tearing of the wind. As long as one feels uncomfortable heat, One naturally wishes to move in the cool air. Since I know it will bring some relief to my lungs, I am quite willing to accept the dangers of travel. Our boatmen have had to anchor the boat for two days, I turn my withered face to my servant to make an inquiry. Unless it is going to be fierce again this morning, I am told, They will at once let me continue my long voyage. I shall lean across the table, gaze from the deck, And watch the cloudy hills, passing me, float away.

CCCLII YO-LU-SHAN AND TAO-LIN MONASTERIES

South of Jade Springs stands the extraordinary Yo-lu-shan Beside the winding woods and ravines of Tao-lin. The entrance to Yo-lu-shan towers above Tung-t'ing's shores. The foundation of Tao-lin stretches into Lake Red Sand. In the halls, the cold air even in midsummer will chill Buddha's bone; But heavenly music always issues from the angelic figures surrounding the incense-burner. Every foot of ground is covered with the evergreen grass from snow-topped mountains, Each of the monks is comparable to a pearl from a distant sea. The dagobas rival palace walls in splendor; The kitchen has the same refreshing scent as the pine groves. These bells might make one think that lotus-blossoms and double-headed birds sound alike; Those boards inscribed with golden characters are dazzling in the sunlight.

It might take one too long to find the fairyland across the eastern sea; Nor can one be sure of the existence of blissful heavens in the extreme west. I am, therefore, pleased with passing this place in the evening of my life; And the hospitable welcome is as comforting as the warmth of the spring sun. Where else could a white-headed man like me go, If he does not choose a site near this heavenly neighborhood to build a hut? The fine custom of the legendary Peach Blossom Valley has ceased to exist, But the soil of the equally famous Tangerine Sandbar is still rich. Moreover, life in the T'an-chou Prefecture is wholesome and conservative; There are no boisterous sounds in the courtyard of the prefect.

Many good men in the past have hidden away from a degenerate world; It is now fortunate for me to find a happy land for refuge. I shall not consider it too late to seek shelter among these old and wise monks. What good will it do me to reach out for wealth, prominence, or fame? Having been long fond of poetry, I am accustomed to enjoying quiet retreats; Continuing to study Buddhism, I shall not lack inspiring companions. Every turn or fold of the landscape shall be absorbed into my bosom, Every bird or flower shall be my friend. In his days of exile, the great Sung Chih-wên wrote a poem on the wall; I am grateful he still left something for me to portray.

CCCLIII   STOPPING FOR THE NIGHT AT HEWN ROCK STATION

We stopped early because the guests and the workmen were tired, And we might as well enjoy the beautiful landscape of midspring. A storm might come without warning; We do not dare leave the boat unmoored. As the evening colors fade in the inlet, Countless stars begin to twinkle. The new moon has not appeared; Our bluish lamp has gone out.

Among the poor, there are extraordinary people, both good and bad; In time of trouble, there is little kindness or gratitude. I, too, have been careless— A habit with me for years. Confucianism warns men to beware of danger; In the Canon of Changes the teaching is well stated.

CCCLIV SOUTHWARD

The stream of peach blossoms flows toward us between two shores of spring, As our white sail winds through the maple forests on both banks. As refugees, we have been moving from one place to another— The further from home, the more tears dampen our clothes. Aged and infirm, I am steadily traveling to the south; Remembering my gracious Sovereigns, I turn frequently to gaze to the north. My whole life constitutes a bitter song; I have found none to appreciate such sad music.

CCCLV EARLY SAILING

Every quest is preceded by a hundred scruples; Confucianism is indeed one of my troubles! And yet, because of it, I have many friends; And despite my age, I have continued to travel. We started early today and the boatmen are too lazy To study the wind and adjust the sail right.

Wise men of ancient times would not expose themselves to any chance of danger; Why should we hurry now at the risk of our lives? Black serpents are leaping in the rolling waves; A yellowish fog is spreading to meet the rising sun. Is it miasma that comes to hasten the end of life? I feel fatigued, I lean on something, and I sleep.

My servant comes to help me with my morning toilet, And the bronze mirror clearly reflects my withered face. Haphazardly I pin the cloth cap on my head; I feel ashamed of myself as I glimpse the flowers in the forest. I hear there were pirates on the river last night; I rejoice that they can rob me of only an empty purse.

Having come a long and hard way to be a guest, One can make few appeals without injuring one's self-respect. Among the ancients, there were good men who refused to compromise and starved to death; There were able men who humored the world and received rich gifts. These are mutually exclusive examples; The trouble with me is that I want to follow them both!

CCCLVI FERRY CROSSING

The Hêng, the great mountain of the South, is now near us; The Hsiang River turns here to flow east. A mild wind helps us as we pull with our oars— As we watch the spring sunlight floating above the mountain clouds. I turn to look again at the Ferry Crossing; I realize there are thick maple forests in the region. I see shining fish struggling within tight nets, While I hear orioles singing carefree tunes. Even trivial creatures know the difference betwen freedom and bondage; Sympathy and compassion should be but natural to the human heart.

In the pot, there is still some leftover wine; On my knees, I place the silent lute. I am no longer impressed with the claims of wisdom or holiness among the ancient great; I shall dozingly loosen my robe to welcome the fine air upon my breast.

CCCLVII MY FEELINGS (TWO POEMS)

2

Lawlessness became widespread in a tottering nation; My longing and grief grew as I looked back upon the golden times of great sovereigns— As I sailed up the Hsiang River through Hu-nan And sought in vain for the burial grounds of Emperor Shun in the dusk. A submerged fish will avoid a baited hook, A running deer will not cast back a lingering look. I have a nature—open, free, high-spirited— But I am now trying to make it different and distorted! Bound I am, and delivered to the pursuit of clothing and food— To seeking out sympathetic friends in distant places. After braving the wind and waves of the spring For hundreds of miles up the tree-lined sandy river, I could find no auspicious days to continue the sail upstream, And a new season of the year has come to pass. I have abandoned the old homestead to the accumulation of dust; I have more than once troubled the boatmen to make uncertain trips.

Besides the troubles of age and illness, I am tied To numerous trivial mundane necessities. Eternity is just one undifferentiated grave; Why bother to add one more name to it? I fear I might disgrace these enchanted surroundings, Hence I persist in my unwise plan of going further south. Since I am willing to accept all the murky poisons there, I shall, of course, banish all fears of hardship on the way. Tigers and wolves are threatening the central sections of the Empire; How can I hope to dwell long in the places I have passed? Ko Hung and Hsü Ching of ancient times Also fled the world and traveled this road. Though I cannot compare with them in wisdom; I too am accustomed to moving about. But what more can be done for my exhausting illness, After the acupunctures and cauterizations have almost killed me more than once? My servants grudge the hectic and fruitless use of their service, The boatmen are angered by the long interruption of the voyage.

I hope indeed that we shall one day hoist the sail and gather way, But what the will of heaven is, none can tell. If I can only reach the extreme South, I shall force myself to get up. And to court the friendship of the old Polar Star, I might even stretch my feeble legs atop the fairy mounts of the southern shore.

CCCLVIII STAYING IN THE BOAT: PRESENTED TO THE GENTLEMEN IN THE CITY

Stupidity on top of frequent illness! Thus I have a double excuse for my social failures. I am so deaf that my friends have to talk with their fingers; My hair is too thin to comb.

We have been waiting, in this lake region, for rain, And have had during the summer just shallow mud. While my boat waits for the little river to collect more waves, I have moored it by the long dyke.

Though I set out to the north, I was not returning home, For the boat soon turned toward the west. The bitterness of displacement in the evening of life Is tonight mixed with the tears of separation. The children have more than once written to say That their soup was too thin and tasted too flat. How did I ever come to these straits? In the order of things now, it is difficult to expect justice and fairness. Propped on high pillows in bed, I can see the moon and stars rolling in the water; I can almost hear the repeating drums of the heavily garrisoned city. The wind seems to convey the howling of tigers and leopards; Staying on the water overnight, I am a companion of ducks and gulls.

I was amazed that the trip to the other districts was in vain, And I regretted the separation from my usual friends. Too long has this boat been afloat; Too many sleepless nights have I spent on it. Gentlemen, you are all prominent men with great expectations; Many are those who come to you for assistance. To quench a dying thirst, I have hoped only for a few drops from the overflow; But my scanty provisions will hardly permit many days of waiting. The distance to your doors is too far, if I take a stick and walk; The cost is prohibitive, if I try to engage a sedan chair. While I lament my own humiliation, Who is there that will pity such involuntary plight? Is there really no fishing even in a big ocean? There might be tall ladders to reach the floating clouds. The meritorious achievements that are in one's thoughts Should not be difficult to discern, even though not expressly stated.

Let the generous follow an ancient example of giving away a whole granary, Let me follow another of not wanting to recross a bridge without doing it in splendor. Let it be understood that in my old frame the loyal heart will not collapse; I am looking for a place where no compromise of principles need be made.

CCCLIX SICK IN BED IN THE RIVERSIDE APARTMENT. FOR THE INFORMATION OF GENERAL CENSORS TS'UI AND LU

The kitchen of a sojourner is poorly provided; Though the mat and the pillows in the riverside apartment are comfortable. The illness of my declining years has left me only bones and skin; My thoughts during these long summer days usually concern the generosity of friends. I recall the smoothness of steamed wild rice, And can almost smell the fragrance of water shield soup. These are soothing to the palate and warming to the stomach; Who is it that will bring me enough for a few bowls?

"Facing the Snow" [cccLx], "Silkworms and Cows" [cccLxi], and "The Red Phoenix" [cccLxii] have been generally placed by editors among Tu Fu's T'an-chou poems in the winter of 769. There is nothing in the poems to confirm this assignment. On the other hand, there is nothing to repudiate it.

CCCLX FACING THE SNOW

The northern snow is invading T'an-chou; The clouds of Tatary have made the homes cold. Wind-driven leaves are flying with the snow; Mixed with rain, the flakes seldom show the pattern of a flower.

Though the money in my purse is all spent, It is still easy to buy wine on credit. Why is no friend coming to share the jug with me? I shall wait until the crows come to roost at dusk.

CCCLXI SILKWORMS AND COWS

There must be ten thousand cities in the Empire; And none of them is untroubled by the weapons of war. How good it would be to beat these instruments into farming tools, And let the oxen plow every acre of the many abandoned fields! Oxen on the farms. Silkworms in the homes. Our valiant soldiers need weep no more. Men will harvest grain, women spin silk—they will sing as they work.

CCCLXII THE RED PHOENIX

Do you not see that of the mountains of Hu-nan the Hêng is the highest? On the highest peak a red phoenix cries forlornly. It turns, bends, and stretches to look for its kind; When fatigued, it stands in silence, with drooped wings. Pitying the various birds caught in the nets below— From which the smallest sparrows cannot escape—It decides to share its food with all humble creatures, even the ants, And cares not if all the owls should get angry and hoot.

"Shown to Tsung-wu on New Year's Day" [cccLxiii] and "Another Poem to Show to Tsung-wu" [cccLxiv] would be written on February 1, 770, if my conjecture about Tu Tsung-wu's birth date is correct. We may recall that on a previous festival day, our poet wrote poems to show to his two boys, Tsung-wên and Tsung-wu. On the present occasion, he had something to say to Tsung-wu only. We may assume that the elder boy was then not with him. In a poem written a few months later, our poet mentioned the return of a boy from a long distance. That might have been Tsung-wên. Could our poet have sent him in search of the lost Tu Fêng in the East?

CCCLXIII SHOWN TO TSUNG-WU ON NEW YEAR'S DAY

You cry, and my hand trembles; I laugh, and you will grow tall fast. We have met New Years in many places, But always farther and farther from our home country. I see that we still use the cypress wine for the festival; But my wearisome illness has confined me to a wooden bed. When I teach my son, so full of promise, I am ashamed of not having a better career even in old age. I shall, however, compose a poem and write it on paper myself, While you say the words of felicitation and offer your father the cup. Not knowing the whereabouts of my brother in the East, I sing and shed tears at the same time.

CCCLXIV ANOTHER POEM TO SHOW TO TSUNG-WU

I see you are composing the lines to fit the prosody you have just learned; You have opened the books and spread them over the bed. Try to sing in the style of ancient masters; Don't let your heart be carried away by pretty playthings. You may drink seasonally on festive occasions; Next year you will be as tall as I am. You should learn as much as possible of Confucian ethics, Since you seem already to admire good literature. A boy after his fourteenth New Year's Day should aim To be comparable to some of the three thousand students of the great sage. And remember, only those who understood both morals and letters Were admitted further than the yard, up into the master's hall.

On February 21, 770, Tu Fu went over his file of correspondence, and found a poem which Kao Shih sent him on February 16, 761, when Kao was prefect of Shu-chou and while our poet was living in the thatched hut in Ch'êng-tu. Kao died in Ch'ang-an on February 17, 765, in the position of an Advisory Chancellor (twenty-sixth rung up the official ladder). Our poet now wrote a belated response to this old poem and prefaced it with a dated statement that all of his intimate friends had died except Li Yü, Prince of Han-chung, and Ching Ch'ao-hsien, Prefect of Chao-chou. That Tu Fu did not mention Ts'ên Shên, who was known to be living in Ch'êng-tu in 769, has led modern scholars to infer that Ts'ên died shortly before February 21, 770.

"Written in the Boat on the Second Day of the Cold Food Festival" [CCCXLV] was possibly written on April 4, 770. Two other poems generally assigned to the latter part of the same spring are "Some New Playful Lines on Watching from the Boat the Falling Flowers in the Storm" [cccxlvi] and "Meeting Li Kuei-nien in Chiang-nan" [cccxlvii]. There is only a slight question regarding the former. Remembering our poet's very recent teaching of his son Tsung-wu to avoid pretty playthings in poetry, we may wonder how the playful, beautious imagery in the poem could have been a good example to set for the youngster. Yet, the poem may contain hidden, allegorical meanings which could be understood at the time, but which we are now unable to unravel. The latter poem poses a much more serious difficulty. For centuries, the authenticity of the poem has been questioned and defended. The poet was saying that he had frequently seen Singer Li Kuei-nien in the houses of two celebrities in Lo-yang. In view of the fact that both of these celebrities died in 726, wouldn't Tu Fu have been too young to associate with them? On the other hand, since Tu Fu had said in his "Brave Adventures" [ccxi] that he had ventured into the arena of letters in his fourteenth year, there is no reason to insist that he could not have met Singer Li frequently in Lo-yang, say, in 725, and in the houses of local celebrities.

But, there is also a textual difficulty in the second half of the poem. If Tu Fu now meets Singer Li again in T'an-chou in the spring of 770, would Tu Fu say, "The landscape of Chiang-nan is at its best"? No, instead of Chiang-nan he would very likely use Hu-nan as he did in other poems [ccclxix, ccclxxiii, ccclxxiv]. Did the text originally read "Chiang-nan"? If so, might not this rather light and breezy poem be assigned to a period in Tu Fu's late teens when he was traveling for pleasure in the Southeast? Did the text originally read "Hu-nan" and was corrupted to "Chiang-nan" in the course of transmission? Yet, according to one ninth-century author, the text already read "Chiang-nan." According to another source, old and saddened Li Kuei-nien was actually singing in the T'an-chou area at this time. Perhaps, for the time being, we had better leave the text of the poem as well as its chronological and geographical assignments as they have been transmitted, noting here the problems awaiting solution.

Before proceeding to Tu Fu's activities in the summer of 770, we should perhaps pause to face the question whether or not he had made a trip in the spring from T'an-chou to some place beyond Lake Tung-t'ing. The question arises from two often quoted poems, or rather, from a part of one of them. These poems, under the title "Clear and Bright Festival," have generally been assigned to 769; and the date would be about April 4, 769, for the festival usually occurred 106 days after the winter solstice. But the two poems seem to be spurious, because the lines, with the exception of two, are rather poor in literary quality. Moreover, they portray Tu Fu sailing over Lake Tung-t'ing; but Tu Fu could not have been on the Tung-t'ing on April 4, 769, for he was then a long way south in the neighborhood of Hêng-chou. One of the

poems describes Tu Fu with the right shoulder and arm paralyzed, trying to write something in the air with the left hand. This does not seem
to be true. Tu Fu was able to write a poem on the wall of Yo-lu-shan
Monastery sometime between February 25 and March 14, 769. He was
able to write a poem for his son Tsung-wu on February 1, 770. Moreover, in Tu Fu's collection there is a poem written in response to one
(which is also printed) by a Kuo Shou. This poem of Tu Fu's must
have been written in the spring of 770 in T'an-chou. But Kuo's poem
describes our poet as trying to row a boat!

It seems to me that of the twenty-four lines in the "Clear and
Bright Festival" poems, only the last two are genuine. Some T'ang
writer, a generation after our poet's time, quoted these two lines with
admiration:

The spring comes, the spring goes, above Tung-t'ing's expansiveness;
O white duck weeds, you are killing a white-haired man with sadness!

Perhaps some busybody afterwards picked up these two lines and wrote
twenty-two more to make up two poems for our poet. And these two
poems have since been widely included in anthologies and biographical
accounts of Tu Fu!

But the two lines quoted above originally belonged to a poem the title
of which was said to be "Passing Lake Tung-t'ing." The original, then,
had nothing to do with the Clear and Bright Festival. And, if the lost
poem was genuine, we may observe that our poet might have sailed over
the Lake Tung-t'ing again about the end of the spring and the beginning
of the summer in 770.

CCCLXV WRITTEN IN THE BOAT ON THE SECOND DAY OF THE COLD
        FOOD FESTIVAL

On this fine morning, we are still eating cold food, and I force myself to
sip a little wine; Wearing a hermit's cap, I lean on the stool in a mood
of quiet sorrow. Over the spring river we sail as if in the sky. To my
aged eyes flowers appear as though in a fog. Butterflies, like pretty
maidens, flutter between parted curtains. Gulls, like pieces of white
paper, float down the rapid current. Through thousands of miles of
white clouds and blue mountains, I direct my unhappy gaze to the north
and think of Ch'ang-an.

CCCLXVI SOME NEW PLAYFUL LINES ON WATCHING FROM THE BOAT
         THE FALLING FLOWERS IN THE STORM

A few branches of the blooming peach trees of a home on the riverside
Have stretched out in the spring wind and rain over a flimsy fence.
While the pretty shadows are being quietly lured away by the blue

stream, The jealous wind comes to throw the red flowers the opposite way. The blown petals, escaping such madness, shower my boat And seem to fear the glare of the water as much as the force of the wind. I resent their rude and shameless intrusion into my bosom; I shall make it clear that I receive them not. Long soaked, they fly slowly, and can hardly attain height; Then like feathers, they are caught on the sand and in the grass. A bee and a butterfly are at once alert and lively; But, to avoid the shrike, a timid-eyed dragonfly steals away.

CCCLXVII   MEETING LI KUEI-NIEN IN CHIANG-NAN

You were frequently seen in the mansion of the Prince of Ch'i; And a number of times you sang before the hall of Ts'ui Ti. Now when the landscape of Chiang-nan is at its best—When flowers are falling, here we meet again. Who could have guessed?

If Tu Fu did take a short trip over Lake Tung-t'ing toward the close of April in 770, he could not have stayed long in T'an-chou after his return. Trouble broke out there on May 7. Governor Ts'ui Kuan was murdered by a subordinate general, Tsang Chieh. The city was seized and another rebellion was in the making. As usual, the Tu family had to flee. "White Horse" [CCCLXVIII] records a sad scene at the beginning of the flight, which is described at some length in "Entering Hêng-chou" [CCCLXIX]. After narrating the causes of the sudden outbreak, our poet touches upon the hardship of trying to avoid the beast-like rioters on land. He seemed to be grateful that his family was together. By "our son, having returned from afar," he probably means Tsung-wên, who had been away possibly to the east coast. "The infant girl . . . not lost from our midst" might have been a baby born during the year of sojourn in T'an-chou; and it was possible that the child was momentarily missed in the confusion of leaving the riverside apartment. After describing the sail upstream and the hospitality of Prefect Yang Tsi of Hêng-chou, Tu Fu proceeds to encourage Yang to organize, with the help of a Mr. Su, an expedition against the mutineers in T'an-chou. This Mr. Su was probably the ambitious and talented young Su Huan whom Tu Fu had previously met in T'an-chou. The last part of the poem concerns the destination of the Tu family on the sailing vessel. They were traveling toward Ch'ên-chou, 457 miles by water from T'an-chou, where Tu Fu's maternal uncle, Ts'ui Wei, probably only a cousin of his mother, was then the acting prefect.

CCCLXVIII   WHITE HORSE

The white horse coming from the northeast Bears an empty saddle pierced by two arrows. My sympathy goes to the erstwhile rider Who is no longer here to tell his tale. After his commanding officer was executed,

He probably fought at midnight and was wounded. This insurrection must have brought about many deaths, Oh, my tears will not stop!

CCCLXIX ENTERING HÊNG-CHOU

Since history began there have been wars and insurrections; Whether a dynasty will stand or collapse depends on the sovereign. We had a most brilliant Court; And yet how mad and violent those Tatar hordes were! Ever since old General Ko-shu Han mishandled his command; Every quiet frontier has become a battleground. Both the government and the people have to endure humiliation; Neither the rivers nor the mountains afford means of defense. Each governor general behaves as an independent war lord, Despising the central authority and breaking every discipline. There is now no uniformity among armies and prefectures; All civil and military administration depend on the whims of the commanders.

I grieve for Governor Ts'ui Kuan, a man of unselfish principles—A man accustomed to life's difficulties and hardships. He governed the province as he did his own simple household, And attempted to protect even the humblest and most helpless. Since he had long sympathized with the suffering people, He was always humane and conservative in his administration. He was, however, not well suited for military leadership; For he was too vigilant an economist. His own habits of self-denial led him to insist on frugality for others; And too much worry over waste or loss multiplied for him troubles within his army. Even officers were on rations of wine and meat, they complained, And the men had hardly enough clothing to keep warm. The mutinous leader purposely mixed falsehood and truth to fan A seditious conspiracy which soon broke into the open, Soaking the general headquarters in blood, Plunging the whole Province of Hu-nan into misery. A fierce conflagration burst out at midnight; The heavy smoke swirled up to blacken the heavens. The mutineers even now are dividing grain and silk among themselves; A murderous atmosphere has spread along the Yüan and the Hsiang. The precept that good rewards come to good men is now turned upside down; I turn to heaven for an explanation, but heaven answers me not.

With a shattered spirit, we fled from flying arrows; Step by step, we zigzagged our way through the wild beasts. We had to endure the pricks and stings of thorns and briars; Often we stopped because of swollen legs or blistered feet. Lucky it was that our son, having returned from afar, was with us, And the infant girl, still unweaned, was not lost from our midst. I thought it fortunate too not to be a permanent sojourner in T'an-chou; But so late in life I am ashamed of being so perturbed. Thus we have proceeded drearily by land and by water; It matters not whether we become lost among fishermen or among merchants. I am too old to be of any service to my Sovereign, And my illness has prevented my going to Ch'ang-an to report at Court. Uncertain is my future amid unrefined surroundings; Depressed is my uncompromising spirit.

After passing here and there sandbars and bays, We have turned now into a cove lined with fine bamboo forests. Stopping our boat to the left of the Ch'ên-chou region, We face ahead of us the great city of Hêng-chou. Birds and clouds are circling round the tall memorial pillars; Flowers and herbs send out their fragrance from famed gardens. Market pavilions with trade banners are discernible among the houses; The watch towers stand imposingly on the city wall. Prefect Yang Tsi has a record comparable to the best among the ancients; His talents have made him outstanding among our officials. As a governor, he will strengthen the Dynasty as a stout pillar does a tottering roof; As a member of the Tribunal, he will subdue the unruly as frost does insects. I was yesterday a guest at his feast among brilliant company; His inspiring conversation flowed as easily as the good wine from the pot—Not to mention his invitation to rejoin him for another party. His hospitality has already soothed much of my disquiet. Moreover, he has an expert of military strategy And a literary talent of the first order In his protégé, Mr. Su, Who is braver than the bravest of the ancient soldiers. If a punitive expedition starts from Hêng-chou's advantageous position, Victory can be guaranteed without hesitation. The rebellious atmosphere will surely be swept away; How can the mosquitoes resist such might?

Ch'ên-chou is famed as the historic site of the Tangerine Well; The immortal hills cast a spell upon our boat. We are tired of the hot summer rain during our voyage, And we rejoice to hear of the clear and cool weather in Ch'ên-chou. A maternal uncle of mine is there acting as prefect, And has sent me some brilliant letters, In which his repeated invitations to me Shine among a hundred lines of beautifully written characters. The poet Chiang Tsung was brought up in the home of his maternal grandparents; The statesman Hsieh An gave himself to the enjoyment of landscape. As an ordinary man, I cannot compare myself to such gems of antiquity; I am a humble, shelter-seeking bird shamelessly entering the phoenix forest. Let me be a pupil to the high-minded scholar, My uncle's associate, the esteemed Mr. Chang Ch'üan. Let me dwell as a sojourner in a humble hut in the happy country To watch the gradual rise of the rocs to the heights.

From Hêng-chou southeastward to Ch'ên-chou was a voyage of 271 miles up the Lei River. When Tu Fu and his family had sailed about one hundred miles, they had to anchor the boat for several days because the swollen river, probably owing to heavy rain, was too dangerous.

Magistrate Nieh of Lei-yang, hearing of the interruption of our voyage, sent a letter with gifts of wine and meat to satisfy our needs on this deserted river. This poem was to express my gratitude as much as the rhyme would permit me. When I finally reached the district city, I presented it personally to Mr. Nieh. From the city, the journey by land was only thirteen miles to the Fang-t'ien Station. The boat took one whole day. The river was then swollen, and we anchored at Fang-t'ien.

The Magistrate of Lei-yang sent me a letter Which reached me far down the deserted river. In ancient times, two Niehs, brother and sister, were famous heroes—You must be a worthy descendant of such an extraordinary family. Recently I saw the grandson of State Minister Ti, And he told me that you were an exceptionally good man. Though you come from a family that was securely famous in the Imperial Academy of Letters, Unfortunately, you are still serving as the chief official of a small district.

You heard that I was detained by fierce waves, And was for five days threatened by the flood. Indeed, ever since the mutiny murdered the commander and brought Mourning banners to the shores of the lake, I have been traveling On a solitary boat laden increasingly with melancholy, Passing many places where dangers threatened. Often I was startled to observe the agile movements of gibbons; Frequently I looked up and envied the freedom of the cranes in flight. Your generosity is to me more than if you had slaughtered a fatted sheep; And the pure wine will help dissolve my sadness.

I am not eloquent enough to interest officials in intervention; But I desire very much to see the rebels in the north annihilated. While I was sailing along the quiet shores towards Ch'ên-chou, I heard no news of the troubles at T'an-chou. Now I learn that Ts'ui I brought an army from Hung-chou And that the troops from Li-chou, though few, are strong. The news of these punitive expeditions seems to be real; I can now smilingly take a rest in the pavilion by the pond.

The histories of T'ang give us no complete information about how the insurrection at T'an-chou was finally cleared up. We are told only that Prefect Yang Tzŭ-lin of Li-chou, Prefect P'ei Ch'iu of Tao-chou, and Prefect Yang Tsi of Hêng-chou all sent punitive expeditions against Tsang Chieh, and that Yang Tzŭ-lin, after receiving a bribe, returned to Li-chou. From Tu Fu we learn that his young maternal cousin Ts'ui I, who had been in the service of Governor Ts'ui Kuan, had gotten an army from Hung-chou and had reached the northern outskirts of Yüan-chou when our poet was in Lei-yang. In a poem addressed to Yang Tsi and other dignitaries interested in sending expeditions against the mutineers in T'an-chou, Tu Fu mentioned that he heard that P'ei Ch'iu's armed forces had reached T'an-chou and that several subordinate generals in T'an-chou had thrice memorialized the throne on behalf of the rebellious Tsang Chieh. Our poet called the attention of Yang Tsi and Governor General Li Mien of Ling-nan to the fact that too many similar cases had occurred in different parts of the empire, wherein a murderous usurper had by such means coerced the court to grant pardon and appointment. He wanted Governor General Li and Prefect Yang to restore law and order by seeing that the rebels in T'an-chou should not escape punishment. I am inclined to think that Tu Fu probably met Li Mien and Li's armed forces on the Lei River coming from Ling-nan. We do not know whether Tu Fu ever reached Ch'ên-chou. It is not impossible that his maternal cousin Ts'ui Wei, Acting Prefect of Ch'ên-chou, might also have come down the Lei River with an armed force. They and our poet would naturally sail down the Lei to meet Prefect Yang Tsi at Hêng-chou. It was then that they learned that Prefect P'ei Ch'iu, commanding a navy coming from Tao-chou at the upper reach of the Hsiang, had already passed Hêng-chou and was approaching T'an-chou.

If Tu Fu wrote more poems about how the various punitive forces brought an end to the T'an-chou insurrection, they were not transmitted in the existent collection. My guess is that perhaps the imperial pardon and the appointment of the ringleaders among the mutineers to other places had reached T'an-chou before the punitive forces had attacked the city. At any rate, T'ang history recorded the appointment on June 19 of General Hsin Ching-kao as prefect of T'an-chou and governor of Hu-nan. Nothing further was said about Tsang Chieh and the insurrection.

Perhaps, before the summer was over, the revolt in T'an-chou was already pacified. "Viewing the Rain from the Riverside Apartment and Thinking of Prefect P'ei Ch'iu Sailing with the Navy" [cccLxxi] would indicate that the Tu family was back in T'an-chou and that our poet was thinking of his friend Prefect P'ei leading the navy southward back to Tao-chou.

Thus we see that several days after the temporary interruption of his voyage at Lei-yang, Tu Fu was back in his riverside apartment in T'an-chou. Yet, as early as the middle of the Ninth century, a story had become current to the effect that while Tu Fu was in Lei-yang, "the magistrate sent some roast beef and white wine to Tu Fu. On account of overdrinking, he died in the night. In his collection of poems, there is one addressed to the Lei-yang magistrate." By 945, when the Old T'ang History was compiled, the story had become: "While living in Lei-yang, Tu Fu visited the Yo Temple and was marooned by a fierce flood, for ten days without food. Magistrate Nieh of Lei-yang, hearing of this, took a boat himself and brought Tu Fu back. This happened in 766, and on account of eating beef and drinking white wine, he died in the night at Lei-yang." It would seem that it was the disarranged condition of the collection of Tu Fu's poems, with the poem to Magistrate Nieh at the end, and the careless reading of it, that gave rise to the story relating to his death in Lei-yang.

But the clearest evidence against the supposition that the Lei-yang poem was Tu Fu's last is "Bidding Li Hsien Godspeed at T'an-chou" [CCCLXXII]. The context of the Lei-yang poem shows that it was written in the summer of 770, before the pacification of T'an-chou in June. The poem to Li Hsien was written in T'an-chou in the autumn of 770, for it says that from the earlier meeting of the two friends in T'ung-ku (659) to their present meeting in T'an-chou there had been twelve autumns.

"Late in the Autumn, I am Ready to Depart for the Ching-chao Area . . ." [CCCLXXIII] was probably written before Tu Fu learned of another invasion by the Tibetans, who attacked Pin-chou on October 5. That he did not make the trip to Ching-chao might have been on account of such news. Or it could also have been on account of the illness and death of his infant daughter. These events would surely aggravate his own illness. "Sick with Fever on the Boat, I Write in Bed These Thirty-Six Rhymes . . ." [CCCLXXIV] is very likely Tu Fu's last poem— perhaps he died of that very fever. When he wrote the poem, it was already winter. He died perhaps in November or December of 770.

CCCLXXI   VIEWING THE RAIN FROM THE RIVERSIDE APARTMENT AND
      THINKING OF PREFECT P'EI CH'IU SAILING WITH THE NAVY

Wind and waves are strong in the South; It makes little difference whether the weather is cloudy or clear. While the sun moves across the fields wet with flowing streams; The clouds pour out of the hills into the river. In this upper story, I feel the shakings of thunder; Looking into the sky, I face the whirls of the shower. This rain comes from the extreme south; It must have washed and cooled the armed forces under the great admiral.

CCCLXXII   BIDDING LI HSIEN GODSPEED AT T'AN-CHOU

You and I were once together as refugees in the District of T'ung-ku; Now twelve autumns have passed, and we meet again near Lake Tung-t'ing. I never really deserved the gift of shoes from the palace; I am now fully tired of climbing to the upper story and singing of separation from home. You have a well-mellowed talent that is unique; But once dropped from the Court, you have found it hard to rise again. Unworthy though I am, Li and Tu have often been mentioned together; Now these cold clouds and cold chrysanthemums will double my loneliness without your company.

CCCLXXIII LATE IN THE AUTUMN, I AM READY TO DEPART FOR THE CHING-CHAO AREA AND I LEAVE THIS FAREWELL POEM TO MY RELATIVES AND FRIENDS IN THE HU-NAN GENERAL HEADQUARTERS

The water has risen high in the streams of Hu-nan While the sky declares the lateness of autumn. How can one help weeping when his resources are exhausted? An old man has not the strength to bear too much sadness.

At the General Headquarters, there is a host of able men; In both character and achievement, gentlemen, you are known to excel. Journeying to the North, one will have to brave rain and snow; Which of you will sympathize with the traveler in shabby fur?

CCCLXXIV SICK WITH FEVER ON THE BOAT: I WROTE IN BED THESE THIRTY-SIX RHYMES TO PRESENT TO RELATIVES AND FRIENDS IN THE HU-NAN GOVERNMENT

O Huang-ti and Shun, whose music was to have brought the harmony of the seasons, You might very well have ceased to tune and to play. For your pipes are discordant, And your lute is half dead. You, sages of hoary antiquity, how much do you know of the agony Of one old, sick, and long away from home?

My boat is anchored indeed by the eastern—the better—shore of the lake Where I can watch Orion rising early above the western horizon. But what I hear is like the chilling flute in Ma Jung's poem, And the wind is like that which blew on Wang Ts'an's bosom. And I, like those two poets, am also in a distant region, Sadly longing for the crispy cold of the home country. The clouds here are darkening the latter days of the year With a mist that blurs the white houses in the villages. The green hills piled behind the mapled-lined shores are wet With a drizzling, soaking rain that has lasted too long. And now comes the flaming fever that spreads in a stifling winter. What good will the villagers accomplish by smiting drums to invoke The spirits that can do nothing, or by shooting the birds That merely resemble the owls of ill-luck?

Thus exhilaration vanishes when one begins to enjoy an unburdened moment, And anxieties rush in with an irresistible suddenness. Mine has been a life that wavers between sinking and floating Amid an environment of dreary decadence. Should I not fear that I might be the target of some evil, Since I retain the hatpin of an official status? My persistent remonstrance displeased the late Emperor. My fall followed a misunderstanding of my affiliations. Where will my mad wanderings finally lead? With so little talent, I am hardly worthy of the regard ac-

corded me. I am accustomed to the poorest vegetable soup, thin and unflavored. You have overestimated a retiring man, as if he might rise high. The hermit's stool is cushioned with layers of black hide, And the scholar's clothes are mended with numerous patches. But my songs of discomfort mainly concern the country's misfortune. My shame rises from my inability to subdue the rebels with my writings.

The fragile linen of Shu, which I have worn for ten summers, Has suffered three autumns of hard washing in Ch'u. Since I have been invited to feast in the hall with brocade curtains, Long have I sung the "Song of Permanent Fidelity." Though I know the wholesome simpleness of ancient times could hardly return, I have kept a naïve innocence, unaware of a world of machinations. Of food, I have taken freely a few mouthfuls, more than a little wren can pick up. As for money, I accept only what is right for the donor to give as well as for me to receive. Going home? The old verses about the abandoned spring grass deepen my forlornness. A place to settle down? The Valley of Peach Blossoms has eluded my search. Think not that a person blown about like a thistledown is free from sharp anxieties: Especially since his illness has worsened—and with the help of medicine—Since he had to leave a dead child in a roadside grave, Since he cannot walk without a staff.

It is useless for a stumbler to try keeping step with the times; He might as well halt and be grateful that there are those who understand. Moreover, there are friends who would exert superlative eloquence To recommend the handle of a sword for sharpness! The oceanwide hospitality that receives all streams without discrimination, The mountain height of favors with steep approaches, Are combined in the city palaces spreading out in the freshness and brightness Of the green bamboos by the blue, deep waters. Many there are who, with open faces and engaging smiles, Have kept running and climbing with surprising speed. And yet, tolerance has been allowed one who is too unskilled to flatter; Such is indeed the shining grace of God.

Now the ambitious foe is still relying on his strategic advantages, Some rebellious renegades are still at large, Letters from the Central Plains are rare, And in the North hostilities are thick. I understand that a stranger is liable to the suspicion of abusing the drinking well. I know too that it is not easy to observe the custom of distant provinces. But the bloodshed of war has continued, And the cries of battle have not ceased even now. From his corpse, Ko Hung departed alive. In exile, Hsü Ching still managed well for his family. Hsü had mastered economy, Ko the secrets of immortality. I have failed in both. I have only timely tears.

Thus ended the life of China's greatest poet.

280

"A fame that is to last thousands of years
Will rise after an unappreciated life
is past."

In 813 Tu Fu's grandson, Tu Ssŭ-yeh, called on Yüan Chên, a popular poet and then an official in Chiang-ling, and requested Yüan to write a funeral inscription for his grandfather. Yüan's inscription is devoted largely to a discussion of poetry, and Yüan declared Tu Fu to be the greatest of poets. The portion that deals with Tu Fu's life is very sketchy. It says that Tu Fu died in his fifty-ninth year and that his coffin was temporarily interred in Yo-chou. Mrs. Tu Fu, née Yang, died in her forty-ninth year. The heir was Tu Tsung-wu, who died before he was able to bring the bones of his parents to the family graveyard in Yen-shih for burial. Tu Tsung-wu's son, Tu Ssŭ-yeh, though very poor, was, by begging and borrowing, finally able to do so.

Though Yüan neglected to give any dates for Tu Fu's life, it was his mention of Tu Fu's age at the time of his death that helped scholars, after centuries of erroneous guessing, to determine the correct dates. Yüan also neglected to mention Tu Tsung-wên, Tu Fu's elder son. This has puzzled many scholars. My conjecture is that Tu Tsung-wên was probably considered heir to Tu Fu's deceased elder brother whose name we do not even know. Since he was thus no longer responsible to his own father in matters relating to ancestral worship, his name was omitted in this altogether too sketchy inscription. Contrary to the guess of some commentators who thought the dead child mentioned in Tu Fu's last poem to be Tu Tsung-wên, the boy was certainly alive a number of years after the death of our poet. When General Li Ch'ang-nao was prefect and governor at Kuei-chou during 773–781, he employed Tsung-wên, who was then probably in his twenties and had the ranking of a Reader, second or third step up the official ladder. Apart from such meager information, we know nothing more about Tu Fu's children and grandchildren. Centuries later, one or another Tu popped up here and there to claim a descent from our poet. None of the claims can be substantiated.

A note by the great statesman and historian Ssŭ-ma Kuang (1019–1086) states that Tu Fu died in Lei-yang and was hastily interred there. The final burial took place sometime during 806–820 in the District of Kung, and Yüan Chên wrote the text of the funerary tablet. On the strength of this hardly reliable note, the people of Kung have asserted that our poet was buried in Kung and not in Yen-shih. Now and then there would be literary polemics on the contention between the two neighboring districts.

The so-called "Grave of Tu Fu" in Lei-yang has been even more famous. The compilers of the local history of the district point to the numerous poems by visitors to substantiate the claim. The earliest of these poems was said to have been written by the great essayist and poet Han Yü (768–824) who, being so near to the time of Tu Fu, might indeed be a good authority. But that poem must be declared a forgery, for the style is very inferior to that of Han Yü's other poems; it was not found in the early collections of Han Yü's works.

Such claims about the resting place of Tu Fu's remains, are, however, entirely understandable, since numerous localities in the land, along the track of his extensive travels, have vied with one another in erecting temples to honor the memory of the unfortunate sojourner discovered to be the nation's greatest poet. Indeed, what Tu Fu had said of his friend Li Po is even truer of himself:

> A fame that is to last thousands of years
> Will rise after an unappreciated life is past.

I cannot claim to have fully understood Tu Fu, the poet. I believe I have a fairly accurate understanding of Tu Fu, the man. He appeared to be a filial son, an affectionate father, a generous brother, a faithful husband, a loyal friend, a dutiful official, and a patriotic subject. He was not only a good man, but also a wise one. His profound studies of history and literature enabled him to understand the strength and frailties of human nature, the bright and sordid possibilities of politics. Some of the observations he made of the eighth-century T'ang empire are still true of China now; some may even be found to be true of other nations.

A NOTE ON PRONOUNCING CHINESE NAMES

INDEX

In the present book, the transcription of Chinese words follows what is known as the Wade-Giles system. It is not the only system in use, but it is the most widely adopted one in writings on Chinese subjects. For readers who have no knowledge of Chinese, the following table of rough sound approximations may be of some help.

a as *a* in *father*	*ŭ* as *u* in *fur*
ai as *I*	*ü* as *ü* in German *über*
ao as *ow* in *how*	*üa* as *ua* in French *tuable*
e and *eh* as *e* in *let*	*üeh* as *ue* in French *suette*
ei as *ay* in *lay*	*ch* as *j* in *jump*
ê as *u* in *pun*	*ch'* as *ch* in *church*
i as *i* in *pin*	*j* as *wr* in *wren*
ia as *ya*	*hs* as *sh* in *she*
iao as *eow* in *meow*	*k* as *k* in *skid*
ie and *ieh* as *ye* in *yet*	*k'* as *k* in *kid*
ih as *e* in *her*	*p* as *p* in *spot*
o as *o* in *orange*	*p'* as *p* in *pot*
ou as *ou* in *soul*	*t* as *t* in *stall*
u as *u* in *rude*	*t'* as *t* in *tall*
ua as *wa* in *waft*	*ts* and *tz* as *dz* in *adze*
ui as *way*	*ts'* and *tz'* as *ts* in *cats*
uo as *wo* in *wobble*	

The consonants *f*, *h*, *l*, *m*, *n*, *ng*, *s*, *sh*, *w*, and *y* sound as they do in English.

In parentheses following the entries, modern names of approximate sites of T'ang cities are preceded by asterisks. The longitude and latitude figures given are from the *Chinese Postal Atlas,* 1936.

Tung Cho, 106, 107
T'ung-ch'üan (district; site southeast of *Shê-hung), 192
Tung-k'o (village), 144, 147
T'ung-ku (district; *Ch'êng chou; Ch'êng hsien 105°40′E, 33°45′N), 144, 153, 154, 157, 158, 278
T'ung-kuan (pass, 110°15′E, 34° 35′N), 91, 92, 93, 94, 98, 99, 100, 108, 111, 116, 239
Tung-mêng Hills, 38
Tung-p'ing (prefecture; before 742 and after 757 Yün-chou; *Tung-p'ing chou; Tung-p'ing hsien 116°20′E, 35°55′N), 93, 103
Tung-t'ing (lake), 145, 169, 199, 200, 202, 257, 261, 262, 264, 271, 272, 273, 278
Tu Number Two, 19
Turfan (89°05′E, 42°55′N), 62, 65
Turkestan, 43
Turks, 42, 43, 93, 98, 99
Tu Shên-yen, 16, 17, 18, 20, 26, 34, 86
Tu Shên-yen, the first Mrs., 18, 20
Tu Shên-yen, the second Mrs., 18, 20, 29, 35
Tu Ssŭ-yeh, 281
Tu Tsi, 74, 77, 187, 194
Tu Tso, 34, 144, 147
Tu Tsung-wên, 223, 225, 230, 269, 270, 273, 281, 282
Tu Tsung-wu, 110, 230, 261, 269, 270, 271, 272, 281
Tu Tzŭ-mei (see also Tu Fu), 16, 157
Tu Wei, 68, 69, 257
Tu Ying, 33, 50, 103, 138, 210, 214, 230
Tu Yü, 16, 20, 31, 32
Tzŭ-ch'ên Hall, 124
Tzŭ-chou (prefecture; 742–757 Tzŭ-t'ung chün; *T'ung-ch'uan fu; San-t'ai hsien 105°05′E, 31°05′N), 178, 189, 190, 191, 192, 193, 194, 195, 196, 197, 198, 199, 200, 207

Uighurs, 42, 98, 100, 102, 111, 117, 119, 126, 134, 144, 146, 150, 192, 202
Underwood, Edna Worthley, 7

Valley of Peach Blossoms, 70, 265, 280
Vermilion Phoenix Tower, 122
Virgil, 1

Waley, Arthur, 5
Wang, Army Inspector, 229, 237
Wang, Cousin, 164

Wang, Prefect of Han-chou, 194
Wang, Prefect of Lang-chou, 196, 197, 198
Wang, Secretary General, 204, 206
Wang, Vice-Prefect, 173
Wang, Young Inspector, 257, 258
Wang Chao-chün, 223, 225, 228, 229
Wang Ch'iang, 223
Wang Ch'ien, 173, 174, 179
Wang edition, 14
Wang Han, 26, 56
Wang Hsi-chih, 194, 212
Wang Ssŭ-li, 126
Wang Tsai, 167, 169
Wang Ts'an, 243, 245, 257, 258, 260, 279
Wang Wei, 44, 45, 123, 124
Wan-nien (district; 748 Hsien-ning; 758 Wan-nien; *Hsien-ning hsien; Ch'ang-an hsien 108°55′E, 34° 15′N), 19
Water Gate, 231
Wei (river), 22, 27, 51, 57, 73, 81, 89, 106, 132, 146, 239
Wei (or Wei-chou Prefecture; 742–757 Chi-chün; *Wei-hui fu; Chi hsien 114°05′E, 35°25′N), 104, 150
Wei, Empress, 41
Wei, General Censor, 169
Wei, Hermit, 139
Wei, Kingdom of, 165, 222, 242, 248
Wei, Madame, 212
Wei, Mrs., 104, 230
Wei Chien, 48, 49, 53
Wei Chien-su, 85, 94, 95, 98, 99
Wei Chih, 109
Wei Chih-chin, 263
Wei Ch'i-hsin, 180
Wei-chou (prefecture; 742–757 Wei-chün; site near *Ta-ming hsien 115° 05′E, 36°15′N), 139, 140
Wei Chün, 260, 261
Wei Fang-chin, 94, 95
Wei Hsiao, 144, 146
Wei O, 95
Wei Pan, 164
Wei Po-yü, 229, 230, 257
Wei Tsi, 54, 55, 56, 58, 59
Wei Yen, 166, 167, 169
Wên I-to, 4, 17
Wên River, 39
Wên-tsung, Emperor, 6
Wên Wêng, 233
West Apartment, 221, 222, 227, 229, 230, 231
Western Capital (see also Ch'ang-an), 99, 111
Western Capital (see also Fêng-hsiang), 122

298

I

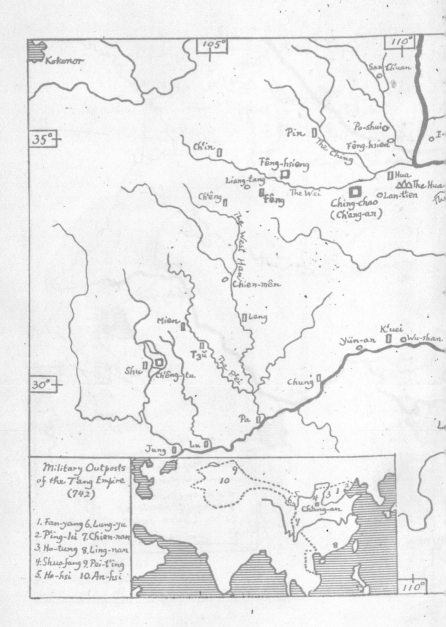

Kokonor

105°

110°

San Ch'uan

Po-shui

Pin   The Ching   Fêng-hsien

35°   Ch'in

Fêng-hsiang

Liang-tang   The Wei   Hua   The Hua

Ch'êng   Fêng   O Lan-tien

Ching-chao
(Ch'ang-an)

The West Han

Chien-mên

Lang

Mien   K'uei

Yün-an   Wu-shan

T3ǔ

Shu   Chêng-tu   The Pei

30°   Chung

Pa

Jung   Lu

**Military Outposts
of the Tang Empire
(742)**

9
10

2
5   1
6   4   3
Ch'ang-an

1. Fan-yang 6. Lung-yu
2. P'ing-lu 7. Chien-nan
3. Ho-tung   8. Ling-nan
4. Shuo-fang 9. Pei-t'ing
5. Ho-hsi   10. An-hsi

7

8

110°